The Fort McClell
POW Camp

Camp

The Fort McClellan POW Camp

German Prisoners in Alabama, 1943–1946

JACK SHAY

McFarland & Company, Inc., Publishers
Jefferson, North Carolina

LIBRARY OF CONGRESS CATALOGUING-IN-PUBLICATION DATA

Names: Shay, Jack.
Title: The Fort McClellan POW Camp : German prisoners
in Alabama, 1943–1946 / Jack Shay.
Description: Jefferson, North Carolina : McFarland & Company, Inc.,
Publishers, 2016 | Includes bibliographical references and index.
Identifiers: LCCN 2016003117 | ISBN 9781476662350 (softcover : acid free paper) ∞
Subjects: LCSH: Fort McClellan (Ala.)—History—20th century. | World War,
1939–1945—Prisoners and prisons, American. | Prisoners of war—Alabama—
Fort McClellan—History—20th century. | Prisoners of war—Germany—
History—20th century. | World War, 1939–1945—Alabama—Fort McClellan.
Classification: LCC D805.5.F662 S534 2016 | DDC 940.54/7276163—dc23
LC record available at http://lccn.loc.gov/2016003117

BRITISH LIBRARY CATALOGUING DATA ARE AVAILABLE

ISBN (print) 978-1-4766-6235-0
ISBN (ebook) 978-1-4766-2227-9

On the cover: Prisoner Hermann Haugg's drawing of the view
downhill from the POW camp; from the camp newspaper,
October 1, 1944 (author's collection)

Printed in the United States of America

*McFarland & Company, Inc., Publishers
Box 611, Jefferson, North Carolina 28640
www.mcfarlandpub.com*

In memory of
Staff Sergeant John Edward "Jack" Shay and Marie Shay,
who never imagined their oral and written memories
would form the basis for a history of the
Fort McClellan POW Camp.

—Their son, the author, Jack Shay.

Table of Contents

Preface

*"If you want to talk some more about this,
give me a call."*

This was never intended to be a book.

I grew up idolizing my father, who thrilled me with stories of World War II. He spoke of his brothers, who saw intense ground fighting and flew combat missions. But, as was typical for many who survived wartime violence and then had to shift 180 degrees and resume normal civilian life, they never spoke about it. My father did the speaking for them.

But he also related his own experiences guarding German prisoners of war in Alabama, a state I associated only with the frontier Indian fighter Davy Crockett (then a national idol because of a lionizing TV series) and the Creek Indian War. And I came to understand that not all army service involved combat. My father maintained that a soldier was a soldier, whether holding a rifle at shoulder arms on a parade ground or cocked against a shoulder while sighting a foe from a foxhole.

I also helped my parents send letters and Christmas cards to former German prisoners and the GIs who had guarded them. My mother often looked at black-and-white photographs from that prisoner of war camp in Alabama, a place called Fort McClellan near a city named Anniston, and reminisced about the people and the times. But I was too young to record their names or even remember who was who in the group shots.

I collected stamps in those years, too. And some of my favorites were profiles of Adolf Hitler on various Deutsches Reich denominations. I knew he was a "bad guy," and that lure, similar to youthful booing when cinematic villains appeared on screen, produced an undeniable fascination.

I played with World War II toy soldiers. When I took my toy guns outside, I strapped on Dad's helmet liner, my favorite of his Fort McClellan souvenirs. But only in my teens did I begin recording his wartime stories and writing them down. When he was stricken with a lingering illness that stripped him of all his faculties, I asked Mom to write down her memories.

Both had often spoken about their POW camp years as though they were the most memorable of their lives. Dad never had the chance to return to Alabama. But I took Mom there twice in the 1980s to reconnect with people from long ago.

After their passing, I discovered my parents' McClellan mementos, memories in their own handwriting and some I had transcribed, and more than 100 photographs I had never asked them to identify.

I returned to Anniston in 2007, hoping only to establish contact with anyone who could identify the people and places in the photographs.

I didn't know it, but that trip would induce this book.

The first person I encountered was Elmer Wheatley, then deputy director of the Calhoun County Economic Development Council, whom I met at the Anniston Chamber of Commerce on August 17. He offered a contemporary map and directions to the Joint Powers Authority, then controlling much of the area occupied by Fort McClellan before its 1999 deactivation.

That same day, Dan W. Cleckler, then executive director of Anniston–Calhoun County Fort McClellan Development Joint Powers Authority, and Linda L. Mann, the executive secretary/office manager of the Joint Powers Authority, both in the former post headquarters building on Headquarters Road, pinpointed the location of several surviving post features and supplied different maps of the current McClellan complex.

Joan McKinney, who had worked at the fort "from 82–94 [1982–1994] as the Director of Protocol and then the Community Outreach Coordinator in the Public Affairs Office," heard of my visit from Elmer Wheatley and emailed me on October 17 with an offer to "answer any questions" and "take you around the camp if you return."

Along the way, other people I talked with got the idea that I was planning a book on the POW camp. Early in 2008, I realized I just might be the likeliest candidate to do that.

I had a wealth of information from my parents, even if in disjointed and undated bits, ranging from the 1960s to the early 1990s. Additionally, I had visited with three of their army buddies from the POW camp: Sergeant Jack S. Steward four times; Sergeant John J. George three times; and civilian employee Essie Woodward twice. I remembered what they had said. And in 1987 and 1988, my mother and I had visited a former POW, Robert Suberg, in Solingen, West Germany. I had asked specific questions and taken notes.

But all this had been done just for background information on my parents' wartime experience. I never expected any of this to end up in a book.

When I finally realized I should properly record these memories before they were forever lost to time, it was too late to ask more specific and probing questions. Or to try to identify Ollie Odus Tutterow, Henry and Elsie Landseadel, Harry L. and Ruth Springer, "Swede and Arlene," and other army friends among the raft of nameless faces in the photographs.

The challenge became how to properly assimilate the personal information with my parents' documents, including copies of military orders, camp reports, work detail sheets, notes hastily written on scraps of paper, letters, manuals, and all the photographs.

My dad had taken basic infantry training at McClellan, suffered an injury, joined the POW camp military police, and then accepted a position as a mess hall sergeant for the MPs (and later the officers) who ran the POW camp. My mom had taken a civilian job in the GI post exchange (PX), then transferred to the POW camp headquarters, and finally ended her wartime career in the personnel department on the main post. They came into contact with most of the American GIs and civilians who operated the camp, as well as a fair number of the German POWs.

My father went from a private to a private first class (PFC) to an acting sergeant to a staff sergeant (with one or two other temporary and lesser gradations along the way). Simultaneously, he served as an MP, an acting mess sergeant, and a mess sergeant. Compounding the matter is the military's use of descriptive qualifiers for each rank. For example, a sergeant could be a staff sergeant, a tech sergeant, a sergeant first class, and so on (successive ranks all within the general umbrella of "sergeant") and also a gunnery sergeant, a mess sergeant, a commissary sergeant, etc. Further complicating the issue is the army's penchant for alternating actual ranks with occupational titles ... and sometimes simultaneously employing both. On some of my father's official papers, he is listed as both mess sergeant and sergeant, among other variations. The text reflects these variations.

I attempted to augment my parents' memories with reminiscences from their friends. That meant combing through address books, surviving Christmas cards and letters, and the Internet for updated addresses, names of relatives, obituary notices, and anything else that might help in contacting the right people. When I came across new addresses or next-of-kin information, I sent out long letters explaining my identity and intentions. The success rate was about 50 percent, and I accepted the reality that not all descendants of good friends of my parents shared my passion for preserving the past.

Joachim Metzner, in a way my counterpart in Germany (because he is concurrently collating and annotating his father's wartime diary entries and the POW camp newspaper he edited), experienced the same frustration. As he commented in an April 1, 2013, email, "By the way: I wrote to this person with the same name [as that of a former POW in McClellan], but I got no answer. We know that he can't be our man based on his age, but I was a little disappointed to get no answer at all."

At the same time, I began archival research on extant McClellan POW records and references in newspapers of the day.

In Anniston, Joan McKinney allowed me access to her extensive files containing documents, news clippings, magazine articles, and photographs of Fort McClellan. She agreed to interviews on June 23, 2008, and November 29, 2009, and used her house as a staging ground, replete with refreshments, for a group interview with several Calhoun County residents familiar with Fort McClellan.

Dr. Joseph A. "Joby" Walker and his wife, Mary Beth, the son and daughter-in-law of Dr. Carlos A. Walker, a GI housing landlord, consented to long interviews on June 24 and October 2, 2008, and November 29 and December 1, 2009. They also provided additional information, maps, and photographs. Mary Beth arranged for interviews with Mary Elizabeth Johnson, Betty Mabry, and Rita Springer, all of whom shared personal reminiscences of the POWs. Joby did the same with Meredith Aderholdt, whose father had supervised POW work details. Additionally, he invited me to address a weekly Rotary meeting in Anniston.

Tom Mullins, the director of the Alabama Room for Genealogy and Local History at the Public Library of Anniston and Calhoun County, turned over the files of Fort McClellan, assisted me in researching the tornado that struck just weeks before the official closing of the POW complex, generously conducted microfilm research on my behalf when I couldn't visit his archives, provided information and photographs of my parents' friends formerly affiliated with the camp, and located (through Betty Bowman) another friend of my parents, Margaret Newman. He also recommended several interview subjects, including Eugene Steppe, a member of the 382nd Military Police Escort Guard Company.

Eugene devoted an afternoon to the public library in Anniston, poring over old photographs and hand-drawn maps, helping identify terrain features and buildings. He ended our conversation by giving me his address and phone number, saying, "If you want to talk some more about this, give me a call." I never had the chance to thank him adequately or take him up on his offer. He passed away too soon after our meeting.

Margaret Newman, a retired navy veteran, school teacher, administrator, and author, helped identify some figures in old photographs. ("I don't think you should be concerned about the soldier in the picture," she once wrote. "I don't think he was a special friend of your parents. He was someone your mother talked with in the PX where she worked. She got me a date with him. I do not recall what we did but from the pictures we must have had a good time.") In a letter dated February 18, 2009, she suggested a long-ago series written by a county historian, sagely concluding, "Maybe nothing is here but that is research! A sentence is good!"

She also arranged for me to interview Steve Bakke and Thom Cole at her 90th birthday celebration in Anniston on April 2, 2011. Steve is a military expert and collector of militaria who provided overall insights. Thom is a world traveler and historian who has turned his home into a veritable museum of historical and military artifacts, implements, and documents; he gave me an intriguing look at his collection of items relevant to Fort McClellan.

Rita (Johnson) Wells, who worked in the POW camp headquarters building with my mother, recalled her memories of governmental civilian life and drew an informal map of

Media consultant and interview assistant Betty Casey (far left) with three Annistonians who contributed significant information for this book. The Annistonians are, left to right, Margaret Newman, Rita (Johnson) Wells, and Thom Cole (Anniston, August 2013) (author's collection).

key features in both the POW and American camps. She also opened her house to me for two daylong interviews and graciously provided an assortment of fruit and cracker hors d'oeuvres, sweets, and beverages.

Regarding the map, she wrote, "I am enclosing the map I have drawn to the best of my ability. So many years have flown by since the camp was closed and demolished, my memories are hazy. At that time the activities going on were much more interesting than the layout to someone my age." She also paid my parents wonderful compliments and, on October 4, 2008, wrote, "You ... made Wednesday a wonderful day for me. It was great making new friends and enjoying long-time ones while viewing those photos of former experiences with people of the past. It felt like I was again in the company of Marie & Jack Shay and that was a happy experience for me."

Archivists and personnel at the National Archives—Darryl Bottoms, Gedra Martin, Ken Schlessinger, and Don Singer—provided advice and background on which World War II domestic front files might prove helpful and which were most likely not worth the effort during several days of searching in late September 2008. Beth Lipford, a former Department of Interior colleague and friend, pointed me in the right direction, made several recommendations on which archivists to seek out, and shepherded me through the painstakingly slow process of winnowing useful information from the tonnage of print matter contained in the Archives.

My own initiatives led me to emails with Bill Brownell and James Bonner, as well as interviews with Phillip Tutor and especially James and Dean Bonner, who shared photographs of paintings and pictures done for Dean's father by a POW. In addition, I was able to track down Clark J. Miller at his home in Pennsylvania, where he related his experiences as a guard for POW work details.

I collected the notes taken from the interviews with Robert Suberg on three separate occasions (August 28 and 29, 1987, and September 23, 1988) and put them in a more coherently chronological order. They offered a firsthand look at camp life from an insider's perspective. His widow, Edith, provided me with his photographs taken by POWs in the camp.

Other people or children of those who had known my parents at McClellan came through with anecdotes, memories, or photograph identifications. They included Ruth Allen, who had worked with my mother in the camp; Mary Jo Berardone, the daughter of Sergeant Joseph A. Spinelli and his wife, Mim; Janice Erfle and Rodney George, the children of Sergeant John J. George; and Jack E. Steward, the son of Sergeant Jack S. Steward.

Klaus Duncan of Jacksonville, instrumental in the annual POW cemetery observances, provided photographs, information, and, most valuable, an aerial map of the POW camp complex from 1944.

Joachim Metzner, the son of *P.o.W. Oase* editor Paul Metzner, sent nearly 100 emails with photographs, copies of illustrations and text from various issues of the newspaper, translations of important portions of the text, answers to my dozens of questions, and some questions for me as well. During the course of our communication, we shared so much information, often of minute detail, that I felt as though this book should bear the names of both Shay and Metzner equally.

On October 16, 2013, I wrote Joachim, "I wish both of us had more time with our fathers ... especially now that we have forged a common bond. They could provide so many answers to questions that we have. We were fortunate to have them … but I wish we could have had them a little longer than we did." He replied that same day: "It would have been nice, if they had the chance to exchange and combine memories. Maybe they do today, looking at and wondering about us struggling with some questions."

It's a pleasant thought, and I think both our fathers would appreciate how their sons—having never met in life—have collaborated so rigorously to keep their memory alive.

Introduction

"A nice break in a nasty war."

No soldier likes the uncertainty of captivity in the land of the enemy. Yet it is an inescapable facet of the hellish art of war.

World War II became the most vicious conflict mankind has yet seen in terms of global reach, devastation, and casualties. It spawned record numbers of dead and wounded, as well as those whose spirits were broken and whose souls were seared. An estimated minimum of 60 million people, both military and civilian, died. Hundreds of millions of others had their lives drastically interrupted or irrevocably changed.

Among the untold millions of prisoners—soldiers, sailors, airmen, and medical personnel, as well as political, ethnic, and cultural civilians, and the unwanted and unloved—who were held against their will, some 435,000 came to America to be interned for the duration of the war.

They were the lucky ones.

They entered a sprawling country, a land of bounty ready to greet them with a friendly curiosity and treat them with a degree of humanity they could not have imagined, a nation with no "ethnic cleansing" concentration camps, no pogroms, no death squads.

More than 600 detainment centers—some small and temporary, others large and permanent—throughout the United States stood ready to accommodate them.

Of the dozens of major prisoner of war (POW) camps, a handful achieved the superior recognition of being well-run and well-regarded, presenting minimal problems and eliciting commendations from all concerned. One, in particular, received repeated high marks from international inspectors and personnel on both sides of the enclosure—captive and captor alike.

The Fort McClellan POW Camp, like the main U.S. Army training post to which it was attached, became a model facility. From the Spanish architectural idiom of the buildings to the beautifully landscaped lawns and gardens, the scenic meandering stream to the arched pedestrian stone bridges, the main post was the envy of military installations around the nation. Its POW camp could not be expected to boast the same features; it was, after all, a containment facility. Yet it managed a neat appearance far better than many other such holding pens.

More substantively, McClellan's German prisoner of war camp was spared a heavy influx of intensely ideological captives, whether supporting or vilifying the governing philosophy of Germany's Third Reich. Throughout its nearly three-year existence, the camp saw no reported prisoner-on-prisoner executions (something stigmatizing other camps) and few escape attempts, inmate strikes, and suicides. The American administrators sought to educate the prisoners, occupy their time with wage-paying work, and encourage their pursuit of artistic and athletic pastimes.

Whether by design or chance, McClellan's camp held remarkably talented writers, musicians, artists, artisans, and athletes connected to one another by the common thread of the uniform they wore. Two of the artists left behind a series of highly personal murals decorating the walls of the American Officers' Club—somewhat unique among POW camps. And McClellan still holds a cemetery, with annual memorial services, for POWs ranging from privates to a general.

This book tells its story.

Of the thousands of publications detailing various aspects of World War II, only a few have examined the POW experience in America. Some have dealt with the issue in national terms—why the camps came into existence and how they were governed. Others have taken a regional approach, surveying camps within a district or state.

This book presents an in-depth look into a single POW camp. It also breaks with the established norm by including whole chapters on the physical makeup and events of the adjoining American military installation entrusted with its operation. It provides a view of POWs juxtaposed with American guards and sheds considerable light on the civilian employees who interacted with both groups.

It also offers personal reminiscences in the words of the principals and their descendants. This narrative includes substantial excerpts from diaries, letters, memoirs, military orders and reports, and American and German newspapers, registering the pulse of the camp as experienced by all who were there and rescuing once-important words from historical oblivion. Dozens of intimate photographs—some taken by the prisoners themselves, and most never seen by anyone other than the subjects and their families—are likewise presented.

No prior publication has put the terrain, makeup, and operation of a camp, as well as a view of the interacting personal lives, under such a revealing microscope. No other publication features as much documentation for all the aspects of a single camp.

This book captures the actual participants in highly emotional, personal moments of honest introspection and follows them through their subsequent years. It emanates from an author who grew up in the postwar years, the offspring of parents who served in the camp, maintained close ties with comrades on both sides, and saved illuminating souvenirs and documents. Subsequent archival research and formal in-person interviews substantiated and augmented the material collected by his parents.

The people who populate this book are presented as neither heroes nor villains—simply men and women thrust together by an unexpected twist of fate in a common place most had never heard of before.

Yet, for virtually all the thousands of intersecting lives at this "model camp," whose faces and words are herein presented for posterity, their time together became memorable, even pleasant. For them, McClellan became, in the words of one person, "a nice break in a nasty war."

1

Some World War II
Background

"Pearl Harbor woke us up.
It woke America up,
and we were never the same again."

World War II began on September 1, 1939, when Germany, long exhibiting bellicose designs on neighboring countries under its infamous führer, Adolf Hitler, invaded Poland. It became the dominant Axis partner, aligned with other fascist or dictatorial nations— notably Italy under its prime minister, Benito Mussolini, and the Soviet Union under its dictatorial leader, Josef Stalin.[1]

England and France, the two other major European powers, opposed the Axis. France quickly succumbed to the German military juggernaut and for the bulk of the war remained an occupied territory. England valiantly fought on, assisted by materiel from the United States. But the December 7, 1941, Japanese attack on Pearl Harbor (an American base in the Hawaiian Islands, then a U.S. possession) brought America into the war alongside England, Canada, Australia, New Zealand, and other English-speaking possessions or former possessions in Asia, all of which constituted the Allied Forces.

The Pacific phase of the world war was already raging, pitting the empire of Japan led by its prime minister, General Hideki Tojo, against the Allies. Pearl Harbor provided a bracingly harsh bucket of water in America's face. As Marie Shay, soon to be intimately involved with a prisoner of war camp in Anniston, Alabama, a place she had never heard of, later recounted,

> In the years before the war, we thought the turmoil in Europe and Asia was beyond us. It just didn't concern us in our everyday lives. Who went to Europe in those days but the wealthy? Most of us never saw a map other than in school. The Rhineland and Pearl Harbor were only names to us. China and Japan were on the other side of the world. They might just as well have been on the moon, for all we knew or cared.
>
> It wasn't that we were ignorant. We were just wrapped up in our own personal lives, and we never thought the conflict would reach us here. It was Europe's problem. The Depression hurt most families, and we were still trying to catch up and make ends meet. We had nice diversions to get our minds off the unpleasantness from overseas. Movies and books and dances. Not that everything was rosy, but we were primarily concerned with just getting by.
>
> The politicians and people in government knew more about this than we did. Oh, there were a few who followed events in Europe. Grandpa [her father-in-law] read the newspapers and he followed the news on radio. He was a smart man, and he would always tell us, "Things in Europe are not good. There's going to be trouble there, and it might come here to America."

But we had just gotten married [1937] and, when you're in love, conditions halfway around the world don't concern you.

Pearl Harbor woke us up. It woke America up, and we were never the same again.[2]

Just prior to America's entry into the war, the politically astute generally believed that if Germany and its partners triumphed over England and the European mainland while Japan conquered the entire Asian and Pacific expanse, the Western Hemisphere would be either isolated from the rest of the world or next in line for conquest.

Certainly, troubling military events prior to the war pockmarked much of the world with unrest and invasion, leaving the remaining nations wary. Mussolini's Italy had invaded and conquered Ethiopia (Italian East Africa) on the East African mainland and Albania on the Balkin Peninsula, just across the Adriatic Sea. Hitler had annexed the Rhineland, Austria, the Sudetenland, and Czechoslovakia in Europe. Japanese forces had marched into the northern portion of China (Manchuria), just west of the Sea of Japan, and then China proper.

On August 23, 1939, just a week before the German attack on Poland, Stalin's Soviet Union and Hitler's Germany, neither liking nor trusting the other, formulated a nonaggression pact, an alliance guaranteeing Soviet cooperation in the imminent occupation of Poland and an agreement to supply Germany with materiel in exchange for Soviet rights to portions of Poland, the Baltic countries, Rumania, and Finland, key states with access to water routes and seaports.

After the invasion of Poland, German territorial seizures increased. Hitler tore through the western European countries of Denmark, Norway, Holland, Belgium, Luxembourg, and France, isolated Great Britain, and took control of eastern Europe by subduing the Balkan Peninsula, from Hungary and Yugoslavia to Greece and Bulgaria. By mid–1941, Germany controlled almost all of Europe, except Great Britain and a few countries hoping their neutral status would allow them to ride out the war without major devastation.

On September 27, 1940, three years after joining Germany and Italy in a political stance against Communism, Japan expanded the union of the totalitarian Axis powers into a military one.

On June 22, 1941, Hitler invaded his on-paper ally, the Soviet Union, in a drawn-out campaign that would ultimately doom him and check further territorial aggression.

The December 7, 1941, attack on Pearl Harbor immediately plunged America alongside Britain and its allies into a war to the death with Japan, Germany, and Italy.

Italy controlled some of North Africa, primarily Libya, which was directly south of Sicily and the southernmost part of the Italian mainland. Italian forces stood there to protect that portion of Africa from the British, New Zealanders, and Indians who occupied Egypt and its strategic location guarding the Suez Canal, which connected the Mediterranean Sea to the Red Sea, Gulf of Aden, Indian Ocean, and the British colony of India.

The first major combat in what became the North African campaign, also known as the Desert War, occurred in September 1940 when Italian Marshal Rodolfo Graziani moved against the British at Sidi Barrani in western Egypt, close to the Libyan border. Three months later, the British Army of the Nile, under General Sir Archibald Wavell, had pushed the Italians back into Libya, to Benghazi, collecting some 130,000 Italian prisoners along the way.

Hitler responded to the Italian troops' inability to hold North Africa by providing reinforcements, chiefly his Deutsches Afrika Korps armored units under the leadership of General (and later Field Marshal) Erwin Rommel, soon to become famous as the wily and successful "Desert Fox." Arriving in Tripoli, Libya, on February 12, 1941, to help the Italian commander, General Italo Gariboldi, Rommel quickly seized offensive control. Two months later, he had chased the British out of Libya (save for one bastion in the coastal city of Tobruk) and leapfrogged into Egypt. With help from German Luftwaffe air attacks on the British bases around the Suez Canal and Peninsula, Rommel's combined Italian and German forces took the fight into the heart of coastal Egypt. A year of stalemated conflicts ensued, with Rommel scoring several victories but unable to smash through the Tobruk lines and capture the British Commonwealth Allies.

The 25,000-man garrison of British, Australian, New Zealander, and Indian soldiers at Tobruk finally fell into Axis hands on June 21, 1942. The 8th Allied Army retreated into Egypt with Rommel in pursuit. Taking up positions at and near El Alamein, on the coast of north-central Egypt, the beleaguered Allied troops came under the leadership of eventual Field Marshal Bernard Montgomery, who proved a formidable match for Rommel. For nearly two weeks beginning October 23, 1942, Montgomery's British, Australian, New Zealander, Highlander, South African, and Indian forces maintained a relentless engagement with Rommel's Afrika Korps. They nearly incapacitated Rommel's entire 240-tank army and sent him retreating west in early November.

Then, on November 8, 1942, fresh Allied forces, comprising Americans and British, invaded northern Africa via major incursions on the beaches of Casablanca (Morocco) and Oran and Algiers (Algeria) in Operation Torch. The invading armies, under the command of then–Lieutenant General Dwight Eisenhower, forced the Axis forces ever eastward across Africa, as Montgomery's Eighth Army pursued Rommel westward.

The German Wehrmacht (Army) and its Italian allies took refuge in Tunisia, roughly in the middle of northern Africa. For a while, the tide turned in favor of the Axis, wedged between two Allied armies but receiving reinforcements from Italian Sicily, less than 100 miles northeast across the Mediterranean Sea.

On February 14, 1943, Eisenhower's army, driving beyond the Atlas Mountains, approached the Eastern Dorsal Mountain range, 50 miles from pushing the Axis into the Mediterranean's Gulf of Gabès. And on the eastern flank, Montgomery eyed Mareth, less than 100 miles from the Allied advance line. In desperation, Rommel charged the American lines, shoving the Yanks 50 miles back on their heels to the Western Dorsal Mountains. History recorded the engagement, which lasted until February 22, as the Battle of Kasserine Pass. But it turned out to be Rommel's last gasp. Jaundice, fatigue, and the frenetic pace of combat had taken a toll on him. On March 9, he returned to Germany, his defense of the North African continent a valiant but certain failure.

The Allies, meanwhile, closed in for the kill. In March and April, the pincer arms of the twin armies kept the Axis foe retreating ever northward in Tunisia. On April 23, a combined effort to quash Axis resistance began. Montgomery's British Empire troops moved north to Tunis. Recovering from the American setback at Kasserine Pass, the U.S. II Corps took Hill 609, pushing on toward Bizerta, another coastal city, a few dozen miles northwest of Tunis, as the British First Army occupied the strategic Longstop Hill.

Finally, on May 7, 1943, the Allies took the last Axis holdouts in Tunis and Bizerta. The Germans and Italians retreated to the Cape Bon Peninsula, the part of Tunisia closest to Sicily. But even that wasn't safe. The Allies secured the northern tip of the peninsula and wedged the Axis forces into the Menzel Temime area of the eastern seacoast, bottling them up by land as well as by an air and sea blockade. With nowhere to go and no new men and armaments to rejuvenate their spirits, the overwhelmed Axis army surrendered on May 13. Estimates vary, but perhaps as many as a quarter-million soldiers instantly became captives in a strange land, their immediate safety in jeopardy, their future in doubt.

The North African campaign had proven disastrous for Hitler and Mussolini, with whole divisions—an estimated 350,000 soldiers—killed or captured. The African continent was lost, and the Allies had strong bases from which to launch the invasions of Sicily and then Italy, moving ever northward to the heart of Germany. The failed North African campaign foreshadowed the Normandy invasion and the ultimate Allied penetration to Hitler's capital city of Berlin. Though no one knew it when the encircled Axis soldiers surrendered on May 13 on the Cape Bon Peninsula, Hitler's dreams of a continental, if not global, empire would end in the Axis surrender of May 7, 1945, less than two years later.

The campaign made heroes of Field Marshal Bernard Montgomery and his "Desert Rats," who had outlasted the best of Rommel's men, and American generals Dwight Eisenhower and Omar Bradley, who would end their military careers as five-star generals of the army, as well as another American general named George S. Patton, who became a household name, a near-mythical figure, and a human cachet to his men, who would, to their dying days, proudly boast, "I fought with Patton." Tobruk, El Alamein, Kasserine Pass, Tunisia, and even Casablanca went down in the storied annals of military exploits.

The Axis armies merely went down to defeat. The Allies often directed rancor against their vanquished opponents. Eisenhower declined to meet German General Jürgen von Arnim, considering him not a defeated foe but a representative of "a completely evil conspiracy" designed to spread inhumanity, bigotry, and persecution under the guise of rampant fascism.

German Field Marshal Erwin Rommel alone came out of the Axis North African campaign a hero to his homeland and an admired tactician and strategist to students of military history. His glory days behind him, he came to a tragic end on October 14, 1944, when Hitler forced him to poison himself, the result of discovering Rommel's connection to the failed July 1944 plan to kill the Führer with a concealed bomb. The German people were told Rommel had died of wounds suffered on July 17 when a Royal Canadian Air Force airplane had shot at him in his staff car. The men who served under him in North Africa and ended their wartime service in POW camps only later learned the truth of his ignominious end.

It was these men—and their comrades captured earlier in the North African campaign—who wound up at first in holding pens, euphemistically termed "processing" centers, on the continent in secured places like Casablanca and Oran, among others. There they were medically inspected and, if time and circumstance permitted, assigned serial numbers that would serve as a crosscheck to their individual names throughout their captivity. Then, when logistics were right and troop transport ships available, they were relocated to permanent stockades and camps in England and North America.

They were a varied mix, ranging from battle-hardened veterans to raw, wary recruits. Some were Nazis (a nickname taken from the sound of the first two syllables of the Nationalsozialistiche Deutsch Arbeiterpartei—in English, the National Socialist German Workers'

Party), melded to the philosophy of Germany's ruling party; others were mere draftees, conscripted from the ranks of schoolboys and civilians. Some were not even German, but rather men from countries allied with or annexed to the Fatherland. They spoke Polish, Hungarian, Dutch, Czech, French, Finnish, or any of the Baltic or Balkan languages. Some were in their 30s, even 40s, but most were teenagers and young men in their early 20s. They tended to look the same—windswept, sunburned, fatigued from months or even years of fighting enemy artillery and the constant onslaught of intense sand, fleas, and temperatures soaring well over 100° (sometimes even at night), as well as bitingly cold temperatures in the winter. Their uniforms were similar: dull olive tunics or khaki shirts, and matching pants or shorts, plus tan ski caps or steel helmets, complete with goggles to keep the blowing sand and grit from their eyes. They might be from the 5th Light Division (later the 21st Panzer Division) or the 5th Panzer Regiment, the 10th Panzer Division or the 15th Panzer Division, the Afrika (and later 90th Light) Division or the 164th Light Afrika Division or the Italian Mobile Corps (Ariete Armoured and Trieste Motor Divisions). But they were individuals with aspirations and dreams, likes and dislikes, and loved ones back home, their lives suddenly interrupted in a manner they could not have dreamed of a scant few years earlier.

But they shared one unmistakable trait: To the men who held guns on them, who had bested them on the field of battle, they were only enemy soldiers who had to be dealt with— a bothersome distraction to further pursuit of the war. Soldiers everywhere, in all times, only want to end the fighting as soon as possible, preferably with their side on top, and then go home in "glory" to resume normal lives. But for the captured tens of thousands of Italian and German soldiers, the war would still go on, only without them. They were destined not to fight again. Their war was over. Ahead of them lay the uncertain duration and conditions of captivity in a strange land behind wire fences, knowing no one but each other.

Of the roughly 435,000 Axis prisoners—the majority German—who came to America, many of them from the North African campaign (and later the D–Day invasion and the final battles in the European Theater), about 1 percent ended up in a hastily constructed internment compound on the southwestern fringes of Fort McClellan in a southern state called Alabama, a place precious few had even heard of. They didn't know it at the time, but, for the overwhelming majority, they had arrived at one of the best places any of them could have selected, had they been given the choice—a facility that military personnel and international inspectors alike called the model camp, one of the best in the nation, perhaps the very best.

2

Anniston and Fort McClellan

"The model city of the New South."

The modern capital of Calhoun County in northeastern Alabama, Anniston came into existence after the Civil War.

Samuel Noble and Daniel Tyler (the former of English descent, the latter from New England) determined that the significant ore within the county could foster a successful business. In 1872, they mounted the Woodstock Iron Company and initiated a settlement built around the business. It became an industrial development named Annie's Town in honor of Tyler's daughter-in-law. Eventually, elision rendered the name into the familiar Anniston.

Within two decades, Anniston became a self-sustaining community with major industries, including iron furnaces and a cotton mill, in addition to hotels, inns, banks, churches, schools, and the state's first electrification operation. It was the fastest-growing community in Alabama. Southern newspaperman Henry Grady called it "the model city of the New South."[1] A half-century after its founding, it boasted additional textile operations and more than a dozen iron foundries, enjoying its designation as the international leader in the manufacture of cast-iron soil pipe and fittings and the state bellwether in textiles. By the start of World War II, 38,000 people resided there.

It no longer holds its former economic status and currently lags behind Birmingham, Mobile, Montgomery, and other larger cities in economic vitality, recognition, and tourism. Today, Anniston contains a population in the low 20,000s; excellent restaurants; a well-developed commercial strip along its main thoroughfare (Quintard Avenue/State Highway 21/U.S. Highway 431); a couple of comprehensive museums (the Anniston Museum of Natural History and the Berman Museum of World History); a historic district with Byzantine, Georgian, Gothic, Greek Revival, Italian Renaissance, Queen Anne, Richardsonian, Romanesque, and Victorian architectural structures; and a fine assemblage of modern, well-appointed twentieth-century houses on the eastern slopes where plutocrats once resided.[2]

In the late twentieth century, Anniston received a literary poke in the eye from Thomas J. Watson Jr., the son of the founder of IBM, in his autobiographical *Father, Son & Co.*, co-written with Peter Petre. A member of the mobilized National Guard in the months leading up to America's entry into World War II, Watson was sent to the army post at Fort McClellan for training as a military pilot in the 102nd Observation Squadron. He wrote that "Anniston ... was hot, wet, and boring." He recalled his days being numbered after the Japanese attack on Pearl Harbor: "We knew we'd never stay in Anniston ... they'd ... send us out to fly bombers."

But he stayed long enough to get married. The wedding party lodged in "a cheap hotel near the base" with "spittoons in the lobby." Because "There was no florist in Anniston," his father, Thomas J. Watson Sr., arranged for the delivery of roses from a florist in Atlanta, Georgia. He was married in the "post chapel," where "they were banging out a wedding every fifteen minutes." His honeymoon covered his entire two days of military leave and occurred in "a brick cottage in Anniston" with "ivy-covered trellises."[3]

Its industrial heyday over, Anniston had already been overtaken by the larger cities in Alabama. And Watson was the scion of a prominent, highly successful international businessman, the highest-paid CEO in America. Anniston could not be expected to measure up to the excitement of the urbane, multifarious, polyglot New York City metropolitan area.

But Fort McClellan was another matter. In a short time, it had become an attractive military showpiece, the pride of the U.S. Army, a fort often called a model for others to emulate.

Prior to Fort McClellan, the army had designated the Anniston area as the site of Camp Shipp, a short-lived facility from August 1898 to March 1899 during the furor over the Spanish-American War. The 3rd Alabama Volunteer Infantry called this area home for a brief period, and it also served as a hospital for influenza patients.

But it was Fort McClellan that put Anniston prominently on the military map.

According to the "Information Hand Book for the Soldier," published by the Infantry Replacement Training Center (IRTC) at Fort McClellan after the outbreak of World War II, "Its beginnings are back at the turn of the century when the old Fourth Alabama Artillery banged its practice shells against the surrounding Choccolocco mountains. The partly-donated 18,380-acre camp site became government property in 1917 and was the training ground for National Guard units brought together from North and South for the famous Blue and Gray (29th) Division of World War I."

Fort McClellan began as Camp McClellan in 1917, when the U.S. War Department set aside land on the northeastern side of Anniston for World War I army training. The nearby Choccolocco Mountains to the east, wedged between Anniston and the Talladega National Forest, had earlier provided artillery training when the above-named Fourth Alabama "banged its practice shells" against them. On March 17, the United States paid $247,000 for 18,952 acres. The following July 18, it was designated Camp McClellan, a training ground, in large measure, for the 29th Infantry Division (New York National Guard), comprising men from several Mid-Atlantic states, including New Jersey.[4]

The name came from Major General George Brinton McClellan, the famous Civil War commander of the Union Army of the Potomac from July 27, 1861, until early November 1862. His most famous battle occurred on September 17, 1862, at Antietam, which produced the most casualties of any single day of combat in American history, before and since. Famed for organizational and training precision, inspiring loyalty in his forces, and a reluctance to fight unless he could be assured of victory at minor cost, he was relieved of command on November 7, 1862. McClellan then resigned from further military service. A New Jersey Democrat, he opposed incumbent Abraham Lincoln in the presidential election of 1864, declaring the Civil War a disaster that intruded on individual citizens' rights and calling for a settlement to end the conflict. He won 45 percent of the popular vote but lost in an electoral landslide, 212–21. He became New Jersey's governor from 1878 to 1881 and concentrated, in part, on state education and military preparedness. During the Civil War, he gained a reputation for being able to speedily craft a successful fighting machine from a collection of untrained recruits of differing talents. He was also a handsome, magnetic man averse to seeing soldiers slaughtered and maimed on the field of battle. His autobiography (*McClellan's Own Story*) was published posthumously. He died in 1885, not even 60 years of age, never imagining his name would live on in a twentieth-century fort in the Deep South of the former Confederacy. The designation of the camp in McClellan's honor was a shock for Annistonians, many of whom had lived through the Civil War and had to come to grips with a Yankee name living in perpetuity in their own backyard. But the economic prosperity that Camp/Fort McClellan fostered over the decades helped Anniston overcome its misgivings.[5]

During and after World War I, the military units training at McClellan's rapidly built temporary structures included the 5th and 6th Divisions; the 27th Division of the New York National Guard; the 29th Infantry Division; the 1st, 2nd, and 3rd Development Regiments; the 157th Depot Brigade; the 11th and 12th Training Battalions; and the 1st Separate Negro Company of Maryland. Over the years, the 4th Tank Company, 22nd Infantry Regiment, and 69th Anti-Aircraft Coast Artillery were among those units stationed on the premises.

In 1926, despite a disinclination to retain all the camps hastily constructed for World War I, the federal government authorized the erection of several permanent structures at McClellan, including headquarters and hospital buildings and officers' quarters and barracks.

On July 1, 1929, Camp McClellan officially became Fort McClellan, one of the nation's permanent military sites. The subsequent Great Depression retarded McClellan's conversion. But as part of the economic recovery in the 1930s, money was earmarked for interior roads, an airstrip, and more permanent buildings, most in the Spanish Colonial Revival idiom.

In 1940, with the possibility of direct American participation in World War II looming on the horizon, the fort once again became a training center. Another major expansion took place as more facilities, including five theaters, a 12,000-person amphitheater, and a couple dozen warehouses, rose to accommodate the heavy influx of new recruits, draftees, and mobilized Guard units. The size of the military reservation more than doubled as additional hilly Choccolocco land to the east was bought; the acreage increased to 42,286.

Also in 1940, the War Department established the Anniston Army Depot on land west of Anniston proper, noncontiguous with Fort McClellan. Anniston saw further buildup to its west when the government bought 22,168 acres north of the Anniston Army Depot for use as a practice firing range for tanks, artillery, and mortars, eventually called the Pelham Range.

During the war years, an estimated half-million soldiers trained at McClellan, at first for eight weeks under the Branch Immaterial Replacement Training Center (BIRTC) program; in 1943, this changed to nine weeks of basic training with an emphasis on European-style warfare under the IRTC designation. Other specialized training also occurred: black soldiers in the then-segregated Buffalo 92nd Infantry Division underwent preparations from 1942 to 1943, and a detachment of Americans of Japanese descent shared information on tactics employed by the Japanese military.

The Fort McClellan Military Reservation also obtained a "corridor of land [which] now connects it with Talladega National Forest and makes the reservation's 440,000 acres available for maneuvers and combat field problems," according to the "Information Hand Book for the Soldier."

Fort McClellan became one of the country's largest military centers and, because of its spacious lawns, manicured flower gardens, and Spanish-influenced architecture, one of the most scenic.

Joan McKinney, the fort's director of protocol and public affairs office's community outreach coordinator during a portion of the 1980s and 1990s, recalled the symbiotic relationship between the fort and the community: "They [Fort McClellan] interacted so much with the community. The community gave property to the Department of War. Originally, they [various portions of the fort complex] were farms, little bitty homesteads. The community raised $300,000 in three days to pay the farmers to give their land."[6]

Following World War II, McClellan served as a training facility for the Allied occupation of the defeated nations. Then, in November 1946, the fort became a recruit training center. That designation was short-lived, however, and the fort was placed on inactive mode on June 30, 1947.

The fort was reactivated in January 1951 to support activities for the National Guard Training Brigade and the Chemical Corps Replacement Training Center. Over the years, an ever-changing and sometimes-overlapping array of various schools operated on the premises: Advanced Individual Training Infantry Brigade (for Vietnam War training); Chemical Corps School; Combat Development Command Chemical-Biological-Radiological Agency; Confinement Operations; Department of Defense Polygraph Institute; Evasive Driving Courses; Military Police (MP) School; Military Working Dogs; Reserve Officers' Training Corps (ROTC); Special and Security Operations; and Women's Army Corps School. On average, 10,000 members of the military and 1,500 civilians were stationed or worked there in the post–World War II years, making it one of the largest employers in a multi-county area.

Despite achieving some singular accomplishments—initial permanent site for the U.S. Women's Army Corps Center (WACC); first female (Major General Mary E. Clarke) commandant of a major U.S. Army location (commanding general of McClellan, 1978–1980); and the only army post holding three major missions (1969: Army Chemical School, Military Police School, Training Brigade)—McClellan was permanently closed in 1999, with an official ceremony on May 20.

At this writing, portions of the former fort complex still host the Alabama National Guard, National Guard Officer Candidate School, and the Department of Homeland Security's Center for Domestic Preparedness.

The rest of McClellan's acreage, including the Spanish-influenced buildings constituting most of the fort's visible landmarks, has been spared the wrecking ball, governed first by the Fort McClellan Joint Powers Authority and later the McClellan Development Authority for private economic development. The current residential and commercial community of "McClellan" occupies some 10,000 acres dedicated to multiple and adaptive use. And in 2003, the Department of the Interior's Fish and Wildlife Service began the transformation of 9,000 acres of former army training land into the Mountain Longleaf National Wildlife Refuge.

At this point, McClellan remains a work in progress, its long-term future anyone's guess.

But in a western angle of the former fort, an area now given to a housing development, the most intriguing aspect of the fort's storied past once existed: a model World War II POW camp where thousands of Germans and a couple hundred Americans—mortal enemies on the battlefield—lived in relative harmony.

3

First Arrivals
in the POW Camp

"As the train drove away,
we saw in the distance
the symbol of freedom disappear—
the Statue of Liberty."

Much smaller than the United States and teeming with captured foes, Great Britain needed help in complying with the planks of the 1929 Geneva Convention (formally the Geneva Convention of July 27, 1929, Relative to the Treatment of Prisoners of War), which mandated humane and dignified treatment of enemy captives. Initially wary of housing German prisoners on American soil for fear of mass escapes, resultant internal terrorism, and uneasiness among its citizens, America agreed to oversee 50,000 Axis prisoners captured in the North African campaign. But the sustained Allied triumphs yielded increasing numbers of prisoners, overwhelming Great Britain's incarceration capacity, and the United States later agreed to accept three and a half times that number. And even that 175,000-man total eventually doubled. Accordingly, some 30 camps were constructed on American soil in 1942, with many more to follow.[1]

Historian Arnold Krammer wrote of "511 POW camps across the country, as well as … hastily converted CCC [Civilian Conservation Corps] camps, high school gyms, and local fairgrounds" in his *Nazi Prisoners of War in America*, first published in 1979.[2] Thirty-one years later, historian Antonio Thompson wrote of "more than six hundred camps" in his *Men in German Uniform*.[3] In 2012, *German POWs in North America*, an Internet site, offered the following: "[P]risoners were processed then distributed to one of the main camps, which numbered over 150 by wars [*sic*] end, or smaller branch camps. The total of United States camps, which eventually numbered over 640, were located primarily in the South and Southwest, far from the critical war industries of the Midwest and the Eastern seaboard."[4]

Krammer listed a total in excess of 371,000 German POWs (from a broader field of more than 425,000 total enemy prisoners) in America. He wrote, "Since it was … impractical to shuffle camp populations which often averaged between 8,000 to 12,000 prisoners, the answer was to distribute the men to smaller camps…. Thus began the branch camp network, ultimately a total of 511 small satellite camps…."[5]

Thompson numbered 371,683 German POWs as "having entered" U.S. facilities "by the end of May 1945." "The War Department issued an official statement in August 1947 that all 435,788 POWs held in the United States, with the exception of the seriously sick or injured and twenty-four escapees, had returned to Europe," he wrote. "This included not only the official number of 378,898 Germans but also 51,455 Italians and 5,435 Japanese."[6]

It is not within the scope of this book to determine the precise number of prisoners or the location of all internment centers, whether full-fledged forts, labor camps, detainment facilities, temporary holding quarters, base camps, branch camps, and the like. Not all of them existed for the same duration of time. They were located in nearly all of the then-48 states in the union, though in compliance with regulations stipulating how close they could be to large population centers, coastal areas, international borders, and factories or plants essential to the war or the nation's security. They were built or converted from previously existing structures, such as CCC camps or fallow fairgrounds, wherever and whenever needed, and lasted (some for months, some for years) as long as necessary for the ever-changing needs of the War Department.

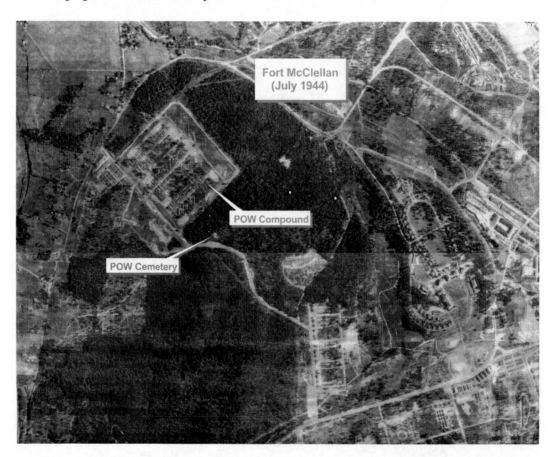

Aerial view, looking north, of the POW camp and a small portion of the Fort McClellan post. The "POW Compound" tag should more correctly read "POW Camp" (which consisted of three individual "compounds," so named). Features include Surrey Hill at far left; Pelham Road (to the right of Surrey Hill), curving right as it approaches top of photograph; the POW camp and the American military camp; the POW cemetery and a portion of Baker Road just below; heavily forested Wygant Hill and Blue Mountain Ridge; and the headquarters area of the main post, including Buckner Circle and Remington Hall (Officers' Club) (courtesy of Klaus W. Duncan).

The POW camp at Fort McClellan opened in 1943 for a projected complement of 3,000 internees—German soldiers from the Afrika Korps. The fort's historic building inventory report, authored by Mary Beth Reed, William R. Henry Jr., and J. W. Joseph for the U.S. Army Corps of Engineers in 1993, stated that the camp was "established at Fort McClellan in June of 1943" after "McClellan's camp was completed in May 1943."[7] Neither the first nor the largest camp in America, it became the model camp, one of the most desirable places to be.

Despite the general layout of most camps conforming to existing military paradigms, some variations occurred. The key element, in abiding by Geneva Convention standards, was to ensure that POWs received housing comparable to that employed for the host country's own soldiers. If American GIs lived in barracks on a military installation, POWs were to be housed in such structures. If GIs slept under tents while awaiting better lodging, POWs could expect the same.

McClellan's camp officially opened as an active internment center at the beginning of July 1943. The first complement of prisoners, some 400 captives, arrived at 5:30 p.m. on Saturday, July 3.

Prisoners came to McClellan by train, having first crossed the Atlantic Ocean via ship and entering the United States through military bases in the port cities of either New York or Norfolk, Virginia. They first stepped on McClellan soil at a siding of the camp spur of the Southern Railway near the Middle Gate (alternately called Center Gate and Baltzell Gate for Colonel George Franklin Baltzell, McClellan's commanding officer during 1934–1936). They then marched to the western outskirts of the post and south to the brand-new POW camp.

The Tuesday, July 6, 1943, issue of *The Anniston Star* explained under the headline "M'CLELLAN RECEIVES NEW WAR PRISONERS" and the subheading "One Load Comes In This Morning, Another Monday Night":

> More Axis prisoners, probably over 1,000, arrived at Fort McClellan late Monday [July 5] afternoon and early this morning, but no information about them could be released by Colonel Martin H. Mean[e]y, commander of the Internment Camp because of military regulations.
> Those who saw the prisoners en route from the railroad to the Internment Camp were confident that they were Germans and that they were enlisted personnel.
> The first Axis prisoners arrived Saturday night [July 3] and in one instance, several of them were known to have given assistance in fixing windows in one of the barracks.
> While military authorities have been prevented from giving out information about the camp, its capacity and the number of prisoners on hand, speculation has been to the effect that other prisoners likely will come later.
> Colonel Mean[e]y's organization in charge of operating the camp was well in its routine before the prisoners arrived and the strictest enforcement possible is the order for both the letter and the spirit of rules and regulations.
> Just what the prisoners will do in the camp remains to be seen. It is known that prisoners elsewhere have been given the opportunity to work in agriculture and it may be that such is in the offing for those in the Internment Camp at Fort McClellan. So far, no information has been forthcoming on this point.[8]

The arrival date received corroboration in the July 9, 1943, issue of *The McClellan CYCLE*, a weekly newspaper "published each Friday by and for the men of the Infantry Replacement Training Center, Fort McClellan, Alabama." It began publication on September 11, 1942, by the Branch Immaterial Replacement Training Center and ran for the duration of the war and beyond, with its editorial office "across from the Post Swimming Pool." The

The POW camp and a portion of the American military camp, looking north. Features include Pelham Road (upper left corner); the American camp, including the headquarters building and barracks (below Pelham Road); the POW camp, divided into equal thirds, one for each compound, with interior roads on a northeast-southwest slant; the POW greenhouse (far right corner of camp); and the cemetery with Baker Road below (courtesy of Klaus W. Duncan).

brief, one-paragraph story on the bottom of page 1 said simply, "The first group of Axis prisoners of war arrived at Ft. McClellan Saturday night and they are now confined to the Internment Camp. Another group of prisoners reached here Monday morning."[9]

The army's monthly rosters of camp strength indicated that "400 PW's [sic] arrived at Ft. McClellan" on "3 July 43 1730 o'clock."[10] The camp's German-language POW newspaper, *P.o.W. Oase*, which began publication in the fall of 1943, concurred. In a story from the July 14, 1944, issue, Unteroffizier (Sergeant) Heinrich Baumann of the 1st Company wrote of his arrival on July 3, 1943 (translation by Joachim Metzner, the son of the newspaper's editor):

The train gave a jarring hoarse sound of its siren, just like an old ocean freighter and stopped panting [chugging]. We stepped out.

At first we were very astonished to see so many soldiers for our reception. In a march formation, 5 in a row, and escorted by U.S. soldiers to the left and right, we eagerly entered the camp—the camp has its name in honor of General McClellan. With mixed feelings we passed the gate. The calendar said the 3rd of July 1943.

Halt! In small groups of 20 men, we were channeled through a barrack in which we were ... checked again (we were rid of any small animals [that is, deloused of any parasites] ... already in the harbor of Newport News [Virginia]), were allowed to dress again and then we got into our living barracks.

I have to admit, the organization was not bad, in a short time everybody has got his bed and bedding. A good purification from the travel dust in the washing room (full appreciation for this...) was the next thing to do. Afterwards we had to report for eating. We were ... surprised because, after the last restless days, we had really clean, well-laid tables, which gets us our moral back [lifted our morale]. The whole dining area shows German cleanliness and we poor devils felt good again after a long time, especially because the meal was good and sufficient....

Tired as dogs, everyone slept well that first night.[11]

Nearly 40 years after the camp opened, Dewey Welch, a former GI assigned as a guard, recounted his memories to Staff Sergeant Dan Coberly for a retrospective feature in *The McClellan News*:

About May or June [actually July] 1943, the prisoners began arriving. I went down and helped bring them off the train.

The pro–Nazi's [*sic*] were really mean. I remember they broke another prisoner's arm one time. They had quite a few fights among them in the early days. They used to holler back and forth trying to start something.

Sergeant Coberly also interviewed Edward Hooper, another guard with early memories of the camp. "There was quite a mixture of them—SS, Gestapo, and regular soldiers," the latter said. "Later, we tried to separate pro–Nazi's [*sic*] and the anti–Nazi's. We didn't have much luck."[12]

Ruth Allen, a civilian government employee whose army husband, Ray, worked on the main post, saw POWs arriving from her home across Pelham Road (the current State Highway 21/U.S. Highway 431/McClellan Boulevard) from the post and also from the post exchange (PX) in the American military camp (directly across from the POW camp), where she worked from 1944 to 1945.

They [trains] had unloaded them at a railroad crossing. And we could see the train coming. And then after a while, there would be a lot of 'em [POWs], probably several hundred of them. And they would be walking under armed guard. And they were carrying duffel bags like we carry a purse. And then they went in, up into the camp. They were a sorry-looking bunch of men. We saw these rows of prisoners walking by, and they were kind of pathetic. And then they were split up [into individual areas of the camp].

I often saw them from the PX. There was kind of a hill up to their camp.[13]

Not all the captives remained in McClellan; many were transferred to other camps in the state or region. But McClellan initially processed all POWs designated for internment within the state.

Paul Metzner, later the editor of the prison camp newsletter, voiced the thoughts of many prisoners, curious over what awaited them, when he wrote of his own arrival at McClellan on August 7, 1943:

Through the dark night races the PW-Express [train]. Direction unknown. Like shadows, trees, houses and mountains race by and finally one gives up trying to penetrate the darkness with tired eyes that again and again want to close. And then suddenly the light of the young day does lift the landscape out of the blackness into our field of view: deep green expanses of lawn with white wooden houses amid flower beds in summery colors, roads, country houses, lakes, mountains, water ... it may be that it is one of many weekend developments [getaways] to which the big city dwellers flee and in it experience nature and themselves as human beings again after the hours spent in the unrest and impersonality of the sea of stone [cities].[14]

And what did he and the first batches of prisoners think when entering the camp? Undoubtedly, most would have felt some discomfort and unease. Shakedown inspections, much like today's airport screenings, are never fun. Seeing the few possessions one owns fingered carelessly and perfunctorily by alien hands is always unsettling. On top of that, few German prisoners spoke English; few American GIs spoke German. The internees were in a strange land most had never visited even as civilians. And while being assigned new quarters in guarded buildings in the Deep South, they were about as far from their native homes as they could have imagined they would ever be.

But some pleasant surprises awaited. The white or cream-colored clothing initially issued them (preparatory to the blue denims with yellow-stenciled "PW" lettering) was clean, the barracks comfortable and new, and the food warm and good.

In reminiscences penned in September 1991, former POW Alfred Arens recalled his entry into McClellan nearly half a century earlier (original spelling and punctuation intact):

> On july 3., 1943 we entered Fort McClellan. The first impression was excellent. Get in your mind: we were tired, exhausted soldiers who were hunted in the last days in Tunisia like hares by spitfires and thunderbolds, day and night. And now new, clean barracks. The highlight in this evening was a meal of turkeys big like eagles served by men in white jackets: we thought we had arrived in paradise. Naturally, in the following days and month the life got more normal, the normal life of a PW.[15]

Erhard Eifler, another McClellan POW, wrote a similar recollection that same year: "At the 18th of August [1943] probably, I arrived at the Camp.... I felt great, because I knew that this bad war was over for me."[16]

The highly literate Paul Metzner recorded a very thorough account of the first impressions of a typical internee. His son, Joachim, who inherited his father's written memories, arranged and annotated them in subsections. On November 17, 2012, German scholar and teacher Joni L. Pontius paraphrased Metzner's diary entries in the *Teil 3 August 1943–Frühling 1944 (Part 3 August 1943–Spring 1944)* section:

> He wrote of the irony of arriving at Fort McClellan by train, a prisoner in a strange land, tired and just desiring to sleep, and seeing guards with rifles to prevent the prisoners from making a break for it and running off into the wooded areas near the road, as if they knew where they were going, as if they actually could somehow escape and survive in a new surrounding they knew nothing of.
>
> Then he writes of seeing the internment camp, a tall wire fence, and all the barracks appearing to be a dark grayish-green in color, and the guard towers rising higher above the barracks. And then hundreds of other prisoners coming out to welcome them and wearing light-colored sports clothes, leisure clothing, not the German uniforms, but the typical leisure clothing of the prisoner.
>
> And then they enter the camp by the main gate, and the sentry closes the gate behind them.

And they look at the guard tower nearby, and it is obvious to them that they have lost their freedom, at least for as long as they are to be in captivity.

And they are split into groups of 20 men and taken to be inspected. They then are taken to their barracks, the gray-green buildings raised up from the ground by cement pedestals or blocks at the corners. And they are given their new sets of clothing, two pairs of light-colored shirts and trousers, white socks, blue coveralls, bedding, razors, combs, and soap. And he writes of how they are refreshed after showering and surprised to find running hot and cold water from the sinks and showerheads and good bathroom facilities in good working order.

And they slept better that first night in camp, more comfortably than they had the previous two weeks, when traveling to the camp. And even though they're farther away from home, they felt a better sense of security and comfort in the United States. And they attend a church service the next day, which is Sunday, August 8, listening to the words of Chaplain Rindahl, a Norwegian chaplain in the United States Army, who gives a sermon on faith in a common God.

And they have access to a canteen where they can buy nice nonessentials like cigarettes, beer, chocolate candy, sweet items, mirrors, orangeade, sports apparel with the ten cents they receive every day in the form of coupons, canteen three-dollar checkbooks.

And he says they are allowed to send mail back to Germany, once per week, one letter and one card per week. The paper has been specially prepared to deal with the issue of invisible ink.

He wrote of receiving a new assignment on August 16, working in the battalion headquarters as director of recreational activities, sports and entertainment or leisure activities. He was involved in courses that taught math and English and implementing a team chess tournament for the four companies of the third battalion [Compound 3].

He wrote that they played ping-pong against [American] Captain [Woodrow] Wallace [the plans and training officer] who sees his POWs as men, not only as workers. And he [Wallace] isn't afraid to play with them in singles or doubles table tennis. And he says it would be interesting to see if a parallel circumstance existed in Germany, but he doubts it.[17]

Twenty-four-year-old captured German artist Christian Höschle arrived at McClellan on July 23, 1943, two weeks before Metzner. He later wrote his autobiography, *Hast du nichts so bist du nichts*, which included chapters on his years at McClellan.

Born May 19, 1919, in Wendelsheim (within the later state of Baden-Würtemberg), Höschle began drawing with charcoal at the age of four. In 1936, he embarked on an "apprenticeship in a nearby artistic metalworking shop," where, according to Joachim Metzner's translation, he excelled and "was asked to make a relief portrait of the 'Führer.'" It was sent to Hitler as a birthday present from the town of Tübingen (near Wendelsheim). Young Christian received a written acknowledgment "promising him a free place at [an] Artistic school in Munich in the future."

But service in the Third Reich beckoned. After a civilian assignment, he was called to the military on December 12, 1939. He became a sergeant and went to Tunisia with a tank detachment. He was captured on May 12, 1943, following the defeat of the Afrika Korps.

"At first they fell into the arms of the British and the treatment was OK," wrote translator Joachim Metzner. "Then the French were responsible for the transport and the situation became worse. When they reached their final African Camp in Casablanca the Americans took over and … [those] weeks were much better in [terms of] food and treatment. Christian Höschle started to make souvenirs out of tin cans and lids, mainly Ashtrays and ornamental plates and the American soldiers swapped them against extra food and cigarettes. On July 6th the big Journey across the Atlantic started and Christian Höschle tried to cheat [pass] the time doing drawings, which he soon could sell to the US–staff on the boat. At July 19th they entered the New York harbor."[18]

"He was impressed with America," Joni Pontius said, translating the McClellan chapters.

He arrived in the New York Harbor during the night. At 4 a.m. on July 20, he had a good breakfast, and he saw the skyline at 5 a.m. At 6, they were put in smaller boats and transported across the harbor to the railroad yard. They were fingerprinted, and military police kept the curious onlookers away from them. They were stunned by the upholstered seats on the nicely decorated Pullman cars.

And then he wrote, "As the train drove away, we saw in the distance the symbol of freedom disappear—the Statue of Liberty."

They traveled through Pennsylvania, West Virginia, Kentucky, Tennessee, and into Alabama. He found the train ride exciting and interesting because of the expanse and beauty of the land.

They arrived at Fort McClellan on July 23. And he wrote, "My intention was to make the best of this forced situation. The thought even slowly came to me that perhaps there would be the possibility of staying in this land of unlimited opportunities."

They got off the train about a kilometer outside of the camp, and they marched to the camp. To their left and right, standing two meters away, were soldiers with machine guns. They weren't sure if it was an honor cordon or if they were afraid of them.

They went through the gates, and an American major stood in front of them, patting his stomach and saying, in essence, "Now you'll eat well" in broken German—"Jetzt aber schnell gut essen."

Shortly after, cigarettes and drinks were distributed.

The right[-hand] camp [Compound 3 of the POW camp's three sections] was for underofficers [noncommissioned officers] up to hauptfeldwebel [translated as master sergeant in a 1945 World War II German-to-English manual; see "Note on Rank" at the end of Chapter 3 in chapter notes], and he was assigned to that camp because he was an unteroffizier [sergeant]. The middle and left camps [Compounds 2 and 1, respectively] were for the troops [enlisted men]. [Other reports and memoirs indicate that this division of men by rank did not always occur as described by Höschle.]

He guessed there were about 3,000 POWs there. And they had nothing taken away from them [not always the case in Allied POW camps and detainment centers]. "We were even allowed to keep our uniforms," he wrote.

They went into clean barracks—no bunk beds. Each bed had two quilts and two wool blankets, a white sheet, and a pillow. Then after they had gotten their beds, they were led into a shower room for a warm shower. "After so many weeks and months to stand under a warm shower again!" he wrote.

They were given two pairs of shoes, one pair of cotton pants, two pairs of wool pants, one wool jacket, five pairs of socks, four pairs of underwear, four undershirts, one raincoat, one pair of gloves, one belt, and handkerchiefs. "One must say," he wrote, "that the Americans had prepared for our reception."

"After we were freshly showered, clothed, and shaved, we had to go to roll call and were officially greeted by the camp commander [Colonel Martin H. Meaney]," he wrote. And Meaney said that they would be treated according to the Geneva Convention. He left them with the remark that it wasn't up to him to make their fates worse but, if they held onto their famous German discipline, they could together make the best of their situation.

Then they were taken to the mess hall and were astounded when they saw the quantity and quality of the menu.

The following days passed by with immunizations, medical records, fingerprinting, and ID information.[19]

All surviving memoirs of McClellan's first arrivals tell similar stories of such unexpected but welcome hospitality.

4

Descriptions of the
POW Camp

*"The pine trees which surround the camp
give it a pleasant aspect."*

The Fort McClellan POW Camp conformed to existing standards.

As Antonio Thompson wrote in *Men in German Uniform*, "POW camps consisted of one or more compounds, each normally housing 1,000 men … separated by barbed wire. The men in each compound further divided into companies of 250. An average compound, therefore, had four companies."[1]

McClellan's camp was designed for one enclosure with three separate compounds, four companies in each compound, and approximately 250 men in a company. It was a rectangle, approximately 2,000 feet along its front and back and 1,400 feet on either side, laid out on a hill north of Baker Road (a post road east of the civilian Pelham Road), on the western section of the McClellan complex.[2] The front side of the camp paralleled Baker Road.

The view from Surrey Hill, looking across Pelham Road. In the foreground are a rectangular sign (far left) proclaiming "Fort McClellan ALABAMA PRISONER of WAR CAMP"; the white guardhouse at the junction of Pelham and Baker Roads; the POW camp headquarters building (immediate right of tallest tree); and the American camp warehouse complex. In the background, on either side of the guard tower, is the POW camp (author's collection).

A remarkable photograph, again from Surrey Hill, showing the rectangular sign, Baker Road (center of photograph), and guardhouse with closed gates on either side. The POW camp is to the left of Baker Road, and the American camp is to the right. The MP on duty is barely visible in front of the guardhouse, and another MP and a woman are seen conversing nearby at the road edge (author's collection).

Karl Gustaf Almquist described its outward appearance following his December 21–25, 1945, visit on behalf of the Young Men's Christian Association (YMCA) War Prisoners Aid Program:

> On a highway [Pelham Road] about four miles north of Armiston [*sic*], Alabama, we find the barbed wires indicating the Prisoner of War Camp of Fort McClellan. It appears so suddenly that it is possible to pass without observing it…. Outside the fence life is going on normally, with rather heavy traffic on the highway, one-family houses along the road, and the beginning of the countryside, with cattle from the farms crossing the highway. Inside the fence you will find a rather big, transitory "town" with its own life.[3]

McClellan's main post headquarters area occupied land east of the camp. Only two-thirds of a mile, as the crow flies, separated the Officers' Club (later named Remington Hall) from the easternmost point of the camp. The post headquarters building—the fort's nerve center—crested an elevation known as "the hill" a shade under a mile from the camp. But heavily forested hills—Wygant Hill and Blue Mountain Ridge—between the camp and the headquarters area prevented either location from clearly viewing the other.[4]

The camp's three compounds were laid out in as many parallel sections, each on a northeast-southwest axis and perpendicular to Baker Road on the south. Each was separated from the others by interior fencing and included a central road splitting its length in half, with parallel rows of barracks and other "temporary" buildings on either side.

According to the German-language camp newspaper, *P.o.W. Oase*, the gates separating the interior compounds from each other were sometimes open (allowing free access) and sometimes not. As Joachim Metzner recounted, "The 3 compounds were separate in the beginning (1943), then joined and separated again in 1945," meaning "the pow could pass

A view from atop the guard tower near the middle road (foreground) entering the center of the POW camp. To the left are portions of Compounds 2 and 3 and the twin rows of stakes supporting the enclosing barbed-wire fencing. Another tower is visible at top center. On the right is Baker Road. Despite the direction of the vehicles, Baker Road was a two-way thoroughfare. A quartet of MPs stands in relaxed formation near the guardhouse (courtesy of Alabama Room, Public Library of Anniston and Calhoun County).

freely between the 3 compounds for quite a long time." When interior gates cordoning off one compound from another were closed, signs proclaiming *Durchgang Verboten* ("No Entry") stopped passage.[5]

Christian Höschle agreed. "The three gates within the main gate were as a rule always open, and this meant that we could visit troops," he wrote in his autobiography.[6]

Each dormitory barracks, built in typical military shotgun style, rose a foot or more above the ground on thick blocks placed underneath the corners. Small wooden staircases at the front and rear allowed access. Each barracks was 20 feet in the front and rear and 40 feet along the sides. The single-story buildings sported sloping roofs rising to pointed ridgelines at the apex. Each featured a pair of single-width doors at the entrances and several square or rectangular windows and portholes along the sides. Inside the huts, wooden bunks along either side accommodated about 20 men. Surviving illustrations depict the beds in rows parallel to the front width of the barracks (perpendicular to the 40-foot-long sides). Stoves with vertical piping rising to the roof rested on elevated platforms, and wooden benches, seats, and tables provided space for leisure activities like reading and writing.[7]

Erhard Eifler, interned in McClellan from August 1943 until April 1946, became one of the camp's longest-resident POWs. He later reminisced:

A view of the middle road going up the hill of the POW camp, bifurcating Compound 2. Baker Road is at the bottom of the illustration, separating one of the buildings in the American camp from the dozens of POW structures. The main entrance into the POW camp is flanked by an open gate and the main guardhouse. Guard towers are visible at bottom left and left of the top of the middle road. Illustration by POW H. Geyer from the introduction to Collection II of *P.o.W. Oase* (author's collection).

POW Hermann Haugg's depiction of the inside of a typical prisoner barracks. From *P.o.W. Oase* #47, September 7, 1944 (author's collection).

I was ordered to go to Camp [Compound] 3, 3rd Btl. Our boss [supervising American officer] was Capt. Welles [possibly Captain Woodrow W. Wallace], I believe. We were about three thousand german POWs, one thousand in a camp, as far as I remember. 12 POWs slept in one of the barracks…. The barracks had round windows, like portholes. In the middle of the building stood the big oven that we could feed with wood or coal, if necessary.[8]

The various visitation reports by international inspectors or members of the U.S. military provided details of the camp's structure. A September 2, 1943, report on "Camp McClellan" filed by "A[lfred]. Cardinaux" of the neutral Swiss Legation recorded the following:

The camp for prisoners of war is completely separated from the [U.S.] military camp. The barracks are built on the slope of a wooded hill, and the pine trees which surround the camp give it a pleasant aspect….

At the time of the visit, there were 3012 German prisoners of war:

663 non-commissioned officers
48 members of the sanitary personnel
2301 soldiers

Total 3012

The spokesman is Willy Utz….

The camp is a former fort, remodeled to house prisoners of war. Consequently, the barracks are different from those existing in Army camps and other camps. Some of the windows are made of thick cellophane and cannot be opened. Other windows are provided with screens to keep out mosquitoes. This system provides light as well as ventilation in the barracks. Each barrack is heated by means of two coal stoves.

These buildings are as spacious and as comfortable as in other camps. The American soldiers on guard duty live in barracks similar to those of the prisoners [but outside the POW camp].

The following buildings are provided for each company:

> 8 housing barracks [an underestimate or miscount]
> 1 barrack for kitchen and mess hall
> 1 barrack for shower, basins and toilets
> 1 barrack for recreation center

There are also a canteen, an infirmary and a school for each four companies....

The hospital is constructed in the same way as other military hospitals. There is an operating room and an X-ray room. At the time of the visit, there were 52 patients in the hospital, 8 of them with jaundice. The other cases were the following:

> 14 diseases of the respiratory tracts
> 9 fractures and lesions
> 17 surgical cases: hernia, bladder, extraction of shrapnel
> 4 syphilis cases

...Twelve members of the sanitary personnel are permanently attached to the hospital and are paid 80 cents a day. These men accompany the prisoner labor detachments working outside the camp, and carry with them a First Aid kit. There is a dental clinic in one of the infirmaries, where the prisoners and the American guards are taken care of.

The dentist told the representative of the International Red Cross Committee that the prisoners of war had very bad teeth. At the time of the visit, 1086 extractions and 102 fillings had already been made....

The kitchen and mess hall are in the same barrack; they are separated by a counter. The tables seat six; they are arranged in two rows. The dishes are of chinaware....

Laundry tubs are provided for the prisoners' personal laundry in the shower barracks. They are given the soap needed for the purpose....

Books are lacking as yet, but since the time of the visit we have sent a certain number of *Soldatenbriefe* [German information books] and other books which had been furnished us by the German Red Cross....

The prisoners have been able to organize English courses, and they will organize courses on a larger scale as soon as they receive the text-books they need....

The prisoners have built stages in the recreation halls and they have bought musical instruments with canteen profits....

The canteen is provided with all the articles needed. Each company has a prisoner representative on a committee which makes decisions as to the use of canteen funds.

As the camp is constructed on the slope of a hill, there is no space large enough for an athletic field. At the time of the visit, the prisoners were leveling athletic grounds, and when this work is finished there will be adequate space in each sector for basket ball and volley ball. The large athletic field, next to the camp, cannot be used as a football field as it is also on the slope of the hill. The prisoners intend to make a vegetable garden there and the Camp Commandant hopes to be able to provide a football field outside the camp....

The camp Commandant has provided the prisoners with electric tools and they have established a cabinet-making shop where they can build furniture and other articles.[9]

A "Report of Visit to Camp Prisoner of War Division, Provost Marshal General's Office" on December 13–15, 1943, and bearing the signature of Captain Edward C. Shannahan, provided a more extensive description of the camp. It listed 3,002 enlisted POWs and two officers and identified "Oberwach[t]meister [Tech Sergeant]" Willi Utz as the "Ranking Prisoner of War Spokesman."

The camp is located in the northern part of Alabama ... and presents a very pleasing appearance. It is surrounded by the timber covered slopes of the southern foothills of the Appalachian Mountains. The camp itself conforms generally to the standard plan for prisoner of war camps with the exception of the hospital which is a part of the Station Hospital of Fort McClellan and the recreation area which is being built across the road from the compound area. As the field originally allotted is entirely too hilly to be of practical use, the original area will be planted as a vegetable farm this next season. Groups of trees within the compounds provide shade for the prisoners during the hot Alabama summer and lend beauty to the camp. The barracks for the prisoners are painted olive drab which blends very well with the surrounding foliage and further assists in beautifying the camp....

The barracks provided are 20' × 40' Caribbean type buildings. Not more than twenty men were quartered in any of the barracks visited by this officer. However, the buildings are dark and cold in view of the light construction and the fact that the sides are meant to be raised to provide light and air. This is impractical at present as the temperature is low at this time of year. Experiments are being made to provide more air and light by cutting windows in the sides of the buildings. At the time of this visit, a program of winterization was started to make the barracks more livable....

Each latrine is equipped in accordance with AR 40–205 and in addition has ten laundry tubs per two hundred and fifty man company. Footbaths are used in the shower rooms and the facilities are inspected regularly.... Each kitchen has a steam sterilizer and all appeared to be exceptionally clean and well kept....

Eight standard GTAM [guard] towers are in use at the camp. These towers are manned by

A revealing photograph taken from a guard tower on the western side of the POW camp. From left to right are the American officers' complex (long building near horizon); buildings in POW Compound 1; a soccer field; and (beyond the soccer field and to the right) much of the American camp, the main guard tower, the warehouses, and the top of the headquarters building (author's collection).

two men, one remaining inside the tower and the other man staying on the catwalk outside. Emergency spotlights are mounted on the towers and may be switched freely from the camp current to an emergency electric system of wet cell batteries....

The standard double fence of hog wire topped with a three-strand overhang of barbed wire is used. There is approximately twelve feet between the fences. The area between the fences has been cleared entirely of grass and other obstructions so a clear and unimpeded view of the area is available to the guards. Therefore, any prisoner getting between the fences would be silhouetted excellently....

In general the field of fire from the towers is good. However, the rolling terrain allows for many "blind spots." They have been covered by the relocation of some of the towers, but one tower remains in a hollow from which the machine guns cannot cover as much fence line as they should....

All buildings, both within and without the compound areas, are at least seventy-five feet from the fences....

No attack or sentry dogs are used at this post....

Each compound has a small, well-equipped infirmary for the treatment of minor injuries, with a daily sick call held in each of the infirmaries. The prisoner of war hospital is maintained as a unit of the Station Hospital and the prisoners receive the same treatment as Army patients. At present, there are forty-eight prisoners as patients in the hospital....

The Provost Marshal General furniture sets were being installed at the time of this visit. Other furniture made by or bought by the prisoners is being installed also. Each compound has a 20' × 100' building to be used as a recreation room and, in addition, each company has a 20' × 40' building for recreational purposes....

Well-equipped woodworking and carpentry shops are available to the prisoners in each of the three compounds. There is also a barber and shoe repair shop available in each of the compounds....

The library is small and equipped with books which the prisoners call "old fashioned." It was found that the majority of the books are of a religious nature and other books which were published more than twenty years ago....

Lieutenant Colonel [Laurence D.] Smith, the Camp Commander, had the following recommendations to make....

That a field house or building of similar type be erected within the compound to be used in inclement weather as a general recreation building and also as a movie house and chapel....

That heavy farming equipment be issued to the camp for the maintenance of the proposed farm....

The camp itself shows the results of hard work on the part of the prisoners. The barracks area and the interior roads are well taken care of, sports fields have been hewn from hillsides, and many other small inovations [sic] have been constructed to make life more pleasant.[10]

Helpful though these reports are in piecing together a camp that no longer exists, their details are not always sacrosanct. For example, an aerial photo taken in 1944 clearly shows clusters of 12 same-size barracks for each company, not the eight mentioned in Cardinaux's report. And in an October 21, 2012, email, Joachim Metzner, referencing his father's issues of the camp's prisoner newspaper, wrote, "[I] went again through a poem of my father 'Unser Lager' ['Our Camp'].... I read rhyme #5 describing company no9, which he belonged to ... and in our twelve barracks...."[11] In a follow-up email three days later, he added, "I just went through the article about 'his barrack' again and got 22 men (himself included)— So the limit was not 20."[12] This clearly indicates 144 barracks, each with a potential capacity of 22 men, for a total resident population of 3,168—more in line with reality than Cardinaux's figures.

The POW newspaper often provided a near-photographic description of the camp,

Hermann Haugg's view downhill from the POW camp. The barracks buildings are parallel to one another on both sides of the sloping path in the center. The larger buildings jutting into the path or at different angles include mess halls, recreation centers, canteens, infirmaries, classrooms, carpentry shops, barber shops, and the like. Haugg also shows various officers' quarters in the American camp on the hill just above dead center. From *P.o.W. Oase* #50, October 1, 1944 (author's collection).

A view from a guard tower looking in a southeasterly direction across the entire camp, showing the symmetrical orientation of the barracks, one group perpendicular to another, with shared common buildings on a diagonal. The greenhouse is the long building in the top left corner (author's collection).

filling in gaps left by the vagueness or errancy of the American reports. Poring over the issues for information on the camp's various infirmaries, Joachim Metzner commented:

> I just read an article again called "A POW got ill" and found: 3 buildings (with chimneys [for contaminated waste incineration]) normally called dispensaries, but the one in Camp [Compound] 3 is a little different, it is used as hospital and officially called dispensary and additionally it is the source of ice water for the whole camp!...
>
> [T]he different one in Camp 3 that is used as hospital was called infirmary. In that they also made smaller surgeries.[13]

The official American reports, resulting from scheduled inspections, were filed in military offices and rarely received wide viewership. And for nearly the first year of the camp's existence, most residents of Anniston and even members of the military stationed at McClellan knew little, if anything, of the internment center's particulars. However, that changed with an item published in *The McClellan CYCLE*, an on-post publication for American military personnel. Corporal William R. Frye's "Inside the PW Camp: Pin-Up Girls, PXs, Nazi 'Heils' Found Behind Grim Stockade" offered this glimpse in the May 12, 1944, issue:

> Under constant MP guard, behind a high wire stockade more than 1000 Nazi veterans of Marshal Erwin Rommel's once-vaunted Afrika Korps are today living a GI life as prisoners of war at Ft. McClellan.
>
> Rows of hutments decorated by spectacular pin-up girls, familiar-looking mess halls and latrines, even PXs and dispensaries occupy the company areas in the stockade by the Anniston-Jacksonville highway.
>
> Army authorities have now stripped away the secrecy which had previously veiled the Prisoner of War Camp and have disclosed many once-forbidden facts to an inspecting party of civilian and Army newspapermen. A CYCLE reporter was in the party.
>
> Now out from "under wraps" is the fact that Uncle Sam has 183,618 Axis prisoners of war

The interior of the POW camp. The main building is at an angle from the barracks on the right and would have served a different purpose. A large stone, bearing a company inscription and the German eagle, stands at left. Such a personal statement, constructed by the POWs, would have required approval from an American officer (courtesy of Edith Suberg).

interned in 99 base camps and 104 branch camps in the United States. Of these 183,618 men, 133,135 are Germans, 50,136 Italians and 349 Japanese.

Captured in Africa

At the McClellan base camp, there have been interned, at one time or another, more than 2000 Nazis who were captured at the climax of the African campaign, at Cape Bon. They were the rear guard of Rommel's broken army, trying to protect the escape of the main body. About half of these men have been "farmed out" to branch camps in this vicinity. All but six are enlisted men. (Officers and enlisted men are in separate areas). They're all Germans: no Japs or Italians are here.

You step inside the heavy gates with pipe dreams you have heard about a Prisoner of War Camp running through your head. It's a feather-bed life, you've been told, with prisoners coddled, eating steaks and French fries on silver platters. Or, it's a miniature Nazi Germany, with "heils" and Nazi salutes and a sinister Gestapo at work.

The truth is more prosaic but just as interesting.

Arranged in "compounds" are rows of one-story wooden hutments, a little larger and a little more tightly constructed than most McClellan huts, but otherwise much the same. Each compound is divided into companies, and each company has facilities similar to those of a training company: a mess hall, a latrine, a supply room, and the huts.

Has PX, Guardhouse

For each compound there is also a canteen (PX), a dispensary, a dayroom, a headquarters, and a workshop. The camp boasts an attractive chapel, a display hall for prisoner art work, an outdoor auditorium in the process of construction, and a guardhouse.

You go inside the first hut with the inspecting party, and a non-com shouts his German equivalent of "ten-chut!" The men line up at attention beside their individual bunks, wearing the faded uniform of a German soldier. The blue denims with "PW" in yellow are their fatigues, which they wear while working.

The men are young. You learn that some are only 15 years old; the average, 20–22. Many are light-haired and typical Hitler "Aryans"; some fall far short of that Nazi standard. They look as self-conscious as a trainee at general's inspection. Occasionally one will smile with what might be a mixture of friendliness, fear, and derision.

The barber shop is a sight to warm the heart of any American GI. It has an enviable collection of pin-up girls on the walls. German barbers give the shaves and haircuts.

The PX is smaller than most branch PXs at McClellan, and sells primarily tobacco, toilet goods, soft drinks, beer, and miscellaneous small articles. Payment is made in coupons, because the PWs never have money. They receive coupons for their work.

Inside the chapel, built on the pattern of most Army chapels, is an altar decorated with flowers, and rows of well-built wooden pews. There are two American Army chaplains, one Catholic and the other Lutheran. The prisoners are 43 per cent Catholic, slightly over 50 per cent Lutheran, and the rest miscellaneous. The chaplains say there are few atheists.

Nudes At Seaside

Like other buildings, the mess hall and the latrine are scrubbed within-an [sic] inch of their lives as if for general's inspection. Both are similar to the ones GIs use. German cooks and a German mess sergeant pride themselves in the pastries they prepare to go with the meals. Food is the same "in quality and quantity" as that of American soldiers. It must be under the provisions of the Geneva Convention.

The display hall for art work shows portraits, landscapes, and still life in crayon, oils, and other mediums. One Nazi soldier has drawn a yacht club by a seaside bay, with nude girls lounging artistically on the shore or waving to the sailboats on the water.

Evidence that may preserve their taste for music can be found in the fact that they asked, and were granted, permission to build an outdoor auditorium for orchestral concerts. At present, it is well on the way to completion.[14]

Recreational and cultural amenities for the POWs existed in a number of shared public fields and structures within the compounds: dayrooms, dispensaries, orderly rooms, reading quarters, and a library. The companies had their own kitchens and messes, the compounds their own exercise and sports fields.

Electric poles and wiring supplied power throughout the camp, and culverts carried runoff water alongside the interior roads slicing through the hilly terrain. The prisoners beautified the fronts and sides of their individual barracks with flowers, shrubbery, and rock gardens complete with miniature houses and other decorative features.

Rita Wells—who, as the youthful Rita Johnson, just beyond her years of formal education, worked in the headquarters building outside the POW camp—later recounted her memories:

The camp was very crudely constructed. The buildings were just put up for the POW camp.

You would get to the camp from what is now called Shipley Road [formerly Baker Road] from Pelham Road [the current McClellan Boulevard or Highway 21]. Shipley Road has since been straightened to a degree.

A chain link fence surrounded the compound.

No civilians were ever allowed in the compound, but we could see some of the activities within the compound. There was a basketball court and a soccer field in the compound that we could see.[15]

Eight guard towers were placed around the perimeter of the camp to observe prisoner movement and monitor activity. Each was constructed as a roughly angled circular enclosure, with white paint around the windowed sides. Green paint covered the roofs, support beams, and scaffolding beneath each tower's elevated platform. A curvilinear catwalk surrounded the enclosed portion of the tower, wide enough to support an armed MP ambling around its circumference. A yard-high railing protected the catwalk. Inside the enclosure, reached by a door, another MP sat and kept a log as he remained within radio communication with other towers and military personnel outside the camp. Ladders leading to retractable ports in the flooring provided access to the towers from below.

The towers were high enough off the ground—a couple dozen or so feet to the catwalk, and well above the roughly 10-foot-high "hog wire" fence enclosing the camp—to provide a fairly unobstructed view of a portion of the terrain.

The eight towers' positions (one in each corner of the rectangular layout and another in the middle of each of the four sides) guaranteed complete coverage of the camp. This format allowed each side three observation posts (including the corner towers, which were shared by two sides).

The towers were connected to one another by a path surrounding the camp, just beyond the double rows of wire fencing, a dozen feet apart, hemming in the enclosure. The twin fencing, about 10 feet high, with three strands of angled barbed wire on top, isolated the towers from inside interference. Access gates, wide enough for vehicles to pass through, stood at key entrance points alongside gatehouses manned by MPs, granting passage to guards at various interconnecting junctures.[16]

The MPs worked in rotating shifts to avoid the strain of long hours in the intense Alabama summer sun and heat, as well as, later, the bitter winter chill. Lights in the towers aided nighttime observation.

In 1943, Private Clifford Prior of the 382nd Military Police Escort Guard Company (MPEGC) wrote his "Ma," Goldie M. Terry of Rochester, New York, several letters describing life in the towers (original spelling, punctuation, and grammar left intact). "I am on guard to-night 2½ on 2½ off you remember I told you about this post before," he wrote on October 22. Seven days later, he penned, "I am on guard as usual thats the only thing I ever do because its our job. I am in a tower this time and its the best job we have its real cool to-night but in the tower we have a coal fire to keep us warm. So you see we have modern improvements here ha ha."

On November 2, he wrote, "I am on guard at the prison hospital to-night 4 hrs on and 8 off not so bad I can get more sleep this way…. It's the same old grind down here nothing new so far on the camp." And on December 16, he added, "The weather down here is real cold not as cold as up north but damp cold that cuts right through you and gets your bones chilled it was 14 above last night but I had a real warm tower and kept warm by the fire so it was not so bad."[17]

Edward Hooper, also of the 382nd Company, recalled his impressions of guarding the Germans: "Well, they really weren't too much of a problem. You know, there were at least 7 towers with 50 caliber machine guns in each one. They weren't going anywhere. I'll tell you though, they kept the area very neat. I was always impressed with how clean they were. And I'll tell you another thing—there was just no comparison between them and the boys in our own stockade. The POWs weren't nearly as much trouble." His fellow guard, Dewey Welch, remembered having "three Military Police Escort Guard companies, with four platoons each," with "3–5 guards walking between towers and three in each tower. We changed guards every six hours, after each pulled two hours on the ground."[18]

A long, rectangular greenhouse, with parallel sections, each reaching a roofed apex and joined together on their inner sides, stood at the northeastern point of the camp, just outside Compound 3 and beyond the barbed wire enclosure of the main camp, yet within the view of the guard tower in that angle. Begonias, carnations, chrysanthemums, ferns, pansies, and a number of other flower and plant species thrived inside the twin peaks of the greenhouse. Outside, expansive botanical gardens created an enveloping canvas of greenery dotted with the colors of vegetation in bloom, broken only by shade structures intended for the enhanced propagation of various species and a couple of storage shacks. Paul Metzner, the editor of *P.o.W. Oase*, described it in the November 22, 1944, issue (as edited and translated by his son):

> The greenhouse was located behind the 12th company ("outside," as my father wrote) near the rear watchtower. It was 13m[eters by] 33m and stood in the middle of the Botanic-garden area (size: 3000m^2)....
>
> The building was ready in September 1944, but the work on the flower and vegetable-patches outside started earlier.
>
> Soil was bad, but they got some dung from a cow-field by truck (With the help from Sgt. Cowgill).[19]

Civilian government employee Marie Shay, herself a gardener, appreciated the different specimens on display both inside and beyond the greenhouse. She remembered decades later:

> We [she and Sergeant John E. "Jack" Shay, her husband] often went to the greenhouse and the gardens when we were done working for the day just to see such beautiful, luxurious colors. We'd walk through the greenhouse and along all the paths through the shrubs and flower gardens outside. They had marigolds and petunias, morning glories, roses, carnations, coleus,

The double greenhouse and gardens as seen from a guard tower (author's collection).

zinnias, asters, glads [gladioli], just about everything. We were friends with the German PW [short for POW] who worked there. It seems like he was always there. We talked with him and took his picture. I'm not sure but what Dad [her husband] didn't have him on one of his work details or maybe was in charge of him there at the greenhouse for awhile because they knew each other quite well.

We took some pictures, but the black-and-white film didn't do justice to all those beautiful colors of the flowers and blossoming shrubs and bushes. We just enjoyed sitting there on the steps outside or walking through all the tables inside with these beautiful flowers of all description. They were so striking. That PW and the others who helped him did a wonderful job with all those flowers.[20]

The POW was Oberfeldwebel (First Sergeant) Erich Thurow, as later identified by Joachim Metzner: "I wonder if your father's friend from the greenhouse was the German leader of the greenhouse. If it was him, then I can tell you his name: Ofw Erich Thurow."[21]

A POW cemetery was established just a tenth of a mile

Erich Thurow and a fellow POW in the greenhouse (author's collection).

beyond the eastern boundary of the camp but separated by a dense tree line. It would ultimately hold the graves of 26 German and three Italian POWs, the majority of whom died in captivity elsewhere and were brought to McClellan for interment. During the war, it was named and numbered P. W. Cemetery T-3547, with a large black and white marble Iron Cross at the head of typical military tombstones. A four-foot-high, ranch-style fence enclosed its inner space.

5

Life in the POW Camp

"We lived every day at McClellan
happy to be safe from the war,
yet wanting to be with our families."

Though McClellan could hold more than 3,000 prisoners, new transfers and arrivals constantly affected its population. The camp's monthly roster sheets told the story.

The first contingent of prisoners—an even 400—arrived on July 3, 1943. Three days later, 417 more entered. On July 12, 934 more (including one Italian POW) came, bringing the total population to 1,751. A fatal accident on July 29—POW Willi Waechter dying when a truck overturned—decreased the total by one as July drew to a close.

The August population swelled to an official 3,012 at month's end, as newer POWs arrived: 56 on August 5, 39 the next day, 417 on August 7, 500 on August 15, and 304 on August 29. But a steady stream of transfers of POWs to other camps, for a variety of reasons, concomitantly occurred: on August 7, the lone Italian POW went to Camp Como, Mississippi; 50 Germans went to Hunters Run, Pennsylvania; and one German wound up in Camp Alva, Oklahoma. Additionally, the practice of sending companies or squads of Germans to other areas for what was termed "detached service" began. For a one-month detail, starting August 28 and ending September 29, 1,250 German POWs went to several locations in Georgia—the Americus Army Airbase, Turner Field in Albany, Army Air Field in Bainbridge, and Spence Field in Moultrie—on a peanut harvesting assignment.

By the end of September, 3,019 POWs remained at the fort and 1,250 worked a Georgia detail. At the end of October, the official tally was 3,011, with 1,000 detailed to harvest cotton in Mississippi. At month's end in November, the camp's roster included 3,005, with 1,250 men picking cotton in Mississippi and peanuts in Georgia. December's final figure came in at 2,997, with 760 men on Georgia details.

The following year, 1944, the first full year of the camp's operation, the familiar trend continued. Official end-of-month figures, accounting for new arrivals and men transferring in, as well as current POWs transferring out to other locations, listed:

January—2,987
February—2,988
March—2,737
April—2,489
May—1,342 (after more than 1,100 men had transferred to other locations)
June—1,335
July—1,336

August—1,338
September—2,050
October—2,942 (bolstered by the arrival of 1,000 POWs on October 28)
November—3,101
December—3,087[1]

A report stemming from a February 23–24, 1945, visit to the camp by Maurice Ed. Perret indicated a population of 3,065 German prisoners, including 209 detailed to Camp Clanton, Alabama. A July 1945 report by Captains W. J. Bridges and C. E. Tremper accounted for 2,546 men, including those in Clanton.[2]

Regarding non-German POWs, no one interviewed for this book recalled Italians in the camp. Nor did the author's parents ever speak of any Italian prisoners. It seems likely that any Italians interned at McClellan resided there only briefly, pending transfer to other locations.

This constant fluctuation continued until the official deactivation of the camp on April 10, 1946, with diminishing numbers in late 1945 and early 1946, when large numbers of POWs left McClellan for eventual repatriation to their homeland.

The POW officers at McClellan also varied. At first there were none. By October 1943, however, two had arrived. On February 12, 1944, four more medical officers transferred to the camp. The officer population rose to nine on April 22, 1944, when three additional medical personnel arrived. One officer left on September 6, reducing the total to eight. By the end of October 1944, the total stood at five. On November 13, a nonmedical officer, a chaplain from Camp Como, arrived to increase the total to six once again.[3]

At full capacity, the camp had three compounds, each with four companies (numbered 1–12). Assuming an equal distribution of men, each company would have had about 250. But as work details elsewhere in the South claimed hundreds of McClellan's internees at a clip, and the camp's population dipped well under 2,000 (and sometimes under 1,500), it would have made sense to consolidate in order to conserve utility costs and reduce maintenance.

Some POWs changed company assignments. For example, Paul Metzner, the editor of the camp's POW newspaper, began in Company 9 and wound up in Company 7. His son offered this explanation in a March 21, 2013, email: "[C]ompanies were sometimes transferred in total to sidecamps for a longer time (work duties) and … men [remaining at McClellan] … had to be integrated into another … [remaining] company, but that is only an idea." Albeit a likely one, as he had suggested in an earlier (July 10, 2012) email: "I guess, if a company was away in a side-camp … the barracks were closed and remaining men (ill or other jobs) transferred to other companies." It would have saved on operational upkeep.[4]

And though the full capacity of McClellan was always listed as 12 companies, the numbering could change. In the December 6, 1944, issue of *P.o.W. Oase*, a chart enumerating the distribution of companies yielded the following information: Compound 1—Companies 1, 3, 4, and 5; Compound 2—Companies 6, 7, 8, and 10; Compound 3—Companies 9, 11, 12, and 13. The apparent reason for the shift? The transfer of Company 2 to Branch Camp Clanton.[5]

Reassignment—sometimes welcome, sometimes not—always had the potential to disrupt a sense of normality. As Joachim Metzner wrote in an April 9, 2012, email, being sent "to another camp was sometimes very bad. Once, someone who ... [was scheduled] to play at the [POW camp] theatre in the evening, had to leave the camp towards a side-camp and they had to replace the actor for the role in a few hours (The replacement did the job with the help of a prompter). The same problems for the [POW orchestral] group 'Sorgenbrecher,' who had to permanently exchange members."[6]

In an October 28, 2012, email, Joachim translated his father's account of a new company's arrival and subsequent assignment to living quarters:

An interview with the new 10th (company)
The conscientious chronicler [editor Paul Metzner's self-reference] records: September 3, 1944, arrival of a new Company in strength of 248 men from the camp McCain. Company commander is OGFR. Thiel. McClellan will be the new main camp for them and the men will live on the earlier [assigned area] of the 12.Kp. [Company]....

He further explained:

The numbering [of companies] was not the same as in the early dates [of the camp's existence]....
[T]he early "African" [Afrika Korps] inhabitants of McClellan, who built up the camp in some way [interior and exterior improvements] were proud of their company and company number....
It would be ... bad ... for them coming back after peanut harvest and [having to] live in other barracks and get a new company number; it is like losing identity and home.[7]

Despite the presence of American MPs in the guard towers and on roving patrols, and American officers assuming overall direction, POW noncommissioned officers enjoyed the perquisite and responsibility of supervising camp activities. Such a program ensured a degree of order and a natural prisoner chain-of-command, and it retained the discipline desired by all armies, whether in war or peace. Each POW barracks in every company had its own reporting hierarchy, enabling privates and corporals to look to their noncoms for orders, task assignments, and so forth, much as they would had they not been captured. Ultimately, the U.S. officers in charge announced specific programs, changes, improvements, new policies, and disciplinary measures and listened to POW requests and complaints. But it was the noncom cadre among the prisoner ranks that made the camp hum along a daily pattern.

Staff Sergeant Jack Shay (a private during his time as an MP) remembered the light touch administered by the captors on captives:

Technically, we had the run of the camp, all areas, depending on what company you were in and your duty station. You could be in any of the towers or on the catwalks. Or you could be patrolling the compounds or going with our photographers or officers or the CO [commanding officer] on inspections or checking out problems. But you wouldn't go in the camp unless you had authorization. The PWs had their own guys in charge. And we generally stayed clear of them so long as they kept their noses clean and played ball with us [obeyed camp rules].
They [POWs] were a pretty good bunch, for the most part. We had no big problems, no breakouts. Oh, maybe a couple squabbles here and there, but nothing to write home about.[8]

Much of the camp's daily activity came to light in periodic reports. In a September 1943 International Red Cross report, the prisoners sported "all the clothing they need," and several were, even at that early juncture in their internment, receiving "letters from their families." The report by "Mr. A. Cardinaux" also said:

The representative of the International Red Cross Committee talked freely and without witnesses with the [prisoner] spokesman and with the [POW] company heads....

The various problems in question were discussed in a very cordial atmosphere. The Camp Commandant is very much interested in the prisoners and would like to help them as much as possible in the organization of their school.

Morale and health among the prisoners are excellent.[9]

Captain Edward C. Shannahan's December 1943 report provided a peek into the camp's day-to-day existence, both within and outside the three compounds:

Two daily prisoner counts are held, one at revielle [*sic*] and the other at retreat. The prisoners do not actually stand retreat. A perimeter motor patrol is maintained during the night and during periods of sudden darkness in the daytime....

There are but two officer prisoners at this camp who are members of the Medical Corps. The officers live in the guard house within the compound area and expressed no complaint about this arrangement. Quarters are being erected to take care of them and should be ready for occupancy shortly....

The treatment appeared to be good and the prisoners well disciplined....

This [kitchen/mess] equipment is the standard, post camp or station issue with the exception that tin cups and plates are substituted in some cases....

Wherever possible, substitutions are made to suit the national taste of the prisoners....

A small garden was maintained during the past season and the dividend was excellent. For next season the Camp Commander [Lieutenant Colonel Smith] has leased a plot of seventy-five acres in the vicinity of the camp. He expects to have very good results from the garden....

All of the [prisoners'] garments noticed were marked correctly with "PW." No national uniforms are marked....

There are only two officers at this camp and none of their clothing has been marked in any manner....

All of the prisoners have been issued winter clothing and are well equipped. The Camp Commander has been having difficulty with shoes for the prisoners. All of the shoes issued are reconditioned and it is almost impossible to ascertain the correct sizes....

The daily sick call averages between eighty-five and ninety prisoners. There is no evidence of malingering on the part of the prisoners....

One patient is suffering from battle neurosis....

No motion pictures are available to the prisoners at the present time. Inasmuch as the prisoner of war camp is located at some distance from the main post, it is not considered practicable to utilize the facilities of the Army Motion Picture Service on the post....

Sports kits have been received from The Provost Marshal General and the War Prisoners' Aid. In addition, the Camp Commander has purchased other supplies from canteen profits. The supply on hand is sufficient for the needs of the prisoners....

Each compound has its own small orchestra. At the present time, the Camp Commander is attempting to accumulate sufficient instruments to organize a symphony orchestra. Theater groups are maintained also by each compound, which groups periodically give plays for the benefit of all the prisoners....

A sufficient supply of small tools is available but, in view of the purposed farming program for the coming season, a need for heavy farm equipment has arisen....

Mail arrives at the camp direct from Germany necessitating its return to the District Postal Censor.[10]

The POW newspaper, established in October 1943, provided a concise summary of leisure activities during the camp's first half-year of existence in the January 27, 1944, issue. Camp adjutant and spokesman Willi Utz wrote of 85 cabaret evenings, 80 company evenings, 10 theater evenings, 5 record "concerts," and 3 poetry readings, as well as 20 performances taken to those prisoners confined in the camp hospital. He estimated an attendance aggregate of 45,000. Some presentations were staged only for individual companies, others for the compound, and still others for the entire camp (with several renditions to accommodate all prisoners who wanted to attend).[11] In a December 9, 2012, email, Joachim Metzner wrote that if "45,000 visitors attended," then "every comrade saw about 15 performances on average."[12]

Utz listed approximately 5,000 hours of classroom education from about 20 permanent teachers, with current participation numbered at 1,000. He also credited relief agencies, such as the War Prisoners' Aid, with supplying more than 1,000 books (most in German); 70 sports game balls; 20 pairs of boxing gloves; 660 games; 70 painting sets; 70 tools for modeling, carving, and other crafts; and 3,000 notebooks, exercise books, and stationery or school materials. POW Christian Höschle, in his autobiography, likewise attributed supplies to the efforts of the German and International Red Cross units and "especially the National Catholic Welfare Council and the POW Welfare Committee of the YMCA."[13]

In May 1944, following a Swiss inspection of the camp, U.S. State Department official Parker W. Buhrman counted 9 officers (all medical personnel), 501 noncommissioned men, and 873 enlisted men, all German, for a population of 1,383. He wrote glowingly of the camp's morale:

> The general morale or discipline ... [of] this camp is outstanding. It is one of the best camps to be found anywhere.... It is a well seasoned organization....
> The representative of the Swiss Legation informed the camp commander that there were no complaints of any character on the part of the prisoners....
> This is a first-class camp in every particular.[14]

Regarding the medical personnel, *P.o.W. Oase* editor Paul Metzner mentioned a few of the officers, all engaged in practicing medicine—Doctors Gohlke, Göppel, and Heilmann—in the February 18, 1944, edition. And in a 2014 email, his son identified a prisoner named Kussmaul (possibly Alfred Kussmaul) as another doctor.[15]

In the May 19, 1944, issue of *The McClellan CYCLE*, Corporal William R. Frye provided another look into the camp in "Inside PW Camp: Bomb Stories Bunk, Nazi Prisoners Say; Call War News 'Lies'":

> Nazi prisoners of war at Ft. McClellan read stories in American newspapers about the bombing of German cities—and they don't believe it. They toss the stories off as "propaganda," PW officials have discovered.
> Just as they were surprised to find that New York had not been leveled by German bombs, as they had been told, these veterans of the North African campaign cannot believe Germany is losing the war, and distrust the news they hear over the radio and see in the papers.
> An official inspecting party which recently got the first look-see inside the McClellan PW Camp learned these facts from Washington Army officers who conducted the tour.
> As the high-ranking American officers walked down company streets of the two compounds, prisoners raised their right hands high, palms out, in the Nazi salute. The officers returned the salute in traditional American fashion.
> Under the Geneva Convention, prisoners of war are subject to military discipline similar to that which governs soldiers of the confining power. Thus the Nazis are required to salute American officers, and Uncle Sam's Doughboys under similar circumstances, would have to salute German officers. The officers return the salute. German PWs here use the "heil" when uncovered, the Ameircan [sic] salute when wearing a head covering.
> Ft. McClellan has a clean record on escapes: not a single prisoner has slipped outside the stockade AWOL. (Some go out under guard to work.)

Few Escapes

All over the United States, there have been 285 escapes. Only a few who got out have stayed at large for more than 48 hours, and none has been able to accomplish any sabotage, according to Lt. Col. Earl L. Edwards, assistant director of the PW Division of the Provost Marshal General's Office.

Colonel Edwards said one trainload of Italian prisoners was in a train wreck, with the cars knocked completely off the tracks and overturned. The Italians merely picked up the guards' guns and handed them back to them, not a one trying to escape. "We don't imagine the Germans would act that way," he added.

All PW privates are required to work at least eight hours a day, six days a week. The noncoms and officers may also work if they request it. They are paid 80 cents a day for a full day's work. This is in addition to the 10 cents a day allowance given the privates and the standard $20–$40 monthly pay given officers, the amount depending on the rank. There are only six officers at McClellan.

"Prisoners are treated humanely and fairly," Colonel Edwards says. "They are treated as soldiers of an opposing army, and not criminals. However, strict discipline is maintained and in no instance are the prisoners pampered. This treatment may be summarized as 'fair but firm.'"

Colonel Edwards said the Nazi Government is quick to retaliate if our discipline becomes too stiff, and that this is the reason for many of the privileges which are misinterpreted as pampering by some civilians. If withdrawn, American boys confined in Germany would feel it.

There isn't much trouble with discipline, Lt. Col. Laurence D. Smith, commanding officer of the McClellan camp, says. Chronic troublemakers are segregated.

The men are said to have a Gestapo of their own to discipline non-Nazis and men who get too friendly with the American system. Asked about this, Colonel Smith said, "It may exist, but if so we haven't seen any evidence of it. We haven't tracked anything down."

The prisoners get both German and American newspapers, but the American papers are censored by an officer in the camp headquarters who clips any item "which would increase our problem of maintaining discipline," Colonel Smith explains.

"We censor items about race riots, strikes, and the like, but leave in all war news and most of the editorial comment. The want ads have to be clipped because they might include messages in code."

Most of the men disbelieve the war news, feeling it comes from some American equivalent of [Minister for Propaganda and Popular Enlightenment Joseph] Goebbels['] office—an office they have learned to distrust. Those who take bombing stories seriously sometimes have occasion to worry about families or friends who lived in the city. PWs are limited in the number of letters they may write, but not in the mail they may receive.[16]

In a November 1944 report concerning an inspection by Werner Tobler and Eldon F. Nelson, several recreational activities received high marks: "The recreational program ... is very well developed. There is a camp paper, movies are shown regularly, there are radios, a good school program and several art projects." This report also commended the camp's management:

> The representative of the Swiss Legation told the State Department representative informally that he regarded this as one of the two best camps that he had visited in the United States. He spoke very highly of the commanding officer, and the other officers of the camp....
>
> This is one of the best camps that the writer has visited and the camp commander appears to be a very able person; understanding and humanitarian in his attitude toward the prisoners of war.[17]

Edouard Patte inspected the camp on December 11, 1944, and wrote:

> The University with twenty-five teachers has a one thousand two hundred student enrollment who are taught every conceivable subject. Sport activities are mainly centered around a football

and handball championship where sixty teams are entered during this winter season. Other activities like theater, movies, orchestra continue, as in the past, with great success.

I had at the end of my stay at the Fort a most unusual experience in visiting the attractive little zoo, built by a POW who had been a circus attendant in Germany. After having been taken to the airarium [sic] where beautiful birds of all colors and shapes— thirty-eight different species—were kept, I was given for a few minutes a handful of snakes, half asleep, cold, coiled, black, silvery, gray, brown. I must confess my preference for handling other animals. Then, as long as the alligator [lizard] and the turtles were hibernating and therefore not ready for a social call, we passed to the next little house with flying squirrels, possums and raccoons. The POW entered a small enclosure, moved a few stones, awoke a beautiful fox and tried with much skill, poise and persuasion, to teach him to obey his voice. It lasted ten minutes, all of them packed with tense interest. First frightened, then sneaky, then calmed, then obedient, at last the captive animal tamed by a captive man learned the lesson; but as soon as the POW has disappeared it certainly forgot it! The circus man had a smile—or was it a grin— when he said to me: "Sir, neither man nor animal can ever learn anything when being a captive!"

Then after "the taming of the fox" I met the prisoner chaplain and theology students. They were a group large enough to constitute a small seminary, priests, monks, pastor, students and seminarists. I had a general meeting with them. We reviewed the religious situation, on the up-grade fortunately; large attendance at the services. The chaplains are badly in need of better books, and I was exceedingly sorry to be unable to give them any hope of better religious literature in German before several months. We have had with the German POW theologians of Fort McClellan one hour of true fraternal fellowship....[18]

The zoo Patte visited was probably in Compound 3. Joachim Metzner identified it as the largest collection of animals in the camp in a February 18, 2013, email that also addressed the issue of pet cats and dogs, as well as doghouses outside various barracks:

[I] found in the newspaper, that dogs were not allowed anymore ... they were tolerated in the beginning but ... becoming too [many] ... they got forbidden in spring 1944....
And I found articles ... that ... biggest zoo was in Compound 3.
Some paragraphs tell about all the different kinds of animals they held.
Example ... [of] some birds: Hairy woodpecker, Morning dove, blue jay, chirping-sparrow, English sparrow, sparrow, Myrtle-warbler, Summer-tanager, blue birds....[19]

The May 18, 1944, issue of *P.o.W. Oase* devoted nearly two pages to camp animal collections or zoos. Under the heading "*VON ZOO ZU ZOO*" (which linguist Chania Stymacks loosely translated as "From the Zoo and to the Zoo"), Paul Metzner wrote of lizards, crabs, dogs, cats, bluebirds, bees, rabbits, pigs, and other species. As Stymacks explained, "He describes 'fliegenden Eichhoernchen' [Eichhörnchen], which translates as 'flying squirrels' and says that they have a habit of being nocturnal, and at night they jump around screaming. But one gets used to everything, especially if you are the one who keeps them in their confined cages."

The POWs could watch a number of 16mm films on a regular (usually weekly) basis; the movies were projected onto screens by fellow internees in their various compounds. Because of the relatively limited seating in the day/recreation rooms where the films were screened, it routinely took a full week for one film to be viewed by all who wanted to see it.

The May 6, 1944, *P.o.W. Oase* included a report of prisoners watching the 1940 American film *One Million B.C.*, featuring Victor Mature, Carole Landis, Lon Chaney Jr., and giant lizards and dinosaurs. As Stymacks translated, "They liked it very well because of its curiosity."

The May 12 issue told of prisoners seeing their first German-language film. It became the headline feature on page one. According to Stymacks, "'We saw the first German film in America.' They were shown *The Old and the Young King* [*Der alte und der junge König*] with Emil Jannings and the fights with his strict and duty-bound father. The first king of the Prussians. And they were sorry they couldn't play the film for the external or outer [branch] camps." The Whitsunday ("Pfingsten," late May) 1944 issue likewise commented on *Emil und die Detektive*, which "gave them much joy, even though it was a children's movie. They went repeatedly to see it because it had scenes of Berlin and Germany."[20]

One 1945 report declared that 90 percent of the prisoners availed themselves of the cinematic offerings, with musicals and comedies being the most requested. A list of "Films desired, which until now have not as yet been ordered," compiled in late 1944, included *Flash* [that is, *Flesh*] *and Fantasy, Government Girl, Powers Girls* [*The Powers Girl*], *Sensations of 1945, Stage Door Canteen,* and *Step Lively,* as well as several German films, including *Blumen aus Nizza, Der junge und der alte Koenig* [*Der alte und der junge König*], *Emil und die Detektive,* and *Konzert in Tirol.* That same list noted, "Our film program is settled and filled up till" May 1, 1945.[21]

Perret's February 1945 visit prompted the following report:

> Each sector [compound] contains an infirmary with a sanitary officer responsible for medical inspection. An American doctor comes daily for the special cases. The serious cases are taken to the hospital. At the time of our visit, there were 26 patients....
>
> These patients are suffering from various mild maladies (sinusitis, dermatitis, cellulitis, mild nephritis, etc.); or they have had accidents, wounds, or fractures....
>
> An officer and a private of the sanitary corps work as dentists....
>
> The prisoners have established a large open-air theater where they also show motion-pictures....
>
> The camp has 4 small football fields and a field of regular dimensions. Several tennis courts are being laid off. Last summer, the prisoners had several opportunities to go bathing [swimming], but since an American soldier was drowned, they have not been allowed to go....
>
> Every Sunday, two Catholic services and a Protestant service are conducted by prisoners; during the week, they have assemblies and supervised study.

The report also listed a total of 3,727 volumes in the library, 3,438 in German and 289 in English, covering fiction and nonfiction (technical, textbook, religious, and medical) topics.

Among the courses offered at that time in the "very complete study program" were classes in agriculture, architecture, commerce or business, economics, engineering, law, mathematics, and foreign languages, including English, French, Greek, Italian, and Russian. Certain classes addressed specific needs or interests, including coursework for noncommissioned career and reserve officers and "preparation for Master's examination." The classes took place during daytime hours, ranging from as little as one or two to as many as 36 hours per week, and attracted more than 500 participants. A gamut of evening courses in various foreign-language, business, clerical, history, math, science, and technical subjects drew anywhere from a half-dozen to dozens of participants each, with English, as might be expected, attracting a high number. A total of 894 men reportedly attended evening classes from January 23 to February 21. The report also averred that "more than 40 professors" provided the classes and that "2 students are taking correspondence courses with the University of Michigan."[22]

The January 20, 1944, *P.o.W. Oase* published a report of current courses covering English, French, and Spanish languages, mathematics and business, history, and mechanical and farming skills, submitted by Oberfeldwebel (First Sergeant) Martin Alstedt, training manager.

Various American reports, while pedestrian on the surface, provided an inestimable service to posterity by recording the names of POWs engaged in exceptional service, thereby supplying identities that might otherwise have been lost to history.

On March 1, 1945, the camp library and school consisted of the following staff members, all POWs: Oberwachtmeister (Tech Sergeant) Walter Scherer, director of studies; Unteroffiziers (Sergeants) Hubert Schaupp and Kurt Sund, librarians; and Unteroffizier Hans Kraemer (or more likely Krämer), bookbinder. The instructors, POWs all, were Ernst Berthold, Wilhelm Böhmichen, Karl Braun, Hans Bruchhagen, Heinz Dethloff, Heinrich Engelhardt, Paul Ferley, Fritz Gottschlich, Kunibert Gramlich, Gustav Harant, Alexander Hart, Siegfried Hartmann, Rudolf Hattinger, Gerhard Haulitzki, Martin Hauschild, Hans Helbig, Kurt Hoffmann, Josef Hoiss, Georg Hubricht, Theodor Huetsch (probably Hütsch), Helmut Kaspuhl, Albert Klumpp, Kurt-Guenter Koch, Guenther A. Krueger (probably Krüger), Rudolf Krumlinde, Alfred Kussmaul, Alois Lehner, Konstantin Merk, Paul Metzner, Rudolf Ostrowski, Karl Pannholzer, Johann Pohl, Arnold Puetz (more likely Pütz), Hans Ring, Frederich (possibly Frederick) Schlosser, Walter Schmidt, Willi Schnoeckel (probably Schnöckel), Alfred Schobora, Helmut Schoenhoff (undoubtedly Schönhoff), Herman Schroeder (probably Hermann Schröder), Severin Seitz, Walter Specht, Werner Sperling, Josef Teipel, Wilhelm Ulrich, Hans Wahl, Hans Waitz, Karl Woltering, and Valentin Ziegler.[23]

Both American chaplains (whether priests or ministers) and German chaplains (POWs who also happened to be clergymen) provided religious services throughout the duration of the camp's existence. In 1945, a census determined that 55 percent of the POWs were Protestant, 35 percent Roman Catholic, and 10 percent of differing or no affiliations. But not all those identifying themselves as Protestant or Catholic attended weekly services. Protestant Bible classes or prayer groups attracted a small proportion of attendees.[24]

The most popular activities involved diversions from the standard monotony and trepidation of internment centers. The main recreation room and some of the smaller dayrooms offered phonographs and collections of 78-rpm classical, operatic, and popular music recordings of recent vintage, tables and chairs, decks of playing cards, assorted board games (chess, backgammon, checkers, and the like), and ping-pong tables and apparatus.

Boxing was a popular universal sport, and classes taught the fundamentals of pugilism. A full range of sporting activities, including track and field events like broad jumps and shot puts, handball, and so forth, also occurred.

Organized team sports dominated. European football—the American soccer—was king. The sport that many people around the world referred to as "the great equalizer" proved very popular in the camp and inspired hundreds of participants to vie for league championships.

"Soccer was not big here in America," Staff Sergeant Jack Shay commented. "We liked baseball. It was America's pastime. It was our game. Some of the GIs followed college football, too. Pro football wasn't that big at the time. But baseball was very popular. Our GIs played it and talked about it. We'd talk about Joe DiMaggio and Ted Williams. Hank Greenberg. Bob Feller. Those guys were in the service during the war. Stan Musial. Dixie Walker. Johnny Vander Meer. The Yankees. The St. Louis Cardinals. The Detroit Tigers. The St.

Soccer was king in the POW camp, being by far the most popular athletic pastime. From *P.o.W. Oase* #67, March 10, 1945 (courtesy of Joachim Metzner).

Louis Browns. And boxing was very big, too. Joe Louis. He boxed at McClellan for a promotion. And then we looked at the PWs across the road [Baker], and they're playing soccer!"[25]

P.o.W. Oase artist Hermann Haugg's illustration of a scene involving the 7th Company's gymnastic equipment—even parallel bars, vaulting horse, and so forth—for the October 19, 1944, issue made it appear as inviting as a park.

Translator Joni Pontius commented on the prevalence of athletics: "Some of the written material talks about the prisoners taking part in constructing their own sports fields. Some of the companies had grounds for various games and sports contests. One was 70 by 40 meters in size. And one sentence mentioned that the prisoners had to clear a few hundred cubic meters of dirt and dig out some trees to make a field and then level it off so it was playable. I gathered that in the fall of 1943 one of the inner camps [compounds] had three small soccer fields. And there were dozens of games between a number of teams, very much like play in an organized league."[26]

Music was also an important part of POW life. An enumeration of the "List of records we still have in the Camp," dated "6.12.44," included over 300 records of various types of music, especially symphonic, chamber, operatic, choral, march, polka, dance, and popular. A public address hookup amplified the recordings to allow a louder broadcast. A survey determined that the POWs enjoyed light concert music (a mix of popular songs, marches,

Hermann Haugg's sketch of an exercise field for the 7th Company. From *P.o.W. Oase* #53, October 19, 1944 (courtesy of Joachim Metzner).

and classical excerpts) and radio programs, followed by news and comedy programs, and classical, jazz, and swing offerings.[27]

Following a May 1–4, 1945, visit, Edouard Patte called the camp "one of the most attractive bases in the U. S. A." He noted a seemingly greater appreciation for sports than for scholastic endeavors:

> School is not prospering. Sports are, however, exceedingly popular; a championship tournament has been organized, with 300 contestants in handball, 120 in faustball, 66 in ping pong, 70 in tennis, 45 in boxing and 42 in light athletics. The uniforms for the teams were made out of onion sacks, dyed in various colors, and tailored in camp.
> Church activities are well attended, with Sunday and weekday services, which I attended. I was much impressed by the sense of devotion.

Within the same period, Patte also visited McClellan's side camps at Clanton and Sibert, both in Alabama. He found the former "On landscaped grounds, with much green and shrubbery … well repaired and enlarged," and the prisoner population "All working in compounds, sawmill and lumberyards" and enjoying "1 small canteen, with day-room attached; 2 ping pong tables, various games," and "*Movies* twice a week, very good, on local contracts," as well as a library of "80 fiction and 50 other books, in exchange with base," and "Some very good records." He observed a reduction in the latter camp's facilities "on account of the transfer of 40% of the prisoners ... to other units" and noted that the orchestra and school had been closed; in addition, he noticed an interest in the POWs receiving "our German movies" to supplement the camp's "games and a fairly good library."[28]

McClellan's POWs had their own compound canteens, offering a smaller amount of the supernumerary goods and services available to GIs and civilian personnel in the main post canteens. A 1945 POW report mentioned electric ice cream refrigerators and 20¢ haircuts in the canteens.[29] And during the hot summer months, prisoners could wear short pants within the compounds.

Among the most welcome camp features were the regular rations of very substantial fresh and warm food, virtually all varieties. As POW Erhard Eifler recalled:

> We really got enough to eat, especially this unforgetable [*sic*] white bread which we never saw before in Germany. And the food during wartime in Africa was quite bad. The kitchen in the camp was of course a main institution for us. The POWs themselves prepared and cooked the meals. We had a lot of fruits, like apples, oranges and pears. Besides water we had the possibility to drink tea, coffee, and to buy milk or even "Redcap" beer [in the canteens]. 200 cigarrettes [*sic*] costed 1,20$ [$1.20] in the cantine [*sic*], a beer 20 cents, I think or even less.[30]

POW Christian Höschle echoed Eifler's assessment. As Joni Pontius translated,

> He wrote that there was never a day without meat—beef, pork, lamb, chicken. And pastry, vegetables, milk, fruit. "We were all convinced that we wouldn't have been fed this way at home with mother."

A scene, drawn by a POW, of a typical moment in one of the camp's several prisoner canteens. From *P.o.W. Oase* #59, November 29, 1944 (courtesy of Joachim Metzner).

He said, "We could not understand that a land like the U.S.A., which was also in a state of war, could maintain such an abundant standard of living. They also had to supply their allies with food and weapons. Thus, it was a land flowing with milk and honey. We felt like we were in a golden cage. We were also aware that the American prisoners in Germany never got food like this."

Höschle was so impressed with the abundance of food that he wrote of white flour being used to mark lines on the soccer fields. That never would have happened in Germany because of bombings and food shortages.[31]

The canteens and recreation barracks became places to relax and unwind. Beer (albeit of the reduced 3.2 percent alcohol-content variety) could be obtained at the canteens in exchange for the money coupons the POWs received to use for goods and services. Limitations on how much watered-down alcoholic beer or wine a POW could obtain at any given time ensured that the camp would be free of boozy Germans staggering around and creating either disciplinary problems or public spectacles.

To circumvent the proscriptions, some prisoners relied on their knowledge of home-brewed concoctions and created stills in deep recesses within their barracks, crafting rough, barely passable, but potent beverages that would never be commercially served. No statistics indicating the breadth of such activity have surfaced, but it certainly existed. POW Eifler wrote of one such still: "[W]e also destilled [sic] brandy in our barrack which was forbidden. It tasted awful, but we got drunk, which was helpful once in a while, when we got home-sick.... But after some weeks the american guards realized the smell in our barrack and discovered the hole in the bottom of our barrack. So we had to give up our 'Black forest' destillery [sic]."[32] Höschle concurred: "We distilled our own Schnaps from oranges and peaches, which was, of course, forbidden."[33]

The prisoners received permission to have their own farm. Called simply "The Farm," it seems to have been the brainchild of First Lieutenant Zimri M. Addy, initially in charge of Company 1 in Compound 1. Located in Weaver, a little more than a mile north of the camp, it was popular and mentioned in *P.o.W. Oase*. As Joachim Metzner remarked in a July 10, 2012, email:

> My Father wrote an article about the PW-Farm in the Xmas-issue 1944 of the newspaper....
> It was rented by the camp from an American Farmer, who was away in the army for some time (only the land and some barns and sheds were rented, not the house in the middle). Rented Size around ⅙ square mile.
> The idea came from Lt. Addy.
> It was a lot of work (seems, that the land was not used for some years) partly done by the PW by hand, but they also used tractors. The German "Farmdirector" was Stabsfeldwebel [Master Sergeant] Schaer and the work began in spring 44.
> ⅓ of the land was taken for corn....
> Other vegetable[s] did not come very well, maybe because it was too dry. But they had some cucumbers, beans, tomatoes.
> The harvest was given to the POW-companies and to the guards-company as well.
> For 1945 ... [plans were] to get some young plants from the greenhouse and manure from the defecator [sewage treatment area] of the fort ... (which was not far away from the farm).[34]

The makeup and activities within the camp remained fluid. The June 16, 1945, *P.o.W. Oase* referred to the addition of more coops for chickens, pigeons, and rabbits and gardens for cucumbers and tomatoes, as well as the placement of curtains on the open-air stage "because entry was not free anymore!" Two weeks later, the July 1 issue reported the arrival of billiard tables, the transfer of 300 men (mostly from the 9th Company) to Camp Jackson in South Carolina and another 100 to Camp Sibert, and the internal relocation to Company 9's barracks of POWs formerly assigned to Company 13. Additionally, the open-air stage had been refitted and readied to show films to 800 viewers at 15¢ a head.[35]

Was the camp liberal enough to allow prisoners to have cameras? For years the consensus answer was simply no. Cameras were not sold at the POW PXs and likely would have been confiscated if they had arrived in packages or been discovered in shakedown inspections. POWs returning from offsite work details should have—and presumably would have—been subject to either visual or physical scrutiny.

Joachim Metzner addressed this question in a March 23, 2013, email:

> There is an article in the paper telling about old days, when the soldiers photographed a lot, but "here as pow in McClellan the law is different—and we have to accept that" … "we hope that the drawings in the Newspaper will be a replacement for photos to watch and talk about later with our beloved when we are back home[.]" That indicates clearly, that it was not allowed to take photos.[36]

At least the ban on photography was in place at the time this newspaper article was written. But Paul Metzner left McClellan for reassignment to Rhode Island in the summer of 1945, and his last issue was dated July 15 of that year. The camp went on nearly a year longer.

Could the army's policy at McClellan have liberalized in that last year? Or could certain POWs have flouted the rules and sneaked a camera and film into the camp?

Rita (Johnson) Wells, who worked in the camp's headquarters building until it was closed, said, "They discouraged cameras."[37] But she was talking primarily about the civilian employees. Annistonians Steve Bakke and Thom Cole, both military authorities and collectors and conversant with McClellan, said it would have been "fairly easy" for handy POWs, skilled in the art of photography, to make a camera.[38] And it's very possible, even probable, that GIs shared some photos they took inside the camp with the POWs.

Robert Suberg, who lived as a POW in McClellan during Paul Metzner's stay and remained there after the latter's departure, spoke of "making pictures" when interviewed in 1987.[39] Furthermore, the author received photographs of the camp and various POWs from Suberg's widow, with the understanding the photos were German in origin.

Focusing on the spiritual aspects of the camp in his report of September 16, 1945, when World War II had ended and Germany was under the authority of the occupying Allied forces, Inspector Patte wrote:

> The religious life in the camp, does not seem to have been greatly affected by the new situation of Germany. There is as much indifference as in the past, and a little bitterness; however, the influence of the Church is not negligible, even according to the spokesman who is not a churchgoer. The students in theology have the possibility, at night, to study under the ministers in charge and have access at all times, to the Catholic and Protestant library, in the Sacristy of the chapel. I asked for a young Catholic student, the permission to remain at Fort McClellan rather than be transfered [*sic*] to another side-camp, in order to remain under the sponsorship and leadership of the Catholic Father for his studies. The Executive Officer [Captain Charles Sturm] told me of his desire to cooperate in the matter, provided the student would keep working at camp as a regular POW.
>
> I had also two conferences with the spokesman, who mentioned that the educational program, the artistic and musical program were as good as ever, with their splendid symphony orchestra and their arts studio.[40]

The nondenominational POW chapel on the north side of the middle road in Compound 2, with the main guard tower in the background. From *P.o.W. Oase* #61, Christmas 1944 (courtesy of Joachim Metzner).

One of the last looks inside the camp came from a report filed by Karl Gustaf Almquist detailing his visit of December 21–25, 1945. He especially highlighted the role of the YMCA, which he represented, and the spiritual health of the camp as it wound down operations, preparing to release the last of its inmates for eventual repatriation in Germany:

> Until recently the camp had about 2,300 prisoners of war; today it holds only a few hundred....
>
> The spokesman told me that the camp was being deactivated and that they expected to be transferred shortly after New Year's Day. All activities, therefore, had been stopped. Formerly they had had all the activities which were permitted, such as instruction in English, History, and other subjects. The attendance at the classes, not the least at the English classes, had been extraordinarily high. In this connection I want to mention how well many of the prisoners of war were graduated from a class in English for advanced students. The Post Commanding Officer attended the graduation exercises.
>
> With pride they showed me the big library, where there were many books which had been distributed by the Y.M.C.A. It was understandable that they had no further wishes in this direction. The spokesman, however, wanted to express the thankfulness of the whole camp for our assistance. He also wanted to let me know how his comrades appreciated our organizations.... "We are so happy to have an opportunity to read and learn during our captivity. Maybe all is not in vain. We have learned a great deal here which will help us in the future. We still have hope for the future," he continued in a humble voice.

They had an orchestra which the American authorities and the prisoners of war spoke of very highly. Some of the orchestra members were still in the camp and they wished to know whether they might keep the instruments which they had used for a long time and which they really loved. After I informed the Commanding Officer that it was our intention to let the men keep their instruments, he was glad to confirm this as Camp Commander. In this way the camp received a Christmas gift for which they were very happy.

The conversation with the pastors shed an interesting light on their work in the camp. It was impossible to mistake the good friendship between the ministers of both confessions. Is not this a good sign for the future? Circumstances had obliged them to share each other's thoughts on faith and creed. Looking at the chapel, which was nicely decorated, I could see that neither confession dominated the building. It was a room for services and meditation. A man was just decorating the altar for Christmas and building a nativity scene which would illustrate the holy Christmas story.

The pastors, a group of laymen and I spoke of the future role of the Church. Seriously they discussed the problem of whether the Church had failed in Germany during the last twelve years under the Nazi regime. Both pastors had suffered greatly during that time. The Lutheran pastor could not obtain any position and was obliged to move from one place to another. The [Roman Catholic] priest was nearly taken to a concentration camp. It was a rather sad story about inhuman suffering and persecution for the reason only that they were steadfast in their faith. Systematically, the Nazi leaders tried in all ways to break down their courage. However it always is impossible to fight against the true Christian spirit. Now they hoped to found and build a new church at home, to help children, women and men in their great need. A faith at the same time humbel [*sic*] and strong burned in their hearts…. They hoped for understanding

A photograph from the "Compliments of Headquarters" souvenir booklet showing "the priest [who] was nearly taken to a concentration camp" by the Nazis as punishment for his faith saying mass in the chapel (author's collection).

and help from the Christians in America and other countries in this most difficult task. I was glad to bring greetings from the Church outside barbed wires....

During Christmas I divided my time between the services at Fort McClellan and the Prisoner of War Camp.... The services in the Prisoner of War Camp were very well attended. The sermons were deep, hopeful and encouraging, built upon the Christian message for Christmas....

When I finally left Fort McClellan, I left friends on both sides.... My impression was that the work of the Y.M.C.A. and the Ecumenical Commission had been constructive and of permanent value.[41]

Even six decades after the closing of the camp, people recalled select incidents. Rita (Johnson) Wells remembered a singular experience involving a rather recalcitrant POW:

I was a clerk typist in the administration section of the camp's headquarters. I worked with some of the prisoners in headquarters, and I saw others. They would have a large "PW" stamped on the front and back of their shirts and the seat of their pants and the fronts of their legs, halfway between the knees and the hips, and on the arms.

We had an incident once where one man had to get on solitary confinement for two weeks. He wanted to be paid for the time he stenciled the "PW" on his clothing. After the initial issue of clothing which the PWs got when they arrived in the camp, they had to stencil the "PW" on all further clothing they

And here is the same Roman Catholic chaplain, Father Josef Müller, in a photograph he gave to the author's parents (author's collection).

acquired. All the stenciling equipment was there, and he wanted to be paid for his stenciling. He wanted 10¢ an hour. Then he refused to wear his clothing. I guess it was on principle. He was put in solitary for one week on bread and water. We noticed this when his 201 file, his documentation file, came to be typed. All his vital information, good and bad, was typed into that. After two weeks, he still refused. And then he was released. And we found out that his POW friend had stenciled his clothing for him because he felt so sorry for him.[42]

But incidents like that were the exception.

Well-known Annistonian dentist Dr. Joseph A. Walker was simply the teenaged Joby Walker, living on Surrey Hill, across Pelham Road from Baker Gate, during World War II. He could clearly see Compound 1 from the elevation where his house sat. "Of course, I heard them [POWs] singing and playing German songs. I could easily see the fence around the camp, and I saw them playing volleyball."[43]

Joan McKinney spent more than a dozen years in Fort McClellan long after the war, serving as the director of protocol from 1981 to 1989, and then as the public affairs coordinator until 1994. She has since dedicated much of her time to accumulating information, records, and photographs on many aspects of the fort, including the POW camp. "Fort

McClellan was a model prisoner of war camp," she said in 2009. "Everyone said that. You could play there, you could work there, you ate well. And McClellan was known even among the prisoners as a good place to be by networking. Now Aliceville [a camp in west-central Alabama, near the Mississippi border] was a much larger camp, but McClellan was the model camp."[44]

The prisoners agreed. Klaus W. Duncan of Jacksonville, Alabama, instrumental in preserving memories of McClellan, translated several issues of *P.o.W. Oase*. Some of his translated tidbits referred to prisoner reactions:

> There was an infirmary but POWs preferred to be treated by their own German Doctors. Doctor Lampen Scherf [Lampenscherf] was the chief doctor....
> When they arrived at McClellan, they were so happy. For the first time [in a POW camp] they saw trees, hill[s], and woods. McClellan was well organized. They loved McClellan because it reminded them of home.
> The camp stage was the center of communication. The main topic was always what company would leave McClellan. Nobody wanted to leave. Companies frequently moved to places of work. One company left for Clanton to harvest peanuts. They disliked Clanton.[45]

Private Clark J. Miller, who accompanied POW work details as a guard for a couple of weeks at the end of his basic training cycle in early 1945, remembered hearing how prisoners felt about life in captivity. "They had [it] better than we had," he said in 2010. "They didn't want to go back. They had it better here."[46]

Such remarks echoed the sentiments expressed by the POWs. Unteroffizier (Sergeant) Heinrich Baumann extolled the merits of the camp, as well as its policy of allowing prisoners to retain as much of their Germanic heritage and identity as possible, in a story from the July 14, 1944, issue of *P.o.W. Oase*. Having spent one year in the camp at that point, he wrote both nostalgically and optimistically (translation by Joachim Metzner):

> Do you remember the days, when everyone helped to develop the areas of the companies to look good? Much earth had to be moved (just like on a construction area for roadwork), drainage ditches were built, lawn was seeded, sports fields created and a lot [of] other things were done. Yes, we can say that we made an OASIS out of the desert. Everything has developed into something good. The inner room of the barracks was turned [made] to look cozy.
> Do you remember how much zeal and diligence there was to build tables and benches, nearly elegant chairs and neat small cupboards? Small lampshades were glued, pictures painted, models of planes and tanks tinkered and a lot more to have a personal feeling in the rooms.
> How receptive we were in those days for every variety, the opening of the canteen or the first cinema show of advertising films of Philip Morris or others. Although some comrades wondered about films showing wrestling, others enjoyed that, just like seeing struggling bears or lions in the zoo.
> This small entertainment developed suddenly, when gifted comrades got together and gave us hours of joy with some cabaret shows. But there was a lot of difficulties, the lack of a real stage, the question of costumes, missing props.... But these problems were solved because of the talent to organize.
> A newspaper ... was born to entertain us with contributions from the readers ... telling ... us something worth knowing. And see: there was Jupp Kraemer with his tenacity [born] of his Rhinish roots (...he was from a region near the River Rhine) and [with] a lot of optimism [he] wrote down sheet music by heart and founded a little band called "the Heimatsender" (... Heimatsender = broadcasting station of home) that brought enthusiasm to all comrades with uncounted evenings of Entertainment. That band developed into the band we know today in the "Batl. 1" [Compound 1], entertaining the comrades several times. In camps [Compounds]

2 and 3 other musicians founded smaller and bigger bands with the same goal to blow away the sorrows—and that was reached 100%.

Sometimes someone takes … to … sitting at the open air stage in the evening, watching this or that play. This stage, built … [by] the German soldiers, could also [just as easily appear to] be located in a small town at home. Greater plays with dominating [dominant] woman roles are no problem anymore, because some comrades are able to play this in an outstanding way— and one can forget, that it is a man under these nice arranged clothes of a woman and sometimes one can fall in love a little bit with this leading lady. But especially the stage scenery and set decorations are very good and need a special compliment. The guys are creating a magic theatre world with only a few colored cloths and wooden ledges.

In sports everyone has his joy, no matter if it is in an active or passive way. When I think about the league games in soccer and handball on the constructed sport fields everyone has to admit that we really have something useful for the health of our bodies. A big "Well done!" for the grounds men who understood to involve so many to help. Sometimes the enthusiasm between sports men and visitors was that great, you could believe you are attending a big sports event with 2 big teams at home. One time we even had a "real commentator" with megaphone.

If I see all this that was created with such ridiculously small resources in one year, it makes me think that we can be proud of our achievement—and that our "business card" presented to our host American state will remain a good memory when we are back home again in hopefully not too long a time. Let's continue on this path and then we will not return to our homeland as alienated men.[47]

In his customary lyrical mode of expression, Paul Metzner wrote of a typical evening in the camp at the approximate two-year mark of the enclosure's existence. In the May 30, 1945, *P.o.W. Oase* issue he remarked on how a stroll through the camp would yield certain sights and sounds at "6 o'clock in the evening when the day's work is done … for a city of 3,000 men." "I think it's worth it, to wander with an open mind through the camp and realize that, despite all, life pulsates everywhere," he wrote.

Metzner described the following: the headcount at the close of the workday; the ongoing work for the second-shift POWs in the kitchens; the gathering of the athletes and spectators for handball, soccer, fistball, tennis, or gymnastics; the opening of the canteens and, "depending on the stock," a crowd of patrons either "greater or less"; the activity in the library, a "meeting place for intellectuals" who shrug off their imprisonment and "seek the reading of classics, novels, travelogues and descriptions of nature," voracious readers who desire to "get drunk on literary works"; the barracks where "the bookworms … behind the newly purchased book, [have] taken refuge in the world of dreams," focusing "on his book, which has become his friend"; the classes and the work that goes into the lessons, because "You never regret what you have learned, only what you have missed"; haircuts in the barbershop and, "Incidentally, free quotes from [German writer Johann Wolfgang von] Goethe!"; visits to the camp dentist "and the 'torture chair' waiting for the victims"; rehearsals for musical or dramatic performances, or individuals just practicing on their musical instruments; taking in a movie from hard backless benches—"it would be pleasant to sit on a padded seat in one's local movie theater and watch a movie with a close friend, but behind barbed wire we can't be picky and have to be content with two hours of entertainment, particularly if we can see a German film"; the chess matches and table tennis games in progress throughout camp; washing clothing in the sinks of the laundry rooms, where POWs of necessity became "their own washer-women" and came to appreciate all the more the chores of their "mothers and women"; and the "songs from the chapel uniting the worship community."

"The darkness has fallen," he summarized. "With slivers of light from the lamp poles, the barracks, and the kitchen windows.... We know every corner, every look over the fences that surround us. How often have we looked out to those distant hills that resemble the mountains of our homeland in their silhouettes! ... How long will we experience this? Yet we look ahead to the day when we will recall this time in McClellan and say, 'This was once our life, and now it is only a memory.'"[48]

Robert Suberg spent much of his time in captivity at McClellan. In a 1987 meeting, he indulged his memories of being removed from both the horrors of war and the comfort of loved ones, placing things in perspective, painting a more melancholy picture of a captive's life (even in one of the best camps), and enunciating the universal feelings of all those who are captured:

I can't say that we were happy to be POWs in Alabama. Does any man want to be captured and a prisoner in a strange land? Does any man ever want that? But there is nothing good in war. Just unhappiness. Misery. Suffering. On both sides. Hunger. Blood. Death. You want to be with your family back home, safe.

But when we were captured and made prisoners, we were not happy at being captured, but happy to be in the U.S. and not Russia. We lived every day at McClellan happy to be safe from the war, yet wanting to be with our families. We were sick in our hearts, homesick. You miss your home when you are away and locked up somewhere else. But what can you do? You are many thousands of kilometers away from home. You do the best you can. You make friends with your comrades, and you hope to see your friends and families in Germany again someday.[49]

6

The POWs:
Who Were They?

*"People think we were all Nazis, like Hitler.
But we were not."*

Most of the names of the thousands of McClellan's POWs are currently unknown. Military authorities expunged all POW personnel records from McClellan's files after the closing of the camp or transferred them to centralized federal sites. National Archives staffers uniformly aver that most records of interned personnel were subsequently shipped to the prisoners' native countries for disposition.

The relative handful of known duty rosters, sick lists, camp inspections, and the like yield only a scattering of names. Consequently, generalities abound.

In an intriguing overview published in the July 14, 1967, issue of *The Anniston Star*, Bill Plott quoted a somewhat negative picture gleaned by at least one contemporary observer of the camp's residents:

> The Alabama Review ... carried an article on Alabama's POW camps in a recent issue.
> Dr. William Stanley Hoole, the author, quoted a Washington newspaper correspondent who described the Camp McClellan facility as the "largest and best" POW camp in the U.S. but added that newsmen could "feel the sneers of the prisoners as they passed through the place."
> "They seemed cocky, even about their capture," the newsman continued. "Their attitude is reflected in the German legend which they put around a huge sun-dial they have built. It says, 'For us the sun never goes under....' For the most part they are service troops.... They are good looking soldiers, but most of them are rather short. Nearly all carry the Aryan superiority look, which they were taught by the Hitlerites...."
> In general, the prisoners at Fort McClellan were a quiet, obedient lot despite the "cockiness" described by the Washington correspondent.[1]

Thirteen years later, Staff Sergeant Dan Coberly referred to the same information in his "Stalag U.S.A." newspaper series:

> The *Montgomery Advertiser* described Camp McClellan POWs as:
> "Greatly depressed by the turn of the war, but still persisting that Germany was superior to all the world."
> "They are in excellent health, well-fed and with bright, shiny uniforms. By contrast, the younger men were bedraggled and worn from previous campaigns."[2]

Steve Bakke, a lifelong devotee of twentieth-century international politics and warfare, has scrupulously amassed a storehouse of knowledge, connected to this period, as well as a sizable collection of militaria.

Most of the prisoners who ended up at Fort McClellan were what would be considered rank-and-file soldiers, not hard-core Nazi adherents. The ones who were known to be hard-core Nazis were separated out beforehand and were sent to other camps. Those camps were more like prisons. It was my understanding that the SS [for "Schutzstaffel" or "guard detachment," an elite German quasi-army originally intended to safeguard Hitler] troops were sent primarily to England for internment.

In Europe, the Axis powers included Italians who were basic conscripts. And then you had the fascists who, more or less, fought in Russia. The Germans, most of them, were young conscripts, not necessarily Nazis. They were captured in North Africa, Sicily, and southern Italy. They were the ones who came to many camps here in America, including McClellan. I'm not saying there were no fascists in McClellan, but most, from everything I've studied, were primarily just Germans conscripted into the army.[3]

As might be expected, the POWs came from disparate backgrounds and occupations—some just beginning their lives' work, others seeing their vocations interrupted by the call to arms.

A December 1, 1943, occupational summary identified 169 different professional backgrounds for the 2,994 men then in the camp. It highlighted professions producing the most vocations: automobile and "body repair" mechanics (107); bakers (100); barbers (29); bricklayers (54); butchers (103); career soldiers (56); carpenters (114); chauffeurs (125); clerks (142); cooks (18); electricians (60); engineers (17); farmers (528); gardeners (33); laborers (171); locksmiths (139); machinists and machine builders, designers, installers, and technicians (43); mailmen (17); mechanical engineers (64); merchants (163); metal workers (20); painters, whether automobile, sign, or commercial (70); plumbers (30); salesmen (83); shoe repairmen (24); smiths, whether black, copper, gold, or tin (41); stone cutters and masons (16); students (93); tailors (37); teachers (16); and toolmakers (21).

The smaller categories included 6 architects; 4 artists; 2 bartenders; 6 brewers; a bridge builder; 8 chemists; 3 chimney sweeps; a cigar maker; 5 contractors; 3 dentists; 3 diamond cutters; 3 distillery workers; a dressmaker; 9 druggists; 14 estate administrators; 4 firemen; 8 foresters; 2 glass cutters; 6 hotel workers; a hunter; 2 insurance clerks; 9 interior decorators; an interpreter; a jeweler; 3 lawyers; a Linotype operator; 4 lithographers; a lumberjack; 2 medical doctors (both officers); 6 miners; a musical instrument worker; 4 musicians; an opera singer; 3 opticians; an organist; a potter; 13 printers; 4 radio repairmen; 11 railroad inspectors and workers; a reporter; 6 roofers; a sculptor; 4 seamen; 2 shepherds; 2 ship builders; 2 stewards; 6 surveyors; 2 tax collectors; 7 telephone linemen, operators, and repairmen; 11 tractor operators; 3 typesetters; 6 wagon repairmen; 8 waiters; 4 watchmakers; a watchman; a water pilot; 14 weavers; a well builder; 7 woodworkers; and 9 listed with no occupation.[4]

In his autobiography, Christian Höschle wrote of McClellan as a reservoir both receiving and incubating talent. When he arrived on July 23, 1943, he quickly found an inordinately high number of professors, music teachers, engineers, language teachers, top athletes, artisans, and craftsmen. "Because we were an elite troop, it was obvious that we would be occupied with culture, science, and crafts, and everyone could indulge his own hobby," Höschle wrote. He also mentioned that German ingenuity impressed the Americans: "Soon there was a saying among the Americans—'If you give a German prisoner a tin can, he will immediately make a radio or a machine gun out of it.'"[5]

Fortunately, the names of many accomplished prisoners who passed through McClellan are known. For example, the formal interpreter for the camp was First Sergeant Willi (sometimes spelled Willy) Utz. And Werner Möller, interned in the 7th Company, worked as a clerk and interpreter in the works project director's office from late 1944 to late 1945 in a "superior manner" and studied American history in one of the camp classes.

P.o.W. Oase, published in German from October 1943 until July 1945, contained "over 500 names overall," in the words of the editor's son, Joachim Metzner, but most were mentioned in passing, such as the participants in sporting events and dramatic presentations: "Sometimes the first name is missing, but in the army the ranks are very often more known than the first name, so no wonder. In some cases I found ... the home region or home town and/or the age of the people."[6] In numerous emails, Metzner highlighted prominent POWs who made enough of an imprint to merit inclusion in one or more of the newspaper's issues.

The camp's largest, fullest, and presumably most professional orchestra was Sorgenbrecher, a German name roughly translated as "Blues Breakers" (as in "Banishing the Blues"). The musicians often changed, based on the availability of POWs with musical talent and the habitual transfer of various POWs from one camp to another. The February 3, 1945, *P.o.W. Oase* listed the members at that time (with additional information provided by Joachim Metzner in 2013 and 2014 emails): Gerenot Dietrich, Franz Fehrenbach, and Heinz Ohmacht on trumpets; Wilhelm George and Franz Schrimpf on trombones; Rolf Geissler, Otto Konhäusner, Werner Philip, and Bernhard Ververs on saxophones; Adolf Happold on bass and accordion; Axel Hofmann on piano; Otto Stürzer on bass and guitar; and Jacob Frantzen on percussion. Joachim subsequently discovered that Konhäusner, who was also a clarinetist, later became a recording artist and may have worked at the National Theatre in Mannheim, West Germany, in his postwar years. He also called Franz Fehrenbach a "great trumpet-player" and "after the war here in Germany a well known musician at a big radio station."[7]

Unteroffizier (Sergeant) Heinrich Baumann also played violin in Sorgenbrecher. He arrived at McClellan with the first batch of POWs on July 3, 1943, and hailed from Karlsruhe, just south of the famed medieval and university city of Heidelberg. Another man with the same surname also played handball in the camp's athletic leagues.

Franz Beer excelled in soccer, so much so that his name appeared in 21 issues of the newspaper.

Ernest Berthold was a natural athlete, the best tennis player in the camp, and skilled in table tennis as well.

Hans Bruchhagen worked in a canteen in Compound 3 and won a long jump (5m20) track and field event.

Fritz Gottschlich submitted at least one item to the paper.

Reinhold Güther, mentioned 26 times in *P.o.W. Oase*, graduated from the Berlin Music Academy and sang in the Municipal Theatre of Greifswald and the City Theatre in Lübeck (both in northern Germany near the Baltic Sea) before his army service. After his release, he continued his operatic career as a tenor in Bremen and at the Opera House in Zurich, Switzerland. He accepted numerous guest engagements in theaters in Bremen, Freiburg, Kiel, Oldenburg (all in West Germany), and Schwerin (East Germany). According to Joachim Metzner, "He sang on the stage a colorful variety of roles in both opera and operetta, and was universally esteemed as an actor. In Zurich he worked with the premiere of [Franz] Lehar's operetta *Spring* in the 1954–55 season and during the 1957–58 season in Oscar Straus' operetta *The Pearl of Cleopatra*. His operatic roles included: Don Ottavio in *Don Giovanni*, Tamino in *The Magic Flute*, the Florestan in *Fidelio*, the title character in *Fra Diavolo* … Rodolfo in *La Boheme*, Alfredo in *La Traviata*, Radames in *Aida*, Lohengrin [*Lohengrin*], and Bacchus in *Ariadne auf Naxos*."

Unteroffizier (Sergeant) Gustav Harant, perhaps an architect or contractor in civilian life, oversaw the creation of construction gangs and helped with the engineering of the outdoor stage. He was also a soccer referee.

Helmut Kaspuhl worked as a set decorator and stage designer.

Rudolf Krumlinde and Werner Sperling helped with the entertainment aspects of the camp.

Rudolf Ostrowski and Arnold Pütz were among the camp's veteran chess players.

Helmut Schönhoff was a botanist.

Unteroffizier (Sergeant) Walter Specht might have been a designer or painter in civilian life; as Joachim Metzner wrote, "He also designed some [of the] Interior of the room [the Schwarzwaldstübele, a dayroom fashioned in 'Black Forest' style]."

Hans Wahl played soccer.[8]

As the war progressed—badly for the Germans—the intellectual complexion of the camp changed somewhat. As translator Joni Pontius remarked of Höschle's book, "He said

POW Robert "Bob" Suberg, wounded and captured in the North African campaign, came to McClellan while still a teenager (author's collection).

that at the beginning of July 1944, four weeks after the Normandy landing [D–Day], the first German prisoners from Normandy came to the camp. But they were not elite troops. They were the last offerings—17-year-old boys to 45-year-old men. Many of the prisoners from the African Campaign stood by the gate to the camp. They saw these new men—thin and tired and with long faces, as they walked to the gate. And they [the African veterans] stormed them [new arrivals] with questions to learn the news. They learned that whole companies had to surrender because they had no munitions. And most of them were of the opinion that the war was no longer winnable, that it was only a matter of time."[9]

Robert Suberg addressed the political identity of the prisoners in a 1987 interview: "When I came to Fort McClellan, I was a young man. We were young boys, many of us. Not even 20 years old. I was 19. And we were not Nazis," he said adamantly. "Maybe some, but not most of us. We were just young boys who were drafted. Loyal to our country, but not Nazis. I know people think we were all Nazis, like Hitler. But we were not."[10]

Höschle agreed. "A few comrades were party members," he wrote, "but not many." He also remarked on an internal change within many internees, a wisdom gained by imprisonment. "He wrote about the initial mystique of Hitler and Germany's perceived omnipotence," Pontius commented. "He said they were caught off-guard because of the many [military] successes at the beginning of the war. But he said that imprisonment gives one the opportunity for developing new ambitions and a spiritual maturity. And with this maturity and recognition which he acquired in his imprisonment, he was able to take part in the later rebuilding of the Fatherland."[11]

Of the several thousand prisoners interned at McClellan through the camp's nearly three years of existence, almost all were German. The camp newspaper was in German. The surviving U.S. Army and international inspection reports mention German specifics, hobby or entertainment activities, and such. Those interviewed for this book spoke of the prisoners as German. Rosters, where available, of work details or other groupings of men bear German names. Contemporary newspaper accounts, whether in the local civilian newspaper or Army periodicals, referred to the prisoners as German. In *The McClellan CYCLE* of May 12, 1944, Corporal William R. Frye wrote, "They're all Germans: no Japs or Italians here."[12]

It undoubtedly was true at the time. But according to military reports, McClellan had a brief Italian presence. The POW cemetery contains three Italian prisoners of war brought from Camp Como and reinterred on November 7, 1945. Annistonian Joan McKinney, who has scrupulously tried to salvage any and all records of the fort's history, addressed the issue as follows:

> I don't think there were Italian prisoners kept at McClellan. I have lots of clues that lead me to that conclusion, but don't have specific documentation. I believe the information evolved because there were three Italians reinterred there ... and the cemetery is so named [German Italian Memorial Cemetery]. I have a camp gain/loss report ... that 1 Italian Prisoner arrived at McClellan on July 12, 1943 and 1 Italian Prisoner was transferred to Camp Como, MS on Aug 7, 43. There is no other mention of Italians, although no nationality was mentioned in subsequent postings.[13]

Three American sergeants—John J. George, Jack E. Shay, and Jack S. Steward—who worked at the camp and spoke to the author on numerous occasions, all referred to the prisoners as German. So did the wives of two of these men who lived with their husbands within view of the camp. Rita Wells (at this writing the only known survivor of the camp headquarters' civilian contingent) in several interviews said she saw, heard, and interacted with only German POWs.

At this distance, the best speculation is that a very small number of Italians, perhaps only one, were ever housed at McClellan, and probably only for a brief interim while awaiting relocation.

7

POW Work Details

"When Daddy was being good to the German prisoners here,
my oldest brother was over there in Germany fighting them."

From the start of POW internment in America, the lowest-ranked men spent the majority of their daytime working on monitored details outside camp confines. These details presented opportunities to learn new skills or hone existing ones, escape the boredom of another day inside the symbolic "four walls" of the camp, see new terrain, and make money, although they were never paid in actual cash (in part to prevent bribery of their GI guards), but rather in coupons, redeemable for goods at their compound canteens.

Captive officers were exempt from such work, unless they volunteered for it. The noncommissioned officers who chose—or were sometimes forced—to work often became supervisors overseeing the privates (and occasionally corporals) who performed the actual labor. Work details occurred on weekdays, with occasional exceptions, including mess hall and canteen assignments.

Conditions differed from camp to camp, whether work was onsite or off, and whether it included evening work or other variables. In *Nazi Prisoners of War in America*, which surveyed camps nationwide, Arnold Krammer wrote of normal wakeup calls for POWs at 5:30 a.m., with breakfast a half-hour later, followed by work details from 7:30 a.m. until 4:30 p.m., with lunch around the noon hour.[1] But not so at McClellan.

Klaus W. Duncan, who translated several issues of *P.o.W. Oase*, wrote, "POWs had to wake up at 6:00AM. Breakfast was at 6:30, and work started at 8:30. 5 P.M. trucks brought POWs back to camp."[2]

In his autobiography, Christian Höschle remembered a 6 a.m. wakeup call, with time to make his bed and clean the floor and barracks, shave and shower at 6:30, stand roll call at 7:00, and eat breakfast at 7:30. Work details followed. He mentioned that although the lower officers (sergeants) could be called on to work as supervisors, there were those who chose to eat, play cards, and lie in their beds—"lie in your lazy skin," as he phrased it. Being an artist as well as a sergeant, he chose to work in his "studio" (he was given a building in which to paint outside the compound, and he was free to come and go).[3]

Surviving U.S. records, GI memories, and the pages of *P.o.W. Oase* indicate that the hours of work details varied, depending on the nature and location of the work. In the January 21, 1945, *P.o.W. Oase*, Paul Metzner wrote, "The following article gives an overview of a working day of the camp. The abundance of work projects makes it impossible to thoroughly talk about the individual projects but an attempt is made in the coming episodes to elaborate on the work of some of the more significant commands."

He enumerated several work details—hospital and mess hall kitchen labor—that required early wakeup calls, some at 4:00 a.m. and some for double shifts (with commensurate time off the next day). Other work details began at 7:00, when the POWs would line up at the gates for truck or other transportation to their work locations. The jobs included common labor, carpentry work, roofing, painting, landscaping, tree removal, automobile mechanics, piano tuning, and working in the wastewater treatment plant, "which the Americans" call by "the beautiful epithet Coca-Cola Plant." Counting also those engaged in writing, teaching, gardening, and plumbing, Metzner assessed the "daily total work" force to be "approximately 1,300 men." Lunch occurred at noon, with quitting time at 4:30 p.m. "But only just for almost all. The kitchen commands may remain in service until 18.00 [6 p.m.].... And for those regulated by special interests working hours [last] into the night."[4]

The POW details at first tackled the grunt work forming the bedrock of operations at the camp and post. But as those tasks were accomplished, prisoners received permission to work beyond the fort itself, in the Anniston community, and sometimes far afield, dozens of miles away—even across the state line into neighboring Georgia. Logging and land clearing needed steady manpower, and the agricultural fields of the countryside required constant sowing and reaping, as well as supportive tasks. Individual business owners and farmers employed POWs under contract at prevailing American labor wages; the POWs received their customary 80¢ a day, with the remainder (after allowable employer deductions for lodging and/or transportation) going to the federal government.

On the McClellan post proper, POWs engaged in various stonework and landscaping projects. In a July 1955 compilation titled *The History of Fort McClellan*, Major Mary C. Lane wrote:

> Of the 3,000 prisoners interned, approximately 1,340 worked each day.... About 200 prisoners were used daily for excavation, drainage, and clearing projects on the main reservation; 170 cooked the meals and did kitchen police details at the Post hospital; other crews baked the bread for the 30,000 troops in training; repaired vehicles used on the Post; salvaged materials such as tin cans and scrap paper; and worked for civilian contractors on various projects in the neighboring communities.[5]

Prisoners routinely cleared, drained, and excavated areas of the post, always with an eye toward furthering the beautification of the "showplace" fort, and they also worked in kitchen details for the permanent post staff and constantly revolving trainee cycles. Numerous installations on the post always needed painting, and motor vehicles required repair. POWs laid out patios, erected chimneys and stone walls, and planted shrubs and flowers. But the figures constantly changed, as the available pool of POW labor rose and fell with additions and transfers.

In one of the first reports on camp life, conducted after a September 2, 1943, visit by the International Red Cross Committee, A. Cardinaux wrote:

> Maintenance work in the camp presents no difficulties. The cooks, hospital orderlies, clerks, etc., are paid 80 cents a day....
>
>   566 prisoners were doing various types of work in the military camp and on the neighboring farms, and 360 were doing improvement work in the camp. At the time of the visit, 1250 prisoners were away from camp, harvesting peanuts within a radius of 400 kilometers, for about three weeks. Those prisoners work under the supervision of the regional military camp authorities. They live in tents and their food is prepared in field kitchens. A mobile canteen allows for the purchase of various articles.[6]

Captain Edward Shannahan offered a snapshot of some of the work done by POWs in his mid–December 1943 report:

> There are twenty-nine prisoners who claim a Protected status. Of this number, nine assist in the infirmaries, one man assists the dentist and two others are employed in the medical ward of the hospital. The Chief of Surgical Service at the hospital refuses to allow any of the prisoners to work in his wards in view of the experiences he had with them when they first arrived. The Protected Personnel would give their own interpretation to orders issued by the surgeon. He would not stand for this and ordered them removed from the hospital. He stated he will not reconsider his decision unless ordered to....
>
> Two side camps are maintained, one camp of two hundred prisoners located at the Bainbridge Army Air Base, Georgia, and the other camp of three hundred prisoners at Spence Field, Moultrie, Georgia. Both of these side camps are administered by the base camp. However, all of their rations and supplies are supplied by the posts on which they are located. In addition, several details work out of Fort McClellan. These men are given sandwiches for lunch with the balance of the ration received in the regular mess....
>
> Transportation is supplied by contractors. The Camp Commander stated he has had to caution several contractors on the type of vehicles they use for the prisoners and also on the quality of the drivers. Some of the vehicles have been in [a] very bad state of repair and the drivers very reckless. On one occasion he was forced to cancel a detail as the type of vehicle supplied endangered the lives of the prisoners and the guards riding in it....
>
> Sanitary measures at the side camps are standard Army installations and are considered excellent. On the contract details working out of Fort McClellan, however, the latrine facilities are makeshift and barely suffice. As these details are of such short duration, it is not considered economical to erect latrines. Straddle type latrines with a latrine screen are presently being furnished....
>
> Lieutenant Colonel [Laurence D.] Smith, the Camp Commander, had the following recommendations to make.... That working gloves be issued in addition to wool gloves for labor details during the winter months....
>
> The Camp Commander apparently is very interested in the work of the prisoners and is attempting to find projects on which they might be employed.[7]

The Internee Work Schedule for December 13, 1943, provided a typical accounting. On that day, Cavalry First Lieutenant Zimri M. Addy, commanding the "P.W. Bn. 1" (or 1st Battalion, comprising the 1st, 2nd, 3rd, and 4th Companies, in Compound 1), oversaw the overall distribution of work details. A total of 997 PWs were accounted for: 36 working in the main post utility yard; 18 in the engineering repair shop (6 with the shoemakers, 12 with the tailors); 10 in the "Recl Yard"; 2 painting the Service Command Unit (SCU) 1437th mess hall; 2 working in the POW Headquarters building for Lieutenant Jacob Scholom; 11 working under contract to "Mr. Lagarde"; 8 serving as cooks in the 1437th mess hall; 3 more in the visitors' building; 2 serving in the chaplains' office; 10 working as florists; 10 more in the machine shop in the supply building; 2 painting for "Captain [Woodrow W.] Wallace"; 12 working on a drainage area; 10 performing either cleanup or drainage work in their own compound (that is, Compound 1); 2 painting; and the remaining 859 on detached service (538), earmarked as company or battalion overhead (143), in the hospital (18), in company area (128), or sick in quarters (32). Unspecified numbers of American soldiers in the 382nd, 383rd, and 433rd MPEG companies oversaw the details.

That same day, the camp's 2nd Battalion (comprising 5th, 6th, 7th, and 8th Companies in Compound 2) accounted for 1,005 prisoners, including the pair of officers who were medical doctors. Members of the 383rd supplied escort and guard protection, and First

Lieutenant Carl T. Whitehead signed off on the work schedule. The various activities included work at the post engineering office, sewage disposal plant, post cemetery, post garden, electrical warehouse, 1437th SCU area, and the PW camp motor pool (a smaller motor pool for GIs operating the POW camp, just across Baker Road). Among the specified tasks were typewriter repair, painting, pinball setting, cleaning the ditch near Middle Gate, and painting "Capt. Larkens [Edward B. Larkin's] office." Included in the aggregate were men assigned to overhead, sick in either hospital or their quarters, and on detached service in Georgia and Mississippi.

The total personnel for all three compounds that day amounted to 3,005: all prisoners working for pay (877); those who didn't qualify for paid labor (209); those not working for myriad reasons, including sickness and exemption (926); those on detached service (991); and the medical doctors (2).[8]

In a May 1944 report (following a visit by Dr. Rudolf Fischer of the Legation of Switzerland), Parker W. Buhrman, a U.S. State Department representative, wrote of a side camp at Evergreen, Alabama, halfway between Montgomery and Mobile in rural Conecuh County, operated by McClellan and utilizing 100 men "in pulp wood cutting and highway construction."[9] Another report, following an inspection by Werner Tobler of the Swiss Legation and Eldon F. Nelson of the U.S. State Department in November 1944, supplied the following:

> ...1108 men were engaged at paid labor on the day of the visit. A few of these were on contract labor outside of the post and some had paid jobs within the compound. The rest were employed on various post details.... At the side camp all employable men were working. Some were cutting pulp wood, some telephone poles, and others were engaged in agricultural labor. The side camp at Clanton, Alabama, is located 125 miles south of the main camp and is constructed of former C.C.C. buildings.... The side camp at Evergreen, Alabama, mentioned in the previous report was transferred to Camp Rucker....[10]

Maurice Ed. Perret's February 1945 inspection contributed additional information:

> About half of the prisoners of the camp work, namely the privates and a certain number of non-commissioned officers. Most of the men in the American military camp are in charge of the current work. The principal details are those of the kitchens and canteens (250 men); bakeries (50 men); construction, repair and maintenance of roads (168 men); repair and upkeep of equipment and of shoes (63 men); repair and upkeep of vehicles (100 men). Inside the camp, 208 men have assumed responsibility for paid employment; among these are 20 professors. Some men work outside the camp as wood-cutters, or in construction work. In summer, some groups are employed in agriculture.[11]

The report of an inspection by Captains W. J. Bridges Jr. and C. E. Tremper in mid–July 1945, bearing Bridges' signature of July 16, presented tedious evidence of both the military's strict adherence to regulations and an apparent laxness in applying such diligence to prisoners:

> In many cases detail work reports are turned in without signature of using agency or detail supervisor....
> Inspection of work details ... revealed the following practices that do not conform with existing regulations....
> PW's [sic] working on kitchen police details in the Regional Hospital messes, IRTC messes, and at the Enlisted Men's mess at the PW Camp are given every other day off. Therefore, they work only half as long as American enlisted men work when they are on kitchen police detail....

Detail No. 22, a Post Engineer detail of 4 PW's is employed within the compound to line drainage ditches with rocks. This does not conform to the requirements....

Prisoners of war are transported by truck to the Officers' Club. The QM [quartermaster] subsistence detail No. 73 is returned to the PW Camp by truck in the afternoon, and the IRTC Ration Breakdown Detail No. 91 is trucked to and from the PW Camp. This transportation does not conform with ... policy regarding the transportation of prisoners to work sites within three miles of the PW Camp....

PW's are given two 10 to 15 minute breaks per day on at least two details where civilians do not get a break. These two details are the IRTC Jap Village Construction and the brush cleaning detail at the Anniston Warehouse Corp.... PW's will be required to work the same number of hours as civilian employees on the same work project....

Many details of PW's work less than eight hours per day, even when the morning and afternoon breaks are counted as working time. This was especially noticable [*sic*] on the Post Engineer Grass Cutting detail No. 56 and the Fertilizer Detail No. 21....

Much of the Post work, which is classed as Priority I work does not fall within the definition of Priority I work....

German leaders on some details do not work and do not understand English, therefore these leaders cannot relay orders to the workers. Several civilian formen [*sic*] expressed the thought that all leaders should be required to work....

The policy in force at the PW Hobby Shop, Detail No. 228, of charging only 80¢ per day, plus 10%, for labor used in repairing or manufacturing articles for U.S. personnel does not conform with the provisions of paragraph 47 [etc.]....

The Anniston Warehouse Corp. had 76 PW's employed on 14 July 1945. The foremen were well satisfied with the work the PW's were doing. Four of these men were sodding a golf course. This is not Priority II work....

A log cutting detail near Tallapoosa, Georgia ... has never reached the task of 1,250 Board Feet, Log Scale, per man day. Disciplinary action, as required by paragraph [etc.] ... has not been administered....

It is recommended that all PW's on kitchen police details, not under contract, be required to work six days per week....

It is recommended that labor within the compound, that is necessary to the maintenance or repair of the compound, be placed on an unpaid basis....

It is recommended that PW's be given breaks only if it is customary for civilians on like jobs to get breaks....

It is recommended that the representatives of the using agencies, that sign the daily work sheets, be required to keep an accurate check of the hours worked by the PW's....

It is recommended that the dailywork [*sic*] sheets be revised so that the supervisor's signature is a certification as to the hours worked....

It is recommended that the Post Director of Personnel cause a survey to be made to determine which details should be properly classified as Priority III work....

It is recommended that all German leaders and interpreters be required to work with the detail to which they are assigned....

It is recommended that all articles manufactured by PW's, for sale through the Canteen, and all labor expended repairing articles for U.S. personnel, be done during the PW's spare time.[12]

P.o.W. Oase also furnished insights into the work details. The October 24, 1943, issue told of a 100-man force detailed to Georgia to harvest peanuts. The "reporter" wrote of arriving on trucks near the city of Americus, nearly 200 miles southeast, for an extended field trip. The next day, groups of 20 men began working on various farms. The writer described a fairly relaxed atmosphere of good-natured joking, living under tents reminiscent of their wartime experience in North Africa, and looking forward to the respites sandwiched between the loud calls of "Break!" and "Break's over!" He wrote of moving on to Moultrie for more peanut harvesting, then finally returning to McClellan to relate their experiences to friends, over peanuts, and wonder whether in a few weeks they would buy in their canteens some confection made with peanuts they had themselves picked.

In the November 9, 1943, issue, Paul Metzner wrote of a work detail climbing aboard a truck outside the main gate of the camp and traveling 75 kilometers through Anniston and its environs to a farm. He extolled the "excellent road, similar to the German highways," and commented on the prettiest part of Anniston, a residential section with a wide street and tree-lined median, a thoroughfare flanked by "neat" houses with front gardens. He took in the bucolic scenes and signboards promoting nearby fishing, boating, and swimming areas that stirred up memories of past days in "our home country across the ocean." And after harvesting the corn, "it's back to the camp" because "the working day is done and slides into the evening," in which the farm workers become once again Germans "in the uniform suits of POWs."[13]

Years later, Alfred Arens recorded his memories of the details (original typescript intact):

As a corporal I was not obliged to work but I—and most of the others—worked voluntarily because of the payment of 80 cts instead of 10 cts for non-workers. In this way I baked bread in the Fort McClellan's bakery, learned to harvest cotton and peanuts and to discern black-snakes from rattle-snakes (what some inhabitants did never achieve). In springtime 1945 we built imitated Japanese villages for training purposes of the GI's, since ... the US was planning to invade Japan. During these years, we came during the harvest-time also to Georgia, Mississippi, Florida and Tennessy.[14]

Former POW Erhard Eifler also wrote of his work activity while interned at McClellan from August 1943 to April 1946 (original typescript):

During the first year I worked outside the camp on a farm near Anniston. The farmers was Wiley, I think. We harvested peanuts, cotton and millet. I got 80 Cents for 80 pounds of cotton. The work was o.k. and we could earn some extra money to buy special things in the cantine....

After one year I had to work as a fireman or stoker. For a twelve hour [shift] I had to take care of the heating of officers homes. Therefore I got a bycicle to tour around at Ft McClellan. I did this job also about a year.

Then I had to change my duty-work again and helped in the hospital kitchen starting at 06 p.m. until 01 a.m. There I baked thousands of pies. This job lasted about 5–6 months....

We didn't have connections outside of the camp other than with the work. With the monthly 3$ salary we could earn another 20$ per month with our work.

I also remember my last job in Ft McClellan, when I worked at the post motor pool and as a mechanist I fixed cars. Each POW had an american civilian aside [overseer]. My colleague was Mr. Bowman. He gave me once a very nice golden fountain-pen. I still keep it as a souvenir.... I also have to add, that I built the destillery [undoubtedly at the covert behest of certain GIs] in the motor pool.[15]

Chania Stymacks translated much of *P.o.W. Oase*, including the May 6, 1944, issue, in which

Page 3 has some information on peach tree pruning in North Carolina. The writer says that parts of our camp left to do farm work. Parts of the 9th and 10th Companies and the 11th Company had to go to North Carolina to Fort Mackall to work on a peach plantation. They sent a report back to Fort McClellan. It's quoted in the newspaper.

Some of the barracks in North Carolina were not finished. And the prisoners had to put streets in and ditches around the tents. And they had to build tables and chairs and benches and closets. And our sportsmen, they mean athletes, helped out putting in a new sports field.

McClellan lost some of their musicians in this transfer.

They took 18 hours to get from McClellan to North Carolina.

All the POWs except for a very few go to work. The details were 10–60 men strong. The first week they pruned trees. And the plantings were very large, 80,000–200,000 trees. And they said, "Wouldn't it be nice if we could have a harvest, but it's only May." Others went to the forests to cut trees or worked in the warehouse or did work to eliminate mosquitoes around the camp so that "the dear little animals" wouldn't eat them up. They said their days were filled with work. And at night, at the sound of *Taps* in the camp, they took their well-deserved rest so they could be fresh by the first sound of *Reveille* and be ready for work.

Back in McClellan, the 5th Company and parts of the 6th and 7th Companies went on a trip to Florida, and they will be in the same area as the 9th and 10th Companies.

He [the writer] refers to McClellan as the stem camp, as the main camp, and writes about so many groups being sent away to other satellite camps. The 4th Company went to Evergreen in southern Alabama. And he asks the other groups that have been externalized or sent away to send him reports for the paper.[16]

In his 1980 series on German POW camps and McClellan, Staff Sergeant Dan Coberly interviewed several GIs for their memories of prisoner work details:

"Sometimes we took them by truck to Pell City [Alabama] to work in the lumber mills. I think they also picked vegetables on a farm in Weaver...," [Edward] Hooper said....

Marvin Wilder [also listed as Wildes] served as a medic at the camp.... "I remember the prisoners were always working, building something or fixing things."] ...

Luther Mitchell also worked at the camp during the war years. He was responsible for landscaping and gardening. At one time over 300 POWs worked for him. They began building a green house but the project was never completed. Mitchell was drafted instead.

"Many of the flowers we grew were used at the Service Clubs and the Officer's Club," Mitchell said. "I remember some of the men got shook up by an electrical storm that damaged some of their barracks. They were just prefab, wood and tar paper shacks.

["]The prisoners said to me after the storm 'We were in the middle of the war, but it wasn't as bad as this!' They sure were scared. I guess they'd never seen such bad weather in Germany."
...

Gene Lucky ... used to be a ... Corporal at the Camp. ["]I was in charge of 8–10 POWs from time to time, and used them to spread out tents, maintain field kitchens and bivoac [sic] equipment. It was all kind of silly, really. The MP's [sic] would march the prisoners in under heavy guard, and then leave them there with me. We didn't have any guards or any guns. Just supplies."][17]

Dr. Joseph A. "Joby" Walker, who grew up on Surrey Hill, just west of the camp across Pelham Road, recalled seeing "the PWs going out in those two-ton trucks on work details and singing German songs. I remember those heavy trucks with the canvas over the ribs going out toward Weaver [one mile north of the camp]. The prisoners were young, good-looking, tan, and singing. They worked with their shirts off."[18]

Working at the camp headquarters, Rita (Johnson) Wells often heard and saw work details coming and going:

They [the army] had contracts with other civilian companies on [work] details. There was a cutting-wood detail. These companies contracted with the camp.

They had a roll call when they loaded them [POWs] in a truck at Baker Gate. The POWs wore blue jeans uniforms, and the letters "PW" were embossed at the knee and the shirt and across the hips.

They were never housed anywhere else and always came back each day from work details, at least the ones that I saw.[19]

Landscaping and any pick-and-shovel work were among the most taxing assignments performed by POWs. This drawing by POW Albin Sagadin (published in *P.o.W. Oase* #44, August 17, 1944) is titled "POWs at work." Prisoners on such laborious details and in steamy weather received permission to work without shirts and in short trousers (although the pick-wielding man at right, bereft of footwear, was probably an anomaly). The men are clearing land on the hill near the American officers' buildings. In the distance are all three guard towers fronting Baker Road and the entire expanse of the POW camp (courtesy of Joachim Metzner).

When working on details, the POWs wore their standard prisoner garb, generally consisting of a dark blue tandem of trousers and shirt with light-colored (either yellow or white) "PW" stenciling in various places: the shirt sleeves, either above the elbows or just below the shoulder seams; the back, either even with the shoulders or centered; sometimes the front, even with the chest; the trousers' knees or thighs; and across the buttocks. When jackets or overcoats were worn in cold weather, the stenciled letters appeared on the outerwear as well. Likewise, when overalls, undershirts, or vests were issued, the stenciling appeared in the same locations whenever possible. If cream- or khaki-colored clothing was worn, the letters were in dark black coloring. Most often, the letters were horizontal. But it was not uncommon to see POWs sporting clothing with vertical lettering, particularly on shirts above the elbows.

Margaret Newman grew up on the "Brick Pike" (Pelham Road), just opposite the camp. "I saw the POWs hanging by the fence [of their camp] watching traffic go by," she recalled. On April 19, 2009, she spoke with Mrs. John (Loretta) Edwards and recorded the following:

John Edwards was connected with the Central Presbyterian Church, Anniston during WWII. In addition to his church work, during the spring and summer he worked at a peach orchard in Menlo, Georgia, as an office worker. Prisoners from the POW Camp at Ft. McClellan picked peaches. John knew a little German so [he] talked with them some. One day a prisoner was missing. He was found behind a tree asleep.[20]

Annistonian Steve Bakke heard numerous accounts of prisoner work details. "I was at a family reunion in the 1980s," he noted in 2011. "It was a family reunion for a friend of mine. And one of her relatives, a great aunt or cousin, I'm not sure which, remembered, when she was 13 or 14 or 15, the German POWs coming into Georgia from McClellan, especially during the cotton harvest. A lot of 'em were sent in to pick in the orchards and fields. And a lot of the owners of the cotton fields had migrant workers. And as she was getting older and getting more [romantic] attention from the POWs, her mother made her come into the house." He added, "I've heard stories over the years about the POWs picking oranges and lemons in Florida. And I can remember a friend telling me the Germans had pretty much free rein when they were on these details and could even go into stores."[21]

Ferrol L. Aderholdt of nearby Jacksonville was a lanky 34-year-old woodworker and master craftsman when he began civilian employment as a senior equipment repairman in the quartermaster branch of Fort McClellan in October 1942. He continued working for the fort until June 30, 1947, when McClellan was temporarily deactivated, and he left as the foreman in the wood and metal section of the Quartermaster Repair Shops. In his nearly five years of employment on the post, he frequently oversaw prisoner details. In 2009, his son Meredith, also of Jacksonville, recounted his father's wartime civilian service:

He was born in Calhoun County, and he lived in Calhoun County all his life. As a young man, he went to work with his father and grandfather in woodworking. And he was highly skilled. He made furniture. He even made caskets.

He had an offer to work for the Roosevelt family in New York. There's a family in Anniston, the Kilbys, and they had a foundry. They were pretty rich, and they took him down to Warm Springs, Georgia [where Franklin Delano Roosevelt underwent water therapy for his polio-stricken legs]. This was probably around 1927 or 1928, maybe even later, sometime around when Roosevelt was governor [of New York] or maybe running for governor. And he met Mr. Roosevelt, and he shook his hand. Mrs. Kilby was telling Mr. Roosevelt what a wonderful worker he was. And then he met Mrs. [Eleanor] Roosevelt, and her family was interested in having him do some work for them up in [Hyde Park,] New York. And they asked him to come on up to New York and do work for them and stay there. But he decided he didn't want to come up to New York.

Later he built a home in Bonnie Brook, Alabama, that looked like that place in Warm Springs [the "Little White House," FDR's retreat built shortly before he became president in 1933].

Before the war, he had been running a woodwork shop down at the mill here [Jacksonville], and he was a pretty well-known furniture maker.

During the war, he went to work at the post. He did repairs for the Army Depot. And he was in the quartermaster shops on the post. And they had German prisoners come in and help. Now they [POWs] couldn't work for the [U.S.] war effort; that was against the rules. But they could fix cots and chairs and things. He had at least one other civilian working for him, too. But every day, he had six or eight prisoners.

One time, he saw an accident. This was on the fort. They [POWs] did a lot of things, a lot of work details at the fort. This prisoner was gluing a big block of wood, and the glue hadn't set yet. And this piece was really built up quite a bit. And this one part came out and hit him in the head. It was in a lathe. He might have been making a big plate or saucer. It was spinning real hard. The sad part is the guy knew better, but he was in a hurry. They [POWs] knew what they were doing. These guys weren't amateurs. And my dad felt kind of sad about it."

Ferrol Aderholdt continued his association with the fort into the 1950s, when McClellan was again activated. He died in 1974 at the age of 67.[22]

James Byron Wester, Sr., was another local civilian contract employee at McClellan. His son-in-law, James Bonner, spoke of Wester's relationship with the POWs: "From what I understand, he was in the paint shop. He was a civilian with authority over the paint shop. They used the prisoners for work details. They painted the buildings. And they'd send 'em up to Cedartown, Georgia [about 45 miles northeast of the camp by current roads], to do painting."

"He did wallpaper jobs and house painting," Bonner's wife, Datha Dean (Wester) Bonner, said of her father. "He was born around 1900, and he died in either 1970 or 1971. I was born in 1944, so everything I heard about the prisoners came from other people. I know he was very good to the prisoners. And when Daddy was being good to the German prisoners here, my oldest brother was over there in Germany fighting them."[23]

Pennsylvanian Clark J. Miller was not even 18 when he was drafted into the army on November 10, 1944. Before embarking for Europe for the final furious months of combat, he guarded POWs on work details. As he recounted in 2010:

I had 12 weeks of training. It was originally 17 weeks, but it went down to 12 weeks because they needed men. I was in the infantry. I took a troop train down to Fort McClellan from Indian Town Gap [Pennsylvania]. They told us when we got on the train where we were going, but not before. It was a secret.

When they were getting us ready for shipping out, we had our details. One of them was guarding some of the prisoners. They picked out the better ones, and we took them out for details. We took them out to gather garbage on trucks. [U.S. Army] Companies A, B, and C—they would take turns. They would take one or more of us from each company. I was in Company B, 25th Battalion, 2nd Pennsylvania Division. This would have been in February 1945. I remember Captain Livingston. And 1st Sergeant Moran from Reading, Pennsylvania. Master Sergeant Trimmerman was overall [in charge]. There were four platoons in Company B. Five hundred men in a company. The barracks was on the left side of the railroad area [on the post], the northwest side, I think it was.

Maybe six or twelve soldiers would be detailed to guard the prisoners that day. And we'd pick up usually two men [POWs]. A

The teenaged Clark J. Miller, who guarded POW details before shipping out for combat in Europe (courtesy of Clark J. Miller).

few times, three or four prisoners. We'd march down to Pelham Road to the POW camp and pick them up.

We were handed an M1 rifle, usually a carbine, a smaller version of the M1. Six to 12 of us marching down all the way from the barracks [on the post] to the POW Camp. The MPs knew who was coming down, and they were highly disciplined. They'd brief you on what your detail was that particular day. We weren't supposed to go into the camp. They'd bring the POWs out to us.

And if there was a garbage truck—I'd say a ton- to a ton-and-a-half-size truck—the driver was a GI. I'd go in the back of the truck toward the cabin. And a lot of the time the POWs would walk alongside when the garbage truck got full.

Your rifle was in a position that you were ready to shoot, even from the hip, if you had to. You didn't have it at your arm, left or right.

The detail might last three-quarters of a day or all day long. You got up at 5:00. Had reveille. And you were assigned your detail. A lot of times during the training, we'd get up at 4:00 and have your training exercises, then move out on your POW detail. This was toward the end of the training when you were just waiting for orders to ship out.

This was winter in Alabama. We'd see snow, but it didn't last long. You might have two inches at a time. Maybe three or four, maybe less, would be the most I'd seen. There was a lot of rain, but that didn't stop you on your details.

I remember the prisoners on the details. They talked in German, and that's what aggravated you 'cause you didn't know what they were saying or if they were planning anything. You really had to be on your toes. And they wouldn't talk much. Very rarely did you get one that would talk English. Or maybe could talk English. Now and then they would. I would say a lot of 'em were young kids. Like me. Teenagers.

One time, I remember, they got into a scrap between themselves, and it was hard to break 'em up. They almost were coming to fighting. Don't know what it was about.

But most of the time they behaved pretty well. But you had to be really stern. It was one of the details at Fort McClellan that you were a little uneasy about. But otherwise, you didn't care. One detail was like another.

Miller left McClellan "in late February or early March. I took a troop train to New York City, and then I went to England and the European theater. I arrived by troop train, I traveled by troop train, and I left by troop train. And when I got to Europe and the fighting, it was rough. But I don't talk about that. Ever. I'll just say I went in the army as a kid. And I matured in a hurry." He finished his service as a PFC and was discharged in 1946.[24]

Numerous POWs spent their working time learning the craft of baking bread and various pastries. Publications on America's POW camps always list bakeries as among the most common places for POW labor.

Mess Sergeant Jack Shay oversaw meal preparation for the GI mess halls in the American military installation, across Baker Road from the POW camp. Among the scores of POWs he supervised during that time were Franz Beer, Walter Beier, Helmut Engelke, Alfred Goldhardt, Georg Kügle, August Lobitz, Karl Merbold, Alfons Mildenberger, Karl Mildenberger, Ernst Schmidt, Heinz Schumann, Gerhard Sommer, Robert Suberg, and Erich Wetzold, all from the 7th Company.[25]

In postwar years, an arched stone bridge with a macadam deck spanning the South Branch of Cane Creek (just north of what, during the war, was known as Middle Gate Road, now Baltzell Gate Road) was identified as a likely POW project. The bridge was designed as a pedestrian crossing, more decorative than functional, owing to its location a few dozen yards west of a larger bridge for both people and vehicles. But because of its position just

```
                              Prisoner of War Surgeon
                              Ft. Mc. Clellan, Ala


                                      1 January 1946

In accordance with Par 12 AR-30 305 the following PoW's foodhaendlers on detail
# 125: Mess Hall 1463, were found  free from any contagoius disenses:


     NAME                    RANK           ISN          Co.#


     Goldhardt, Alfred       OGefr.         30734        7

     Schumann, Heinz         OGefr.         30728        7

     Merbold, Karl           OGefr.         29790        7

     Lobitz, XXXX August     OGefr.         30564        7

     Schmidt, Ernst          Gefr.          30193        7

     Engelke, Helmut         Gefr.          245          7

     Wetzold, Erich          Gefr.          29722        7

     Suberg, Robert          Gefr.          29728        7



                                        HENRY T. BROBST
                                        Capt. MC.
```

A typical work detail roster, dated New Year's Day 1946 (author's collection).

north of and down the hill from McClellan's post headquarters area, it commanded attention and became a scenic backdrop for photographic memories. A plaque ("THIS BRIDGE WAS BUILT BY GERMAN PRISONERS OF WAR DURING WORLD WAR II") was placed in the northeastern end column. But though the bridge was there during the war, questions remain concerning its construction. In 2009, Joan McKinney said, "I'm not sure how much stonemasonry work the POWs did. The plaque was put in only in the last four or five years. I think the WPA [Works Progress Administration, alternately referred to by others as Work Projects Administration] put that bridge in before the war."[26]

Rita Wells, who grew up near the camp and eventually worked in the headquarters building, remembered seeing the bridge in place before the camp was built. POWs, however, did work on the walls lining the South Branch and cleared wild growth from the creek bed beneath the bridge, perhaps causing the misattribution.

Many POWs took pride in creating a homey physical environment in their living quarters. That meant transforming their barracks into welcoming buildings where they could pass time as well as sleep, beautifying the grounds with flowers and rock gardens, placing

An eight-man work detail, wearing "PW"-embossed clothes, in the American camp. Despite one newsman's account maintaining that "most of them are rather short" (see "The POWs: Who Were They?" chapter), this group appears quite the opposite. Robert Suberg, second from right, was six feet tall. Sergeant Jack Shay, who supervised this group, commented, "They were generally young, strong, lean men in good shape and with well-developed muscles who looked like they might be good athletes" (author's collection).

wooden or stone walkways between buildings, and installing handrails over ascending terrain. Joachim Metzner described some of this internal work activity as follows:

[They began] with a lot of work to create good drainage ditches with small bridges to their barracks. Doing some internal work in the barracks (mostly the space in the barracks was divided into 2 areas to have a living area and a sleeping area) [and] building new little cabinets from old wooden boxes. Then adding some makeover on the outside of the barracks. More work was done to have stairs (if needed) or nice ways [paths] between the barracks of a company, erect[ing] some fences.... A special barrack ... got a totally new designed interior ... in "Blackforest"-style [the Schwarzwaldstübele].[27]

The roofed POW stage, open to the air at its proscenium and constructed on the right side of Compound 2 up the incline from Baker Road and near the top, became the crowning glory of prisoner internal work. Quoting information contained in his father's newspaper, Joachim Metzner explained:

In the early days theatre play was done in the entertainment rooms [of the various compounds]. With a little stage at the end of the barrack they had a very long audience room ... not an ideal

The open-air stage, a fully functional theater, built by POW labor (courtesy of Edith Suberg).

solution and only smaller plays or vaudeville were shown ... there was an idea [need] for a real stage very soon.

Following an article in the newspaper # 33d: In Fall 1943 a stage building was started between the entertainment room (barrack) and a work shed in Batl/Camp 2, but due to fears regarding a possible fire the ... [half-finished] building had to be torn down....

Shortly after this Uffz-. [Unteroffizier or Sergeant Gustav] Harant presented a drawing of a bigger stage and this was accepted by the camp-leadership ... (the American and the German) at the 4th Jan 1944. The work started at 10th Jan 1944 and it was finished by Whitsun (...5th June...). This was located in the area near the edge [dividing line] of company 7/8 (2. Batl.)....

The size: play area 7m[eter] × 7m plus

Height: 9m

Light: 6000 W

plus ancillary room

The opening [premiere]: The ... Orchester [orchestra] under the leadership of "Uffz. Reinhold Güther" ... played a military march of [Franz] Schubert.

Then a stage play "Der Bürgergeneral" from [Johann Wolfgang von] Goethe was done.

From now on the Big stage was [a] center of entertainment.

Each week 2 times or more ... American and German films....

Music shows and theatre plays ... [for] example: "Krach um Jolanthe" from German Author "August Hinrichs"; comedy "Nachtrabe" from POW Gerhard Schulz, comedy as well as orchestra-evenings (parts of "Othello" and other serious music).

In 1945 after the war was over, things got more complicated [changed].... Now cinema costs 15Cent and the stage got visual covers to prevent ... spectators, who do not pay. They now had 800 official seats.[28]

The stage was professional in every way, with a dressing room, rear storage chambers for props, and an overhead structure for stage flies. As Joachim Metzner wrote, "They had a bridge … for light and hanging stage sets in the top over the playing area."[29] It became a junior version of the Hollywood Bowl, with curved tiers of seating in the form of benches fanning out on a gentle slope in front of the proscenium. Because of its benches and relatively sheltered location "behind the 8th company, where the land goes up" into forested expanses approaching the northern extent of the camp, it became a gathering place, even when no performances occurred.[30]

Unfortunately, all that work of beautifying their camp came to naught shortly after the war, when all the buildings were razed to make way for a suburban housing development. Not a single structure remains.

8

The Artistry of the POWs

"These were highly accomplished people,
not just average soldiers."

McClellan's prisoners included gifted artists, sculptors, woodworkers, illustrators, writers, poets, dramatists, and musicians. As Joan McKinney assessed, "These were highly accomplished people, not just average soldiers."[1]

In his December 11, 1944, inspection report, Edouard Patte noted a pronounced emphasis on artistic avocations (original syntax intact):

> Since my last visit, four barracks were set aside as art-studios. Within them are working a few painters, sculptors, toy makers, and handicraft addicts who do some commendable work. Those little studios with self-made benches, old canvas frames, tin cans full of red, blue, yellow, black and white, with paintings of European landscape, of marines, of winterscenes, of still nature,— cheese, sausages and beer, or glorious bouquets of geraniums—, with portraits of soldiers, of Arabs, of nude women or of a child, offer a striking resemblance to the typical Montparnasse penthouses. I ignored whether a would-be Picasso is among the POW's but I do know that you will find amidst them sincere artists who have found in painting, drawing and sculpturing the best outlet for their inner force....
>
> Col. Schmidt [Smith] has helped these men in setting apart some space, in ordering material and equipment, and in attempting to secure in the various canteens of the Fort a ready market for the finished work. Weaving, leather work, wood carving absorb the time of one hundred and twenty men in special workshops. This is the outstanding achievement of this camp, very skillfully coordinated by an experienced handicraft leader, who goes from building to building to check constantly on the quality of the products.[2]

The "four barracks ... set aside as art-studios" arose in 1944 in the space between the southeastern boundary of Compound 2 and the outer fence of the camp, close to Baker Road and right of the camp's main gate. Christian Höschle commented on these buildings in his book. "In April 1944, he noticed a few barracks on the edge of the camp, each 12 feet by 12 feet," translator Joni Pontius noted. "He said nobody knew what they were for at first. But they had to vacate their atelier, their studio, and had to move to these artists' barracks, and they [camp artists] were dispersed two or three in each barracks."[3]

Höschle also provided information on some of the camp's young artists:

> He wrote there were about 60 men who wanted to paint, and you had to apply for painting classes from a teacher. There was this Hungarian who had studied in Munich....
>
> Christian said he liked to use oils. One [painting] was a sailboat on the water. And one of his first portraits in oil was of his friend, Albert Effinghausen, who also enrolled in the painting class....

One of his friends was Hubert Maiburg, a graphic artist. Hubert was also a student, and he and Christian developed into the best portraitists in the camp....

The Americans brought photos of their family members to Christian to paint. And he also did a self-portrait.[4]

In the decades since the camp's closing, two other artists—unknown for half a century—assumed near-mythical status for a controversial work rarely seen.

"The Military Showplace of the South": Fort McClellan, Alabama, a Historic Building Inventory, a report submitted to the U.S. Army Corps of Engineers in June 1993, included the following information:

> One of the remodeling tasks undertaken ... was the furnishing of the bar in the newly designated Officers' Club. The fitting out and decoration of this room was assigned to Prisoners of War ... the bar was unfortunately replaced between 1982 and the Present.... The POWs, however left another legacy in a different medium:
>
> > What they left—a cycle of paintings on the walls of the bar...—is like torture. There are 17 murals, and with violence, oddity and mystery they encircle the room and capture it (Freeman, *The Anniston Star*, 1979).

The murals range from the genteel to the disturbing, covering the upper five feet of wall space on each wall. Whether they present a single storyline or simply present a variety of themes is arguable. On walls with doors, the painters framed their work around the door, making an obstacle an asset. They are clearly the work of several individuals, some scenes showing more mastery over the art than others. The murals on the south walls show fairly well-to-do individuals engaged in family life on the parapet of a castle.... Three scenes are depicted on the east wall including a courting couple, a young woman pensively touching a dove and two soldiers sharing a drink.... These scenes are pleasant in aspect but not of the same caliber, in theme or rendering, as those painted on the remaining walls. The mural on the west wall is perhaps the most disturbing, showing a violent conflict between men armed with daggers, billy clubs, and stones. The men are powerfully built, in some instances hands and feet are grotesquely enlarged.... Hiding behind a corner, a passive man looks on at the violence holding his hand to his mouth. Viewers have described the scene as apocalyptic and have considered it to be inspired by the paintings of Michelangelo.... Another mural of this ilk, painted on the side projection of the fireplace, shows a violent scene in which one man, possible [*sic*] injured, lies in a prone position while another man with a spear, eyes an approaching snake. Again, hands and feet are grossly distorted....

Four of the murals are possibly connected. They follow each other in position around the room and involve conflict between soldiers and civilians in a village setting. A woman, the central character, appears in most of the frames. While she differs facially and in size in each frame, her clothing, in style and color, remain[s] the same. In the first mural, a petite older woman is standing on a chair possibly mixing food in a bowl. Out of her window, she can see two soldiers approaching.... In the next scene, a soldier is speaking to a lady who is looking out of a window. He holds a bouquet of roses behind him as if to surprise her. A young boy is shown on the other side of the window on the ground.... The soldier, woman and boy share the same facial characteristics but the boy's hands and feet are distorted. A view of village life lies behind this scene featuring a skeletal looking man and a young girl. In the next scene, a woman wearing the same clothes as the woman in the window is offered money by a soldier.... In the fourth, which takes place on a quay, a soldier has stabbed another soldier while two women scream in anger.... One of the women is clothed in the same colors as the woman in the previous mural but to accommodate the door opening she has been diminished in size, becoming dwarflike.

The themes presented within these murals appear familiar and then again unfamiliar. Mixing twentieth century elements with traditional folkloric, possibly operatic, and Biblical images, the artists created a room with views that have remarkable power. The murals were purportedly begun in 1943 and finished in 1945 by a group of German POW's [sic]. The names of the painters are unknown but at least four artists were interned at the camp in 1943.... The manager of the Officers' Club between 1941 and 1945 recalls that three men produced the murals. She notes that the painters were loners, not mixing with the other POWs who were given other tasks to complete in the building and that they were part of Rommel's Afrika Corps captured in North Africa.... A restoration of the murals in the late 1970s indicated that the painters used organic material, such as egg and clay. Further while no signatures were discovered, "Anno 1945" was written on one panels [sic] as well as "Saga" (Soga?) and at some distance "Belau." Another possible clue to the identity of the painters lies in two signed paintings attributed to POWs. The first is a copy of a Rubens painting completed by Paul Weingarth, the second a landscape scene painted by Heinz Hippold now hanging in Fort McClellan's Public Relations Department. Either men [sic] may have been responsible for the murals but it is equally possible that others may have been involved.

To date no information has been found indicating who supervised the painters. Where setting is shown, the artists tried to maintain consonance with the Spanish flavor of the building. However, the themes within the murals suggest that the POW's [sic] were allowed to paint whatever topic they chose. In essence, they favored views which few Americans would choose as backdrops for social drinking. This trait lead [sic] to their being paneled over in the 1950s until the late 1970s when they were uncovered by [Rolf] Von Helberg, a warrant officer. Von Helberg led in the restoration of the murals and campaigned vigorously for their uncovering. One of the murals which was water damaged was repainted by Von Helberg. Unfortunately, he was not aware of the existence of slides taken of the original murals so his recreation was not guided by the original....[5]

The above summary referred to information contained within the September 16, 1979, edition of *The Anniston Star*. Staff writer Laura Ann Freeman's two-page, eight-photograph piece, titled "POW art: Vibrant, sometimes masterful, work of German soldiers uncovered at Fort McClellan," utilized the limited information known at the time and described the bizarre brutality of some of the murals:

[A] cycle of paintings on the walls of the bar in the Officers' Club—is like torture.
    There are 17 murals ... with violence, oddity and mystery....
    Almost two decades ago the Army covered the paintings with wood paneling. Apparently, they were considered unpleasant....
    Now, the paneling has come down....
    [Rolf] Von Helberg was one of the forces behind the movement to uncover the paintings and, by his accounts, it was a fight....
    Yet, on the eve of the official opening of the Officers' Club after a redecorating project, Von Helberg worried about a small group which wants the murals covered again....
    On the north wall, above two doors, are painted visions of murder and despair. Brutal foreshortening of hands and feet force an almost unspeakable element of outrage, as if the paintings scream.

Freeman wrote further of the limited knowledge of the paintings' origins only three decades after their completion:

To explain the paintings may be impossible, for even specifics about the works ... are hard to come by.
    The Army's memory is short. files [sic] on the prisoners were either destroyed or marked "unrecoverable" after 25 years.
    Nothing original dealing with the POW life or art remains in the office of the Chief of Military History in Washington....
    Ewing Steele.... From 1941 until 1945 ... manage[d] the Officers' Club and the 54 POWs, including the artists, who worked there.

"There were three of them. They worked all day long. I can't remember who they were, but they were painting their moods. The pictures on the walls were the moods of those boys and they must have been in bad moods," she recalls....

"The ones that painted stayed to themselves and didn't have much to do with the other boys," she says.

Freeman also quoted several regional experts who were consulted when the paintings were accidentally unearthed. Ted Weeks, then the curator of the Birmingham Museum of Art, while declining to term the artwork "great," described one violent panel as "Wagnerian" in scope "and says the man portrayed gazing at the writhing fight scene may suggest, 'mankind as an observer looking upon chaos in a rather inactive way.'" She also included remarks from Dr. Martha Simpson, a teacher and quondam professor of art at Jacksonville State University, who called the paintings "very ambitious and very successful."

Rolf Von Helberg, Freeman wrote, "with 15 years experience as a commercial artist, is convinced the entire cycle is a story of some kind." She added that, in an earnest, well-intentioned effort to fill in an area where the paint had been removed or damaged, he repainted one mural, attempting to fill in the empty areas with likely expressions or probable designs, only to later discover, in a hitherto-unknown file, photographic slides taken of all the panels.[6]

However conceived, the murals failed to match the heroic, patriotic domestic art prominently displayed throughout the United States during the war, and they fell short of much of the fine European artistry collected by American connoisseurs. Central figures in various murals appear as brooding, hulking, menacing, and misshapen brutes, some even dwarflike, often drawn in stiff and unnatural poses in a bizarre world of violence and discomfiting dread. Observers considered the disconcerting images—intruding so graphically and obscuring the more pastoral scenes—either a foreboding, apocalyptic glimpse into the inner soul of humanity or a visually metaphoric rendering of the uncertainty of mankind in captivity.

American officers of all ranks had access to the club and could have easily seen the grotesque images splashed on the walls as poor ambiance for a clubhouse meant to provide a relaxing respite from a world-engulfing war. As Mike Oliver, a reporter for *The Birmingham News*, wrote in 1982:

> The writhing bodies seem out of place in the lounge of the Officers' Club....
> It could make even an army man a bit uncomfortable while trying to relax with a few drinks. Maybe that's why the writhing bodies ... were covered with wood paneling for 30 years....
> Rolf Von Helberg ... supervised the restoration of the Officers' Club....
> He speculated that the wives of McClellan VIPs in the 1950s pushed for the murals to be covered....
> "Over the years, rumors persisted that the murals were obscene," Von Helberg said. "So it was passed down from commander to commander not to uncover the walls.
> "When I ... in 1978 ... was assigned as branch manager of the club, it was in need of renovation.... I took it on myself to look behind the paneling. I saw (the murals) and said let's rip it."
> Von Helberg said that he received static from the Officer's Wives Club and wives in general because the rumors persisted that the murals were obscene. He said he got orders to cover them back up but "I have a dialect and don't always understand English."
> If the murals prove one thing it is that one man's smut is another's art.[7]

The murals subsequently underwent several treatments, including one in 1985. As South Carolina art conservator Catherine Gambrell Rogers wrote in 1998, "Restoration work is documented on the murals by a[n] inscription/signature by the restorer which reads 'Mural Restoration//Kay McFarland 1985.' It is located on the mural to the left of the fireplace...." She also included a full list of 16 murals, complete with locations:

North Wall
    Mural #1: Man with red slippers.
    Mural #2: Group of men fighting with large rock.
    Mural #3: Two men with bird, animal, and woman with red top.
East Wall
    Mural #4: Woman at window and old man begging.
    Mural #5: Man with snake.
    Mural #6: Woman in red dress with soldier with coins.
    Mural #7: Two soldiers with two women.
South Wall
    Mural #8: Two men with rock wall.
    Mural #9: Man with woman with umbrella.
    Mural #10: Woman in red dress with birds.
    Mural #11: Two men drinking wine.
    Mural #12: Landscape with mountain and castle.
West Wall
    Mural #13: Wall of fort.
    Mural #14: Boats at sea with fort.
    Mural #15: Children playing with blocks.
    Mural #16: Man and woman on castle steps.[8]

In the fall of 1998, and with the final closure of the fort less than a year away, Rogers undertook the $15,000 task of cleaning and stabilizing the murals. Aamer Madhani reported on the assignment in the September 26, 1998, issue of *The Anniston Star*:

[A]reas where paint has chipped will be replaced and discolored areas will be touched up. The thin layer of filth covering the panels will be removed without harming the integrity of the artists' creations.

The scenes range from depictions of family life to a conflict between men armed with daggers. The quality and detail of the work varies. And while none of the panels are Michelangelos, they hold the common thread of historical value that merits saving....

The POWs were allowed to paint whatever subject they chose. Their choices were romantic and Eurocentric in nature, evidently not a pleasing backdrop for American officers who took refreshment in the club....

There is not much information about the prisoners who created the murals. Their names are unrecorded, but it is known that at least four were being held at the camp in 1943.

In 1979 ... The Anniston Star reported that the artists ... were loners and rarely mixed with the other prisoners.[9]

Writing in *The Birmingham News* on November 10 of that year, with the restoration ongoing, Rose Livingston added a few more details:

The artists and their intentions are more fascinating to the historian than the finished product, which covers walls in a former officer's club that now serves as a tax preparation center.

The 17 murals lining the upper five feet of the plaster walls appear oddly unrelated, varying from scenes of hand-to-hand battle to romance. Some are bloody....

"It's a pessimistic outlook," said Al Reisz of Reisz Engineering, a consultant.... "They'd been through a lot of combat." ...

During that time [World War II], the officer's club was being remodeled and its decoration was turned over to some POWs with artistic leanings ... the walls were covered with scenes apparently left up to the imagination of each painter....

Reisz ... was ecstatic that the workers discovered two signatures in the process. Reisz plans to use the names to research the artists' lives in Germany after the camp closed....[10]

The artists' names turned out to be Albin Sagadin and Herbert Belau. Their long-delayed discovery touched off several attempts to learn more about these men.

Perhaps more than anyone else, Annistonian Joan McKinney, a transplanted Marylander who spent the better part of two decades as a government employee in various high-profile positions at Fort McClellan in the 1980s and 1990s, has virtually adopted the murals as a pet project. In 1999, Tim Lockette interviewed her for a piece in the *Gadsden Times*.

Formerly the director of public affairs at Fort McClellan, and now a contractor with the base, McKinney is the base's resident expert on the ... artifacts they [POWs] left behind....

McKinney said the theme of the murals is "the struggles of mankind." ...

The only thing the scenes have in common is their setting—they all take place in a sort of Italian Renaissance landscape. Even the costumes don't quite seem to match....

She's convinced that some of the images contain inside jokes.... With so little information about the artists, it's hard to know how much of the painting is symbolism, and how much is happenstance....

When the restorer found a signature on one of the paintings—"Sagadin"—researchers were able to identify him as Albin Sagadin, a German private who participated in an art show mentioned in the prisoners' newspaper.

A friend ... looked up the name on a Web-based directory.... The first number he dialed was the right one—but Sagadin's wife said her husband had died just three weeks before.

Albin Sagadin was a 26-year-old student at an art academy in Dresden when he was conscripted into the German Army.

He and at least one other artist—whose signature reads "Bolar" or "Bolau" [Belau]—mixed their own paint, using egg whites from the mess hall as a base. Prisoners at the base were notorious for their ability to scrounge up art supplies....

One of the female figures in the photo may have been a picture of Sagadin's first wife, who died in the late 1940s. Sagadin reportedly told his second wife that he had painted a picture of his first wife during his stay in the camp.

Sagadin tried to return to the United States after the war but was denied entry because of a lung ailment.[11]

In a piece for the fall 2007 *Alabama Historical Association Newsletter*, McKinney wrote, "The works are attributed to two POW artists.... Both signatures are visible on the murals; the date of 1945 appears below Sagadin's name on the south wall. Bolau's signature (could also read, "Belau" or "Balau"), appears on the north wall."[12]

Since then, more information has surfaced regarding the painters, if not exactly how and why they were commissioned in the first place. A November 1944 report on conditions in the camp averred, "This camp boasts of a person who is said to be one of the best contemporary artists in Germany."[13] No further identification was provided. It seems likely, however, that Albin Sagadin was the artist of note.

"When Sagadin was tasked to do those murals, he probably asked Belau to be his apprentice," McKinney ventured. "He probably was training Belau to follow in his style."[14] In a 2012 email, she wrote:

According to Joachim [Metzner], Beleau is described … as having no formal training….

So, here's … [a] theory as to why Beleau was selected: If I were a classically trained artist (Sagadin was trained at the Dresden Academy of Art) and was commissioned to do this large body of work, I think I'd want an apprentice who would follow my instructions and not attempt to execute his own interpretations of what the painting should depict. I'd want a follower, not someone who felt they were my equal….

And regarding Sagadin, she added, "Sagadin died at age 83. He tried to come here in 1953 but was denied permission. He probably had TB, a communicable disease."[15]

According to information supplied by Albin Sagadin's widow, Maria, as well as data on the Internet, he underwent three years of study at the Dresden Academy of the Arts before his military service, which resulted in his subsequent capture and internment. He died in November 1998 at age 84, which would have put him in his early 30s when working on the murals.[16]

Meta Kordiš, curator of the UGM Maribor Art Gallery in Slovenia, shed additional light on the artist's background in an August 28, 2012, email to Joachim Metzner (syntax intact):

Albin Sagadin was born 1914 in the village Slivnica near Maribor. First lessens of painting he received from prof. Žagar in Ljutomer [Slovenia]. Before the II WW he was as an amateur exhibiting in Murska Sobota [Slovenia] (1939) with other painters. Solo show he had in Lendava [Slovenia]. During the German occupation of Yugoslavia [then encompassing Slovenia], he went to Dresden [Germany], where he studied. He was drafted in German regular army. Later in Africa capture by the USA. Then you know the rest. In the year 1946 he came back to Slovenia. He joined Maribor artists club. He was active as an illustrator and restorer of frescos. In the attachment you may find the only data we keep of him in our archive. It is in Slovene.

The attached document, dated 1951, added that he was repatriated in November 1946.[17]

In the January 7, 2000, issue of *Stars and Stripes*, a military periodical, Richelle Turner-Collins described Sagadin's artistic style:

He first painted in a realistic painting style, using bright pastel colors and small brush strokes that is best shown in his paintings of city scenes of Salzburg, Austria. They were done after he was released from the POW camp and while he was working with Americans in Salzburg. They show the development of his own special style, one that is similar to that of French Impressionist Claude Monet but that also includes the broad, deep brush strokes similar to those of Vincent Van Gogh.

The same style can be found at the wall murals at Fort McClellan, which were completed in 1945, shortly before Sagadin returned to Germany….

"He really liked being in Alabama," Maria Sagadin said…. "He said he really wanted to go back but he had a lung sickness and could not."

Maria Sagadin said her husband sought American citizenship while still a prisoner, but was refused because of his lung illness.

When Sagadin returned to Germany, he worked during the day as a salesman to support his wife and daughter, Carmen. In the evenings and on weekends he painted. He did it for love and not for money. He often refused to sell his paintings. His wife's home is decorated with many of his artworks.[18]

Information on Herbert Belau, whose correct surname only came to light in recent years, was provided by his daughter, Susanne, in communications with Joachim Metzner. Excerpts from her written account follow:

Herbert Belau was born [December 8, 1921] in the province of Neuhof close to Heilsberg in East Prussia [Germany].... Assisted by 20 workers, his father Egbert and his mother Susanne ... farmed 500 hectares of land and raised cattle, hogs and horses....

At the age of thirteen, he ... left home to go to a progressive boarding school ... in Bieberstein near Fulda. This is where he made important friends.... Also, he was fascinated by his art teacher Rudolf Kubesch, who specialized in abstract art. In 1941 during WWII, H.B. was drafted into the army and he had to leave school but was still able [to] receive a high school diploma.

Stationed in Italy in 1942, he was trained as a dispatch rider and transferred to the German Africa Corps to Tunis in May 1943 at the time when these troops capitulated. Captured, H.B[.] was then brought by ship to the USA to Fort McClellan, Alabama, where he lived as a POW until the camp was closed in April 1946. He spent an additional year as a POW in England.

H. B. returned to Germany in 1947. He went to Göttingen where his sister was living after her flight from the Soviets, who had occupied East Prussia. Both parents had died there. In November 1947, H.B. enrolled in the State Crafts School in Kassel [then part of West Germany], which incorporated the local crafts school and the school of fine arts. After six months, he took a leave of absence to become a stonemason in Göttingen. By 1949, he enrolled as a student at the School of Arts in Düsseldorf. He studied art in the class of Prof. Ewald Mataré until 1954 and became one of the sculptor's most talented students....

Being well trained as a craftsman, H.B. got several student jobs ... [in] religious art and sacred buildings. After graduating, he became a self-employed artist concentrating on religious art. He created figures of the Madonna, crucifixes, scenic reliefs, candelabras, doorknobs, fonts, fountains, etc. Some of his artwork, however, was somehow controversial.

As such, his Virgin Mary wooden statue, which B. had built for a new church in Kaiserslauten, was not consecrated by the bishop, because he considered it to be too modern and even blasphemous. This was a scandal at that time—and a topic for an article, which appeared in the reputable weekly paper DIE ZEIT....

H. B. married Ursula Starck in 1953.... Herbert and Ursula had three children ... and lived until their divorce in 1968 in Düsseldorf. In order to get the custody for his children, H.B. gave up his self-employment and took a job as an art teacher at the Humboldt High-School in Neuss. At the same time, he set up a studio in an old mill close to his home and used it to work on his art. Using a different format and a new technique at that time, he created wood and linocuts, engravings, drawings, small plastic art, wood, paper and clay work.

In 1986 H.B. was diagnosed with cancer. The illness was treated, but it eventually led to his death in 1990.[19]

Joachim Metzner provided further details: Belau's repatriation to Germany occurred on July 1, 1947; he "became a teacher in later years because of the insecure income of an artist"; and he died on August 29, 1990, at age 68 in Neuss, near Düsseldorf. "Based on the age and the fact, that Sagadin was older and had already studied in Dresden/Germany, Sagadin probably had the leadership in creating the murals but ... Belau was very self-confident and of course had [his] own ideas to contribute."[20]

Neither artist lived to see the current appreciation for their combined American masterpiece and how they are today venerated by people who never knew them.

It is also unlikely that other POWs ever saw the completed works. Sagadin and Belau may have told their compatriots what they were doing, but art descriptions in *P.o.W. Oase* focused more on individual art exhibits in the camp than on the masterwork in progress at a building on the main post they rarely would have seen, even from the outside. A small item in the May 30, 1945, issue mentioned both men by name: "Our painters were not seen so often during the last time. This is because of the enforced work duties, which lead our comrades Belau and Sagadin for months into the fort (painting the officers' mess based on their own drafts)."[21]

Rita (Goodwyn) Springer of Anniston recalled seeing the artists working on the murals when she visited the Officers' Club as a youngster, but she did not know who they were.

I saw POWs around Buckner Circle [the main headquarters and lodging area of the fort], a few together. And they were always doing things and gardening.

I practically lived there at Remington Officers' Club. I saw them painting murals. I don't ever remember seeing more than two there. I remember seeing them up on scaffolding. There was a little bar to the left as you came in Remington Hall, and the door was open. By 4:30 or 5 [p.m.] the bar was still open. And I remember they had the windows open to vent the place because of the artists doing the painting on the walls. They [the murals] were absolutely different from what you would see anywhere else. There were some people living on the post who didn't like those paintings, and they complained. That might be why they covered those paintings with mirrors later on.[22]

Fellow Annistonian Mary Elizabeth Johnson was still a teenage Mary Elizabeth Lloyd during World War II. Graduating from high school in Bristol, Virginia, in 1942, she spent the next four years at Vanderbilt University in Tennessee. But she returned to Anniston each summer to be with her parents, Ernest C. and May Lloyd, and help at the family bakery, Lloyd's Bakery, at 1316 Noble Street.

"I was here in the summer and worked in the bakery," she remarked. "And I saw the boys [GIs] coming in for doughnuts and soft ice cream. I also dated some boys out of the fort, and I can remember going out to the Officers' Club in Remington Hall. I can remember this one time, it was June, July, August, and I was on a date in Remington Hall. I remember seeing a young man on a stepstool or ladder painting. If you come into Remington Hall, and you turn left, there were murals. He would have had his back to me. I just saw him there, painting, and knew what he was doing. It was a one-time deal. In that room, I saw the man painting. But I didn't know who he was. I don't think any one of us going in there ever knew the identities of the artists. We didn't talk to them, and they didn't talk to us.

"At one time, those murals were covered up. I think they're visible now, if you can get in to see them."[23]

In recent years, particularly since the closing of the post and the transfer of Remington Hall to private ownership, the murals, though professionally restored and uncovered, have gone largely unseen. More significant yet, because of base closings after World War II and the long period when the murals were covered, relatively few people have ever seen them, and then only during those brief years when they were visible and the facility was open. Many of those who did see the paintings apparently found them disquieting, violent, profane, disjointed, and too murkily allegorical for leisurely sensibilities to enjoy during off-duty hours. Even after the restorations, when the forgotten murals again went public, they became primarily a curiosity from a bygone era. Because they form the bedrock of the walls themselves, they would be unlikely (though not impossible) candidates for removal and relocation to more appropriate art galleries.

The carved bar had a shorter life span. It was removed at some point in the past, its fate unknown.

When this author viewed the murals on August 18, 2007, he casually strode into Remington Hall, whose front and rear doors were then open to accommodate light maintenance and repair work. No one else was in the building, save a solitary worker. The author spent the better part of an hour entering every room in the building, including the Mural Lounge, the Eisenhower Reception Hall, the General Mary Clarke Meeting Room, and the restaurant before taking some rough measurements and several photographs, among them one of a plaque proclaiming, "WALL MURALS PAINTED DURING WORLD WAR II BY GERMAN POW INTERNED AT FORT MCCLELLAN." A brochure advertising the Remington Hall Meeting Center (as it then was known) included the following description: "The murals depict scenes the POW's [sic] felt best reflected the historical aspect of their homeland, as well as the dreams and possible fears of soldiers from all time periods."[24]

The building closed shortly afterward, and this writer met nothing but shut doors and no signs of life upon subsequent trips to the fort. In the fall 2009 issue of *Alabama Heritage*, Joan McKinney wrote:

> The work of Sagadin and Belau has now been inaccessible to the public for a few years, generating perpetual concern in the Anniston community. Rumors repeatedly surface that the murals are threatened by mold and moisture damage. As long as the structure holding this treasure remains locked and empty, fears will grow. But the recent news that the property has been purchased for an events center brings a glimmer of hope that the murals will once again be enjoyed by the public and preserved for the future....
>
> They are a vivid representation of a fine hour in the American past—when prisoners were treated with such humanity, they were inspired to create a gift that outlived them. The fate of that gift is our collective concern.[25]

Four years after this article was written, the building was still closed, with wild growth sprouting up where manicured lawns and flower gardens had once beautified the grounds. But later in 2013, the building again became available, at least for special groups. "The owner of Remington Hall is opening the building to the public so they can view the murals," Joan McKinney wrote in an email.[26]

Naturally, POW artistry varied from person to person. An analysis of camp activity once listed the capabilities of camp "artists, painters or sculptors" as "good, mediocre, & poor," with the artisans creating works of "what they see around them, or have seen in Africa-Europe."[27] And though the discovery of Sagadin and Belau's murals, because of their immense size, prominent placement, striking visibility, and survivability, has received the lion's share of attention in recent years, the American army and civilian personnel attached to the camp were much more familiar with the names of less-celebrated artists whom they got to know on a personal level.

The modern emphasis on preserving and showcasing the murals, while laudatory, presents an exaggerated notion of their value at their time of origin. Though the murals certainly represent Sagadin's masterwork while at McClellan, their current renown is disproportionate to their contemporary awareness even by fellow internees. How many POWs ever saw the murals? How many even knew about them?

The camp's art exhibits, held at various times, attracted a far greater level of visibility and appreciation. The May 1, 1944, *P.o.W. Oase* featured a story of one such display. Under the heading of *Durch die Ausstellung* (Through the Exhibitions), the paper devoted two and a half pages to various artists. As Chania Stymacks recounted in November 2011,

> It mentions a number of prominent artists.
> Hermann Haugg. He did *The Fox and the Snow*, a pen drawing, and a self-portrait. He won an art competition in Germany. He was 33 in 1944. He did a lot of the drawings and the cartoons in the newspaper.

Christian Höschle of the 9th Company. He was an artisan. He excelled in competitions in Germany, and he had a number of special achievements. He was 24 in 1944.

Hubert Maiburg. He did portraits in oil and coal. He was a graphic artist.

Albin Sagadin of the 5th Company. He was 30 in 1944. He studied in Germany, and it says he wants to finish his education in Germany after the war. He had several portraits in the exhibition, all in oil.

Herbert Belau. He was the youngest in a family of painters. He came from East Prussia. He had just started to paint in the POW camp. He loved painting as a schoolboy. One of his paintings was done from memory of his homeland. It [the article] says, "I seek the art and technique of picture making, and one has to feel the mythology of the object." He says he has been caught by art, as if it's the deepest part of his soul, and it will become a part of his life in the future. He was 22 in 1944.

It says the exhibition is finished, but they're working on new pictures. And that dissatisfaction is the strongest motivator of their actions. And it says that, "We shall observe the works of the comrades, and they shall be a piece of our POW existence and of the history of the camp and the comrades who painted them." It also says that the prisoners have seen very few of the remarks on the paintings that were made in the American newspapers.[28]

Translator Klaus W. Duncan listed the works of the quintet of exhibiting artists: for Haugg, "Radierung, A Championship Game, Sketches about life in camp"; for Höschle, "At the Grave of the Fallen Panzer Member (Friend), Panzer Battle, Sunrise at a Funeral, Soldier Behind a Barb-wire Fence, Sailboat"; for the 26-year-old Maiburg from 9th Company, "Corporal Lippert (portrait), Corporal Werner, Centuries Meet, Bust of a Lady"; for Sagadin, "Portrait—Officer Maier [Meier], Portrait—Oberwach[t]meister Schmitz, Portrait—Oberwach[t]meister Schrodt, Self Portrait, Ladies by the Lake"; and for Belau, "2 Kids About the Camp, Birch Trees in the Summer, Portrait of a German Sergeant, Portrait of a German Soldier, Sketch of Someone's Head."[29] Belau also executed a portrait of a fellow prisoner named Karl Woltering.

Translating other issues of P.o.W. Oase, Stymacks again highlighted Hermann Haugg, who alternated landscape illustrations of camp life taken from various points of view with humorous or editorial-type cartoons. "Haugg did many of the illustrations. There can be no doubt that he was talented. His cartoon meanings are subtle. Maybe personal [idiomatic and allegorical] jokes. But his drawings of scenery and views of the camp are very clear and straightforward."[30]

In his story on the Officers' Club murals for the Gadsden Times, Tim Lockette interviewed local historian Kimberly O'Dell, who told him, "My great-uncle knew one of the prisoners. He'd bring him boxes of matches, and (the prisoner) would burn them and use them to make charcoal drawings."[31]

The murals and the issues of P.o.W. Oase left a visible legacy. But no such fate awaited the prisoners' musical and theatrical offerings. It seems likely that none of the musical or dramatic POW performances were recorded or filmed.

With a population ranging from more than 1,000 to slightly in excess of 3,000 at any given time, the camp had dozens, if not several hundred, musicians. Their own individual instruments were back home, but their talent could be harnessed in practice sessions and staged performances. It required only time, willingness, and new musical instruments and sheet music acquired from the Prisoners' Aid Committee of the YMCA, the Red Cross, outright donation from some other source, or purchase using the profits generated by the camp's canteen program.

A camp orchestra and choral group formed. At one time, each compound boasted its own orchestra, though smaller in size. The report resulting from Maurice Ed. Perret's February 1945 visit identified 30 men in the orchestra and 80 in the chorus. Both groups performed programs of light classical or concert pieces customary to the musical tastes of the day. Sorgenbrecher, the camp orchestra, provided monthly "concertos" for the prisoners from January 1944 to February 1945, according to a report covering that period.[32]

Rita (Johnson) Wells spoke of frequently hearing the POW musical groups from her clerical post in the headquarters building: "We heard this beautiful music coming from the corner of the compound when we went out to lunch. The orchestra often played popular American music."[33]

The POWs also staged live theatrical performances. According to one report, approximately 30 POWs were either skillful or unabashed enough to lend their talents to the shows, most of which were lighthearted romps or comedies.[34]

In mid-spring 1944, they put on a one-act play called *Gaston* by Amand Fürth. According to translator Chania Stymacks, "There was one female role. And the actor playing the 'girl' was seen as maybe too genuine and eager [too real]. Guards with weapons came to pick up this 'girl.'"[35]

The "girl" was actually Gefreiter (PFC) Günter Sylvester, who, for whatever reason, seemed to specialize in performances requiring him to "dress in drag." As Joachim Metzner

Hermann Haugg's impression of a scene from *Krach um Jolanthe*, a comedy performed by the POWs. The illustration is from *P.o.W. Oase* #55, November 2, 1944 (courtesy of Joachim Metzner).

wrote, because of the absence of women among the POWs, "He was the man for woman[']s roles—I found his name around 10 times in the paper." And the above incident involving "guards with weapons" occurred when American MPs apparently mistook the actor for a real woman somehow smuggled into the camp, unaware that "she" was actually "Sylvester outside the entertainment room, maybe for a cigarette."[36]

Often dubbed "spectacles" and "comedies," the plays occurred in numerous places within the camp, chiefly the open-air stage in Compound 2, various recreation rooms, and company dining rooms. In April 1944, the play *Sommerregen*, a comedy by H. V. Schumacher, was mounted in the 10th Company dining room. The following month, the actors presented Johann Wolfgang von Goethe's comic *Bürgergeneral* on the main stage. Around this same time, the 9th Company dining room saw Hugo Weitz's *Unschuldig verheitratet*.

Vaudeville burlesques and music hall skits also became popular: there was *Tropenexpress* "for the whole camp" in November 1943; *Alles für Herz* in the 10th Company's dining room in January 1944; *Froh und Heiter* in the 9th Company's dining room in April 1944.

Heinz Fischer, one of the POW newspaper's assistant editors, wrote a preview of *Tropenexpress* in the November 15, 1943, issue, in which he proclaimed "for the first time the participation of all three battalions [compounds]." He called the program (translated as *Tropical Express*) a colorful evening of "two happy hours" and invited the POWs to "ride with us through the world of the sunny South" with "colorful, cheerful pictures of exotic countries." "All aboard!" he wrote. "Take a seat! The Tropical Express starts!" He credited Hermann Gülden of the 2nd Company, Otto Hiss of the 3rd Company, and Werner Rundshagen and Paul Weingarth of the 5th Company as being the production's leading lights.

For Christmas 1943, the 9th Company staged a musical program with solos, whether musical or narrative, by the following POWs (listed by last names only): Distner, Dombeck, Habenicht, (Paul) Metzner, and (Johann) Rohregger. Joachim Metzner wrote, "The ... program for the internal [company] festival ... of Kp9 [Company 9] survived. A few Xmas songs are listed, sung by the choir or sung all together." As he further explained:

> Singing was the first and easiest way of entertainment (because you don't need any instruments) ... and was very common. Soldiers ... used to sing while marching and ... Germans are traditional [famed as] singers ... there ... [might have been] a choir ... [for] every company.
>
> Singing for themselves, or, if they were really good, singing for other comrades ... [on] the stage of the entertainment barracks was a nice pastime for both, the singers and the listeners....
>
> Very soon [thereafter] instruments were available and smaller ensembles started to rehearse for performances on stage.
>
> Others started with stage plays and ... the American leadership of the camp was an active supporter for all these activities.[37]

Christian Höschle likewise recorded the therapeutic value of music: "We sang a lot and forgot that we were prisoners."[38]

The POWs also applied their talents to handicrafts. The camp hobby shop produced many wooden souvenirs and bric-a-brac sold either in the POW canteen or privately, or else given to others, especially American GIs with whom certain POWs formed an attachment.

"They made a lot of pieces in their hobby shop," Rita (Johnson) Wells said during one interview. "A lot of things fashioned from wood. And these pieces here," she added, pointing to a collection of molded German heraldic medals she owns. "I don't know where they got the lead from, unless maybe from the print shop. And these were not discovered until a shakedown of their personal things. Somebody told me they [POWs] took the keys off a piano and inlaid them in their wood craft items. They were creative."[39]

In the May 1, 1944, *P.o.W. Oase*, Albin Sagadin stated, "I prefer to work in oil, watercolor, and charcoal. The subjects of the paintings can be quite different: landscapes, fantasy, portraits, symbolism. It's hard to say which images are best. For an artist is always on a creative quest and must never be satisfied with his work." Spoken like an artist who just happened to be an imprisoned soldier, as opposed to a soldier who liked to dabble in painting.

9

P.o.W. Oase—The Camp Newspaper

"They're nice turns of phrase, nice paragraphs.
It's really beautiful stuff."

German-language newspapers or newsletters, sanctioned by the U.S. leadership and published with some American oversight by the POWs themselves, surfaced in camps throughout the country. As Arnold Krammer wrote in *Nazi Prisoners of War in America*:

Within a very short time, every camp in the country began publishing its own newspaper.... Written entirely by the prisoners and mimeographed on the camp machine, these papers were surprisingly sophisticated, carrying such things as poetry and short stories; crossword puzzles and word games; a weekly calendar of events; sports news; announcements of plays, concerts, and films; technical articles ranging from anatomy to photography; clever cartoons and comic strips; and, finally, a page of classified ads. They were remarkable efforts by the prisoners.[1]

McClellan was no exception. For nearly two years—mid–October 1943 to mid–July 1945—of the camp's 34-month existence as an active detainment center, the German POWs received the morale-boosting benefits of a newspaper published in their own language. Often called *Die Oase*, the paper was more accurately titled *P.o.W. Oase* to distinguish it from another newspaper of the same name formerly published in North Africa for the Wehrmacht. *Oase* simply meant "oasis"—a cool, refreshing watery break in a desert atmosphere or a welcome respite from anything unpleasant or odious.

Joachim Metzner, the editor's son, was adamant about the distinction:

Another important thing ... it is "PoW-OASE." There was already a paper named OASE while they were in Africa—I don't know, who made that. They took the name "PoW-OASE" as a little reference to that other paper, but wanted to underline, that now they are making their own POW-newspaper and McClellan was their Oasis.[2]

Translator Klaus W. Duncan commented:

In order to understand the foreign POWs at McClellan, one must read their writings and attempt to understand their thoughts.
    The Oase ... gave us an inside look at what life was like at McClellan's POW camp.
    As I read and translated the various issues, I felt that I was part of this period....
    The Oase and mail were always censored and translated into English. This made publication a slow and difficult process....
    At Aliceville there was always a sense of unrest and mistrust. While translating the Oase, I never saw this feeling of resentment at McClellan....
    The Oase newspapers were published weekly ... to provide the POWs with some sort of news from home in the form of literary essays, news, comic strips, puzzles, math problems, word problems and scientific essays.[3]

Of course, some U.S. supervision had to occur. As Joachim Metzner wrote, "The paper ... [had] to be given to a censor and must be translated ... 2 days before printing the original."[4]

P.o.W. Oase benefited from having a highly literate prisoner at its helm throughout its run. Obersoldat (PFC) Paul Metzner, born on Valentine's Day (February 14) in 1901 and a product of Stettin, Germany (the current Szczecin, Poland), was 42 when captured on May 13, 1943, in Tunisia. His incarceration disrupted a promising career.

Though educated as a teacher from 1918 to 1921, he stared unemployment in the face shortly after his education ended in the early years of the Weimar Republic. Jobs were scarce following the economic devastation wreaked on Germany in the aftermath of World War I. As his son pithily said in describing the economic landscape, "No job, because the government has no money in those years."

Paul took various jobs, including working in an insurance firm from 1922 to 1924, and then began a half-dozen years of working as an assistant editor and then managing editor for Stettin newspapers. In 1929, he relocated to Berlin to enroll in courses necessary to qualify for a career in education. In 1934, he achieved his goal of being a tenured teacher.[5]

He had been among the older candidates in 1942 when, against conventional military logic, he was drafted into Hitler's Wehrmacht. As Joachim explained, when Paul reached the customary age to enter the military "(around 20) there was no general conscription due to the regulations after World War I (peace treaty of Versailles). So ... he did not [join the military]. He was then called to the army in spring 1942, getting a quick military training and then moved here and there until being sent towards Afrika ... and that [his subsequent captivity] was the end of his [military] career."[6]

Transferred into American custody by his British captors at the close of June 1943, Paul was transported to Casablanca on July 21 and two days later began the journey that took him and about 1,850 other POWs to America. Arriving in New York on August 4, he was put on a train and, by a circuitous route that stopped in Cleveland and Sidney (Ohio), Marion (North Carolina), and Decatur and Birmingham (Alabama), arrived in Anniston on August 7.

His scholarly background and urbane mien made him a natural to edit the paper. In recent years, Phillip Tutor of *The Anniston Star* has written several stories and columns on POWs and Fort McClellan. In a full-page story published on May 3, 2009, he summarized Paul Metzner's life in a few brief sentences:

Paul Metzner, the erudite editor of *P.o.W. Oase* (courtesy of Joachim Metzner).

Paul Metzner ... was no ordinary German soldier. Paul was in his early 40s when he was conscripted ... after working as a sports journalist and mathematics teacher....

Paul Metzner was eventually transferred to a camp in Rhode Island [Fort Philip Kearny (often spelled "Kearney"), named after a Civil War Union general killed at Chantilly, Virginia, in 1862], where he worked at a re-education facility called "The Idea Factory" and helped edit Der Ruf, a national German-language POW newspaper designed to preach the value of western-style democracy to the prisoners.[7]

But first came McClellan.

Fortunately, the entire run of *P.o.W. Oase* still exists. Paul's son has every issue. Additionally, select issues reside in disparate collections in both Europe and America, including those belonging to several Alabamians (among them Joan McKinney and Klaus Duncan), as well as the author.

Joni L. Pontius—a lifelong German teacher and scholar who traveled throughout Europe, lived in Köln, West Germany, from 1972 to 1973, and returned to Germany for an extensive visit in 2011—translated much of *P.o.W. Oase*'s material for this book. Her translations follow.

The first issue was published on October 10, 1943. It was printed on 8½" by 11" cheap pulp paper. Issue 1 carried an illustration by artist Hubert Maiburg (using the acronymic "huma"), spread out over the top half of the first page, of a typical Saharan scene—a blazing sun over a rolling terrain with palm trees, cacti, and a stone well—with the words *P.o.W. Oase* artfully sprawling across the landscape. The bottom half, immediately beneath the place and date of publication (*Camp Newspaper of the Prisoner of War Camp Fort McClellan, Alabama, U.S.A.* and *10.October 1943*), greeted readers with the headline "In Preface":

> When you, my comrades, are holding this first newspaper of your camp in your hands, the name "PoW Oasis" could surprise you. And yet it has been chosen with forethought as the embodiment of your fate and mine.
>
> There in North Africa, in the area of the oasis, we sat together and read the battlefield newspaper "The Oasis," heard the voice of our comrades in it, read the experiences, the jokes, the poems, the articles, solved the puzzles, and it was like a small piece of home for us.
>
> And now we are united in the same camp, you and I and all whom fate has driven to the camp at Fort McClellan. Foreign are the tongues around us, and foreign is the life outside, and we stand in the foreign land like an oasis, which is set apart from the world around it.[8]

Regarding Paul Metzner's take on the origins of the paper:

> I'm stuck with serious but nice work: a camp newspaper, for which the adjutant has appointed me as editor, should surprise the comrades for the weekend. No example is available, so I can freely create without the influence of defined models or norms. Of course, it's worth it to travel the slippery slope of censorship from time to time (edition 1, in German and in English translation, was given to [American] Lt. [Vincent S.] La Rosa on October 4) but it works. Only the little word "Stacheldraht" ("barbed wire"), actually the typical embodiment of captivity, is crossed out.[9]

Translator Pontius offered additional information: "He was satisfied with the newspaper's first issue [given to the various barracks two days before the official date of publication].... And he said that every barracks was satisfied with that model by the 8th of October. It received approval from the camp spokesman, someone named Utz [Willi Utz, the camp interpreter], who held it out as satisfactory. The prisoners of war especially liked the math in the paper, the features that promoted higher math skills and things that stimulated thinking."[10]

Today of immense value to historians attempting to piece together vignettes of camp life, the issues achieved an intrinsic value even when published. Furthermore, Paul Metzner recognized the original and future worth of the newspapers' content in his Christmas 1944 summation of his literary child when he wrote of collecting sequential issues in separate bound volumes (comments and translations follow):

Metzner comments on the newspaper generally and its reason for being ... the sentence word order is rather peculiar in many spots, but I tried to strike a balance between the original as written and its intended meaning, as I understood it. The syntax is less than perfection in English....

"It is certainly not actually common to collect newspapers in a special edition from one's own library. Newspapers are usually only fleeting friends that quickly become worthless and are allowed to disappear when they have done their duty, entertained us for a few hours and perhaps given some excitement.

"The accompanying exception, however, which the first collected volume has found, gives us the justification and obligation to also publish the following collected editions 26–50 of our POW-OASIS as a definitive chronicle of a half year of POW life in Camp McClellan. It was spring when we wrote number 26, and week in and week out we have carried the camp newspaper into your barracks with the consciousness that it qualifies as a substantive part of your POW experience. Perhaps you were not in agreement with everything, found the sports reporting too long or too short, the articles not specific enough, the puzzle section too encompassing, the type not clear enough but a newspaper written in a POW camp may and must indicate the special nature of this circumstance under which it was born.

"We have gone to pains, and here I thank my co-workers Heinz Fischer and Helmut Klemm for their constant contributions, which must be their own reward, to improve the paper, and we were grateful for each contribution and the expanded publication image of the POW-OASIS. To the few comrades who contributed articles, pictures, Feuilletons ('leaves' in French; literary stories; a very literary term!) we give thanks; they have with their works helped to construct the creation of Collection II of the OASIS that we now place into the hands of all of our comrades as a small part of their own diary, which will in later days be read, when McClellan belongs to the past.

"Fort McClellan, Alabama, USA.
Christmas 1944

Metzner
Head writer."

In the margins of her translation, Joni Pontius added, "The papers have been bound together and are in the library. He says that the paper is there as part of their prisoner experience, like a diary, week in and week out."[11]

A serious journalist who transformed his editorial job into the labor of a historian, Paul Metzner accompanied several work details to get an accurate feel for the experience. As his son explained in an August 2012 email, "My father did some jobs just for one day by himself to make articles of the experiences—Working as a baker—Peanut harvest—Timber."[12]

Though Paul served as editor-in-chief, he received help from Heinz Fischer and Helmut Klemm, who became coeditors. Additionally, a number of other POWs contributed articles, submitted questions or amusing space fillers, and drew cartoons or, most important for later generations, scenes from everyday life in the camp.

In 2012, Joachim Metzner provided nutshell descriptions of the paper's luminaries:

P.M. [Paul Metzner] was the leading editor and his hobby was the puzzles and chess problems in the newspaper. Normally he did the articles with some emotive background (i.e., essays about work efforts inside and outside of the camp).

His 2 colleagues were Heinz Fischer and Helmut Klemm.

Specialties of Heinz Fischer were articles around entertainment (theatre, concerts, variety etc.) and sometimes he took an active part of entertainment events in the camp by himself.

Helmut Klemm in the first instance did the articles and pages around sports....

Hermann Gülden was titled ... leader of the department <leisure activities>. An interview followed [in #50], in which Hermann Gülden tells about the start and the development of concerts or public gramophone playing....

I think, there was a close relationship between H. Gülden and the OASE, because he coordinated culture events, which were announced by the paper or ... [which] had articles....

Hermann Haugg was the main ... [illustrator] for the paper!!! He did some of the bigger drawings as well as a lot of the little drawings between the articles.

Beside him the following ... were important contributors [illustrators] for the paper:

Uffz. [Unteroffizier or Sergeant H.] Geyer (no first name known)
Uffz. Christian Höschle
Hubert Maiburg...
Uffz. [Walter] Specht...
Fw (Feldwebel) [Staff Sergeant] Zehentner (no first name known).[13]

Joachim also identified master illustrator Haugg as being "from Munich and 33 years old (in 1944) ... [where] he worked as a lithographer."[14]

Most issues had a page labeled Die "Bunte Seite" (loosely translated as a page for miscellaneous items, often humorous or tongue-in-cheek, which modern audiences might call "The Lighter Side"). Those pages featured some of the finest caricatures and cartoons by talented people, including Oberfeldwebel (First Sergeant) Hermann Haugg of the 6th Company, who could have had careers in journalism if they had so chosen.

An informal historian who avidly chronicles his father's significant contributions to documenting prisoner life during World War II, Joachim Metzner has painstakingly gone through the 800 single-spaced pages of the collected issues of P.o.W. Oase seeking any and all information that would be helpful to researchers, collating, cross-referencing, and translating. He highlighted those who assisted his father in submitting stories, poetry, reflections, features, and illustrations:

I just extracted the amount of contributions (articles, drawings ... with name authors):

Paul Metzner 107
Helmut Klemm 56
Heinz Fischer 54
Hermann Haugg 29
Willi Utz [the camp spokesman, who may have submitted only official announcements] 22
Hubert Maiburg 17
Feldwebel [Staff or Tech Sergeant] Kranick 13 (Kranick contributed crossword puzzles often, but nothing else...)
Uffz [Unteroffizier or Sergeant] Geyer 8 (made some drawings/cartoons...)
Hermann Gülden 7...
Heinrich Baumann 7 (did some articles...)

Joachim also gave additional information:

Willi Utz ... [who went] to Aliceville in early 1945 and [was] replaced as Camp-spokesman....
Christian Höschle. Also a painter like Haugg and working for Oase from time to time....

Portraits of POWs instrumental in the success of *P.o.W. Oase*, all drawn by Hermann Haugg. Top: Paul Metzner and Hermann Gülden; bottom: Heinz Fischer and Helmut Klemm. From *P.o.W. Oase* #50, October 1, 1944 (courtesy of Joachim Metzner).

Albin Sagadin. Herbert Belau. The two making the murals in Remington hall…. I have some longer text about them displaying some of their work in an internal exhibition and Sagadin made one work esp. for OASE.

Other contributors included Gerd Beyer of the 10th Company; Wilhelm Böhmichen, who proffered an answer to a police-related issue; Unteroffizier (Sergeant) Franz Fischer of the 8th Company; Unteroffizier Rudolf Hattinger, who constructed a crossword puzzle for issue 16 and a biographical story for issue 22; Gefreiter (PFC) Fritz Hedwig of the 1st Company; and Heinz Richert, who submitted several sports items.[15]

Though the paper never published photographs, the illustrations of various compound buildings and surrounding scenery were authentic enough to fill in many gaps in the absence of a complete photographic record of the camp. Joachim recalled one illustration by Paul Weingarth of an 8th Company scene that showed a POW, the stenciled "PW" emblazoned on his apparel, walking in the foreground: "[It is] Funny to see a man with 'PW' on his clothes in this drawing and the sign[ature] for the drawing with PW (Paul Weingarth) below."[16]

Among *P.o.W. Oase*'s poetry was a piece credited to Hermann Gülden in the November 25, 1943, issue. It enthralled translator Joni Pontius, whose master's thesis and PhD dissertation topic focused on the Holocaust poet Paul Celan. She wrote:

> The more I worked with this poem, the more it impressed me.... I'm grateful to have been given the opportunity to read it and get to know it. I think that it's good enough to be included in an anthology of WWII poems.... I did look to see if the author, Hermann Gülden ... was published or a known poet. I didn't find any other writings of his....
>
> The poem is written in dactylic tetrameter, or trimeter, with an extra partial foot at the end:
> Es reitet der Tod seinen Rappen ins Feld
> '/"/"/"/
> die Erde sie dröhnt unter eisernen Hufen,
> '/"/"/'/

Robert Browning wrote "Just for a handful of silver he left us..." in the same meter. As for the rhyme, it does, well and without clichés. The pattern is consistent: abab, cdcd, efef, etc. At the end he flips it around for a strong finish. Whoever Hermann was, he had a real way with words and expressed some powerful ideas without lapsing too much into well-worn imagery, which would have been easy. Okay, death is a reaper on a horse, but still, he did okay. Here it is, rendered without trying to rhyme it, which would have completely compromised the images. It's not Dr. Seuss, after all.

"The following poem was written by a comrade for 'Totensonntag,' on 21.11.43." (Eternity Sunday, the last Sunday before Advent [similar to All Souls' Day in the Roman Catholic Church]. This was first observed by the Lutherans in 1816, and has become an established day in all German states for commemorating the dead, visiting graves, etc. It has legal restrictions as a "silent day," upon which music may not be played in public, or only during certain hours.)

> "There is a reaper, who is called Death.
> Death rides his black horse into the field,
> the earth rumbles under iron hooves,
> and trembling and fear fill the world,
> which greed and ambition and arrogance created.
> Filled with blustering and hissing, the air
> carries the murdering iron burden of Death,
> which full of murderous greed calls for the victim,
> from the scythe his heart's blood drips, so red,
> as ever it pulsed in the body of the youth.
> And the body of the earth rebels at the trotting of the steed,
> yet from the steel arc longs
> the wretched victim of the impact for the softness of the field.
> Corruption to reap,
> Death sows evil in the place of horror.
> The scythe whirs, and he mows powerfully
> into the rows of the bravest fighters.

> From the blade it drips in a bloody gleam.
> In the furrowed soil percolates the red,
> and in graves they bury the harvest.
> There is a reaper, who is called—Death."[17]

The newspaper carried a number of recurring features, including *Weisst du Es?* (Do You Know?). As Joni Pontius explained,

> Its intention was to provide information in a fun, engaging way. Some of the questions were when did Homer live, what does quarantine mean, what German province is the land of 1,000 lakes, what is the capacity of the human lung, how long did Schubert and Mozart live, when was the Panama Canal built? And then it would say that answers would be in the next issue. *Wer Hatte Recht? Who Was Right?*
> He [Paul Metzner] had another feature, basically called *Thinking and Computing*, that had math problems, puzzles to solve, even chess moves. And he would challenge the reader to come up with the correct answer or solution. And he'd publish the correct answers in the next issue. It was ingenious stuff designed to educate and entertain at the same time.[18]

Over its 75 issues, *P.o.W. Oase* included continuing features on the history, geography, and customs of the United States as well as pieces on the cultural, artistic, and literary achievements of Germany. Paul Metzner also excerpted portions of his diary dealing with the universal emotions of those in confinement.

A lifelong linguist who has taught German, French, and Yiddish in America (in addition to English as a second language in the Montessori Gymnasium in Köln), as well as an actress with performances in documentary films and C-SPAN, Joni Pontius currently provides freelance translations of primary documents and book editing services. She spent seven months poring over several hundred pages of German material, much of it from the pages of *P.o.W. Oase*, for this book. Regarding Paul Metzner, she had the following to say:

> He really writes very well. And he has a poetic turn of phrase. It reminds me of some of the poems of Bertolt Brecht, who wrote the same way. He's clearly very educated because he talks about craft things, people doing carvings, and oil paintings, and all sorts of artistic and poetic things. Just the way he puts things. They're nice turns of phrase, nice paragraphs. It's really beautiful stuff.
> There's this one part [a diary excerpt on arriving in America and being consigned to a POW camp]. He says it's August 5, 1943, and he and his comrades find themselves in a land of opportunity. But they're there as uninvited guests, a nice way of saying they're captives. And they know the beginning of their residence here in this country, but they don't know how long they'll be here, because they're deep in the bosom of time, a time that is not theirs to know. That's good poetic phrasing.
> And then he ends this part of his diary, at least the portion that was excerpted in the newspaper, by invoking the goddess of fate, imploring her that they be allowed to see the immense size and uniqueness of America and experience all the good things, the new things that it has to offer. Then we won't object to our fate, he says, and we'll be able to forget and forgive being behind barbed wire. That's his ending. That's just beautiful writing.[19]

Fellow translator Chania Stymacks was similarly impressed. Currently active in a German Club, including its choral society, she experienced some of the ravages of World War II as a young girl. "I was born in Silesia," she recounted in November 2011. "I had the life of a typical refugee. I moved to Breslau (today's Wroclaw, Poland), then to Czechoslovakia, then back to Breslau, then to a refugee camp, then to lower Saxonia. I came to America in 1966 with my husband. I speak German and English and a little Italian and French."

She translated a number of consecutive issues of *P.o.W. Oase*: "Every serial of the news-paper, or for serial you could substitute issue or number, has the same wording underneath *P.o.W. Oase: Lagerzeitung des Kriegsgefangenenlagers Fort McClellan, Alabama, U.S.A.*, that means *Camp News of POW Camp Fort McClellan, Alabama, U.S.A.*" She went on to say:

In serial 26, or you could say number 26, dated April 15, 1944, the first page, under the heading, there's a poem, *In Springtime*, by [German literary figure] Eduard Mörike. Then on the whole second page, there's a private first class in the 7th Company [Gefreiter H. Biggeleben] writing an essay on motorcycle humor. On the third page, there's something called *Der Fachmann spricht*. That means *The Expert Speaks*. And it's on kometen. That's comets. And it goes into the fourth page. The fifth page, the whole page, is by someone in the 9th Company. And it's called *Sports Memories*. The next page is all about sports in the camp, soccer, handball, some other things. Page seven has, we'd say, Feuilleton, that's the word for short stories, or maybe not-so-serious news, small items to entertain. There's something on that page by [German authors] Hans Riebau and Eugen Roth and a cartoon. Page eight has questions and answers: *Du Fragst—Wir Antworten* (*You Ask—We Answer*). There's a question on how to tan snakeskin and pelts. On page nine, he has things that appear in many issues, things like *Denken und Rechnen* (*Thinking and Calculating*), *Weisst Du Es?* (*Do You Know?*), and *Schace* (*Chess*). Page 10 has *Wer Hatte Recht?* It means *Who Was Right?*, and it gives answers to questions from another issue of the paper. It's supposed to give you something to think about, something to see if you know the answers to things it asked you in a past issue. On the bottom of the page you see the name of the editor, Paul Metzner from the 9th Company.

And you see these things, these types of stories and feature articles in most every issue. You see names of people who wrote some of the stories. Number 27, printed April 20, 1944, has something by Sergeant Unruh of the 9th Company and P. Häring of the 11th Company, a humor article by Hans Riebau, something by [Gefreiter or PFC] Blattmann of the 8th Company, and so on. You see this in all the issues.

And there are some unusual and interesting things. In this one [number 28, May 1, 1944], there's a drawing of an elephant, possibly by Hermann Haugg. He did a lot of drawing for the paper. And it wasn't done to show an elephant but to make a comparison. There are words by the elephant. And you must read into the words the hidden message. It means, "You need to develop a thick skin [like an elephant] to be a prisoner in a strange land. Immunity. You don't take everything to heart, seriously."

Some of the jokes and stories are not very funny. Not the way most people think of things funny. Maybe satire, more than funny. One of them [stories] makes fun of the German language because there aren't the suffixes. And it makes fun of high school teachers and other educators who think too much of themselves [pedants].

And there is another one here in number 30 [May 12, 1944] that has a cartoon … [of] some-body who is high-stepping on a ladder, *Der Hochstapler* ["Impostor"]. And it's really about somebody who pretends to be better than he really is.

And in number 31 [May 18, 1944], there's a drawing of a man inside a picture frame. And his head and upper body are tearing through the painting. And the caption is, "He is in the picture." In German, it means he knows what it's all about. The illustration is a word play, a play on words.

Here is another word play [switching to issue 32, undated but bearing the designation of Pfingsten (Whitsunday or Pentecost, late May) 1944]. There are two cartoons on page seven. In the top cartoon, Haugg shows his hair is being cut by his wife and child, and he's making fun of something entirely different. "I don't care for my wife, I don't care for my child," he says [an inverted visual play on words that actually means he is being "shorn" and divested of his wife and child].

The comic page was used to give stories about comical situations, funny things about people.

Number 29 [May 6, 1944] has a whole page on *Meteorological Musings on the Climate of Ala-bama*. It's facts about the weather in Alabama [written by Paul Metzner].

In number 30 [May 12, 1944] he [Helmut Klemm] writes, "This starts the second year of our being imprisoned here. What we are doing here is preparing us for what we will do after the war. The rest of the world sees us as idle. But we prepare for the largest reconstruction in the world. Our entire camp life is in service to this goal. All our schooling courses. Our education. How we use our free time, even in cultural pursuits and sports."

And in other pages of that number, there is a story about Rainer Maria Rilke, a very famous German poet. And a poem by someone who is not a well-known name [the German poet Wolf von Niebelschütz]. It's called *To My Mother*. It's a poem for Mother's Day. The main content is "You loved me when I wasn't yet born, and you loved me to the last breath." There's a long essay on American history, how the Germans see it. And they write about how they played their symphonies and operas of the famous European masters. And a lot about their sports programs.

Number 32 [Pentecost 1944], der Fachmann, the expert [Helmut Schönhoff], speaks about biology, zoology, botanic things.[20]

As stated previously, the newspaper printed 75 issues. The first 49 employed the *P.o.W. Oase* name superimposed over the Saharan desert background. But starting with the fiftieth issue and continuing until the final edition, the wording changed to *POW Oase* (no periods, all uppercase lettering in *POW*). For the sake of continuity, this book will use the initial title.

More striking, the new graphic featured a different cluster of palm trees, cacti, and the well at the far left of the masthead, a guard tower in dead center, a typical barracks at the right, and strands of barbed wire running from left to right across the entire length of the page. The sun pokes into view just right of the tower roof. The illustrator is unknown. As Joachim Metzner explained, "It is not 100% clear. Issue 50 says 'All drawings of this issue Hermann Haugg,' which could include the title drawing. Hubert Maiburg still was … [there] (last notice with issue 72)—But my idea is he would continue to have the 'huma' [for Hubert Maiburg] in his drawings if he did them—so probably Haugg made the title-drawing from issue 50 on." Commenting further on the masthead, Joachim wrote:

> When I first looked at the title-drawings I found that in the beginning they changed from issue to issue a little bit (as if it had to be … [redrawn] for each issue). Then they seemed to have something to "print" it from "a source" to the waxpaper again and again for each issue. Issue 50 (called Jubilee-issue) was something special and maybe they changed the drawing for that reason. Why it became permanent from then?—I don't know. Of course it was more realistic (Watchtower and barracks was the reality). From time to time the drawing was modified … for special reasons (see Xmas issue 1944 with watchtower, snow and xmas-tree).[21]

The location of the editorial office and the printing press is today hypothetical. As in all matters concerning *P.o.W. Oase*, Joachim Metzner is the best authority:

> Where was the newspaper made?
> The only answer I can give is from the mastheads of the newspaper:
> In the beginning I found:
> Barrack at the entry gate to the 2nd Batl. [Compound 2]
> Later: In the Barrack of the Batl. III [Compound 3]
> Or: In the Barrack of the headquarter Batl. III
> In one issue in an article about the tasks of the camp-spokesman I found, that the office of the newspaper was next to the room of the German spokesman.
> How many issues were printed?
> I found (this is at least true for 1945, when the paper was [in] short [supply], maybe they released more [issues] before:
> > 2 issues for each barrack; because I found … that around 20 men lived … [in] one barrack and 3000 men overall in the camp, I calculate around 300 issues. Some additional issues went out to the side-camps, so maybe we have 400 issues in total!!??[22]

The title page of *P.o.W. Oase* #50 (author's collection).

    In another email, he quoted the press run as enumerated in the November 29, 1944, issue: "[T]he count of issues to be given out: 25 issues for each company (2 for each barrack and 1 for the orderly room)."[23]

    Production of the newspaper involved typing the features on a manual typewriter, arranging the pieces along with the original artwork as they would appear on a given page, and then mimeographing them on standard-size 8½" by 11" paper similar to traditional newsprint. Paper was almost always in short supply, and *P.o.W. Oase* wisely utilized its available space. A hectograph was used and, as Joachim Metzner explained, "In issue 53 was an explanation [of] how the newspaper was made...." "Our camp newspaper is not 'printed,' but 'copied.' The necessary wax paper sheets bear no resemblance to the bookprinting related materials.... From such a matrice [matrix] of wax can be made about 10,000 average-quality 'prints.'"[24]

In 1945, the War Department embarked on a secret mission to democratize select prisoners, hoping they would later fashion a viable political republic from the ruins of a collapsed, devastated Germany. Paul Metzner was among those chosen to join an elite group of German literati, under the auspices of the Office of the Provost Marshal General's (OPMG) Special Projects Division at Fort Kearny, a very liberal camp in Rhode Island. He joined his intellectual peers in turning out issues of *Der Ruf* (*The Call* or *The Summons*), a new national newspaper, already in progress since March, to be distributed to German POWs awaiting repatriation, with the intention of inspiring them, through its well-rounded philosophical, cultural, and historical articles, to restore their ravaged country and transform it into a political and economic ally.

Just a couple of weeks before his departure, Paul Metzner prepared an essay on accepting the fall of the Third Reich and rebuilding a better country in what became the penultimate issue of the newspaper (published on July 1, 1945). He concluded the essay with these words: "If someone ... were to call 'Oase' a small 'Ruf,' I could never be angry with him. Because it is better to hear a call than to close one's ears and eyes and persevere in error."[25]

Metzner left McClellan at 9 a.m. on July 12, 1945, with the seventy-fifth issue of *P.o.W. Oase* due on July 15. Following brief stays at Forts Getty and Wetherill, both in Rhode Island, he arrived at Kearny on August 7 (two years to the day after first arriving in McClellan) and commenced work on his new task on August 13.

He signed his essay on the first page of that last issue of *P.o.W. Oase* with his full surname, rather than his oft-used "tz" or "Mtz" (according to his son, identifying his words as "something personal"). His last paragraph read:

> With this issue of the "Oase" we again reach a Jubilee: Number 75, and, simultaneously, my last issue. I started this work more than 22 months ago. I would like this camp newspaper to continue to be a part of the camp until the day, hopefully not so far away, when the last of our comrades will say farewell to McClellan.[26]

A simple sentence or two in that final issue indicated a desire for the paper to continue, even announcing at the bottom of the last page a projected date for continuance ("Folge 76: 23.7.1945," or "Number 76: July 23, 1945"). But it appears that Metzner's absence meant an end to McClellan's POW newspaper. As his son suggested, "Due to the information I got from [historian] Daniel Hutchinson, there were no further issues made after 75 and my impression of the last issues in June/July 1945 was, that my father already made these issues by himself without any help."[27] Joachim later amplified this information in another email:

> It looks like the paper should go on when my father left....
> But reading the last issues he seemed to make them on his own, no Fischer or Klemm signing anything!

On page 1 of that issue 75 he wrote: "I would like if the paper will continue to be part of the camplife.["] But he did not name someone responsible; and … a wish could mean, that up to then no one was found to do it.—I never heard about issues after #75.[28]

No one interviewed for this book had seen or heard of additional issues of the newspaper. Nor did Sergeant Jack Shay, who kept certain issues of *P.o.W. Oase* among his World War II memorabilia, have any beyond number 75.

So what was the impact of those 75 issues?

In his December 11, 1944, overview of camp life and conditions, observer Edouard Patte wrote of the consequences of a chronic paper shortage and passed judgment on *P.o.W. Oase*:

> The camp paper "Die Oase" which was printed every week needs more paper to be continued on a weekly basis. As no priority is available, it will be distributed only once a month, unless the Y.M.C.A. can provide the mimeograph paper. I am reluctant, however, to pass an order to our ware house, knowing that there is a shortage of paper in every American organization. I do not believe that the "Oase" is of such paramount importance for the camp morale to justify the expense as well as the contribution of a special contingent of paper.[29]

The paper met with apparent disapproval from some U.S. censors. In "The Oasis: German POWs at Fort McClellan," Daniel Hutchinson wrote:

> American censors monitored all POW newspapers like *Die Oase* for objectionable content, and several censor reports of *Die Oase* survive, although they are confusing and contradictory. The first dated April 1, 1945, described *Die Oase* as a "very dangerous paper" because of content interpreted by censors as influenced by National Socialism. The second report, issued only two weeks later on April 15, then described *Die Oase* as "nonpolitical."[30]

Nearly 30 years earlier, Staff Sergeant Dan Coberly had written:

> On April 1, 1945, military authorities described the paper as "poor" in makeup and content, "militantly Nazi" and "very dangerous." …
>
> Strict surveillance of *Die Oase* led to the segregation of Nazi and anti–Nazi prisoners. Incoming and outgoing mail was carefully screened for mention of the newspaper's articles….
>
> Meanwhile *Die Oase* editor Obersoldat Paul Metzner was carefully watched. A former High School teacher, he seemed to have "considerable influence among the prisoners."[31]

The April 1, 1945, report referenced above was titled "Report on Camp Newspapers in German Prisoner of War Camps." It identified the name of the camp, paper, editor, publication schedule ("Every two weeks"), types of features, physical size, and number of pages ("18 pp. issue"). It described the "Make-up: poor," "Contents: poor," and "Political Attitude: Militant Nazi." In its "Remarks and Recommendations," it offered the following:

> The camp newspaper "Oase" consists of average articles of average quality. (Sports, recreation, novels, cartoons). The articles of general contents touch PoW-care, the daily life of the prisoners and criticisms of performances within the camp. —A very active sporting life in the camp is revealed by abundant informations concerning sports. A page with mixed contents and cartoons as well as short novels and humorous articles. The section "Novels and Science" has scientific articles and answers to correspondents. The novels are taken from German authors, being well known in Germany, and approved by Nazi authorities.
>
> Very dangerous paper!

Another report from April 15, 1945, offered fewer words, calling the "Value: poor," the "Contents: poor," and the "Political Attitude: nonpolitical." Its "Remarks and Recommendations" pronounced, "The greater part of the 'Oase' is filled with reports accounting for sport activities, camp events and clerical work performed in that camp. Furthermore, There are stories and articles for entertainment."[32]

Neither report bears signatures. Additionally, their assessments of the quality and political orientation of the paper stand in direct contrast to those of current scholars and translators who find the newspaper's content apolitical and remarkably literate.

Camp spokesman Willi Utz wrote of a visit to McClellan by "Herr [Werner] Tobler," a representative of the Swiss Embassy, on November 23 and 24, 1943. In the December 2 issue, Utz remarked that the inspector gave the highest marks to McClellan out of the more than 10 POW camps he had seen thus far, "and he mentioned in his appreciative words, our *camp newspaper.*"

From all indications, the paper proved popular with the interned garrison residents. POW Erhard Eifler, as late as 1991, called it a "special thing ... where you could read the camp news, poems and sport events, sometimes also from abroad. I still have a collection of the news...."[33] Joachim Metzner corroborated that view, having discovered the newspaper's poignant legacy in 2007, 30 years after his father's death:

> He showed me the OASE-newspaper but we did not speak often about that time, as it was ... over for him, when I was born ... and when I might be starting to be able to understand more.
>
> So I have my knowledge mainly from the rediscovered newspaper, which I [have] studied intense[ly] since 2007....
>
> In my eyes it seems, that very soon [after the camp's opening] ... teachers developed the idea of leading their comrades to make the best out of the situation, developing an education program....
>
> And there were appeals in the newspaper to use the time to develop ... skills, which will be needed, once ... back in Germany.[34]

As for Paul Metzner's post–*P.o.W. Oase* years, he left America via ship for a relatively speedy release and repatriation to Germany when *Der Ruf* ceased publication in 1946.

Phillip Tutor of *The Anniston Star* established communication with Joachim Metzner 31 years after Paul's 1977 death.

> We talked about his father's wartime political leanings, and that he firmly believes his father was not pro–Nazi, which contradicts claims made in several aged research papers on Alabama's POW camps. He even sent along a copy of his father's repatriation papers.
>
> The document's date was March 10, 1946. "By (Metzner's) efforts," wrote Brig. Gen. B. M. Bryan, "he has contributed substantially to the success of (the German re-education program) without expectation of special treatment or rewards."[35]

The younger Metzner summarized his father's postwar career in a 2012 email, translating some of his father's own comments, and then adding his own (in italics):

> Coming home in 1946 I was homeless; my family had to abandon our house in East Berlin, because the Soviets occupied the whole part of the town; and so I got to my brother in the area of Uelzen [then West Germany].
>
> *He never went back to Berlin and the house was gone for him; there was only some money compensation in Germany for those, who had lost homes in the East.*
>
> At the 1st of February 1947 I became a substitute principal in Hanstedt.... From then I was at a school in Bevensen. With the 13th of July 1950 I got back the non-revocable status. ... *some time [had to elapse] until the past was clear [cleared by authorities] ... Nazi-activism in the past should not be accepted.*

At the 1st of January 1955 I began my job in Wolfsburg and in March I became vice-principal of school #IV there.

During both my positions I tried to raise the exchange of ideas.... I held lessons for the junior teachers and colleagues about different themes of mathematics, music, sports and historical lectures as "Might, right and despotism" and "German History from the view from Americans."

I acted as a conductor of choral societies in Bevensen and Uelzen.

In Wolfsburg I concentrated ... on my job as vice-principal....

In 1959 P. Metzner became the principal of a new school in Wolfsburg and worked there for the next 7 years, when he had to retire at the age of 65 (standard retiring age in Germany).

In those years he was also very active in local politics and because he was 2 times reelected, this involvement lasted into his early seventies.

Unfortunately he became ill then, had a few surgeries, but did not really recover....

He died at the 14. December 1977 in Wolfsburg.[36]

The "local politics" that Paul Metzner embraced was in his final city of residence, Wolfsburg, then a town of 75,000 residents, where he ran for a councilman's post "with nearly no chance" to win—yet he somehow won. As his son explained, "He was reelected 2 times and this is remarkable, because he changed ... party in between.... He said ... 'I only want to fulfill my duties without constraint and dogmatism.' ... I feel that he [wanted] to think for himself and not let the party decide, what to think about a special problem."[37]

Ironically, though Paul Metzner affected numerous lives and wore many hats throughout his lifetime, in America he is currently remembered more in legacy than he was appreciated in life.

He took his post as editor of *P.o.W. Oase* very seriously and fashioned himself a chronicler of a lifestyle not of his making, yet one he sought to record for whatever worth posterity might bestow. As he wrote on July 5, 1944:

At this time, which is for many of us the first anniversary of our time in the POW Camp of Fort McClellan, we republish the collected issues 1 through 25 of POW-OASE.

The content of those issues is already known to you but we were of the idea that a reprinted collection of those issues could become a good summary of our time here.

At the moment we are in the middle of our captivity, and we don't know how long it will last. But there will come a time when we shall gather our belongings to start our journey back over the ocean. And maybe you, comrade, will include this gray folder [containing the 25 issues] into your belongings just as if it were a part of your own diary, one that you can peruse at home, together with your loved ones, to reminisce about what had happened during your time here.

Maybe the layout is not all that it could be. But please remember that a POW camp has limited opportunities. But you can judge the content. And I hope you come to the conclusion that it is your newspaper. If you were one of our contributors, thank you for your help, and please continue, so that we can eventually say when we go home: we have done our best.[38]

He later bound, as a personal record, issues 26–50, which became available in January 1945.[39]

Collections of issues of *P.o.W. Oase*, important as morale boosters when they were first published, are of even greater value today as generational family keepsakes, and also for the firsthand information on camp life contained within their yellowed pages.

Joachim Metzner pronounced a fitting benediction for his father's legacy:

I just got an email from the son of [Erhard Peter Richard] Eifler [a McClellan POW who died on April 23, 2012, at age 89]. He found the full collection of newspapers [issues] 26 to 50. The paper was reissued for a collection of [issues] 1–25 and later for a collection 26 to 50 (my father took one of each home, you know) and they had many reservations [orders or requests] for that. Maybe these collections had to be bought for money (paper was short and the normal circulation was low for that reason) and this ... shows me the importance for the readers then and later as a memory.[40]

10

Negative Aspects

"A human life was extinguished."

Not everything in this model POW camp was harmonious.

A potential problem in many camps involved perceived or potential Nazi and anti–Nazi behavior.

When America's POW camps initially opened, the only separation among men involved their particular uniform (whether German, Italian, or Japanese) and rank (officers and non-officers). However, it quickly became apparent that hardline German proponents of Nazism, pacifistic soldiers who fought for Germany but not the Nazi ideology, and vocally anti–Nazi individuals would not mix well in captivity. Furthermore, different nationalities, languages, and cultures (German, Austrian, Czech, Slovak, Polish, Hungarian, and so forth) among prisoners who wore the same Wehrmacht uniform did not guarantee such uniformity when removed from combat. Theological and philosophical differences also became more noticeable when men were not fighting a common foe under battlefield gunfire.

In time, these issues were addressed, and prisoners received better scrutiny before being randomly placed in a camp. But at first, many camps saw ingrown problems stemming from this unfortunate dearth of preparation in identifying prisoner characteristics, and McClellan proved no exception.

A report from the camp headquarters bearing the signatures of Commanding Infantry Colonel Martin H. Meaney and First Lieutenant Charles E. Sturm (Field Artillery Adjutant) and dated September 7, 1943, nominated Oberfeldwebel (First Sergeant) Karl Johann Wilhelm Schaeffer (probably Schäffer)[1] for transfer to the POW camp in Alva, Oklahoma, because:

> Close observation of this man by his company commander reveals him to be a Nazi extremist and agitator. His agitation assumes the form of small irritating protests and uncooperative attitude toward the American personnel in his company. This man was selected as company leader and resigned, supposedly because of poor health. This claim of poor health has been disproven by physical examination. It is the opinion of the undersigned that this man's resignation was prompted by the belief that he could better spread his false gospel by being an ordinary member of the company. A majority of the noncommissioned officers in the same Compound with this man have refused to sign an agreement to work and, while it cannot be definitely proven by interrogation of other prisoners of war, it is believed that this man is the cause of this condition. Because of his leadership ability it is believed that this man is a disturbing element within the enclosure....
>
> It is believed that the transfer of this man from this Camp will have a favorable influence on the actions of the other prisoners of war.[2]

Eleven days later, the same commanding officer signed off on another requested transfer to the same Oklahoma camp, this time for Unteroffizier (Sergeant) Guenther (probably Günther) Guse:

> This man was included in a shipment of prisoners of war received at this Camp on 3 Sep 43, from Fort George Meade, Maryland, and was assigned to Prisoner of War Company No. 3. At the time of his arrival he appeared to be cooperative and willing to work and signed an agreement to work at suitable Class II labor when work was available. At that time every non-commissioned officer in this Company had signed the agreement to work. Recently PW Guse withdrew his agreement to work and has tried to influence other non-commissioned officers to do likewise by spreading rumors and complaints against working. He has been overheard to remark "for every month that you do not work in the United States, the German Government will pay you ten (10) dollars when you return to Germany." He has displayed definite Pro-Nazi tendencies and has been a disturbing element within the Compound.[3]

An October 5 request from the new camp commander, Infantry Lieutenant Colonel Laurence D. Smith, identified three more POWs for transfer—Oberwachtmeister (Tech Sergeant) Max Bauckholdt, Wachtmeister (Staff Sergeant) Erich Boensch (probably Bönsch), and Gefreiter (PFC) Andreas Driezen:

> The above named prisoners of war have been reported to this Headquarters as general trouble makers and a disturbing element within the enclosure. These men recently withdrew their agreement to work at Class II labor and have attempted to induce other prisoners of war to do likewise. One of these men was sent out on a work detail and had to be returned to the enclosure when he refused to work and attempted to fight with other prisoners of war who were trying to encourage him to work. By their actions, and because of their military rank, these men could have an important influence on the other prisoners....
>
> It is the belief of this Headquarters that the above named prisoners of war are the ringleaders of this subversive attitude....[4]

On October 25, Smith requested the transfer of two more "trouble-makers and agitators," Oberfunkmeister (approximately Tech Sergeant) Josef Lechner and Stabsfeldwebel (Master Sergeant) Roderich Semmler:

> These men are both high ranking non-commissioned officers and seem desirous of assuming leadership of the company, although it is apparent that all of the other noncommissioned officers of this company are fully satisfied with the present leader. These prisoners of war have misused their rank in demanding special favors from the privates, such as, breakfast in bed and other privileges, and have attempted to influence other members of the company not to work.[5]

Transfers sometimes occurred to protect POWs staunchly opposed to the Nazis, as illustrated in this October 18, 1943, request, signed by Sturm for the commanding officer, concerning the safety of Unteroffizier (Sergeant) Karl Stevens and Gefreiter (PFC) Heinz Milz:

> It has been brought to the attention of the Prisoner of War Camp Commander that the following named prisoners of war have displayed definite Anti-Nazi tendencies. These men are of Dutch descent. During the period of their detention at this Camp, these men have been well-behaved and cooperative in every sense and have caused no trouble of any type or description....
>
> The Prisoner of War Company Commander has reported that there have been rumors within the Company that these men would be beaten up because of their Anti-Nazi belief. These men are at present confined to the hospital as a measure of protection....
>
> It is believed it would be to the best interests of all concerned, and particularly as a matter of personal safety for the prisoners of war, if they were transferred to Camp McCain, Mississippi or to some other Anti-Nazi Camp.[6]

One of the most unusual requests for transfer concerned the case of Gefreiter William F. Kolkmann, a German native who left the Fatherland to try his economic fortunes in America, got married, and only returned to Germany for a brief time (or so he thought) to look after his ailing mother. He became ensnared in the deteriorating political situation there and found himself, against his will, drafted into the German army. Captured in North Africa in 1943, he wound up at Fort McClellan.

Kolkmann left behind a fascinating story of ill luck. Excerpts from his November 3, 1943, request for release and/or transfer follow (original syntax intact):

On January 29, 1905, I was born in a little town, Langwedel, near Bremen in Germany on a small farm, which had been in the possession of our familie for quite a number of generations.... Including myself, my parents raised six children of whom I am the only son.... One Sunday I visited my folks in Langwedel and had a long talk with my father. We were of the same opinion that in Germany it was impossible for a young man to get ahead, and then I told him about my plans of going to the U,S.A. [sic] to try my luck there. Then and there he told me that our farm would later on belong to me, my being his only son as it was customary in Germany. In April 1928 I came to the U.S.A. Quite difficult it was for me to find a job as I could not speak the language. Finally, through the help of some friends of our familie whose ancestors came from my home town ... I was supplied with a job in an ice cream store.... I ... then got myself a job ... as an accountant.... I resigned, as a better job had been offered to me with an investment house. Through hard work after having been in the U.S.A. about two years I became acclimatised, was doing well in business and never dreamed of going back to Germany again.... A few years after the Wall Street crash my firm also became affected and went into bankruptcy. Most of the money went with it. But I took it smiling and got myself a position with a New York Stock Exchange house as a customers' man.

On March 31, 1931 I got married. My wife and I understood each other and we were very happy together.... As my record at the New York Stock Exchange shows was I employed with various member firms of the New York Stock Exchange. In 1939 I passed my examination as a senior customers' man.

Due to the fact that my mothers health was in bad shape and on my fathers advise to come if I wanted to see her once more and at the same time settle the matter of property, I decided to make this trip to Germany.... I could not see the outbreak of another World War for at least a year.

On May 9th, 1939 I left the U.S.A.... After having been absent for over 11 years, it felt fine being home again and seeing the parents and the sisters. A shock I received though by the sight of my ill mother.... But after a few weeks she became much better again.... Everyone knew that her illness only come from worrying and longing for her only son.

When the war broke out it came as quite a surprise to me. I knew, of course, that the war between Germany and Poland could start at any time but I never expected England and France to take up arms at the same time.... But even then I felt that their could be an understanding between these countries again and I decided to wait with my departure untill the war over. My wife, in her letters gave me the same advice. Worried I was when the German employment organisation called upon me and advised me to take a job because every German had to work. I told them that my home and my wife were in the U.S.A. and that I intended to return there. I then was told, that as a German citizen I would have to find myself a job or I would be forced to take one.... Finally, I received notice for compulsory labor with the "Familienunterhalt" in Bremen, an organization which pays out money to the families of soldiers.... After trying again and again during the following years I finally managed to get a release from this job. Life was a torture to me. Letters from my wife came in sparsely and after Germanys declaration of war on the United States, stopped alltogether.... Now I was called upon for service in the army. On the 23 of July 1942 I had to appear. When news came out that the American forces landed in Africa my first impulse was to volunteer for service there, and this way get a step closer to

U.S.A.... I finally got to Tunisia on February 19, 1943.... The next day I had to report to a hospital to drive wounded over to the airport. How happy was I when after a few days work I heard the voice of an American soldier and how surprised he was, learning that my home was in New Jersey. Later on I quite often had the opportunity of meeting Americans and I always made sure that they received the best of care on their transport to Italie. How sorry was I when I received orders for another job, as I felt so much at home with the American boys. When things in Tunisia came to a head and I saw that here the war would be over any day I drove over to the northwestern part of Tunisia, where I knew the American forces were and on May 9th, 1943, exactly four years after having left the U.S.A., I became a prisoner of war....

I knew I would soon be home and see my wife again. Naturally I had a big job now on my hands. The army was not prepared for this mess of prisoners. There were no accommodations for us and in the beginning there was very little to eat. I was busy serving as interpreter day and night, I had to keep the prisoners quiet when there was no food and had to straighten out differences wherever they arose ... we were to be shipped to the U.S.A. ... the camp commander in person came to me and asked [me] to go along home to my wife. He told me I would be called for questioning in the U.S.A. and be released there.... By coming ashore in Staten Island the Leutenant in charge gave me a letter of commendation which I enclose.... Now I am in the P.O.W. Camp, Fort McClellan, Ala., 3d Battalion, leader of which is Lt. [Theron R.] Hearon, and have been waiting to be called for questioning....

My only thoughts and wishes are of my wife, who by cruel fate also had to suffer a lot. Please give me a chance to make life easier for her. Is there still a chance for us to become citizens of this free country or do we have to return to this gruesome Europe after the war?[7]

Smith approved Kolkmann's request and on January 5, 1944, forwarded it to the commanding general of the 4th Service Command in Atlanta, Georgia, writing:

Gefreiter Kolkmann ... petitioned for a release from confinement, presenting ... a complete story of his life, with references. This petition was denied by Headquarters ... Washington, D.C., 26 November....

Because of his business experience and ability as interpreter, Kolkmann was placed in the office of the Prisoner of War Exchange here, in a responsible position. His work there has been excellent....

At a conference this morning, with Camp and Compound Spokesmen, among other things, complaint was made by this group, against Kolkmann, and request made that he be removed from his position. The reason given was that he assumed too much authority and did not show proper deference to his superior noncommissioned officers. Following the meeting, at which Kolkmann was present, he asked to speak to me alone. He thereupon told me that the real reason for the request for his removal was the intense feeling, amounting to hatred, of all the other prisoners of war because he did not share their views and sentiments as Nazis and they knew this. Further, they are suspicious of him because he had lived in the United States for eleven years. He states that he is worried and very unhappy, and asked to be moved from this Camp to another....

I agree in full with Kolkmann and approve his request for transfer to Camp McCain, Miss., or such other Camp where his associates will be more congenial. He can be used to much better advantage somewhere else and will, of course, be happier.[8]

An international inspection of the camp in November 1944 uncovered details about a brief prisoner strike. A report dated November 24, pursuant to the visit three weeks earlier, offered the following information:

[T]he general morale and discipline in this camp is good, however there had been one instance where the main camp went on strike a while ago for about two days. There was an unwilling little group of non-commissioned officers who fomented the strike. The ringleaders of the group have since been transferred. While the strike was in progress, a search was conducted, and after the search the German POWS complained that several private articles, including watches and rings were missing. Upon investigation, the camp commander was able to locate some of these articles, and they were returned to the proper owners. However, the spokesman sent in a list of articles which still were claimed to be missing to the camp commander, and the investigation of this matter is not yet cleared up....

The representative of the Swiss Legation informed the camp commander that the only complaint that was brought up was concerning the missing articles taken during the search....[9]

Referencing a February 1945 visit to the camp by Captain Walter H. Rapp, Major Paul A. Neuland filed a memorandum on March 9:

Upon specific request by the camp commander, Captain Rapp interrogated six prisoners of war of Austrian descent who claimed to be anti–Nazi. As a result of this interrogation, Captain Rapp recommended ... that these six prisoners of war be immediately segregated from the rest of the prisoner of war population and that service command headquarters ... transfer these prisoners without delay to an anti–Nazi camp. Their personal safety seems to be in constant jeopardy because of the presence of three S. S. and Gestapo prisoners and it was recommended ... to immediately transfer these prisoners of war to Alva, Oklahoma.[10]

A little more than halfway through the camp's existence, about a hundred prisoners had been removed at various times from McClellan and sent to other internment centers due to "subversive activities." Camps at Aliceville, Alva, and Opelika, among others, had accepted them.

Journalist Bill Plott wrote of "two instances of trouble" in the camp, including the 1944 strike, in *The Anniston Star* edition of July 14, 1967:

One incident involved the death of a young German soldier who was killed attempting to escape from the camp. Details of the incident have been lost because no newspaper account of the attempt was ever printed. The young soldier and approximately two dozen other prisoners are buried in the German-Italian Memorial Cemetery at the fort. The others all died of natural causes. [Though believed accurate at the time, the information in this paragraph has since been discredited. See "The POW Cemetery" chapter.]

The second incident came in the fall of 1944 when Colonel Smith ruled that German non-commissioned officers could not use privates on KP duty. He directed the NCOs to do their own housework in the camp.

Leaders among the NCOs organized a strike and on a Saturday morning all of them refused to work. Smith put the prisoners on bread and water and by late Saturday afternoon the leaders were requesting a conference. Smith sent word that he would not be able to meet with them until Monday morning. The weekend diet of bread and water brought a quick end to the strike.[11]

Staff Sergeant Dan Coberly echoed some of the above information 13 years later in his "Stalag U.S.A." series in *The McClellan News*:

"Agreeable" prisoners refused to work when their request for certain concessions was denied. After two days of a bread and water diet, all quietly returned to their tasks....

A tornado reportedly destroyed several barracks, injuring two men. Another truck over-turned in Bain's Gap, killing one man. All the dead were buried in the camp cemetary [sic]. United States policy at the time did not allow for bodies to be sent home.[12]

He also quoted former camp GI guards regarding these incidents:

According to [Dewey] Welch, one prisoner died when a truck overturned at Bain's Gap. "The truck had a truck load of rocks and for some reason a POW sat up on top of the pile. Something happened and the truck overturned...."

Another former guard, William A. Burke added a few tidbits of information. "When I got back from the Pacific, I was assigned to the Military Police Escort Guards.... I ended up at Camp McClellan and mostly took prisoners to work in the fields, about 50 men at a time.... Some spoke better English than we did."

"I remember one time when we returned from a work detail a rumor that several men had been killed in a truck accident spread. But as far as I can tell, there were no successful escapes. No one was shot while I was there.["][13]

Rumors aside, only one POW died in a truck accident, as *The Anniston Star* reported on August 1, 1943:

WAR PRISONER DIES IN ACCIDENT AT FORT

Six Other Prisoners Hurt When Truck Overturns

Although he had fought a lost cause and was interned in a war prison camp at Fort McClellan, a youthful soldier of the Axis powers died in a tragedy that struck Friday afternoon at Fort McClellan. The war prisoner was accorded a military funeral Saturday afternoon, and buried on the reservation.

Authorities at Fort McClellan were prohibited by military regulations from making any comment whatsoever in the case and [the] only information available was confirmation of the war prisoner's death at a local funeral home from where the body was prepared for burial.

The accident happened Friday afternoon when a truck overturned. Aside from causing the death of the war prisoner, six of his buddies were said to have been injured also. Rumor was to the effect that none of the other war prisoners were critically injured, but that all were placed in the hospital for further treatment.

Prior to this there have been some other rumors about accidental deaths in the internment camp, but these were unfounded.

The man was Willi Waechter, one of the older POWs in the camp. Born on September 6, 1905, he was a little more than a month shy of his thirty-eighth birthday. He had married a woman named Martha, and he died of a fractured skull and brain hemorrhaging.

If the information on his death certificate is correct, the accident occurred on July 29, 1943, which was a Thursday, not a Friday, as *The Anniston Star* averred. The monthly roster of all POWs interned at McClellan also shows the date of death as July 29. Regardless, Waechter became the first soldier to be buried in the newly christened POW cemetery.[14]

P.o.W. Oase, which began publication in October 1943, later commented on his death:

And the strongest wish remains in everyone: to live to see it [peace] in good health. Indeed, the sanitary facilities in the camp are excellent, but how cruel the game of chance often holds sway. On the high mountain slope above the road, peeping out between the green of the trees, the plaque with the inscription P.W. Cemetery allows us to arrive at such thoughts: there rests a comrade forever from the horrors of war, which he happily survived: shortly after his arrival in Camp McClellan he met his death in a car accident.[15]

Though McClellan had occasional threats of violence or reprisal stemming from personal animosity or antagonism between Nazi and anti–Nazi prisoners, other prison camps experienced very real violence. "I've heard things about executions at some of the camps," said Steve Bakke, a military historian and collector. "Executions of prisoners by fellow prisoners, almost ritual executions. For political reasons. [Nazi] Party reasons. But I never heard anything credible about executions at McClellan."[16]

Margaret Newman, who grew up on the other side of Pelham Road, across from

McClellan, and returned to Anniston following a distinguished career as an educator, agreed with Bakke's assessment. In 2011, she wrote:

> A man here ... interviewed veterans of WWII. He published a book of these. In it one man said his wife worked at the POW Camp. She said that some of the prisoners killed other prisoners because they were ... friendly with the Americans. I told the author that this was a lie and should not have been published.... It looked like our G.I.s weren't doing their jobs. An insult to them and to the Germans who got along with each other. An insult to the ... population that had no contact with the prisoners.[17]

Rita (Johnson) Wells recalled a minor incident involving a prisoner who was caught with an unusual item during one of the camp's periodic inspections:

> I remember this one prisoner had a fox fur. It was a decorative piece wrapped around his waist. He somehow got through the shakedown with it. He didn't tell 'em [the shakedown inspectors] how he came to come by it. When he was caught, he got one week of bread and water [reduced rations]. The Geneva Convention specified that after one week, you had to feed them [disciplined prisoners]. Then you could put them in isolation for another week. He never told them how he got it. They speculated that he did work at the Officers' Club, and an [American] officer was there with someone who wasn't his wife and had to leave in a hurry. They speculated that maybe that was how the prisoner got the fox fur.[18]

Antonio Thompson addressed the issue of ration reduction in *Men in German Uniform*:

> [I]n accordance with Article 55 of the Geneva Convention, placing POWs on a bread-and-water diet. Military regulations stipulated that diet restrictions could not last more than fourteen days, that POWs must be given at least eighteen ounces of bread and unlimited water, and that the restrictions could be repeated after an interval of fourteen days, during which the POWs' diet returned to normal quantity and quality of food....[19]

Rita Wells also recounted a story about two POWs, detailed to Clanton, Alabama, for logging, who escaped to a nearby farmhouse while fleeing a severe storm and were apprehended by the owner, turned over to local authorities, and returned to McClellan for solitary confinement with reduced rations.[20] The full account is in her reminiscences (see Appendix C). In early August 2010, reporter David Jennings recounted her story with a slightly different chronology in *The Jacksonville News*.[21]

Escape attempts were minimal at McClellan, perhaps because of benign treatment, or perhaps due to a philosophy of waiting out the war's conclusion in relative comfort. In *Nazi Prisoners of War in America*, Arnold Krammer quoted a War Department figure of 2,222 Germans attempting escape throughout the entire course of their internment, a quite low figure amounting to little over half of 1 percent of the total German POWs in America.[22]

Private Clifford Prior, stationed at McClellan, wrote of a prisoner escape in a November 2, 1943, letter to his mother, but the incident seems to have happened with American GIs on the main post, not with German POWs in their camp. He wrote (original syntax intact), "The only news to-day is two garrison prisoners escaped and the camp was bristling with guns to-night it means nothing to us though. Because we are only intrested in Prisoners of War and that could hardly be called intrest more than likely a chance to shoot them would be more like it."[23]

Finally, suicides, stemming from a number of personal reasons, occurred in many of the major camps, not in epidemic proportions, but rather as isolated incidents. McClellan

POW Alfred Arens alluded to them in his 1991 reminiscence (original typescript intact): "In the last days of the war when informations came in that the Russians had invaded eastern Germany one or two PW'S committed suicide hanging one morning in the tree of the camp [a likely reference to Karl Krause; see below]. They are buried now on Fort McClellans' cemetery."[24]

Two McClellan POWs interred in the cemetery were suicides, or so their death certificates stated. The first was Joseph Kohl, a 34-year-old corporal in the 2nd Company, reportedly born on December 29, 1909, married to a woman named Maria, and the father of three children. He died January 25, 1944, according to his death certificate, of "Psychosis, type undetermined," and "Probable barbiturate poisoning, suicide." Though his official "Clinical History" report contains numerous contradictions (including listing his age variously as 35 and 42 and utilizing incorrect dates), it stated that he had been in Bainbridge, Georgia, before being admitted to McClellan's station hospital the day after his birthday, complaining of pain in his head and back and confusion regarding his surroundings for the previous two days. He expressed anxiety over not hearing from his family "for months." During the last month of his life, while under observation in the hospital, he was diagnosed as potentially suicidal because of an earlier incident while at Bainbridge. His report termed him "quiet, reserved and moderately depressed," as well as a person who "did not fraternize with fellow patients and spent most of his time reading," bore a "demeanor [that] was psychotic at all times," and was "aware of his surroundings but took no interest in the activity about him."

The "Autopsy Protocol," morbidly clinical (as such dissections must of necessity be) showed the stomach containing "200 cc of fairly thick, yellowish, partially digested food in which unchewed hunks of apple are found." The final note on the report, signed by William E. White, a major in the medical corps and chief of laboratory service, included statements that "portions of brain, kidney, stomach and liver" were sent out "for toxicologic examination," and "A preliminary report indicates large quantities of a barbiturate were present." Kohl's was a sad, tragic case with no clear understanding of what happened.[25]

He was eulogized in the February 3, 1944, *P.o.W. Oase*, albeit with a different date of birth:

A Comrade Left Us

Soldiers are used to looking death in the eye, he who strides with them over battlefields and relentlessly celebrates the harvest. And yet when he calls one from the ranks, strikes him out of the book of the living with a ruthlessly cold hand, those who have become comrades through daily battle stand still for a moment, and wincing inside.... I had a comrade....

And now we carried a comrade to his grave, Gefreiter Josef Kohl, who died January 25, 1944, in Camp McClellan hospital. He was born on September 29, 1909, in Sudetenland, lived and worked there as a farmer, until his Fatherland called him to its colors and commanded him to exchange his plow for a sword. In May of 1943 a bitter fate stole his weapon the same as us, led him as a prisoner of war to the foreign American land, whose earth has now taken him in forever, him and his sorrows and hopes. A human life was extinguished.[26]

Karl Krause, born May 4, 1896, had just turned 49 (very old for a POW) a month before he took his life on June 8, 1945, by means of "Strangulation (self inflicted)," according to his death certificate. His wife was named Anna, and none of his official records listed any theorized reasons for why he killed himself. According to a story in *P.o.W. Oase*, he was in the 8th Company and had been interned since the previous fall. He was buried on June 11.[27]

In his autobiography, Christian Höschle wrote about depression seeping into the camp as POWs became increasingly aware of Germany's inevitable defeat. "He had two brothers in the war, one 17½ and another in Russia," translator Joni Pontius said of Höschle. "And he was lamenting losing those two brothers to the war. 'Sorrow and tears and no end in sight,' he wrote. 'To be a prisoner is a tough situation, and it requires a strong character. Many fall into a monotony that falls into depression and deep melancholy.' He said that to be a prisoner is a far-reaching psychological problem."[28] Joachim Metzner said that Höschle also mentioned "2 older comrades" who committed suicide "shortly after the war," a probable reference to Krause.[29] The other suicide, if it happened at McClellan, is unaccounted for.

The camp experienced another, less violent death on February 7, 1944, when Private Fritz Clemens, a cook in the 10th Company, succumbed to a heart seizure two weeks past his thirty-fifth birthday.[30] And funerals of Axis prisoners who had died in other camps, while not commonplace, occurred with enough regularity at McClellan to occasionally cloak the camp with an aura of sobriety.

Though not of the magnitude of a suicide or accidental death of a comrade, the constant shuffling and reshuffling of POWs to and from McClellan, either on work details or due to transfers to other camps, likewise disrupted the normal flow of avocational activity. As Joachim Metzner explained, "After a few months ... more and more groups of musicians [began] doing programs.... The problem for many of them: the working duties did not allow continuous development. Suddenly important group members left McClellan for months to go to side-camps and sometimes they never came back to the main camp again."[31] It became a constant impediment to harmony and continuity.

11

The American Military Camp

*"They asked would I like to work
at the prisoner of war camp."*

Over its three years of existence, several hundred GIs, on either permanent or temporary assignment, helped secure the Fort McClellan POW camp, but not all at the same time. As Antonio Thompson explained in *Men in German Uniform*:

One American officer commanded each [POW] company with assistance from three sergeants: one duty, one mess, and one supply. Additionally, a corporal acting as clerk, a private, and one cook were attached to each group.... The United States provided one military police escort company for each compound.... The service commands usually provided twenty-two officers and seventy-three enlisted men for a 3,000-man compound, but actual numbers of guards and support personnel varied considerably....[1]

McClellan had three successive full-time commanders, separate from the overall commander of the fort, yet reporting to him. According to army sources, the first was Colonel Martin H. Meaney of the 27th Infantry Division, in place from May 1 to September 30, 1943. Lieutenant Colonel Laurence D. Smith succeeded him on October 1 and served the longest, until June 1945, when the war in Europe had ended. Major Samuel W. Kendall became the camp's final overseer, relinquishing his post on April 10, 1946, when the camp shut down. However, some documents suggest a delay in the camp's transfer to the last commander: a July 16, 1945, report still listed Smith as commander, and in a September 16, 1945, report, Edouard Patte referred to "the new Commanding Officer as Major (presumably the former Captain Edward B.) Larkin."[2]

The army maintained its own compound, complete with headquarters, barracks, mess facilities, warehouses, motor pool, PX, and other ancillary buildings for the hundreds of American GIs who operated the POW camp.

A newspaper clipping in the McClellan files in Anniston's public library summarized Colonel Meaney's background. Bearing the byline of Mary Diskin Brown, it exists in two fragments, with a handwritten date appearing to be "4–22–43":

One of the most colorful and interesting personalities at Fort McClellan at the present time is Col. Martin H. Meaney, commander of the Prison Internment Camp, on the Reservation at Fort McClellan....

While at Fort McClellan with the 27th Division in 1940 and 1941, Col. Meaney was executive officer of the 165th Infantry, formerly the Fighting 69th. When the Division left for duty overseas, Col. Meaney saw service in Hawaii and served as commander of the 108th Infantry, one of the largest units of the Division. Possessed of a more than pleasing personality and gifted with true Irish wit and enthusiasm, Col. Meaney first saw the light of day in County Clare, Ireland.

Coming to America in 1908[,] young Meaney's first position was that of a salesman in one of the city's largest department stores. Always keenly interested in men, he soon became associated with the Police Commission of New York City, serving at the time of his induction to the 27th Division as 5th Deputy Police Commissioner....

If Col. Meaney has a hobby outside his army life, it is his wife, the former Anna Elizabeth Stewart of Brooklyn, N.Y., and his six lovely children....

Under Col. Meaney's personal supervision, work is nearing completion on the Prisoner of War Internment Camp and the camp itself is expected to be ready for occupancy by prisoners of war in the near future.[3]

The disparity in the dates of Meaney's assignment (May 1 or earlier) probably stemmed from the camp's official opening in May (though prisoners did not arrive until July) while it was still under construction.

Like the commanders, not all American officers and enlisted men remained in place for the camp's three years of operation. Personnel changed through the years as soldiers requested transfers or accepted reassignments. A December 14, 1943, roster provided the following list of commissioned officers and their commands:

Lieutenant Colonel Laurence D. Smith, commander.

Captain Ira C. Ballard, executive officer.
Captain Edward B. Larkin, 1437th Service Command Unit and supply officer.
Captain William D. Oxford, POW Compound 2 and Company 5 officer.
Captain Charles E. Sturm, adjutant.
Captain Woodrow W. Wallace, plans and training officer.

1st Lieutenant Zimri M. Addy, POW Compound 1 and Company 1 officer.
1st Lieutenant Theron R. Hearon, POW Compound 3 and Company 9 officer.
1st Lieutenant Frank H. Hooper, Jr., POW Companies 10 and 12 officer.
1st Lieutenant Jacob Scholom, intelligence and postal officer.
1st Lieutenant Malcolm R. Swart, personnel officer.
1st Lieutenant Carl T. Whitehead, POW Companies 6 and 7 officer.

2nd Lieutenant Robert S. Holt, POW Company 11 officer.
2nd Lieutenant Gilbert Hunter, POW Company 8 officer.
2nd Lieutenant Frederick F. Jeffrey, POW Companies 3 and 4 officer.
2nd Lieutenant Vincent S. LaRosa, exchange and special services officer.
2nd Lieutenant George S. Middleton, POW Company 2 officer.
2nd Lieutenant Abraham Rabinowitz, assistant supply officer.

Attached Officers
1st Lieutenant Opie S. Rindahl, Protestant chaplain.
1st Lieutenant Jack Savran, medical officer.
1st Lieutenant Arnold W. Schmidt, Catholic chaplain.[4]

Among the other officers known to have worked in the American military camp, as it was referred to in documents, were Captain Frank R. Duffy (works project director), and Captain W. R. Jenkins (executive officer). *P.o.W. Oase* also identified several other officers: Lieutenant Koher, supply and transport; Lieutenant Warren, personal (probably personnel); and presumably the same Edward B. Larkin, promoted to major, as executive officer.

P.o.W. Oase occasionally included passing references to the American officers. Joachim Metzner commented on some of the more prominent names:

...Lt. (Zimri M.) Addy. According to the newspaper he had the idea for the project "PW-Farm." That farm, around 2 km (~1¼ mile) north of the camp was owned by an American (who was away in the army) and some areas of the farm were already unused for a longer time. So the camp rented ... parts of the farm and let the PoWs ... run it on their own....

[First Lieutenant Theron R.] Hearon and Col[. Laurence D.] Smith had a lot to do with the greenhouse of the camp.

Lt. [Carl T.] Whitehead was involved in the plan with [the] "Schwarzwaldstübele."

I found a man named [First Lieutenant Opie S.] Rindahl as someone from the US–Staff, who was originally ... Norwegian and was working as a chaplain in the camp....

Lt[. Vincent S.] La Rosa [*sic*] received an English translation of the newspaper in Fall 1943, maybe for censorship.[5]

He also singled out Captain Woodrow W. Wallace, who merited "nothing in the newspaper, but P. [Paul] Metzner was impressed in his diary, because Wallace played table-tennis with the PoWs (incl. him)."[6]

The commanding officers—Meaney, Smith, possibly Larkin in an interim capacity, and Kendall—all worked in the POW headquarters building. Attached signs proclaimed it the "PRISONER of WAR CAMP HEADQUARTERS." It commanded a small ridge just northwest of the westernmost edge of the POW camp on the northern side of Baker Road. A side road for authorized vehicles separated it from both the wire fence enclosing the camp and the main guard tower in the western corner.

The main building in the American military camp, the headquarters was a one-story rectangle that held the administrative offices of the camp commander, the camp executive

Some of the civilian staff in front of their entrance to the camp's headquarters building. Marie Shay is in the front row, second from left, while Rita Johnson is at the far right of the same row. Bertie McBrayer is in the middle of the back row (author's collection).

officer, various other officers and noncommissioned officers, civilian workers, and often one or two POWs authorized to work in clerical capacities. Two wooden staircases with attached railings climbed the bank from Baker Road and led to the front entrances, facing the road. Enlisted personnel and civilian workers used the entrance on the left (or west) side, while the camp commander, who parked his vehicle nearby, utilized the stairs on the eastern end, which led more directly to his office.

Rita (Johnson) Wells was a personable young, single woman from neighboring Pelham Road when she began civilian employment in September 1944. More than six decades later, she recounted her memories of the activities and work relationships in the American sector just beyond the barbed wire of the camp:

> I actually got to see the POWs even before I worked in the prisoner of war camp. The prisoners were out working along Pelham Road right by our house. Marvin's [a store] is now there. And I remember taking them a pitcher of water. The guard had them doing some bushy work outside, and it was hot. I took them a pitcher of water with some cups, and I asked the guard if I could give them some water. And he said, "Oh, yes, ma'am, and I'd like one."
>
> I lived very close to the camp. I walked to work.
>
> I filled out Form 57, the standard form for employment. And then I had to go to the main post, the civilian personnel office. I passed the test. And they had a couple clerk-typist jobs open, and they asked would I like to work at the prisoner of war camp. I worked there from the fall of 1944 to April 1946, when the camp closed.
>
> We were issued these red cards with your height and weight and vital statistics and your picture. It was your ID badge.
>
> I was a clerk-typist in the administration section. I worked on weekdays. Our shifts were something like 7:30 a.m. to 4:15 p.m. or from 8 a.m. to 4:45 p.m. Maybe some people had 8 to 5. We ate at 12 every day, Monday through Friday.
>
> There were five typists in my section, all women. Several men were working there, too. Many of them were the post men. We typed the payrolls for the prisoners of war and computed their time sheets. They got either $3 for the month if they declined to work or $24 for the whole month if they worked 40 hours a week, plus the same $3 allowance that everyone got. It depended on how much they worked, according to the Geneva Convention. From time to time, they [U.S. military personnel] would send us down information on various prisoners, whatever instructions they had or if they [POWs] did something extremely nice.
>
> I remember Mr. Strickland was a warehouseman. He issued supplies in one of the warehouses, and they were just across the road from headquarters. He would make coffee, and one of our employees would go and pick it up. They would make a file tray and pick the coffee up in paper cups.
>
> There was no time clock to punch, no buzzer, no clock watchers. You just worked.
>
> On our performance ratings, only one person could be designated outstanding. I was the youngest one there, I had been there the least amount of time, and I got the outstanding [rating]. And there was a little bit of animosity toward me. I had high school and a little bit of business college. And I put my nose to the grind.
>
> Staff Sergeant Harry Klein was my immediate supervisor. Harry Klein was from the Bronx. Periodically he got a box of goodies from home. He called me "Rita Pepita from Tahatee," and he pronounced it "Tah-hate-ee."[7]

The post's official newspaper, *The McClellan CYCLE*, made reference to Harry Klein's appreciation of the gentler sex when newly hired civilians arrived at the camp's headquarters building. In the March 24, 1944, edition, correspondent Sergeant John J. George wrote tongue-in-cheek, "[Then-]Cpl. Harry Klein has taken greater interest in his work at headquarters in the past week or so since the personnel increased in his department."[8] The

A late 1945 staged photograph of a portion of the headquarters' interior from "COMPLIMENTS OF HEADQUARTERS." Left to right: Delemba Nolan, Major Samuel Kendall (standing), Bertie McBrayer, Staff Sergeant Harry Klein (standing), unidentified, probably Cynthia Tompkins, Sergeant Albert "Bud" Jones, unidentified (standing), Rita Johnson, and Captain Sherbert B. Jones. One of the unidentified men is Captain Jacob Scholom. Identifications by the author and Rita (Johnson) Wells (author's collection).

teenaged Rita Johnson had not yet begun employment there when this article was written. But when she did, she quickly became one of the prettiest and most efficient of the young women, a situation not lost on Harry Klein.

"First Lieutenant Florence E. Brownell was the administrative officer," Wells continued.

I remember when these PWs were shipped out, she had to sign her name in three places on the forms. And one time, she asked me to sign her name to help her out. She said, "You can sign my name. You write like me." I stayed until 10:30 at night, doing all the paperwork. When I went home, I didn't know if I was Rita Johnson or Florence Brownell!

Major Kendall was the last commander of the camp. He was there in the months before the camp was being closed down. Cynthia Tompkins was his secretary. She was unmarried. She didn't say she was an old maid. She said, "I'm not an old maid. I'm an unclaimed treasure."

Major Kendall would say the usual greetings but never got into a deep discussion. He was very available. He did most of his work in his office. He welcomed people very cordially. Most of the time, he would go to the main post for meetings. He had total authority over the camp, but he did report to the post commander. I remember after his discharge he marketed Vital-ife.

I don't remember all the people who worked in headquarters because so much time has gone by. But I remember Delemba Nolan and Bertie McBrayer. Bertie was very congenial. Captain Jacob Scholom was the security and intelligence officer. I recall Captain Sherbert Jones. Sergeant Jack Furman worked with us, and I think he was also involved with the PW canteen.

I remember your [the author's] mother [Marie Shay] very well from my time in the head-quarters building. She was a vivacious little lady. Your mother started at the PX. Then she transferred to headquarters. That's when I got to work with her and know her. Then she went to personnel on the post—Fort McClellan. She was a real sweet girl. Lady. We chatted. She was very nice.

Marie Shay returned the compliment—albeit in a reminiscence directed to her son: "Rita Johnson was a very attractive young girl. I was in my late 20s at the time, and she was probably a good 10 years younger. I don't know but what she was the youngest one there. She was from Anniston and a very pretty girl. Some of the fellows, the GIs and the officers, who worked in headquarters kind of took a shine to her, and they would fuss over her. But she was efficient, too. A good worker."[9]

The largest portion of the U.S. compound, a rectangular tract unencumbered by perimeter fencing (unlike the POW camp), contained all the other buildings. It lay across Baker Road to the south, parallel to the POW camp but separated by the road. It extended as far east as a point opposite the middle road through the POW camp, wedged in by Baker Road to the north and Pelham Road to the west. The compound included more than 40 buildings ranging from utility garages half the size of a typical barracks to a couple of ware-houses, one of which was larger than 10 barracks put together.

Rita Wells identified the warehouse area and its environs in an August 27, 2008, letter: "The roads didn't have names at that time and I believe there was only one road between every 2 rows of warehouses, giving each building, a frontage to pavement."[10] (The unmarked, unpaved roads she referred to were only a part of the network traversing the entire expanse of the American camp and intersecting at perpendicular angles.)

The warehouses and repair shops occupied ground closest to Pelham Road. To the southeast, some two dozen barracks, housing the 400 men of the three military police escort guard companies, stood in symmetrical rows. Below them, to the southwest, were

Marie and Sergeant Jack Shay in a jeep in the motor pool. The front bumper clearly identifies the vehicle as belonging to the Fort McClellan Prisoner of War Camp (author's collection).

the motor pool, repair shops, and several auxiliary buildings. "The motor pool was on the very end with ample space for vehicles," Rita Wells remembered.

The ground gradually rose southeast of the barracks, but not as steeply as the hill holding the POW camp. Surviving photographs show terraces, each higher than the preceding one, with wooden staircases climbing the banks. A chapel, a PX, and a mess hall filled part of this ground. The structures were built of the same material as those in the POW camp and, in most instances, looked identical.

A wide drainage ditch, parallel to Baker Road, bordered the camp's edge. Wooden footbridges allowed pedestrian traffic to cross the ditch at regular intervals. The main footbridge connected the camp with Baker Road a little southeast of the main guard tower, with the headquarters building in clear view to the northwest.

Additionally, unpaved roadways from the camp intersected Baker Road at numerous junctures, permitting military trucks, jeeps, and vehicles, as well as authorized civilian cars, to come and go. The motor pool was easily accessible by an entrance road spanning an area where the open ditch became a culvert.

Annistonian Eugene Steppe, who served in the American military camp, constructed a crude map of both sides of Baker Road in 2008 and attempted to identify the approximate locations of buildings forever gone:

One of several footbridges spanning the ditch. In the background are the headquarters building, the underpinnings of the main guard tower, and the stakes holding the barbed-wire fence of the POW camp. The women, all civilian employees of the nearby PX, are, left to right, Ruth Allen, Essie Woodward, and Marie Shay (author's collection).

These barracks were for the MPs in the 382nd Company [pointing with his finger to an area close to Baker Road]. And a little bit over here [southwest] you had the barracks for the 383rd Company.

Then farther up here [east], you had a dayroom and a guardhouse.

Then there was a rise beyond that [to the south], and the land went uphill. Up that hill you had the officers' quarters and their mess hall. Not as far up the hill as the cemetery and on the other side of the road.

It's all gone now. Nothing's left but the cemetery. There are new houses there that have been built after the war. No military connection anymore.

I could have told you a lot years ago, but you forget with time. It's too bad they didn't keep something there.[11]

Side note: When Steppe spoke of the "officers' quarters and their mess hall," he referred to a much steeper rise off Baker Road (which is today southwest of the intersection of Shipley and Foxley Roads).

Hundreds of GIs—some deemed unfit for combat for various reasons (usually health-related), others stationed there after their combat experience or while awaiting reassignment domestically or overseas—spent time at the camp. Some of these included the following enlisted men entering SCU 1437: Robert R. Aguilar, Leland A. Holcomb, Herbert Levin, Louis V. Maranhao, Carl E. McCormick, Ruby Nazitsky, Sidney Silvers, James F. Stuart Jr., and Morice E. Witt.[12] An April 30, 1945, army communication, announcing promotions in the "Headquarters Detachment, Service Command Unit 1463, PW Camp," included Alfred S. Nelson, Gerald N. Oak, John E. Shaller, George F. Shepherd, and Harry L. Young.[13] They were just some of the hundreds, now largely unknown.

In his December 1943 report of the POW camp, Captain Edward Shannahan wrote:

Prisoner of War Camp, Fort McClellan has an authorized overhead enlisted strength of seventy-three [U.S.] men. The actual strength was seventy-one on the date of this visit....

Classes have been held by the officers for all of the personnel. The Camp Commander feels ... that the officers are versed fairly well in the terms of the [Geneva] Convention [on the humane treatment of all prisoners of war]. However, the enlisted men, as is usually the case, do not absorb the lectures very well. The Camp Commander intends to continue the lectures on the Convention and the prisoner of war circulars whenever possible....

There are three Military Police Escort Guard Companies stationed at this post, the 382nd, 383rd and 433rd Military Police Escort Guard Companies. Their strengths are as follows:

	Officers	Enlisted Men
382nd MPEG Company	3	130
383rd MPEG Company	3	126
433rd MPEG Company	3	128

...The Camp Commander stated the efficiency of the companies is excellent. The men are given a slight amount of training.... One hundred and five men are on detached service at the present time, and the balance of the men are kept busy with guard duty and prisoner chasing which makes it almost impossible for any large program of training....

Lieutenant Colonel Smith, the Camp Commander, had the following recommendations to make....

That the Rifle, Cal. 30 M1, and Rifle, Cal. 30, be withdrawn from the ... Escort Guard Companies and lighter, shorter-range weapons be issued in lieu thereof. He states this would increase the efficiency of the men and give them a better chance in the event of an attempted escape.[14]

Among those stationed in the headquarters building was Lieutenant Jacob Scholom, the camp intelligence officer. When Captain Walter H. Rapp inspected the camp on February 26–27, 1945, he included a special section revealing perceived weaknesses in gathering intelligence from within the POW camp. As Major Paul A. Neuland summarized in his field service report the following March 9:

> A talk with the Intelligence Officer, Lieutenant Scholom, revealed that he did not have an organized intelligence system, which would enable him to get information from within the prisoner of war compound. Furthermore, the Intelligence Section had no 201 intelligence files on any prisoner of war, besides the routine personnel records. It was felt that the intelligence officer was not entirely on the job and that he was extremely over burdened with other duties, such as, Trial Judge Advocate of the post, President of the Post Exchange, Council and other similar duties. Captain Rapp explained both to the camp commander and to the intelligence officer, the importance of a well kept intelligence doss[i]er on all prisoners of war and the importance of having a good functioning intelligence system from within the compound.[15]

In interviews from 2008 and 2009, Rita Wells recalled the "overburdened" Lieutenant Scholom, as well as various facets of the headquarters building and the American camp across Baker Road. "The supply room was right here," she said, identifying the extreme western side of the rectangular headquarters building on a map she had drawn. "And next was where Lieutenant Scholom had his office. Then it was all open space. And here," she added, pointing to the eastern side of the building, "was where the commanding officer had his office."

Mrs. Wells went on to say, "I remember your [the author's] father [Staff Sergeant Jack Shay]. His mess hall was straight up the road [Baker] on the American side on a rise to the right. I ate in that mess hall with some of my friends. I remember lunch was 25¢ a meal. The mess hall was for civilians, too. The GIs went through the lines. But the civilians had one table in the corner right. The food was put on the table in bowls for us. It was served family-style. It was good. Especially popular was the crumb cake, flat, split in the middle, and a creamy substance in the middle and tiny crumbs in butter on the top. We had 45 minutes per lunch. Maybe some people had 30 minutes."

The establishment of the POW camp required a serviceable road connecting the camp with the town proper. As retired dentist Dr. Joseph A. "Joby" Walker, born and raised just west of the camp itself, wrote in 2008:

> I was born in 1927 in my family's house across the highway from Fort McClellan's Baker Gate.... At that time, the road from Anniston out to the Fort started at the north end of Noble Street.... Quintard Avenue, the current Highway 21 going to the former base, ended at the hill at 22nd Street in Anniston. The fort road was paved with army brick, 4 × 4 × 8 inches, and referred to as the "Brick Pike." It ended at the railroad at Baltzell Gate. That section of railway was built during World War I as a spur off the Anniston-to-Rome (GA) Southern railroad ... the road from Baltzell Gate to Jacksonville was not paved until later.
>   In the early 1930's army trucks had solid tires, that is, metal rims with about four inches of solid rubber. Thus they rode rough and rumbly, loosening many of the bricks as they went. When the temperature soared during long summer days the bricks would expand and be heard popping up. One had to be alert when driving the pike in order to miss the loose bricks....
>   In 1943, the north end of Quintard was opened up and a two lane concrete road was constructed out to the Fort, replacing the Brick Pike.[16]

A year later, Dr. Walker fondly recalled the motor pool and its location near a favorite childhood haunt: "That POW motor pool was by an earthen dam, with soft earth, clay. We'd put a little motor oil in it [clay] to make modeling clay. Then we'd cut it with a knife and put it into small cubes. I think it amused the GIs."[17]

12

Life in the American Military Camp

"Chicken, beer, and guess what fellows—GIRLS!"

To the combat-hardened veterans of the sanguinary battles of World War II, their comrades-in-arms who sat out the duration of the war on the home front must have seemed (at least at times) lucky stiffs, even slackers. After all, they received the same military benefits, went to school on the same GI Bill, received the same health benefits from the Veterans' Administration, marched in the same Memorial Day parades, and joined the same American Legion posts as those who had risked their lives on the fields of conflict.

But generalities often fail to cast light on the gray shadings between what is black and what is white. Not all combat veterans were self-sacrificing heroes; some were frightened men trapped in hellish conditions. Nor were all domestic-based soldiers goldbricks who chose the easy way out and then exaggerated their service to later generations.

In *Nazi Prisoners of War in America*, Arnold Krammer identified the general perception:

> Those soldiers with few qualifications of value to the war effort were assigned to low-priority areas in the backwater of the war, one such area being the POW program. And most of them knew it. Consequently, the American soldier in the POW program generally viewed his role as that of custodian, far from the "guts and glory" of the front lines. Often torn by conflicting emotions, those involved in the processing of prisoners were understandably grateful for the safety of serving in an area removed from the danger and discomfort of the front, yet they often regretted not fulfilling the heroic expectations of their youth.

And again:

> Every man who was physically qualified for combat duty was shipped out, and only those unfit for overseas duty were available to guard prisoners of war....
>
> [T]he Army Service Forces were often compelled to use "superfluous"—or unqualified—personnel: those declared physically or psychologically unfit; recently retired officers and those destined for a terminal or "dead-end" appointment; combat veterans recycled home; and raw recruits.[1]

Those on the home front, including men who served in America's POW camps as noncommissioned officers and privates, received little "glory" for their roles. Yet they were fulfilling an important, if somewhat tangential, task in their nation's ongoing war.

The servicemen guarding McClellan came essentially from three subgroups: young soldiers, almost always privates, who had just completed or were in the final stages of their basic training and were temporarily assigned to fill a need at the camp before shipping out for the front; veterans released from active duty at the front because of wounds or other disqualifiers; and, most often, those who were rejected for combat duty because of marital or family situations or health issues.

In the 1960s, Jack Shay, an amateur boxer and baseball player in his teens, recounted how he ended up in the POW camp, never expecting his recorded comments to be published:

> I was 32 when the army drafted me. I was married six years. They'd generally draft the younger men first before they got to the married ones and the ones with kids.
>
> Uncle Joe [his brother] was already in the Army Air Corps. He was flying combat missions over the Hump [Burma–China–India Theater] over there in Asia. But he was single and younger than me.
>
> And Uncle Patty [another brother] was in the army with General Patton. He saw a lot of action, and, when he came home, he never wanted to talk about it. He was younger than me and single.
>
> Only Ambrose [the youngest of his three brothers, who was deferred because of medical reasons and served in the Civilian Conservation Corps] didn't go. It was a break for Gram and Grandpa [his parents] not to have all their sons gone.
>
> When I was going through basic training at Fort McClellan, I got an infection from barbed wire. It caused all these spots on my legs [dark blotches of scabrous skin from the ankles to the knees]. They'd scab up and be rough, and then they'd bleed. I wound up under medical care. They never healed properly. They wouldn't let me go into combat.
>
> If it wasn't for that, I would've ended up at Normandy on D–Day along with the rest of my buddies or moving up the Italian Boot [Sicily–Italy campaign].
>
> I was assigned to the PW camp. They had just opened it shortly before, and they were taking in a lot of Germans. They needed GIs to run the place. So they slotted me as an MP.
>
> I was one of the older MPs. But they were all ages. We had some young guys not even 20. Some would be there for the whole time. Others were there only for a couple weeks at a clip,

MP Jack Shay at the gate controlling access to Baker Road and the POW and American camps. The American sector is in the background (author's collection).

and then they'd move out. A lot of 'em wound up going overseas. But the permanent party there at the camp, the cadre, there were a lot of married guys, guys who had families.

It wasn't like we had a free ride. It wasn't all hunky-dory. We didn't see action at the front, so we were lucky in that respect. But we didn't know that going in. It was the luck of the draw where you wound up. Some guys wound up in the Armed Services' orchestras and bands. And the famous ones, a lot of Hollywood actors, did promotional work for the government while in uniform. When Uncle Sam called us, we served, regardless where we went. We all knew how to fire an M-1 [rifle]. We all knew how to dig a foxhole. If the army sent us into combat, we served. If they put us here in the States, we served here.

We [at McClellan] got some quick training [as MPs]. We didn't spend a lot of time in training. None of us spoke German. None of the guys I knew. That wasn't a requirement. You just needed to know how to do your job, how to keep an eye on the PWs, and make sure nothing was going on that shouldn't go on.

They stationed us in the towers and at the entrance gates to the compounds and at the main gate [to Baker Road]. We'd have rifles in the towers, short arms holstered on our belts, and pretty much pistols at the gates.

I got to know most of the GIs who worked there, either by face or name. A lot of 'em were young guys in good shape waiting for orders to transfer to some other post. With the sergeants, the NCOs [noncommissioned officers], it was different. They were what we called cadre or permanent party. They didn't cycle in and out. They might be in the camp on a permanent basis for the duration of the war. Some transferred out. But the ones who stayed became a close group. They were a good bunch of Joes.[2]

Fellow Pennsylvania native Joseph A. Spinelli was in his early 20s when an injury suffered while serving in the 82nd Airborne permanently grounded him. As his brother, Patrick D. Spinelli, explained, Joe started "at Ft Bragg, NC with the 82nd Airborne. Joe made several jumps, one descending too fast that it broke his eardrum and caused bleeding. His Paratrooper career ended."[3] Joe Spinelli's daughter, Mary Jo Berardone, added, "My dad injured his back in Airborne, and they wouldn't let him jump. That's why he went to the POW camp in Alabama. He could have been discharged, but he chose to stay in. He volunteered to go to McClellan."[4] Such stories were typical for those exempted from combat duty who fulfilled the remainder of their service at the camp.

Occasionally, for some, the sequence involved ironic twists. The November 9, 1945, issue of *The McClellan CYCLE* told of one such incident, involving Sergeant Paul Nola Jr., who was captured by the Germans and became a POW before being released and assigned to McClellan:

The Purple Heart, Combat Infantryman's Badge and ETO [European Theater of Operations] ribbon with two battle stars on his uniform, add ... credence to the story of Sgt. Nola's battlefront activities.

The demanding occasion in his case came on the cold, bleak day of last November 14th, when German forces opened the Battle of the Bulge [December 16, 1944, according to military historians] against the weakened defense lines of the U.S. 106th Division....

"People can't realize what the boys went through over there," Sgt. Nola says. "The usual *prison* camp fare was a loaf of bread divided among seven to 10 men, a canteen cup of soup, and a little margarine. There were no Red Cross packages. Some of the guys were so hungry they actually broke down and cried because they couldn't stand it." ...

Sgt. Nola returned to Ft. McClellan in September with 50 points. Now mess sergeant for the PW Camp detachment, he has his eye out on a discharge sometime in December so that he can spend Christmas this year ... at his Birmingham home.... [H]e expects to return to his old position as superintendent of bakery route salesmen. Later on he expects to go into business for himself by operating a café of his own.[5]

In the fall of 1944, PFC Jack Shay went from being an MP at the POW camp to serving as a mess sergeant on the American side of Baker Road. It represented a promotion and a fast step up the career military ladder, if one was so inclined. He obtained the post due to a vacancy and a well-placed recommendation. At first serving in an acting capacity as a Technician 4th Grade, he underwent a crash course in mess hall management, food preparation and presentation, and coordination of special recreational activities. It was essentially hotel management, army style.

The MPs and permanent party GIs ate well. Surviving menus indicate well-balanced meals and varied fare. For example, the 1437th SCU menu for January 17, 1945, designed by Acting Mess Sergeant Shay and approved by Mess Officer Captain Thomas J. Peeples, was typical: breakfast—half a grapefruit, dry cereal, fresh milk, hot cakes/bacon, syrup, butter, and coffee; dinner—fried steak, mashed potatoes, stewed tomatoes, coleslaw, celery, bread, butter, and cocoa; supper—beef goulash, boiled potatoes, leafy greens, sliced onions, dessert, bread, butter, and coffee.

Likewise, the May 4, 1945, menu for the "HEADQUARTERS DETACHMENT SERV-ICE COMMAND UNIT 1463 Prisoner of War Camp Military Police," formulated by Mess Sergeant Shay and countersigned by Mess Officer Sherbert B. Jones, First Lieutenant, CMP, consisted of the following: breakfast—grapefruit, dry cereal, fresh milk, fried eggs, toast, butter, and coffee; dinner—roast lamb with gravy, snowflake potatoes, creamed asparagus, sliced tomatoes, celery, bread, pastry, butter, and coffee; supper—hamburger patties with gravy, hash-browned potatoes, corn on the cob, glazed carrots, onion rings/vinegar, chilled cherries, bread, butter, and tea.

No surviving menus in the author's collection list the notorious "SOS"—chipped beef—although that bane of army culinary fare certainly saw the light of day. As Jack Shay was fond of telling his son in the 1960s, "We used to make SOS. [Expletive] on a shingle. That's what we called it, but it was actually chipped beef on toast with a creamy white sauce of flour and butter and seasonings. A little bacon drippings gave it some zip. You could use ground-up hamburger or thin slices of roast beef. Some of the guys liked it a lot. It got a bad rap, but it was actually very good."

Special occasions meant special menus. Christmas Day dinner for December 25, 1944, put together by Mess Sergeants Carl Rodgers and Jack Shay and approved by Captain Peeples, included roast turkey with giblet gravy, sage dressing, snowflake potatoes, cranberry sauce, candied sweet potatoes, green peas, asparagus tips, celery, olives, pickles, pastry, mincemeat pie, fruit cocktail, ice cream, candy, nuts, assorted fruits, and coffee.

A year later, an undated menu with the heading "MERRY CHRISYMAS [*sic*] AND HAPPY NEW YEAR" featured the following for Christmas dinner: roast turkey with giblet gravy, sage dressing, mashed potatoes, candied sweet potatoes, sweet June peas, buttered asparagus, lettuce salad with mayonnaise, celery, olives, pickles, creamed roll cake, fruitcake, bread, coffee, candy, assorted nuts, cigars, cigarettes, and gum. It was, once again, the creation of Mess Sergeant Shay, with the approbation of Mess Officer Captain Alonzo W. Herdrich.[6]

"The GIs never went hungry," the sergeant remembered. "And we had some real chowhounds. If they didn't like the portion sizes, they'd say, 'Hey, can you spare it?' or they'd come back for seconds until we ran out. And the PWs who made the food for me [under his supervision] ate good, too. The same meals we were preparing. And they got to sample it as they were making it. They liked working in the mess hall."

HEADQUARTERS DETACHMENT SERVICE COMMAND UNIT 1463

Prisoner of War Camp Military Police
Fort McClellan, Alabama

MENU::: FRIDAY 4 May 1945

BREAKFAST: Grapefruit
            Dry Cereal
            Fresh Milk
            Fried Eggs
            Toast
            Butter
            Coffee

DINNER: Roast Lamb W/Gravy
                     Snowflake Potatoes
                     Creamed Asparagus
                     Sliced Tomatoes
                     Celery
                     Bread
                     Pastry
                     Butter
                     Coffee

SUPPER: Hamburger Patties W/Gravy
            Hash Browned Potatoes
            Corn on Cob
            Glazed Carrots
            Onion Rings/ Vinegar
            Chilled Cherries
            Bread
            Butter
            Tea

SHERBERT B. JONES
1st Lt., CMP
Mess Officer

J. Shay
Mess Sgt.

The MP menu for May 4, 1945 (author's collection).

Unexpected moments often produced humorous anecdotes. As Marie Shay told the author in the 1970s:

I remember this one time Dad and I decided to make a batch of fudge just for us. Dad was the mess sergeant at the time. And it was late, after hours, and the mess hall was closed down for the night.

So we went into the kitchen to make the fudge. We had all the ingredients there. We put the lights on and started to make it. And, wouldn't you know it, in comes Dad's commanding officer. I think it was Captain Peeples. And he says, "Sergeant, what's going on here?"

Well, Dad didn't miss a beat. He just blurted out, "Oh, it's something special for the boys, sir. I'm making chocolate syrup for the boys."

So, the captain just looked at Dad, and he put his hand on his shoulder and said, "Oh, that's good. Keep up the good work, Sergeant."

So after he left, Dad said, "That was a close one." So we had our fudge. And the fellas got a special treat, too.

Most of the time, the American camp was comfortably stress-free. The GIs had their own PX, dayroom, chapel, and NCO Club, in addition to access to more of the same and swimming facilities, athletic fields, and movie theaters on the main post.

Like the main fort itself, the American camp had a mix of male and female employees. The women came from civilian ranks and worked in either the headquarters building or the main American complex. The civilian populace increased when 300 positions became available in 1944. *The McClellan CYCLE* announced the openings on March 10:

> Vacancies exist for clerks, stenographers, storekeepers, nurses and dental assistants. Wives of officers and enlisted men in this area receive preference for the jobs. Further preference is given wives of officers and men who are stationed here on a cadre or permanent status....
>
> Those appointed receive temporary appointments. Starting pay for clerks on a 48-hour week basis is $130 per month. Registered nurses start at $1620 a year plus overtime.[7]

The American camp received a portion of those women, including New Yorker Marie Shay, who happily trekked nearly 1,100 miles to Anniston to accept a Civil Service position in the GI PX, which sat very close to Baker Road and served the assortment of products customary to all army PXs. GIs, whether off-duty or on break, enjoyed it as a leisurely hangout.

She first met Ruth Allen there, when both worked for Essie Woodward, the PX civilian manager. Ruth was a young schoolteacher barely out of her teens when she came to Fort McClellan, an army bride following her husband. As she recounted:

> I graduated in 1941 and was teaching school in Nebraska. I met Ray [Allen] in Nebraska. He had been in Tryon, but then he was drafted. This was before Pearl Harbor. We married on his furlough on April 19, 1943.
>
> At first, Ray went to California for his basic training, then clear across the United States by train to another fort to board a ship that took him to Panama for two years. Then he went to Louisiana. I finished my year of teaching at a school near North Platte, as Ray went to Louisiana. Then I joined him after he was transferred to Fort McClellan.
>
> There were quite a lot of PXs in the fort, besides the one near the POW camp. Before I transferred to the PX in the camp, I was a

Ruth and Ray Allen in 1943, the year of their marriage (courtesy of Ruth Allen).

salesclerk at the main PX at Fort McClellan. I worked in jewelry and watches. Then I transferred to the PX in the POW camp.

The PX was oblong. The front door was a double door and inside there were some tables and chairs, but not many. There was ice cream there, I think, chocolate, vanilla, and strawberry. And all kinds of pop. Cigarettes. Some candy. It's where us girls worked. I was pretty much behind the ice cream cans.

Essie Woodward was the manager. Your [the author's] mom, Essie, and I worked in the PX. We were the only women there when I was there.

It was a popular hangout. They [GIs] would come in. We had a nickelodeon there. And they danced with us to the nickelodeon when the MPs were off-duty.

I remember there was a little man, a Negro, who worked in the PX every day, all day. A little bitty man hunched over, and he was in charge of cleanup, kind of like a janitor.

To enter the camp, Ruth, like all civilian and military employees, had to pass through the main gate at the intersection of Pelham and Baker Roads. "Usually, you had to show your badge when you were going by the guard house into the camp. Sometimes, the MPs got to know you. Of course, your [the author's] father knew who I was."

She also saw POWs on a regular basis: "They had a bakery, and they brought down baked goods for us. And flowers from their greenhouses for us. They had a couple of trustees, and they could come in the PX. Not many of them, though."

And the salary? Her July 14, 1945, earnings statement for that pay period yielded the following: $1,506 rate per annum; $57.92 regular earnings, plus $17.38 overtime, for a total gross of $75.30; minus $7.30 in federal tax, $2.90 for retirement, and $10 for other with-holdings, yielding a net pay of $55.10.

"The war [in the Pacific] was still going on when we left Anniston. Ray was stationed at Fort Knox [Kentucky] at that point. I came home in the fall of 1945." But permanent bonds resulted from their time at McClellan:

The PX, Building T-3595, scene of much jollity in the American camp. Marie Shay (left) and Essie Woodward flank an unidentified MP (author's collection).

Your [the author's] mother was already there in the PX when I came. And so was Essie. I had a baby Brownie camera, and we took a lot of pictures of each other.

I remember we spent Christmas of 1944 at the fort and in our little house across from the fort. And your mother gave me a nice photo album for Christmas. It was brown with a design on the outside. Very nice.[8]

But there was one occasion (not during Ruth Allen's and Essie Woodward's time) when someone at the PX made a less-than-favorable impression. "There was this one manager," Marie Shay told the author in the 1960s. "He would always tell us the secret of dishing out ice cream. He had a little accent, and he'd get a scooper and show us how to dip it. And he'd say, 'You rrrroll it, and you rrrroll it, and you rrrroll it,'" she said, demonstrating how he'd skim the surface of the ice cream tub, enfolding pockets of air within the ice cream shavings he scooped into a cone. "It would be half ice cream and half air. Then when he left, I would just go back to giving them big ice cream scoops. I couldn't see gypping the poor GIs. He wanted to treat it like it was a business. The boys would always come to me."

Published weekly for soldiers at Fort McClellan, *The McClellan CYCLE*, along with its news stories of prisoner arrivals and camp inspections, sporadically carried submissions from the American camp correspondents detailing off-duty social or sporting events on the "other" side of Baker Road. The items provided a lighthearted glimpse into the everyday activities of the soldiers stationed at the camp and often belied the notion that all POW camp GIs were out-of-shape rejects.

Corporal Harry Sloan wrote one of the first articles for the October 15, 1943, edition:

Very few PW Campers know that they are represented by a fighting basketball team. With only a few minutes practice, they were able to step out and take their first game in the Fort tournament by a score of 32 to 13. It's a swell little team, and bound to improve as they go along....

Games are every Wednesday at 6:30 PM in the Field House [on the main post]....

The boys in 433 are still wondering how Private First Class Bansbach got lost in a Kansas City RR Station. With his furlough due soon, they expect anything to happen. He'd better bring his flashlight and compass this time.

Private Bayne, Casanova of the 382nd, gets air mail letters from ANNISTON. That's love, fellows!

Sgt. Pot McEntee, Celtic songbird of the 383rd, is seriously pricing marriage licenses.

Cpl. Bill Townsend, and Private First Class Klein, both of 383, enjoying Kansas City scenery this week....

PW Campers will now be able to read about their ... results of camp sporting events in the sports section.

Sergeant Ahearn, president of the newly formed NCO Club, wants 100 percent membership.... He can be reached at headquarters, or see your own first sergeant.[9]

In the October 29 edition, the same writer hinted at potential fraternization between a smitten GI and an unnamed female civilian employee in the headquarters building, noted for its attractive women: "1437 is impatiently awaiting that Halloween party promised for Saturday night [October 30]. Chicken, beer, and guess what fellows—GIRLS! This will be Corporal Cope's big chance to finally date that glammer gal from headquarters."[10] Corporal Sloan continued the soap opera in the November 5 issue, recording some of the events of the Halloween party in the 1437th mess hall:

Big event of the week was the Halloween party.... After an opening speech by Pvt. George Bolus that convinced the company double talk has its merits, a chicken dinner was served that still has the Camp talking.

There was plenty of good old 3.2 [beer], and it seemed to your correspondent that every member had his wife or best girl present. The company officers and both chaplains [American] for the PW Camp dropped in during the evening, and all enjoyed themselves.

Highlights of the party were the decorations, which were exceptionally well done, lending the proper Halloween atmosphere, and the Halloween cakes, baked especially for the occasion. They had everyone reaching for "seconds."

Didn't get a look at Cpl. Tyronne [possibly a joking reference to handsome actor Tyrone Power] Cope's heart throb, as she didn't show up. And Cpl. Merle Gerhard left suspiciously early. Rumor had an Anniston gal as the attraction.

Pfc. Richard Klein, of 383, heard a strange noise the other night, fired five fast shots, and said "Who went there?"[11]

In the November 19 issue, Corporal Sloan likewise teased "Sergeant Wood, also of 433," who had "suddenly decided it is necessary to make lots of trips to the Post Tailor. Some say it's a brunette. We think it's a blonde!"[12]

A week later, on November 26, a new reporter, Corporal Howard Cope (possibly the "Tyronne Cope" of Sloan's November 5 gibe), roasted a number of his colleagues:

Pfc. "Man Mountain Dean" Landseadel, 1437, is reported[ly] going on a diet just to spite Mess Sergeant McGraw, who wanted to draw double rations for him. Jest can't do that, Hank....

Private Billingsley, 433, received an unexpected cold shower last week for failing to do his turn at coal-getting, but it took four fellows to get him wet. More work, in fact, than getting the coal themselves.

Pfc. Otto King is home on business—he says. Others say there is a new star in his love-life that is burning right brightly these days. Could be a little of both, by our book.

Private First Class Black is headed for that long-awaited ten-dayer. Hutmates hope he won't get lost in the home town coal mines while he is wandering around. Six months can make a lot of difference in the life of a mine.[13]

Corporal Cope continued the bantering in the January 7, 1944, issue:

Sgt. Harvey Cash will agree with anyone that says "Brooklyn is the garden spot of the world," but says he doesn't know a thing about New York City. Question is whether Brooklyn is in New York or vice versa....

Pvt. Anthony J. Boccabella of the 383rd does have a recipe for those much talked about "bean patties." If any of the other mess sergeants would like to have it, just call Boccabella any time during the day or night, and he will be glad to give you the book (so would the fellows who have to eat the patties).

Can anyone tell us why Cpl. Norman Britt is spending so much time in town looking for a room?

Cpl. Joseph Spinelli is getting baby's clothes through the mail from friends in Pennsylvania. How about some news, Spinelli?

The state of Tennessee should be proud of Pfc. Otto King. He sent more Christmas cards in one day than the 1347th [actually the 1437th] received in a week. If he keeps that up, the Post Office threatens to stop free mail.[14]

On February 4, 1944, a new correspondent, Corporal John J. George, alternating with Corporal Cope in supplying reports to the CYCLE, credited "Cpl. Joseph Spinelli, 1437th," with the "opening of the NCO Club last Friday evening [January 28]."[15]

On February 18, Cope's final piece was published. He listed the NCO Club's elected officers: First Sergeant Charles D. Gable, president; First Sergeant James E. Wells, vice president; and himself, secretary-treasurer. He continued:

Sgt. Maxie McKinney and his wife are doing a swell job of running the club. Believe me, Mrs. McKinney is a very good cook....

We have been trying to find out just why Pvt. Angelo D'Auria, of the 382nd, spent the afternoon at the cosmetics counter in the five and dime store.

Pvt. Philip Cantone, who just married a Southern girl, should have a good talk with Cpl. Walter J. Theobald, who has that gleam in his eye.[16]

The following week, Corporal George took over entirely, embarking on what would become the longest stint of any correspondent in the American camp. His February 25 column began with a brief explanation of what had happened to his predecessor before launching full tilt into the usual blend of information, gossip, and blather:

Those Yankee-Rebel arguments in barrack number one of the 1437th ceased abruptly when Cpl. Howard W. Cope Jr., left to assume his new duties at Ft. Custer, Mich.

S/Sgt. Dominick F. Longhine, the best fire tender of the 1437th, just got his stove a little too hot. He realized it when he held a damp towel in front of the stove to dry and found it scorched brown a moment later....

Pfc. Paul A. Logano, 433rd, has returned from furlough with his new bride.

Some of the boys from the 433rd MPEG Co. wonder why their first sergeant changed from blond to brunette, and why Cpl. Warren H. Bick lost all hopes of going home February 31 [sic]. Sarge has both answers.

Pfc. H. A. Webber, 383rd (supply room playboy) may tell us about the brush-off from that gal in Jacksonville.

Sgt. John J. (Bean Patty) Battaglino of the 383rd returned to the fold last week from cook school at Ft. Benning. The boys now expect dehydrated bean patties.[17]

On March 17, 1944, John George (recently promoted to sergeant) once again utilized his customary concoction of information, gossip, good-natured needling, and puns to submit another round of news:

The NCO Club held its first Saturday night dance on March 11th and it proved very successful in spite of inclement weather. S/Sgt. Thomas Elswick made his dancing debut and surprised many of his contemporaries....

First Sgt. Charles (Cowboy) Gable had a bit of trouble with his Iron Steed the other day, but managed to come through the accident with minor injuries.

The 382nd MPEG Co. has already taken steps to keep from being caught with their bridges down. A heavy rainstorm almost washed away several of the bridges located from the road [Baker] to the barracks, so now the bridges have all been raised.

Sgt. Joseph (Number Please) Stier has found a hideout for his dull Sunday evenings.

Those Bingo experts, Pvt. Clarence S. McDowell and Cpl. Willie R. Blankenship of the 1437th SCU are looking forward to the next Bingo Party at the PWC Non-Coms' Club.

Motor Sgt. Charles Kent received a phone call from his honey in Talladega [Alabama]; two hours later he reached the other end of the line.

Pfc. Milton (Bugler) Mandor is the versatile man of the company: bugler, truck driver and all around man.

Dan Cupid has visited Pvt. Robert Burger of the 383rd and finally found him a Southern Belle.[18]

The following week, March 24, George wrote about Sergeant Bill DeRoma "spending most of his leisure time on the 1437th mess hall," sprucing up the inside and "planting flowers and shrubs outside"; he also mentioned Corporal Clyde (Horseman) Wofford of the 382nd Company, and he concluded with a note on the 383rd Company and "marital dust" getting "into the eyes of Pvt. James Watson, Pfc. Joseph Baldicini, Pvt. Robert Burger and Pfc. Alphonse (Bainbridge) Via."[19]

Though the weekly columns by Sergeant George and his predecessors, taken together, fall into a routine pattern of folksy "news" that the editor and censors of the time would have easily welcomed and approved, they now—at a distance of seven decades, when much of the information on names, duties, and pastimes of the personnel in the American camp has been lost to the neglect of time—cast a glimmer of light on a subject heretofore ignored.

The columns of Sergeant George (who never thought his "space-fillers" would be of serious interest 70 years after they had been written) bring to life some long-forgotten items. For example, in his March 31, 1944, column, he mentioned:

- Eugene Steppe: "[W]e nominate Cpl. Eugene Steppe of the 382nd MPEG Co. as 'lover of the month.' Gene was seen taking his future mother-in-law on a shopping tour."
- Corporal Jacob Schemel and Staff Sergeants Edward "Buster" Blendermann and Joseph "Chow Hound" Miller.
- Sergeant Carmine F. DeRoma, whose sister ("a striking beauty from New York City") visited her brother and charmed a good portion of the 1437th SCU.
- EmPee, the puppy of Staff Sergeant John Battaglino, who served as the "mascot" of the 383rd headquarters barrack.[20]

On April 14, he wrote of Corporal Everett "Hairless Joe" Schott becoming acting first sergeant of the 433rd MPEG Company; PFC Karl "Beau Brummel" Beutel showcasing his dance moves at the NCO Club; the romantic interest of Private John T. Summer of the 1437th SCU; and Corporal Walter J. Theobald, the mail clerk of the 383rd Company.[21]

On April 21, George immortalized Private Robert Fragle of the 383rd for filling the current Charge of Quarters (CQ) position; PFC Joseph "Casanova" DeSain for plunking down two dollars to buy a rose for "his fair young lady for Easter"; and Corporal Warren Beck for "trying out for a position on the 1437th baseball team, 'The Wildcats.'" Then he threw in the usual humorous barbs at well-known colleagues: "S/Sgt. Joseph (chow-hound) Miller of the 1437th has a rival when it comes to chow since Pfc. Robert E. Budabin came into this unit. The outcome was that Mess Sgt. Bill DeRoma had to arrange to seat the company according to rank so as to separate the two, and thus giving the other boys a break."[22]

In the May 12 issue, he identified PFC Otto H. King of the 1437th SCU as the camp's chief telephone switchboard operator.[23] And the following week, he reported that Corporal Charles B. Draut had become the acting motor sergeant. He also listed the election of officers of the NCO Club: himself as president; Corporal Everett W. Schott as secretary-treasurer; and Staff Sergeants Charles Custer and Joe L. Wood and Corporal Merle L. Gerhard as board governors.[24]

In his May 26 column, he recorded the designation of a new manager of the PX, Mary Jane Sloan, "about a month ago." He also wrote of Sergeant Israel Blatt, on extended detached service, visiting the camp and his "home organization" on the 22nd, and of Corporal Oscar Levine celebrating his third wedding anniversary on the 21st.[25] The June 2 column included bits on Sergeant Joseph A. Spinelli ("a happy man now that his wife is living in Anniston") and also Staff Sergeant George P. Cowgill's "spare time" pursuit of the "study of reptiles."[26]

A group shot of army buddies in the American camp, May 1, 1944, all immortalized in the pages of *The McClellan CYCLE*. First row: Sergeants John J. George and Edward Blendermann and Corporal Merle L. Gerhard; second row: Sergeants Joseph A. Spinelli and H. Klein; third row: Sergeant Joseph Miller and PFC Karl H. Beutel (courtesy of Mary Jo Berardone).

A brief item, carrying no byline, in the June 23, 1944, issue announced the formation of an Enlisted Men's Club with the following officers: Sgt. George, president; Private Norman Preston, vice president; Private Jack Furman, secretary-treasurer; and Staff Sergeants Edward Blendermann and Charles Custer, Sergeants William Dennis and Joseph Spinelli, and Corporal Merle Gerhard as board governors.[27]

An uncredited submitter (whose style was very much like that of Staff Sergeant George) recounted "highlights" of a December 9, 1944, dance "at the P.W. Camp NCO Club," among other gossipy news, in the December 15 issue:

Sgt. William W. Dennis making the debut of his terpsichorean excellence which would have won first prize if prizes were given. (likewise S/Sgt. John Rayburn's first born). A specialty dance, the polka, featuring Cpl. Eddie Krolikowski and his partner, Marie Shay. And last but far from least, one of the finest dance bands on the Fort.

Pfc. Edward (Chattanooga) Schaefer was in such a hurry to get ready for that week-end morale builder that he not only burned up the roads, but also his GI (Garbage Included) truck. MPs who stopped him when they noticed his truck afire were politely informed by Schaefer that he already knew of the fire and that he was on his way to the fire station because, as he figured it, he knew where the fire station was but the firemen certainly didn't know where he was with the fire.

Cpl. Henry (Hank) Landseadel is working on a secret invention for the first sergeant's jeep. The information this reporter can get is that it has something to do with "air brakes." Thinks it will work.[28]

The December 29 issue carried a column by newly promoted Staff Sergeant George about a social event on Christmas Day:

Camp switchboard operator PFC Otto H. King (author's collection).

A large attendance enjoyed the Christmas program and open house at the PW Camp last Monday night. Cpl. Lester Hayden and Pvt. Joseph Krpan did the honors. The program was opened with the showing of a movie followed by dancing and refreshments. A dance will be held on New Year's Eve at the club house with the same fine dance band that has been furnishing the jive in the past.

Pfc. Clarence S. McDowell has a voice like Frank Sinatra, only in hilly-billy style.
The beautifully decorated mess hall of the 1437th SCU was accredited to Mess Pfc. John Shay and Mess Pvt. Carl Rogers [Rodgers?].[29]

Others mentioned in the various columns included Sergeant "Tiny" Henderson and Corporal Edwin Logan.[30]

Sergeant George himself became a celebrity in the camp in early 1946. Married in Anniston's Sacred Heart Church on November 14, 1944, while still a staff sergeant, he had received several promotions by the time his daughter, Janice Joan, was born on the first day of 1946. A story, featuring a photograph of the sergeant with his newborn, ran in the *CYCLE* on January 11, 1946:

> While papa, M/Sgt. John J. George of the PW Camp, looks fondly through the glass, Janice George, born New Year's Day, takes a nap in the arms of Nurse Jennie Lawson. Baby George, born at 1:51 PM on Jan. 1, was the first New Year's baby at the Ft. McClellan hospital, as well as the first in Calhoun County. The child weighs 6 lbs., 12 ozs., and is the first born to Sergeant George and his wife, the former Loretta Gendron of Fitchburg, Mass.[31]

Of course, not every experience in the camp made the newspaper. Mary Jo Berardone, at the time a mere toddler, remembered her father, Sergeant Joe Spinelli, building from scratch a miniature jeep: "He built this jeep for the captain's son. I don't know which captain. It was a gift, I want to say a birthday gift for the boy. This was back in 1945. He built it in his spare time in the camp from scrap parts. He was very talented. He could build anything. Then he put me in it and took my picture in it before he gave it to the captain for his son. So I got a memory and a photograph out of it."[32]

Master Sergeant John J. George holding his new baby, Janice Joan, on the arched stone bridge connecting the mainland to a small island on the main post—a popular photographic spot for the GIs of the neighboring POW camp. Left to right: Staff Sergeant Albert "Bud" Jones, Marie Shay, Evelyn Jones, Loretta George, Janice, and Master Sergeant George (author's collection).

The weekly dances, held at the NCO Club on Fridays from 8 p.m. until midnight, proved popular and welcomed nonmembers and guests. Marie Shay, who attended her share, remembered the live bands playing the standards of the day:

The music was always lively, and we even had singers doing solos. And it wasn't just the GIs. There'd be people from Anniston or Oxford or Jacksonville who'd come up for the music and the dancing. It was a highlight in our camp.

I remember Tulsa Steward [wife of Sergeant Jack S. Steward, who shared a duplex house with the Shays across Pelham Road from the POW camp] coming home on a Friday night or sometimes a Saturday, if there was a special event at the club. And she'd be singing "Saturday Night Is the Loneliest Night of the Week." She was still in the partying mood. She always enjoyed the club dances. Her husband wasn't that much of a partier and not really a dancer. He was more the outdoors type. And Tulsa would always say, "Pa [her nickname for him] just changes his

Little Mary Jo Spinelli seated in the toy jeep her father built for the son of one of the American camp's captains (courtesy of Mary Jo Berardone).

clothes when he comes home and lays across the bed. You two [the Shays] never seem to run out of things to say to each other. Whenever you both get home, it's always yak-yak-yak-yak-yak." So Tulsa took advantage of any dance that was available. She was always on the go.

You didn't have to go with anyone to the dances. You could meet someone there. It wasn't necessarily a serious thing. It was just dancing and listening to music and having a good time. Although there were some romances that started there at the club. Some of the GIs and the girls got a little lovey-dovey.

On February 9, 1945, the NCO Club hosted a "semi-formal Valentine dance" that attracted a "record crowd to enjoy the activities." The Misses Marlis Stedham and Doris Whitley provided "beautiful Valentine decorations" and, along with Miss Virginia Denson, served refreshments. The following week, a "Post-Valentine dance" occurred.[33]

Many GIs also took the bus or drove to downtown Anniston for a break from camp life. Being home to a major military installation, Anniston offered big-city diversions like shopping, dining and dancing, civic functions, and various other forms of entertainment. And though it was a Southern town with equal doses of grace, charm, and decorum, like all places where soldiers trained and congregated, it contained another form of night life.

When Jack Shay first arrived at McClellan in 1943, his wife of six years was still in New York. When on weekend passes, he observed Anniston's distractions for anyone in uniform if he knew where to look—distractions that came from a flirtatious smile or a come-hither look. Nearly 30 years later, he wrote a letter to his son, then in Fort Benning, Georgia, about the temptations in Anniston:

> [W]atch for the company you travel with. You will have more time on your hands[.] You will be getting ... passes....
>
> What I am driving at is when you get to town.... All the camps are the same.... The girls work on the guys and try to get them to have affairs.... Most of them are no good, or they wouldn't be giving their bodies away. Watch and keep away from them, as a lot of them have disease and pass it around. They will call you chicken, queer, and a lot of things, but don't pay any attention to them. Also your buddies may do the same—"Oh, come on, Jack. Don't be a sissy. It's good for you." ...
>
> I know because I went through the same thing during the second war.... I just ignored them.[34]

Though Anniston would never be called the Las Vegas of the East, such fleshly attractions enticed some GIs attached to the POW camp who were only too eager to kiss and tell when they arrived back from their weekend leave.

As for Sergeant Shay, he surrounded himself with a cadre of men who were faithful to their wives and nestled in with his own wife when she arrived in early 1944. But still an occasional "opportunity" presented itself, including one notorious episode just across from the POW camp that he politely—and properly, for the sake of his marriage and the honor of the military—rejected. He told only his wife of the incident. She, in turn, decades later, told the author the details in confidence.

13

Civilian Lodging
for the Americans

*"People were renting apartments
to GIs all around Anniston."*

Hundreds of GIs worked at the POW camp from 1943 to 1946, some for the duration of their military service, others on temporary duty pending reassignment or shipment overseas. The permanent party (particularly those married and with children) often chose offsite lodging. Accordingly, many Annistonians rented rooms, apartments, or houses to military personnel.

Among them were J. Fred and Mary I. Gurley, who lived at 1729 Quintard Avenue, near 18th Street. Their daughter, Betty (Gurley) Mabry, a teenager during the war, remembered her parents' interaction with GI families:

> The house was built for an older couple. But I lived there with my parents from 1935 to around 1953. During the war, my older brother, Fred, was in the army. And it was just a very patriotic time.
>
> My daddy was a tax collector for Calhoun County. And they [her parents] were being patriotic in renting. People were renting apartments to GIs all around Anniston.
>
> We had to add a bathroom because we only had one—so they could rent a bedroom and a bath to the GIs. It was convenient for the GIs because the bus to McClellan stopped at the corner to take soldiers to the fort.
>
> These were GIs and their wives. And I'm sure that some of them would have worked at the POW camp.
>
> They [the renters] had a very good relationship [with her parents]. I do remember this one soldier would leave early and then the wife would go later. And they would go out for a walk [in the evening] to supper to eat because there was no kitchen access. And when they would come back, they would sit and visit with 'em [her parents]. Then they'd have to walk right through our living room to get to their bedroom. The library was to the right of the living room. I was sleeping in the library, so it was inconvenient for me.
>
> I don't know if Daddy ever made any money from the GIs. He just wanted to be patriotic. He rented to people he knew. He didn't want to turn over his house to anyone he didn't know.[1]

Rita (Goodwyn) Springer grew up as an "army brat." She also remembered GI housing: "My father was Colonel Alan Goodwyn, a finance officer. He came to Anniston in December 1939. Then he underwent six weeks of basic training and then to war. From 1942 to 1945, we lived in an apartment building off 10th Street in town. There definitely were army buses going back and forth between the fort and the prisoner of war camp and town."[2]

"We lived in a development where they had trailer houses, just across the road from

146

the fort," recalled Ruth Allen, who followed her husband, Ray, to Fort McClellan upon his transfer.

> There were three one-bedroom houses. We rented there for a while. Mr. [Lee] Harris was the owner of the house. Ours was a little three-room house, or you might call it a cottage. There were three of these in a row. We had the one in the front. Where we stayed was across from the fort, not the POW camp, but the fort. I want to say the POW camp was south of where we stayed.
>
> I rode the bus every morning to work [at the PX in the American military camp].
>
> I worked until 9 [p.m.] or about then at the PX. I know when I got home, it was dark, right around 10 o'clock or so. I used to take the bus. And I'd wait at the guard house [at the entrance of Baker Road] with some of the MPs for the ride. Our house wasn't that far away from the camp. It might have been less than a mile, but you didn't want to walk the road when it was dark.

"We went back there about 20 years ago," she said in 2013, "and we went to see the Harrises. And they had turned it [the development] into a travel trailer park on several acres of land."[3]

The closest private lodging to the POW camp crested Surrey Hill, directly west and within eyesight of the camp on the western side of Pelham Road. It belonged to Dr. Carlos A. Walker, a distinguished dentist who had bought 64 acres on the hillside west of the old Brick Pike. As Marie Shay, who rented the southern half of a "duplex" house from Dr. Walker, remembered, "You could see the camp from our house, just down the hill and across Pelham Road. I don't know but what it was less than half a mile or so away in a straight line."[4]

Carlos Walker was the son of Charles Patrick Walker, a private in service to the Confederacy from April 1861 to February 1865. Wounded and captured at Culp's Hill during the July 1863 battle of Gettysburg, Charles Walker remained a prisoner throughout most of the rest of the conflict. Paroled in February 1865, he later became a Presbyterian minister.

Carlos Walker's son, Dr. Joseph A. "Joby" Walker, who was born and grew up on Surrey Hill and later followed his father's footsteps into dentistry, recalled the history of Surrey Hill and how it came to offer convenient and affordable GI housing:

> The 64 acres had three terraces going down to the Brick Pike. Used to have persimmon trees there. Surrey Hill included about 20 houses or buildings, excluding privies. They included the Newman house [home to Jesse

Dr. Carlos Walker, whose Surrey Hill houses stood directly across Pelham Road from the POW camp (courtesy of Dr. Joseph A. "Joby" Walker).

James Newman and his wife, Bessie Mae Keelen Newman], two buildings near the road, our house [known as the Rock House] and the servant house, the honey house, the white frame house—I was born in that house in 1927—the Simmons house, a barn, about a half-dozen other structures toward the north and the west, the Will Smith house, a bee house, a barn, and about three other houses south of that interior road that wound through the hill. We had apple trees toward the road, across from Baker Gate.

My daddy was born in 1886 in Milton, Florida. He lived there from 1886 to 1904. His older brother, Hurd Walker, had a job with the telephone company in the late 1890s, and he moved to Hagerstown, Maryland, around 1906 with the phone company. Daddy went there and worked with him in the telephone company.

One day, he [Carlos] met a dentist, and he [the dentist] said, "Son, you're pretty good with your hands. Why don't you go into dentistry?" So he went to the University of Maryland–Baltimore College of Dental Surgery. He graduated in 1912, and he came to Alabama—Birmingham. He had an aunt and kinfolk there. He drove to Gadsden [Alabama] and worked with a dentist there and went down to Birmingham on weekends.

And he knew that Camp McClellan was going to come up. So he went to practice in Anniston. In 1916, he bought 64 acres and a farm on Surrey Hill. The white frame house and the Newman house were already there. His daddy had died in 1909, so he moved his mother, young brother, and baby sister into a house going toward Anniston that he had bought. He went to the First Presbyterian Church on Quintard and 10th Street.

He met Irene Aderhold, and he married her on September 18, 1918. And they lived in town a couple months and then I believe they moved to Surrey Hill.

My daddy was quite a man. He could play most any [musical] instrument, and he did sing tenor in the opera here.

He had an accident in the summer of 1910. An engine backed up over his foot at night, a cast-iron steel wheel. It cut part of his foot off, just below the ankle. They [medical personnel] wanted to cut it off below the knee, but he wouldn't let them. He designed a prosthetic, a contraption, a vulcanized rubber toe. And an aluminum shin guard to fit into a high-top shoe. And he could outwalk me, even with that. He could swim. He could walk well. He could move his ankle. And they [people] couldn't tell which foot was wearing the prosthetic with the high-top shoe on."

Dr. Walker also explained the origins of Surrey Hill's name:

While in Hagerstown, Daddy lived on a street named Surrey. And Daddy's mother was a Hurd, and her ancestors were from Surrey, England.

He built the Rock House in 1929. Made it out of fieldstone. All you could see was rock fitted in nicely. You couldn't see the concrete. Daddy tapped onto the water main and ran a pipe to the new house. They had running water, pumping water from the well. Later on, he built a barn. There could have been an old log cabin there, too, before he bought the property. We moved into the new Rock House.

It was around 1940 that we started building shacks for tenants and GIs. Things began to buzz around then. Pelham Road was put in in 1943. The only way to get into McClellan before that was up Noble Road.

There were four other houses on the property before he built your [the author's] daddy's house.

These things were on pillars. We cut off 12 × 12[-inch] timbers my daddy had got. The pillars were one foot square. Hard pine. Daddy had 'em sawed, a foot to two feet high. Then he put in the wooden floor, the inside floor, tongue-in-groove pine. Then he put a wooden foundation on that, 6 × 6, and then the floor joists, 2 × 8 or 2 × 10 inches. The walls were tongue-in-groove pine, about 6 inches, dressed down to about 5¼ inches. Then he built the rafters and decking. He put on asbestos shingles. And inside electric lights that hang down. The windows were on the east and the west, both front and back, and they moved up and down. Your parents were on the south side of their duplex, by the barn.

Inside was the living room. We used to call it the "great room." Then the bedroom which had a bed, a sitting area, maybe a radio. And then the kitchen. And maybe a shared bathroom. They were duplexes.

We put in some outdoor bathrooms.

Also, we put in a servant house. He built the servant house in the back when he built the Rock House. And a honey house. My daddy had bee hives. He loved to work with bees. He was involved with grafting and budding trees. He built a storage house. A barn. Negro shacks. The servant house had a couple blacks.

Will Smith and Johnny Hicks, they were sharecroppers. They weren't in the army, like your folks and the other tenants.

Will Smith worked out a deal with Daddy to live in that house. Will worked, plowed, harvested watermelons and cantaloupes. Will was about 55–60. His son was Fred Smith, and his wife was known as Big Mary. She was about 60.

Johnny Hicks was a good worker. Johnny Hicks was about 30. Now Surrey Hill had copperheads, rattlers, chicken snakes, king snakes. And we used to see Johnny out in the back of Surrey Hill. He went through that tall grass with a stick. We'd say, "Johnny, you're looking for snakes?" And he'd say, "And I'se findin' 'em, too."

We had about 14 houses to rent to GIs, not counting the houses for the blacks, plus ours. We rented the upstairs of our house. And we had housing in the larger houses for five husbands and wives.

The rent was $12 a month. Maybe $8 for some houses. It was extra income. And people [GIs] needed places to stay that were inexpensive. And the Office of Price Administration put the word out to the GIs about Surrey Hill and my daddy's houses. And if any tenants complained, they [the office] would tell you [the landlord] what to do to rectify it. But Daddy never wanted to gouge people. He was one of the most honest men I've ever known. He had integrity, he was lovable, he had good character.

Daddy was very intuitive. How he had the foresight to build all this [the Surrey Hill development], I don't know. He always liked to trade, too. He would put on his old felt hat, an old gray hat, and he went out to trade. During the Depression, not everyone had money. And he would trade dental services for things, almost anything, lumber, watches, whatever. I remember one customer said, "I only have 50 cents," and he said, "Then I'll cut it [the tooth] halfway off for you."

He was very adaptable. And he knew a lot about everything. My brother once said, "Daddy, you're good in emergencies, but you make too many emergencies." And he could be funny. My daddy once wrote my sister a letter, and he said, "Enclosed is a small check." And on the bottom was a small check mark.

Surrey Hill became something of a nature preserve. In addition to snakes and field rodents, Carlos Walker's "game farm" included several other species. "Daddy had all these sheep and goats," his son recalled. "And cats. They belonged to somebody there."[5]

Marie Shay testified to the presence of the animals:

You had to watch where you stepped because there were snakes there. If you stayed on the dirt road, you were safe. And you were all right inside your house, but the house was elevated from the ground by the corner pillars, and you never knew what might be underneath. We always had cats and little kittens coming up to the back porch. And I always said, "Jack [her husband], if you feed them, you'll spoil them, and they'll always come back." But he was a softie, and he always had a big heart for anyone or anything. That's why I married him.

We shared one side of our house, and Jack and Tulsa Steward, and their little boy, Jackie, had the other side. We had a common bathroom in the middle. Jackie was a cute little towhead, and he was just learning how to walk. So they would spread out a blanket or a little rug on the grass in front of the house and have a little picnic. And it was so cute watching Jackie run around the lawn because he was at that age where they do some adorable things. And I'd always tell him to be careful because of all the stones and critters in the fields.

The duplex shared by Sergeants Jack Shay and Jack S. Steward and their families. Left to right: Marie Shay, Jack E. Steward, and Sergeant Steward (author's collection).

There were some Negroes who lived nearby. And they would do odd jobs in the area. Maybe harvesting or picking crops or clearing fields. There was this one man [possibly Johnny Hicks]. And he'd be sitting on the steps of the house eating his lunch, all alone. We talked a little. I said to him, "Why can't you go inside and eat with everyone else? You're just as good as they are." And he said, "No, ma'am. This is where I eat." I felt sorry for him. It was so hot outside in the sun. I never forgot that. We didn't see too many blacks back home [in the North] at the time, and we didn't see how they lived.

Annistonians Jesse James Newman, his wife (Bessie Mae), and their daughter (Margaret) lived in a private house on Surrey Hill and also rented a room to the Shays before they moved to the duplex closer to the POW camp. Jesse Newman was a 43-year educator at numerous Alabama schools, including 25 years at Anniston High School, focusing on industrial and vocational education. A scholarly man known as "Cardinal" and "Professor" in college and who worked as a chemist at Muscle Shoals, Alabama, he not only rented a room to the New York couple but also provided refreshments to other soldiers who wandered by his house on the southern end of Surrey Hill. As his daughter recalled, "Some of the GIs would walk over and sometimes Daddy would cut a watermelon" for them.

The house lay on ground south of the Walker buildings. Margaret Newman wrote of the house and its owners:

About our house…. The original folks homesteaded it and named it Surrey Hill for their home in England. My father bought three acres from Dr. Walker. There is some question [of] where Dr. Walker had our house built. Surrey Hill … applied to a hill that has [since] been cut down.

The house was on a pretty location. My parents planned to build their [contemplated] dream house here. The contractor had the plans when my mother died. The house was never built.

My mother got a cough she could not get rid of about January [1946]. Cancer of the heart and lung. She went to bed February 28 and died April 19, 1946.[6]

As for Carlos Walker, "Daddy practiced dentistry in Anniston from 1916 to 1961," his son recalled. "His last office was 1117½ Noble Street. Then he moved his office to the old servants' house on Surrey Hill. He had no appointments. You just walked into the house. In the early '60s, he stopped practicing, before he had a stroke. He had a stroke in 1964 or '65. He could hardly walk. We kept him at home. We had somebody staying with him. But we had to put him in a nursing home for about the last year and a half. He was being fed through a tube and couldn't talk. Eventually, the tube was removed. We said, "Leave it out." And he died a couple days later. This was August 1967. He was buried in Highland Cemetery [Anniston] with my mother and his mother."

The houses on Surrey Hill endured about a quarter-century after the POW camp shut down. "The property was sold to Jim Martin, a developer from Birmingham," Mary Beth Walker, Joby's wife, recalled. "The sale of the property was about 1971. About a year after that, all the houses were torn down."[7]

Eventually it became unrecognizable. "Surrey Hill has changed now," Joby Walker said. "Commercial development has come in. They cut down I think 10, maybe about 15 feet, off the top in recent years. And they filled in the back, which was originally low. Daddy's home was 60 yards to the west of the Arby's which is there now. But it's all changed."

14

Interaction Between Captives and Captors

"Thank you for being kind to us
& treating us like we're normal people."

McClellan's POWs approved, even extolled, their treatment at the camp.

One of the camp's first inspections, made by Mr. A. Cardinaux on September 2, 1943, yielded this remark: "The prisoners are all satisfied with the quality and quantity of their food. They may have as much bread and milk as they wish."[1] And in a December 1943 report, Captain Edward Shannahan wrote, "The spokesman [Willi Utz] was very well pleased with the treatment the prisoners are being accorded and had no complaints to offer."[2]

In a March 9, 1945, memo to the director of the POW Special Projects Division, Major Paul A. Neuland, the field service branch chief, addressed comments made by Captain Walter H. Rapp in his February 26–27 visit to the camp. Neuland lauded the relationship between internees and the camp's assistant executive officer:

> Captain Rapp found the assistant executive officer well acquainted with his mission.... Lieutenant [A. G.] McCaughrin shows a great degree of tact and skill in dealing with the German prisoners of war and seems to be well liked by his fellow officers, inasmuch as he was once before at the same camp in a different capacity. Since his arrival books, both educational and fictional, have been ordered and those which arrived have been incorporated into the already extensive camp library.[3]

Edouard Patte's early May 1945 visit prompted the following comment on First Lieutenant McCaughrin: "The new German set-up seems to be eager to cooperate, and the Assistant Executive Officer has won confidence."[4] And a report dated July 16, 1945, regarding a July 12–16 inspection by Captains W. J. Bridges, Jr., and C. E. Tremper, even suggested a somewhat lax atmosphere:

> Inspection of Compound No. 1 revealed all barracks visited to be in a poor state of police....
>   Excess clothing and unauthorized articles should be taken from prisoners in compliance with Part II, Section I, ASF Circular No. 202, 4 June 1945....
>   Many prisoners have cut down to sandals, government issue shoes, which is in violation of Paragraph [etc.].... Likewise, issue trousers have been cut to shorts. Prisoners should be charged for same under provisions mentioned above....
>   No PW interpreters were observed wearing white brassard, as required....[5]

But it was the personal interaction between prisoners and guards or detail supervisors that came to typify the relationships between men who would have been bitter foes had they met on the battlefield.

The U.S. military proscribed any GI fraternization beyond answering questions deemed appropriate from prisoners and providing instructions, directives, or orders. These regulations made sense, especially given the significant number of POWs, either stridently Nazi or nationalistic, thrust among other prisoners who, whether German by nationality or simply by uniform, viewed their allegiance more loosely. The heavy influx of prisoners thrown into a country ill prepared to handle large numbers and segregate prisoners based upon ideological viewpoint and likely behavior while in captivity resulted in Germans being separated at first only by official rank. Most of the American guards, untrained in espionage, incarceration practices, and psychological profiling, couldn't tell an ardent Nazi likely to instill his own brand of martial law among his fellow campmates from a poor draftee either "afraid of his own shadow" or secretly nursing a vendetta against the Nazi regime.

Marvin Wildes, a medic at McClellan during the war, agreed with this assessment: "We were always told not to fool with the POWs, so I never got to know any of them personally."[6]

Fraternization included any form of chumminess between captive and captor, whether socializing (eating, drinking, flirting, dancing, dating, exchanging perceived or actual favors and gifts) or passing POW messages or any other form of communication in or out of camp. This prohibition also included the same activity between German POWs and American civilians.

But the rules were frequently breached in POW camps. As Arnold Krammer wrote, "[R]eminiscences of former guards and prisoners often touch upon the warm relationships … which formed between them. Most were based on the mutual disenchantment of people who did not wish to be where they were at that moment: far from civilian life, far from combat, or far from home. Sometimes, it was simply the respect of one good soldier for another."[7]

McClellan was one of the friendlier camps.

At first a member of the camp's military police staff, Jack Shay transferred to the 1437th SCU military police mess hall in the American military camp and then to the officers' mess hall. In those capacities, he oversaw numerous POW work details: "We got to know many PWs on work details or KP [kitchen police] duty. One of the main rules in the POW camp, any POW camp, was not to get too chummy. They called it fraternization. But after a while, you could get a feeling for each guy, if they were on the up-and-up or not. You gauged what their game was, if they were regular Joes or not. If they were okay, you could talk to 'em. You wouldn't say anything confidential, no military secrets. But you could treat 'em decent. Even kid around with some of the nicer ones."

His wife remembered some of her husband's hijinks:

> Dad [author's father] was a great kidder. Always saying something funny. You'd never know it from his pictures because he never smiled for the camera, but he was always saying something funny to the PWs. And half the time, they didn't get it.
>
> This one time when the PWs were leaving [their work detail in the American military camp], they were saying "auf Wiedersehen" to one another and to the GIs. So Dad waved to them and said, "I'll be the same." And they were all smiles. "Oh, Jack's sprechen sie Deutsch!" [Jack's speaking German!] they said. Dad just laughed.
>
> We called the prisoners "PWs," not "POWs." Everybody did. And if one of them was complaining or just feeling down in the dumps, Dad would say, "Too long PW!" to them. They got

to where they'd say it themselves, if they were feeling lonely or unhappy or what have you. "Too long PW!"

They also taught us some naughty words in German. Not on purpose. But they'd swear on occasion, and we kind of knew what the word meant just from the way they said it.

The PWs had their own music, their German songs. "Lili Marleen," "O Du Lieber Augustin," "Ein Prosit," and "Du, Du Liegst Mir im Herzen," and some of their marches. But they got to where they'd like American music just as much. They'd be singing our swing music or Dixieland jazz numbers. Songs by Bing Crosby or the Andrews Sisters or Glenn Miller, Benny Goodman, the same numbers you'd hear in our own PXs or our NCO Club for dances. One of the popular songs was "Don't Fence Me In" [the Cole Porter song from 1944]. And Dad would always be comical and change the words around. He wasn't much of a singer, but he could carry a tune. And he'd start singing, "Oh, give me land, lots of land under starry skies above," and then he'd go, "Don't fox me in!" And the PWs would look at him like, "What did he say?" He'd do it with some of his army buddies, too. He'd change a word or phrase just to be comical.

The PWs were very good to me. Maybe because Dad was in charge of them. But I think they liked me, too. I would fuss over them. I didn't want to treat them like they were beneath us just because they were prisoners. Some of them were very nice, polite young men, very religious, and they'd tell us how they would attend church services.

I remember some of them asked me what my maiden name was and what country my ancestors came from. And when I told them, they'd say, "Your name means 'Little German.'" I think they felt comfortable around me.

I think a lot of them missed their wives or their sweethearts or even their mothers back home. And if anyone smiled at them or exchanged a simple pleasantry, maybe something like "I hope you can return to your family soon," well, I think it just made their day. And they'd take a shine to you.

When I would come to work each morning, they had fresh-squeezed orange juice waiting for me. Every day, they'd make sure I had fresh orange juice. And Dad didn't put them up to it. They just did it on their own. When I think about it now [the late 1960s], that was a nice thing for them to do.[8]

Rita (Johnson) Wells recalled interacting with several POWs during her months in the camp's headquarters building:

I remember Alfred Richardt and Günther Freytag, who worked in headquarters. They typed requisitions for supplies and were supervised by [Sergeant] Harry Klein. There was a small door that went into their area.

Alfred Richardt taught English classes in the compound at night. He filled in for the regular teacher. And he spoke English with a lisp. He would try to pronounce my name, and it always came out "Mith Jonthon."

They gave me a couple of [jewelry] boxes which were made by the PWs in their hobby shop.

Mrs. Wells came to know several prisoners and proved it when she opened a souvenir booklet distributed to POWs when they left the camp in 1946. She pointed to several photos showing unidentified prisoners. "This is possibly D. Pohl Johann, I believe [probably Johann Pohl].[9] And this picture, it says 'Course in American History,' that's Siegfried Zuber, and I think also Theo Kuhner, I think that was his name. And this is Waldemar Schopp in this picture of prisoners getting their certificates from an American history course."[10]

Many POWs eagerly shared their handiwork with GI guards or work detail leaders. Some also sought and received monetary reimbursement. POW Erhard Eifler wrote of one example of craftsmanship for sale: "My friend Oswald [Pauli] and I also made rings out of spoons. We bended the upper edge of the spoon and put a five cent coin on top and grinded

Staff Sergeant Harry Klein, Alfred Richardt, and Günther Freytag in a posed shot for the "COM-PLIMENTS OF HEADQUARTERS" booklet. Identifications by Rita (Johnson) Wells (author's collection).

and polished the coin. Then we sold those rings to Americans in the Camp. That was some extra money for us."[11]

In his autobiography, Christian Höschle wrote of his success in selling some of his work. As Joni Pontius translated:

He said, "I earned more money [in addition to his daily allowance] through my pictures. I was able to buy my wedding rings in the canteen [with this money]."

He refers to the Americans as "Amis." It's a shortened version of "Americans." It's slang, but not pejorative.

He writes about an artistic exhibit in the camp. And he says the Americans realized that they could buy artistic things—paintings, children's toys, small furniture. Most of the items were sold, and, at the end of the exhibit, toys were given to disadvantaged children. He says the painters did the best business. He sold most of his stuff and gave away the rest.

Toward the end of his time at McClellan in mid–1945, he said, "A friendly captain by the name of Dougal came into my artist's barracks. I was busy on a portrait as he watched me a few times, and he asked if I would like to paint his seven- and 12-year-old daughters. And I agreed because the man was nice. He further opined that I should pack up my painting things, and he would pick me up in an hour in an auto. That happened, and we drove into the nearby American camp. Captain Dougal led me into a small troop room that was not used at the time. Here I should erect my atelier. And he thought tomorrow he would bring his daughters. He prepared a pass for me with which I could pass unhindered through the gate. It was soon clear to me why I had to have my atelier outside the POW camp because the camp was strictly forbidden [off limits] to children with no exception. Captain Dougal solved the problem in this manner. The next morning he appeared with his wife and his daughters around 9 in my new atelier. The seven-year-old was called Keela, and the older was Bobbie. Both wrote to me for a long time after the war. Most of the time the mother accompanied the girls and sat in the corner.

"I could have tried to escape because there was no fence, but I didn't think about that. It was going well for me, and where was I supposed to go? The few comrades who fled were generally caught again after a short time."

He mentioned that Hubert Maiburg joined him in the atelier outside the camp. For their work, they got cookies, tobacco, cigarettes, toilet articles, and art supplies. And they [U.S. guards] weren't searching people at the gate anymore, and he could once again bring these rare goods with him to his needy comrades.

Earlier in his narrative, he wrote, "There were always two guards at the main gate [of the camp], bored and superfluous. Why should we go anywhere when we had it so good here?"[12]

Other prisoners gave their paintings or handmade craft or woodwork items to GIs they liked or who may have treated them kindly. In a 1979 issue of *The Anniston Star*, Laura Ann Freeman recorded the memories of Ewing Steele, a civilian who managed the Officers' Club on the main post. "Mrs. Steele also has a painting, done on heavy paper with home-made paints, signed by a POW named Paul Weingarth," she wrote. "The painting is a copy of a work by 17th century Flemish artist Peter Rubens."[13]

Alabamian Bill Brownell recounted a happy incident tangentially involving his sister's first birthday: "My father, William, was stationed at the Ft during WWII and my mother, Nora, worked there during that time as well. My sister was born in Anniston and celebrated her 1st birthday at the fort and ate cake made by the prisoners of war that were there at the time."[14]

An experienced woodcrafter and furniture maker from nearby Jacksonville, Ferrol Aderholdt worked as a foreman in the post quartermaster shops from October 1942 until the end of June 1947. During the POW camp's existence, he supervised anywhere from six to eight prisoners on a daily basis, and he came to know even more on a personal level. Among the souvenirs now in his son's possession are a photograph of POW Peter Schmitt and a chocolate tin embossed with Germanic heraldry and insignias.

Aderholdt kept in contact with several POWs after their repatriation. As his son, Meredith, remembered, "He kind of made friends with some of them. Some of them were nice, friendly people. He corresponded with some of them after the war. When the blockade [prohibiting access to Soviet-controlled East Germany] happened, one of 'em was on the east side, and that killed that [prevented further correspondence]. Another person [POW] was killed in Italy on a motorcycle after the war. But my dad corresponded as long as he could."[15]

POW Karl V. Hövener became very friendly with James Byron Wester Sr., a civilian contract employee who supervised McClellan painting projects. Hövener gave Wester several oil paintings and charcoal sketches.

James' daughter, Dean (Wester) Bonner, spoke of the camaraderie between captor and captive. "I know my daddy was very good to the prisoners. Our family has all these paintings," she said, pointing to several works spread out over the table in her Anniston house, as well as a photograph of the POW artist. The photograph shows a bathing suit–clad man and woman thigh-deep in water in a forest setting, presumably somewhere in prewar Germany. An inscription on the reverse of the photo reads, "this is a long time ago 1935 Karl & Nita Hovener." Of Hövener, Mrs. Bonner said, "Daddy met him just as one of the prisoners for him in his paint shop."

Her husband, James Bonner, identified the paintings. One rests in a plain frame and shows a man cheek-to-cheek with a small toddler. "That's Dean's father and her younger brother, Billie. It was done from a photograph [that depicts the father holding the youngster]. It's either a pencil sketch or charcoal. And it's done on a brown paper bag. Might be all he had to work with at the time." The artist's name is clearly visible in the bottom right portion of the sketch, below the child.

"He also did this painting of Dean," James added. A full-color painting on a canvas 15½ inches wide by 18½ inches long, it reposes in a frame and bears the inscription "Hövener Alabama 1945" in the bottom right corner. The artist modeled it after a black-and-white portrait of little Dean taken by the Ables Studio. "He just finished this one," James said, "and it was wet. From what I understand, that was the last one he finished here.

"And after the war, he mailed some more sketches of kittens and roosters in a canister about 15 inches long from his home on Wilhelmsburger Strasse, Hamburg." One full-color work, 8 inches wide by 12 inches long, depicts a mother cat and her three kittens eyeing with great interest a spider spinning down from a strand of webbing before them. His signature, following the established pattern, occupies the lower right corner.

"He did a painting of roosters," James continued. "And there's an oil painting of a lady on a park bench, about 20 inches by 30 inches. One of her [Dean's] cousins has it. We're thinking there were some more charcoal sketches that he gave my father-in-law, too. We don't have them right now. And he [Hövener] told us [James Byron Wester Sr.] how we should take care of 'em."

Both James and Dean Bonner recalled what they had heard regard-

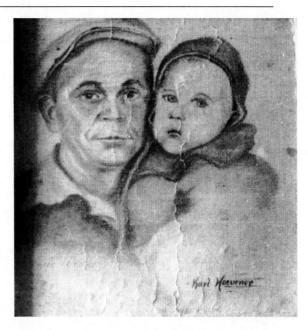

Karl Hövener's sketch of his civilian supervisor, James Byron Wester Sr., and the latter's son (courtesy of James and Dean Bonner).

Little Dean (Wester) Bonner as drawn by Hövener, his last work as a McClellan POW (courtesy of James and Dean Bonner).

ing the relationship between prisoners and neighborhood civilians. "My older sister, Jenny Lee Wester, said they used to take the German prisoners to Georgia sometimes to do work," Dean explained. "Every time the prisoners were going out to Cedartown, the people would go out and wave at them. They were taken out to Cedartown by truck. My mom and dad lived on a hill on the side of the road, and Jenny Lee used to stand outside and wave and holler at the prisoners. This was when the prisoners were in Piedmont [Alabama] on the highway going toward Cedartown, that they [her family] would go out and wave. And this one time there was this man [Arthur Coogler] who lived in the area, and he found this wadded-up paper after they [POWs] came by in a truck. And he gave it to Jenny Lee. And he said, 'This must be for you.' And it said, 'Thank you for being kind to us & treating us like we're normal people.' Some prisoner was thanking us for speaking to them and being friendly with them, even if they were German prisoners. Well, Daddy always told me to treat everyone the same. 'There's no big I's and little You's,' he used to say. My parents said to be good people and to teach us kids to be good to everyone."

James Wester returned to self-employment after the cessation of hostilities. "He was more or less a supervisor over the prisoners who went around the fort and did the painting," James Bonner added. "But after the war, they no longer had a job for him at the fort. So they offered him a job at Pelham Range, but he said no and went into business for himself. We don't know how long he communicated with Karl Hövener or if he wrote to any of the other prisoners. But I guess he treasured these paintings and sketches and handed 'em down to his family."[16]

Janice Erfle, whose father (Master Sergeant John J. George) served among the permanent cadre in the POW camp and who contributed several columns on the American military camp to *The McClellan CYCLE*, recalled a few mementos from the war: "I remember seeing my picture in the newspaper [*CYCLE*] for being the first baby born at ... Fort McClellan in 1946. Other than that, Marlene [her sister] has a [oil] portrait of my Mom [Loretta, who married then–Staff Sergeant John George on November 14, 1944, in Sacred Heart Church in Anniston] that a German painted. I remember that we had a radio that a German had made."[17]

Thom Cole, an Anniston military historian and collector, recalled conversations with a woman who, as a young girl, enjoyed a special relationship with one prisoner in particular: "I worked with a woman in G. F. Wilson, a catalog showroom, a Wal-mart kind of store, in the late 1970s and early '80s. I mentioned to her I was interested in history in general and particularly military history and the history of POWs. And she told me where she lived. And she told me that, as a little girl, the prisoners would be coming down to her father's farm on work details. And she remembered she would be sitting on her father's fence, and they would be coming over to work. And this one prisoner would just pet her hair. This one guy would always come up to her and would give her an apple. She was little at the time. He may have had a little girl like her, and she may have reminded him of her. It was innocent, but she remembered it vividly. And I know she told me that he came over to her and petted her hair more than just one time. He took a liking to her. And they couldn't talk to each other in German or English, so this was the only way he could communicate with her."[18]

Mary Jo Berardone, the daughter of Sergeant Joseph Spinelli and his wife, Mary (nicknamed Mim), was just a baby when her mother brought her to McClellan so they could live together as a family.

Mary "Mim" Spinelli (right) in a jeep while volunteering for the Red Cross at the POW camp. The diamond-shaped design painted on the jeep's side signified the Army Service Forces Fourth Service Command, headquartered in Atlanta, Georgia. It was omnipresent at McClellan (courtesy of Mary Jo Berardone).

After I was born in Pennsylvania, my mother would go to Alabama and then come back with me every six or seven weeks by train. It was always back and forth.

When we were all down in Alabama, she became a volunteer for the Red Cross and got involved with putting on dances and social events.

My dad had a lot of woodworking details with the prisoners. They were learning a trade from him because he had always been in construction before the war. He built a chicken coop for his mom and dad when he was little.

My dad used to hand me to these prisoners, and they just wanted to hold me because they were so lonesome. He would go to where the prisoners were [working a detail outside the POW camp], and that's where they would hold me. I guess he trusted them enough to do this. And they would hold me and then they would cry and cry when my dad had to take me back. They were human. They had families. They missed their kids. And he'd say, "Don't worry. I'll bring her back." And when my mom took me to Pennsylvania for a visit back home, my dad would say, "Mim, as soon as you bring her back, I'm taking her, and we're going over to the prisoners!" I was too young to remember this, but they told me about this later.

Years later, he would tell people, "My daughter was the hit of the POW camp." And I used to say, "Sure, because you'd let everyone hold me."[19]

Her uncle, Patrick D. Spinelli, Joe Spinelli's youngest brother, who served in the Korean War, also remembered the popularity of the cute little girl among the POWs. "He [Joe] worked with German prisoners that were interested in woodworking," he recalled. "Building things to occupy their time. They built a crib for Mary Jo." That crib is still in Mary Jo Berardone's possession, tucked securely away among her mementos.

Patrick Spinelli recounted a remarkable episode involving his brother and an unnamed POW:

> One incident that I remember Joe telling us was when they were working on a project and needed a part they didn't have. A German prisoner told Joe they have it at a hardware store downtown. Joe was puzzled that he knew that. The prisoner asked for some money and he was gone. He returned later with the part, and Joe asked him how long has he been leaving the Camp and why didn't he escape? The prisoner said he had no intentions of escaping as he was treated well by the Americans.[20]

Mary Jo Berardone also remembered her father telling this story during his retirement years. "Here are prisoners that could have walked away, but they didn't want to. They were treated very well. And they certainly got around because they knew where things were in Anniston."[21]

Staff Sergeant Jack Shay received at least eight items from thankful prisoners: a colored pencil sketch of a scene in one of the compounds drawn by Karl Steinmetz on construction paper; an oil paint-

Baby Mary Jo Spinelli, the "hit of the POW camp," whose smile and cuddlesome nature made teary-eyed POWs yearn for home (courtesy of Mary Jo Berardone).

ing of a German outdoorsman clearing a steep mountainous pasture with a scythe, signed by an artist named Baumann; two wooden jewelry boxes, one personally monogrammed; a pair of intricately carved log cabins, each with a sliding mechanism in its hidden core that, when activated, produced a cigarette in a narrow trough on top of the roof; a desk lamp fashioned from a cylindrical artillery shell; and, most impressive, a cabinet standing 28 inches high and measuring 29 inches on its front and 17 inches on its sides, complete with two drawers, an open storage space, and twin hinged doors on the bottom.

"The PWs made some nice woodcraft items that they gave the GIs," he remembered. "And paintings and sketches, whatever they had to work with. Some of the GIs had the PWs make things for them, and they'd pay them. The German prisoners were very good about giving me things for free. They'd knock themselves out to please me. 'One hand washes the other.' If you're nice to people, they're gonna be nice to you."

One item among Sergeant Shay's POW souvenirs, surreptitiously discovered in 1965 by his curious son, was a finely detailed miniature wooden outhouse with German insignia and symbols on its front doors. The doors swung open when a latch was lifted to reveal a wooden figure looking like Adolf Hitler, complete with Charlie Chaplin mustache, as well as a hinged stick sculpted to resemble a private portion of the Führer's anatomy (which, when pulled out, came to attention at a 90° angle to the upright body). The embarrassed son never had the nerve to question either parent about this item's provenance. Nor did his parents ever tell him about it. When he routinely inspected the contents of the house upon his widowed mother's passing, he found no trace of that particular souvenir among his parents' other POW mementos. And he could only belatedly surmise that the carving had proven inappropriate for his parents to retain—and, furthermore, that some POW, whoever he may have been, had a decidedly offbeat sense of humor.

Staff Sergeant Dan Coberly recounted an unusual episode involving fraternization in his 1980 "Stalag U.S.A." newspaper series. Walter Mohr, a German civilian, was aboard a German Merchant Marine charter ship when America entered the war. Ironically, it held more than a thousand American passengers at the time. But the onslaught of hostilities ended its charter service. As Mohr recalled, "We had some 1200 American passengers which we left at Havana [Cuba] and headed for the nearest neutral port. When we got to Vera Cruz, Mexico, we painted the ship and outfitted her for war."

But in coastal waters near Florida, Allied ships intercepted the German ship and captured its 900-man crew. Walter Mohr became a detainee, "sort of a civilian POW." After being paroled by the federal government, he assumed a number of civilian jobs in America before deciding he wanted to join the U.S. Army:

> You should have seen their [the Americans'] faces. An enemy alien wanting to join their Army! Well, they finally got over it and sent me to Ft. McClellan. I ended up as a guard/interpreter for the POW Camp.
> For a long time, the prisoners didn't know I was German. They must have thought I spoke real good German. It was uncomfortable to me. Some of them came from places near where I was born and raised. I didn't dare ask them about home.
> One time I got bit by a water moccasin and was out for 3 days. When I woke up, there they were. I must have said something, for they finally realized I was German.[22]

A brief memoir written by James "Jimmy" Hamilton averred that, on at least a few occasions involving one POW, meals were shared on private property. As he wrote:

> During WWII my dad worked at Ft. McClellan.... My dad became close friends with many of the POWs. One POW had a hobby of carving small animals from pieces of cedar wood. He would send these animals to my Mother and Grandmother. My first cousin ... Buford Rowell [sp?], was a Sargeant [sic] ... stationed at Ft McClellan. He was assigned to guard the German POWs. Buford and my dad saw each other just about daily.... Buford ate Sunday dinner at our house about twice a month. I remember on more than one occasion Buford would bring a German POW to our home for Sunday dinner, I imagine the same POW who carved the cedar animals. I remember the man could speak English pretty good and would sit on our front porch and enjoyed watching the children running and playing. Buford would be driving an army colored sedan and after two or three hours Buford and the man would leave in the car going back to Ft. McClellan.[23]

This would likely not have been sanctioned for too many POWs, if at all. However, security grew increasingly lax in the camp following the end of the war in Europe, and it is possible that such informal "furloughs" might have been quietly granted—or simply taken without fear of serious reprisal.

Another, more subtle interaction also took place, although it was generally invisible and certainly unannounced to the rank-and-file soldiers on both sides of the barbed wire. Toward the fall of 1944 and continuing beyond the end of the war in Europe, a secret yet vigorous policy to democratize the German POWs occurred in most camps. It resulted from the growing attempt to de-Nazify the more malleable prisoners, or at least open their eyes to the principles of democracy prior to their repatriation. Anticipating the end of the conflict in Europe, America hoped to release former prisoners who would extol the virtues of democracy and help in transitioning fascist Germany to a political ally in postwar global relations.

Adjusting the views of a captured people while interned in a foreign country flew in the face of the Geneva Convention and also ran the risk, if it became known, of German authorities attempting to brainwash American POWs into embracing Nazism in their own camps. Accordingly, the program began with top secrecy, and no one beyond the immediate sphere of involvement knew about it. It manifested itself in a greater integration of republicanism within the educational classes offered POWs, as well as an enhanced inspection of the content of newly arriving German-language books intended for camp libraries. Some astute individuals, both POWs and GIs, might have surmised what was going on, though none of the people interviewed for this work professed to know any particulars.

But for most of the people on either side of McClellan's camp, their interactions proved friendly, harmless, and apolitical.

15

Vendettas Among the Victuals

"We are near starvation,
cant you be so kindly
and send us some good to eat."

A notable exception to the humane treatment accorded POWs at McClellan occurred in the spring of 1945. It also played out in a number of other camps across the nation.

When America began learning of Nazi atrocities in the dozens of concentration camps being liberated throughout Europe, as well as the lesser but still substantial sufferings of American POWs during their incarceration in Axis POW camps, the attitude toward German prisoners changed somewhat. It started around the close of the war and continued after hostilities had officially ended, threatening to mar the final memories of life in McClellan for many POWs. As Staff Sergeant Jack Shay explained in the 1960s:

> We treated the PWs very good on the whole. But when the war in Europe was winding down and when it was over, our boys would come back home with stories about the liberation of their PW camps and how they often got scraps to eat. Just potatoes. Or a piece of stale bread and water. A raw cabbage core. Soup that was just water, and they'd run a cabbage leaf or a potato skin through it to give it a little flavor. Coffee so weak it didn't even taste like coffee. And our boys didn't get the rations that the Red Cross sent. They got diverted along the way, or else they just stood in some warehouse in their original cartons and boxes and weren't given to the GIs.
>
> One of our boys [Sergeant Paul Nola Jr.] who was captured during the Battle of the Bulge and was put in a German prisoner of war camp there came back to McClellan when he was liberated. He became a mess sergeant in our PW camp before he was discharged. He worked with me. And he told us horror stories about the poor food our boys got.
>
> We had guys who weighed 150 or 175 [pounds] when they were captured, and they'd come back barely 100 or 120.
>
> These boys would look at how we treated our PWs here. We gave 'em just as good as our own boys. Same portions. Even some of their own German dishes, stews, pork schnitzels, sauerkraut. And they [GIs] would say, "Why are we feeding them so well when our boys go hungry?"
>
> It got worse when we saw films of the concentration camps. All those civilians, innocent people, without any clothes on, just like skeletons, piled up, one on top of another, waiting to be buried. It was hard to watch. And those pictures of survivors. Sad eyes. Bones showing under the skin. And then you looked at our German PWs—all smiles, joking around, eating well, playing ball—it made our boys angry.[1]

In *Nazi Prisoners of War in America*, Arnold Krammer validated those sentiments: "At most such showings [of atrocity films], the American guards were far more impressed by the films than the prisoners, often taking out their hostility on their charges."[2]

In a 1987 interview at his home in Solingen, West Germany, former POW Robert Suberg candidly spoke of a perceptible shift in treatment: "Not all of them [GI guards] were nice. Jack [Shay] was good. He looked at us like we were human beings. But not all of them were like that. We were not Nazis. We had nothing to do with Hitler. We had no part in concentration camps. It was a shame to look at those pictures [of concentration camp victims]. We did not have responsibility for that, those crimes. But we got the blame. When we left Alabama and went to England, it got worse. They treated us like criminals. Not nice. Mean."[3]

In his master's thesis, "Guests Behind Barbed Wire: German Prisoner of War Camps in Alabama during World War Two," John Daniel Hutchinson wrote of a violent episode in one prisoner's life: "Fort McClellan POW Alfred Arens described physical abuse by an American guard in his final days in Alabama. Although Arens remembers his time in Alabama as an overall positive experience, he did not forget the abusive guard. Fifty years later, Arens notes, 'If I could find that individual I would make a special trip … in order [to] give him his kick back.'"[4] And in a 1991 reminiscence, Arens himself wrote (original typescript intact):

> When the war in Europe came to an end, in springtime 1945, *the life got worse in the camp.* One night trucks drove to our canteens and took away the finer objekts which are able to make the life livingworth, chocolate, beer and so on. And we had to suffer a little bit hunger as well. That throws a shadow on the former US-PW-politics beeing suspicious of having treatened the PW correctly as long only as they had to fear retaliation on American PW's in Germany.[5]

Christian Höschle was even more specific in his 1992 autobiography. As Joni Pontius translated,

> "On May 10, 1945 [two days after V-E Day had ended the war], trucks came into our camp with personnel and outfitted with machine guns," he wrote. "And they emptied our kitchen and our canteen. Following the orders of Truman, the new U.S. President, the German prisoners have to suffer and go hungry exactly like their comrades in Germany." And after that, they only had bread and water for four weeks, he said. "The bread was distributed in the morning in the barracks, about 300–400 grams [about 10½–14 ounces] for each man, and thus for four weeks. For the comrades who worked outside the camp, it was strictly forbidden to bring food into the camp. They were thoroughly searched at the gate. In the first days, all prisoners had to stand from morning until evening in the soccer field. It was forbidden to sit on the ground. Security personnel were doubled, and they patrolled with machine guns along the fences."
>
> "We guessed that these measures were taken because the Americans feared a mutiny or an uprising as a reaction to [Germany] losing the war or it may have been a revenge action that Truman ordered. We never knew. It was probably both."
>
> And he continues, "Because of the Geneva Convention of 1929, sergeants couldn't be forced to work. And this international convention was now broken, and sergeants were now forced to work. The delegation of the International Red Cross from Switzerland was no longer seen. The Americans knew full well that they had broken this agreement. Reduced nutrition, forced work for the sergeants, and such chicanery. The Swiss would have certainly protested, but they couldn't have forced entry into the camps. Where there is power, there is right."
>
> "These punishing measures ended after four weeks. The mess hall was again opened, but the provisions were reduced in quality and quantity by 50%. The canteen remained closed. Cigarettes were available in reduced quantity. There was no more beer."
>
> He also wrote that in June, they hadn't gotten mail for a long time, and they hadn't been allowed to write for a long time. "Was it because of the confusion during the end of the war or a jab at the Geneva Convention? We don't know."[6]

Interpreting material contained in the camp newspaper his father edited, Joachim Metzner concurred:

In mid–April and early May, a lot changed in the camp—the gates between the 3 compounds were closed and sports and entertainment were affected.

The USA was obviously sure about the end of the war and tried to change ... the camps during this period ... everyone should work now. In early May the German Camp Spokesman [Willi Utz] was replaced and sent to Aliceville (taken from [issue] # 70).

In issue 72 ... the gates are open again but the rations were cut and no cigarettes and no drinks anymore in the canteen.[7]

Most of the vendettas toward the POWs took the form of reduced rations. It made sense to a nation still in the midst of diverting its essential food supplies to the front lines. The need in the combat zones dictated the policy. And the exposure of Nazi atrocities challenged the forgiving nature of horrified Americans.

"The abrupt shift in attitudes in response to the Holocaust is understandable because evidence of Germany's horrific crimes continues to shock contemporary generations," Hutchinson wrote. "The reduction of food and privileges also seemed the product of victor's justice.... The shift in treatment left a black mark in the memory of many prisoners."[8]

During the early spring of 1945, the War Department began reducing the rations of all POWs while still maintaining caloric fidelity to existing norms. In *Nazi Prisoners of War in America*, Krammer discussed how War Department edicts generally affected food reduction in camps across the nation:

> [R]ations were immediately cut to a maximum of four ounces of meat per man per day, and items which were in short supply such as fats, canned fruits and vegetables, jams, and sugar were substantially reduced. Camp commanders were instructed to implement the following....
>
> a. Meat from swine will be limited to feet, hearts, livers, kidneys, tails, neck bones ... and oily pork not acceptable ... for Army feeding.
>
> b. Meat from veal will be limited to utility grade carcasses....
>
> c. Meat from beef will be limited to shanks, flanks, skirts, livers, hearts, kidneys, ox tails, tripe, brains, and green bones....[9]

Still not bad, considering the malnourishment exhibited in returning American POWs freshly liberated from their incarceration. But the German prisoners did not see it that way, and a diminution in any benefit or accustomed pattern of existence is always viewed as a loss by those affected.

Gefreiter (PFC) Helmut Engelke of Company 7, long detailed to Staff Sergeant Shay, tore a 3½" by 4½" sheet of lined foolscap from a notepad and took pencil in hand to write the following note (original syntax intact):

Dear Jack.!

A happy Sunday wishing you and your wife
Aŭwi and Helmŭt
We are still in the compound, and I guess, that we won't be transferred befor next week. We are near starvation, cant you be so kindly and send us some good to eat, the boy who give you this slip lives on the same barracks with us. Please, see what you can do for us.

turn [sheet] over.

May be if you go with your K.P. till the gate and I think this boy get it through the gate. I hope you are very well and thanks a lot

your former K. P. Aŭwi & Helmut
My kindly regards to your dear Wife

bell bottom troŭsers.[10]

He then folded the sheet twice and entrusted it to the messenger.

This undated incident occurred after V-E Day, when all the American prisoners of war had been liberated and returned to homes or hospitals for recovery, and America no longer feared retribution for the way it treated German POWs. The way this note was delivered may have been an anomaly, and it is not known if other notes like this one passed through McClellan's lines. But conditions had certainly changed from the way they had been at the beginning of 1945.

Fond of bestowing nicknames on those he liked, Sergeant Shay had given Gefreiter Engelke the moniker "Bell-Bottom Trousers" for some reason now lost amid the passing swirl of time, but probably rooted in a 1944 song of the same name, a bouncy melody made popular in a hit recording by the Jesters.

The sergeant kept the scrap of paper with his McClellan mementos, including other postwar letters from that same former prisoner. Years later, in the 1960s, he explained to his son, "We were good to the PWs who worked KP in the mess hall. They were good workers. But things got a little dicey after the war ended. And there was some resentment. I can't vouch for all our GIs. None of the guys I knew ever mistreated them. But I didn't have eyes in the back of my head. You get a bunch of men together, you're always gonna have a couple hotheads."

Several past and present Annistonians have clung to their unwavering belief that nothing out of sorts ever happened at the camp. During

The note, begging for food, from Helmut Engelke and secretly passed to Sergeant Jack Shay (author's collection).

interviews conducted for this book, one person who knew Sergeant Shay said, "I think that note your father had was not from McClellan. It was given to him from someone in another camp." Another erudite person, descended from a former postwar official at Fort McClellan and understandably proud of that lineage, looked the author forthrightly in the eye and proclaimed, "I can't believe we ever starved our prisoners of war or did anything like that. That would never happen at Fort McClellan. I'm sure it never happened. Don't put that in your book. Write a novel."[11]

16

Signal Moments at McClellan

*"The saddest day was when we got word
of President Roosevelt's death."*

Though most of the day-in and day-out activities on either side of Baker Road proceeded with monotonous regularity, a few events precipitated widespread rejoicing, happiness, uncertainty, or sadness.

The camp inspections and exhibits open to select visitors always occasioned redoubled efforts by POW personnel to tidy up their barracks and shared buildings. Art exhibits, particularly those occurring around Christmas 1943 and 1944, gave the POWs a sense of normality and pride, allowing them to showcase extracurricular talents. As the January 7, 1945, edition of *P.o.W. Oase* proclaimed:

Christmas 1943! Our art exhibit has opened the doors of the camp residents and showed them for the first time the work of our artists and craftsmen in their leisure time....

Christmas 1944! A year has gone by, and many of our artists and craftsmen had to put aside the brushes and knives, pencils and files, and so forth and take up the axe and the saw, the shovel and the pitchfork and work on peanut fields and cotton plantations, in forests and garages, kitchens and bakeries. Hundreds of comrades have gone away from us forever to work elsewhere and with them has gone a good deal of our arts and crafts activity....

And now, the second art exhibit of our camp gives us another opportunity [to appreciate new artwork].... But it would be a mistake to consider this exhibit a competition with the first one. The exhibits should be a reflection of the work of our artistic comrades, a harmony that an artist's hand can form from inanimate material like paper, wood, paint, graphite, and metal.[1]

The exhibits featured some of the work of Herbert Belau, Hermann Haugg, Christian Höschle, Franz Huber, Hubert Maiburg, Albin Sagadin, and Paul Weingarth, among others of varying skill and experience. Höschle wrote of one such exhibit in his autobiography:

Eight days before Christmas, there was an exhibition. There were signs in English, and everyone was invited. The camp orchestra was present, the American commander gave a talk, and many U.S. citizens from the region came with their families. And he wrote, "So we got to see now and then a pretty face, but we had to be content with just looking. So we stole [cheated] with our eyes."

And for Christmas 1943, they met in a mess hall and had a fir tree with lit candles. In Germany, Christmas Eve is more important than Christmas. The company leader gave a talk. And they sang Christmas songs. And the Christmas Eve holiday meal left nothing to be desired. They also had little plays and skits in order to be distracted from not being home. Some people read poems. And he said, "On this evening, I felt how happy I was to not yet be married. I noticed how many fathers had tears in their eyes. And their thoughts were certainly more of their loved ones at home than that which was happening around them." They also thought about their fallen comrades. And especially about their fellow prisoners who were in Russian hands who would certainly not have been able to celebrate.[2]

One of the camp's most significant events occurred on April 13 and 14, 1944. As *The McClellan CYCLE* reported on April 14:

An official War Department party from the office of the Undersecretary of War, including representatives of the Army Air Forces, the Army Service Forces, and Army Ground Forces, the Bureau of Public Relations and the Office of War Information, toured the Ft. McClellan Prisoner of War camp last night and this morning.

In the party were 40 newspaper reporters, radio men, newsreel photographers and magazine writers.

Top newspapermen from the staffs of The New York Times, The New York Herald Tribune, The Christian Science Monitor, The Chicago Daily News and 14 other newspapers as well as representatives of the three wire services were included. Photographers from MGM, Paramount, Pathe, Fox, Universal and The March of Time, were in the party.

Maj. Gen. Frederick Uhl, commanding general of the Fourth Service Command, and Brig. Gen. Sidney Erickson, of his office, joined the party from Birmingham.[3]

A subsequent story in the May 1 *P.o.W. Oase* took pride in the way the camp shined when the media had visited. As Chania Stymacks translated, "Fifty representatives of the leading press organs inspected the camp. And they declared that McClellan was the best of the camps they had seen. They said it was among the best five camps in the country."[4]

On the other end of the emotional spectrum, the POWs experienced loneliness when the camp population dropped. From its inception, McClellan supplied other regional, smaller satellite camps with personnel, rarely maintaining its full capacity of 3,000. The May 18 *P.o.W. Oase* addressed this issue on its front page. "It says that there is a long column of trucks ready to take troops to a new work environment," Stymacks continued. "It's expected to last a number of months. But from Washington has come word that the length of the stay is not limited. Camps Bainbridge, Mackall, Moultrie, and Sibert have become developed as independent camps, no longer satellite camps, no longer belonging to the base camp of McClellan. And Blanding and Winter Haven had already been developed as permanent camps. So only those comrades now in Evergreen should be coming back to McClellan. Because of that, the occupancy of the camp has gone down to about 1,300. It has become empty at McClellan, and this has torn apart friendships that have been built over so many months."[5]

P.o.W. Oase always recorded the pulse of the camp. As translator Klaus W. Duncan wrote:

During the week of May 1, 1944, (May 1st holiday for Germans) the POWs celebrated their holiday. The Red Cross brought the following items to the camp: Christmas packages from German families by way of the Argentine Red Cross, 2,000 tubes of toothpaste, 1,000 Get-Well Foot Cremes, 800 candle holders, 725 games of all sorts, 350 playing cards, 1,540 packages of tobacco, 114,000 packages of cigarettes, 325 records, 300 tubes of lemon Toothpaste, 1,000 containers of Nivea Crème, 1,800 candles, 430 Fat Crème, 250 Tubes of body powder, 104 Christmas trees, 480 packages of pumpernickel, 6 record players.[6]

And as Chania Stymacks said, after translating issue 32, "You see, it's not dated. But it says 'Pfingsten 1944.' That means Pentecost or Whitsunday. It would have been late May of 1944. Pentecost is a holiday in Germany. It would compare to what we in America would know as vacation downtime in the summer or the dog days of summer when not much is going on and many normal activities are suspended. In my part of the country, Pentecost is not so much a religious holy day as a national holiday. Even if it's religious in nature, they [Germans] would go to church in the morning and then have dancing in the afternoon. I don't think they had dancing in the prisoners' camp, but it would have been a day to celebrate."

Issue 32 also carried news of another noteworthy event. According to Stymacks:

It's on page five, and it's a special official camp announcement by the Swiss envoy. Its concern was with more freedom of movement and how far the Germans could go to ease their fate as prisoners, meaning to ease the restrictions of being captured. They had to give their word of honor. And it says, we quote the words of the commander that, for certain times, they would be allowed movement outside of the camp. But they must promise not to use this time to escape. These would be limited opportunities, and it was their obligation to obey these time limits. They were to promise not to flee during a walk outside the camp and to not undertake anything that would help them or other POWs to take flight. They were obligated to return to camp and not to exceed [exit] the area that they were allowed to walk around in. They were not to enter into any military activities, not to engage in any actions against the state that holds them. That would mean the United States. They were to declare this. It was the duty of every German POW to follow these directions to the letter.

And they were informed that because they were members of the German Afrika Korps they had a right to an African bonus. And the Swiss envoy showed them the form that would allow them in the future to request the African bonus.

That would have pleased them, whether or not they ever received anything.[7]

But other news events rocked operations, puncturing the camp's comfort aura and leaving pockets of speculation and gossip in their wake.

Around the Ides of March in 1945, a fire in the kitchen of the 8th Company shook up the entire camp. The March 20 *P.o.W. Oase* recorded the details: "In the night towards March 16, the kitchen storeroom of Company 8 caught fire, and the fire department was needed to end the nighttime drama. Nearly the whole camp came running to watch the highly unusual fire. And around 40 men were needed to extinguish the fire."[8] Furthermore, as reported by Joachim Metzner, "it was that heavy, that the fire brigade had to be alarmed…. Nearly 40 men helped to extinguish [it] and a lot of men just gazed."[9]

News reports also came into the camp and created a conversational buzz. According to the journal of Paul Metzner, one such instance occurred in early October 1943. "'The whole camp is in an uproar,'" Joni Pontius translated. "'What we hear is that the Russians are winning the war.' To provide the proper context, the Germans feared losing to Russia more than to the western allies. So any news of victories in the Russian front would have been devastating to them." She went on to say, "He also got the distinction between those [prisoners] who were supporting the party line and those who were learning to think. For example, he writes about the reports in the United States newspapers reporting Italian victories [Allied victories in Italy] and how some of them [prisoners] said they were false. And the reports of Russian victories were really only temporary [German] withdrawals done only for better defense. Some of them [prisoners] said it's all lies, false conclusions of victory, propaganda. And Paul Metzner is writing about those who won't believe. He's calling them out."[10]

As former prisoner Robert Suberg explained in his 1987 and 1988 interviews,

At first we were hidden from everything. Very little news from home. Our mail was inspected and censored. We began to know what we could write and what we could not write. But then they allowed us to read some American newspapers and magazines.

Some of us, I know this, did not believe at first about the American battles [victories] over Germany. We doubted. But later, we knew what was the truth and what was not the truth.

Some of us did not believe that Germany would lose all these fights [battles]. But then you learn to accept truth and facts. If you don't, you live a life of make-believe.[11]

Höschle recalled in his autobiography how the news of political events shaped the camp's emotions. According to translator Joni Pontius:

They [POWs] had a high school teacher who had learned English, and he read the American newspapers to them. They learned about the beginning and collapse of the Eastern offensive in the Citadel and the Allied invasion of Sicily in 1943.

"We further learned of the criminal consequences of the Wannsee Conference of January 20, 1942, the so-called final solution of the Jewish question," he wrote. "We couldn't believe that Hitler committed the greatest crime to humanity in the name of the German people that has ever been committed. Many became afraid and asked themselves, if that is true and we lose the war, then God help us, and woe to the vanquished, and it will be many years until we see home again. A few obdurate Nazis that we had in our barracks became quieter. And because of that we gave free rein to our criticism of German leadership. And they tried to forbid American newspapers from our barracks, but they didn't succeed. The perceptive and logical were in the majority.

"From the newspapers and the radio we learned about the Normandy landing between Cherbourg and Caen on June 6, 1944.

"He who possesses logical thought must recognize that we are losing this war."

And Christian referred to giving up an insane idea of [national] totality which made them [German ruling elite] insatiable and created a state that is no longer moral, at best a regimented and controlled community.

He wrote that the landing in Normandy created great interest. On the one hand, he wished it were another Dieppe [a reference to an August 1942 Allied raid on Dieppe, France, repelled by the Wehrmacht]. But on the other hand, he despaired of the greatest armada in history [D-Day].[12]

The American camp had its own share of memorable moments.

"We always knew what was going on in the world," Marie Shay recounted. "When you worked in the camp headquarters, you'd be aware of things. They made announcements from time to time to the staff. Or you'd hear a rumor, and sooner or later someone would confirm or deny it. When I transferred from the camp headquarters to main post personnel, you'd hear the news even faster because you were at the nerve center. If something very important happened, you'd hear it as it was happening. We had no TVs then, but radios were everywhere. And, of course, you had your newspapers."

She said five events assumed monumental importance in the camp: D–Day (June 6, 1944); the death of Franklin D. Roosevelt (April 12, 1945); Hitler's death (April 30, 1945); V-E Day (May 8, 1945); and the news of the end of the war in Asia (August 14, 1945).

When we heard about the landing in Europe, we [female employees] were so grateful that our husbands were at the camp rather than in the front lines. We were happy that the war was getting closer to being over, but D–Day created a lot of Gold Star Mothers [women whose sons were killed]. I lost a cousin at Normandy [Sergeant Joseph Susedka, buried in the Normandy American Cemetery in Colleville-sur-Mer]. When we realized how many casualties there were, we were all thankful to have our husbands at Fort McClellan and out of harm's way.

But the saddest day was when we got word of President Roosevelt's death. It was a Thursday. He was the only president many of us had ever known. He was the only president I had ever voted for in my life. We used to listen to his fireside chats on the radio. And when he would address the nation and talk about the war, we would look at our map of the world and see the places he was talking about. We had our wartime maps with us in the camp. And we had a stiff cardboard with flat sides [two pieces, creased and notched, imprinted with part of the world on each side] that interlocked to form kind of a globe. We kept it in our little house across from the camp. And whenever the President spoke, we looked at that little globe for the places he mentioned.

He was a wealthy man, but he was for the poor. And he was such a good speaker. He mesmerized you when he spoke.

To top it all off, he died in Georgia. At Warm Springs. It was only about a hundred miles from Fort McClellan. We felt as though we had lost one of our own.

When we heard about it, it was as though everything just stopped dead in its tracks. Our secretaries and clerical workers, they had tears in their eyes. Even some of the GIs. Big, strapping men. And they were weepy.

Someone said the last time we lost a president [in office] was back in the '20s [Warren G. Harding, who died in 1923]. But most of the girls in the office and the GIs were too young to remember him. This was different. President Roosevelt led us through the war. It was a sad, sad time. I don't think we had a sadder day at the camp. When we got together with friends for days afterward, all we could do was talk about the President. You really couldn't concentrate on anything else. You didn't even want to.

Even some of the German prisoners, the ones we knew quite well—they knew. They got the word. I don't think they cared one way or the other, personally. But they expressed their thoughts to us in their broken English.

I remember the ceremonies honoring him around the fort. Flags were put at half-staff. They played "Taps." And patriotic songs. There were services in his honor in our chapel and all the chapels around the post. The amphitheater had a special program. No matter where you went in the camp or on the post or in Anniston, there were flags on display and patriotic bunting and black crepe.[13]

The April 13, 1945, edition of *The McClellan CYCLE* dedicated the entire front page to FDR's death and featured a photograph of the fallen leader under the bold headline "ROOSEVELT DEAD." A hastily written editorial ran on page 11 beneath the paper's publication information:

OUR COMMANDER-IN-CHIEF

As it must to some soldiers, death came yesterday to the Commander-In-Chief of the United States, Franklin D. Roosevelt.

His death, under the most shocking and unexpected circumstances, came at a time when the armies and the navies under his command were beginning to achieve the victories that he foresaw—in the war that he foresaw.

He died in battle as literally as though he had been struck by a bullet.

Just as the majesty of his life touched not only every single American but millions all over the world, so will the tragedy of his passing become a deep personal and individual sorrow to the soldiers and the peoples who championed his conceptions of global peace.

As soldiers of the Army, we dare do no less than we would do for the least of our comrades who fell in battle—carry on in the fight which the President so bravely and gloriously led—so that the certain victory may be the more quickly achieved and the peace may remain a lasting and durable monument to his memory.[14]

The Führer's death occurred on a momentous day for Jack Shay. On Monday, April 30, the same day that Hitler, with nothing left to salvage from the ruins of his Third Reich, plunked a cyanide pill in his mouth and pulled the trigger of a Walther pistol pressed against his head in the musty bowels of his Berlin bunker, the technician fourth grade officially became a sergeant.

The announcement of Hitler's death prompted not only relief but also some speculation in the American camp, according to Marie Shay:

> When we heard that Hitler had killed himself, we rejoiced. At first. But then we were a little skeptical. They [the Western Allies] never found his body. With Mussolini, it was different. They hung him upside down in public. And they took gruesome photographs. But there was some doubt among our GIs about Hitler. Sometime after we got the news, there were rumors around camp that he had somehow escaped and made it out of the country. I don't recall exactly how long those rumors lasted—definitely weeks, even months.
>
> It was like all those conspiracy theories about President [John F.] Kennedy's assassination. You weren't sure what to believe. And everything sounded plausible. In time, we came to believe that Hitler shot himself. But at first there was this undertone about what really happened. I know many of us at McClellan, even after the camp closed, went home thinking it was possible that Hitler somehow made it out alive.

Her son was incredulous when he first absorbed her words, recorded more than two decades after the McClellan years. But historical scholarship has attested to their veracity. As German author Heike B. Görtemaker wrote in *Eva Braun*:

> Countless legends sprang up after the death of Adolf Hitler.... One reason for this is ... that the direct witnesses ... gave contradictory statements later about the exact circumstances of the ... suicide. Another reason is that the Soviet Union [whose forces reached Berlin before the Americans and British] concealed ... for years, the fact that Soviet troops had found.... Hitler ... in early May. Instead of passing the information along, Joseph Stalin, in a conversation with the American special envoy Harry Hopkins on May 26, 1945, spread the rumor that Hitler ... [was] still alive and hidden abroad, possibly in Japan.... Stalin was trying to exploit the death of Hitler ... to suggest to the Western powers that their common struggle ... had to be continued in the war against Japan....
>
> Even at the Potsdam Conference, which took place from July 17 to August 2, 1945 ... Stalin flatly denied ... knowing anything about Hitler's whereabouts....
>
> None ... suspected that the charred remains of Hitler ... had been in the Soviets' hands for months....
>
> In the West, on the other hand, countless rumors and speculations circulated for years about the Nazi leader's whereabouts.... Former members of Hitler's staff ... were also arrested and questioned in the Western occupation zones directly after the end of the war, and they reported Hitler's death ... but there was no material evidence to prove these claims.[15]

"As far as the PWs' reaction to the news about Hitler," Marie Shay continued, "we didn't see any hooting or hollering over there [in the POW camp]. But it was a quiet camp. And the ones [POWs] we saw on a regular basis were nice men. They weren't diehards [Nazi supporters]. I don't think they would have said anything out of the way. They would have kept their feelings to themselves."

In the POW camp, the typical reaction seemed to be not remorse but concern over the long-term future. "When we learned that Hitler was dead and the war was over, we were happy that we would end our days as prisoners," Robert Suberg said. "There was no party [celebration] because of Hitler's death, but we wondered, how will our country look? Almost my whole life, as a young man, a student, and a soldier, I lived under Hitler. He was all we knew. How would our country be now? Who was to be our new leader? We didn't like Hitler. But we loved our homeland. No one wants to lose. So there was sadness. And yet happiness because it was over. And we could go home."

Höschle recorded his memories years later in his autobiography. "On May 1, 1945, the rumor went around that Hitler was dead," Joni Pontius translated. "And he said, 'It was true. He took his own life on April 30, 1945. As one knows today [when writing his auto-biography], in August 1944, following the assassination attempt on Hitler, he explained at a conference that only through the cowardice of the German people, that is, through their unworthiness before history and before him, could the war be lost. And the German people would not deserve to survive.'"

He also recalled the end of the war in Europe: "On May 9, 1945, a long siren wail was sounded in our camp, as throughout the USA. We were not surprised and knew what it was about. The war in Europe had ended. Finally, after a long painful suffering, salvation came. And we knew that the suffering and dying in Europe had ended."[16]

According to Marie Shay:

When we heard of V-E Day, we were all happy. There was cheering all over the [American] camp. GIs and civilians, wherever we heard the news, we just broke out in cheers and smiled at each other. In all our PXs, the GIs would toast each other with beer or soda or what have you. I remember the excitement all around the post and in the [American] PW camp. It was like Times Square in New York City on New Year's Eve. People shaking hands with each other and the GIs lighting up victory cigars or cigarettes. You couldn't hide the excitement and all the hearty laughter at the mess hall in the camp. It was very jolly.

I don't think the PWs did any celebrating. It was pretty subdued in their area. We never really talked politics with them or discussed the war. It was against military protocol to do that. And we didn't rub it in. But I'm sure they heard our cheers and saw us whooping it up. It may have bothered them, but I think they were probably relieved because they'd be released soon.

In the May 15, 1945, *P.o.W. Oase*, Heinz Fischer wrote on page 1 under the heading "Der Krieg In Europa Ist Beendet" (The War in Europe Is Over):

In the first days of May the final decisions occurred on the war areas of Europe. On May 7, the fighting stopped and the five-and-a-half-year struggle ended. Although we may now hope for a speedy repatriation to our homeland, we have to accept the events of the last 14 days [including the violent death of Hitler] in relation to the end of the war in Germany. Until conditions are cleared up and life in our homeland once again normalized, we have to face weeks of worry about our families, relatives, and friends, worries about their lives and welfare. And at the same time we have to prepare ourselves for the trials and tasks that will await us in life there.

On the second page of the same issue, Paul Metzner addressed the task that lay ahead in an essay titled "Current Affairs":

An eventful past lies behind us and a future awaits us, and it will be overshadowed by all these recent events.

It is not the time to comment on all these things from a judgmental position. We need distance and sober contemplation in which each individual must cope with the new situation that seemingly happened suddenly, as though overnight. What a change has occurred in the world.... But we must keep alive the goal of a commitment to our homeland and the will to work in reshaping it.

We want and need to be ready to solve the bitter and heavy tasks that await us when we return. Then we will stand together and rebuild from scratch a country that is our home.

Much will be different then than it was in the past. And it's good that everyone here knows about the challenge and is mentally prepared for it. Facts must be recognized. Facts make demands on us.[17]

The end of the European phase of the war meant for the prisoners both a heightened expectation of a return home and anxiety over when it would happen and what home would look like when they arrived. As Paul Metzner contemplated in the May 30, 1945, issue of *P.o.W. Oase*:

> It is perhaps a good thing that we are at present occupied with a full slate of films, theatrical productions, and concerts and that our work input is increased because it reduces the time when we are alone with our thoughts and, with the recent events, the thoughts of home....
>
> We remain silent.... We remain as prisoners of war and within we ponder, "How much longer?" Our future is still unknown, as it was two years ago when we were captured in Africa....
>
> And the question of our future is always with us....
>
> We look to films and theatrical performances to help us forget ... even if it is to such a tragic film as "Der Meineidbauer." It is easier to see a lighthearted film like ... "Get Hep to Love" [a 1940s musical with Donald O'Connor and Gloria Jean], where we have the right to laugh once again. The right? Yes, because who would profit from a joyless, negative outlook on life? And life has already given us some disappointment and bitterness, and we don't need to further complicate our situation as prisoners of war.[18]

Metzner, in the penultimate edition of his paper (July 1, 1945), also grasped the stark sobriety of being on the losing side and, further, accepting the onus of global censure for taking part, even if by enforced conscription, in a war machine constructed by a hegemonic dictatorship gone mad. He hinted at the emotions and moods he saw and heard in the camp's compounds, whether spoken aloud or merely murmured. He called for a restoration of Germanic energy to help rebuild a war-torn country and create a new economic and political system:

Between Delusion and Reality

> The collapse of Hitler's Reich is viewed in different ways in the POW camps, varying from the deepest feelings of dejection to an awareness of redemption, but also from an eager acceptance to a defiant denial. And yet those who probe deeper into the psyche know that, beyond all these feelings, everything has suddenly become empty.
>
> We have heard the trumpeting of victory throughout the land of the Stars and Stripes, the fanfare calls that would destroy the dream of even the most unquestioningly patriotic German, alive in his soul to the very last, even though he has seen for a long time the inescapable reality. The dictatorial character of the German regime had, for them, made whatever the rulers of Germany said more real than what they could see with their eyes. They had become mindless tools, the only possibility for them under an authoritarian state....
>
> At present, we do not have enough distance from events to adopt a completely reliable position because we have been so caught up in the dogma that has represented itself as the only true and infallible one, demanding allegiance. Yet we do have enough distance to recognize that new paths are opening. Ways to a new future, waiting to be taken. By you and me and many millions. And we want to rely on a new era. The past can help us learn from mistakes....
>
> The USA will not expect us to say "Father, I have sinned" but it will want to see some evidence that we have dismissed the former theories and replaced them with sober findings which, in the words of Major General Lerch, could shape our future. Perhaps many of our comrades will denote all actions taken by the USA in the course of retraining us as inappropriate and perhaps some of us will say, "Let's just go home. Give us some cigarettes and beer and good food, and we'll gladly affirm democracy!" as the solution you want. But will this ensure the Detaining Power that its laws are valid over there in our homeland as well as guarantee that absolutely every single person has renounced the past and is willing to rebuild?
>
> The decision may be difficult. Because many of us have faithfully followed the propaganda and mass psychosis and lost valuable years in war and sacrificed our health. Sacrifices which we undertook in our commitment to the Third Reich. Now we face a decision that we have to meet out of our own conviction. We don't obtain a single-minded unity out of coercion but from the knowledge of a common goal. The future is open for each one of us, and each one of

us is a building block of the building which we will erect, and that building will be called "Germany."

Why am I writing this? Neither to defend the current POW policy of the USA nor to promote a new philosophy—which must be inwardly addressed and not outwardly forced—but to call for reflection and thought.[19]

The biggest celebration, at least on the American side, occurred when the camp learned of Japan's surrender. Marie Shay explained, "When the bombs were dropped [on Hiroshima on August 6 and Nagasaki on August 9, 1945] on Japan, that took us all by surprise. We figured we might be getting good news sometime soon, and, when it happened, pandemonium just broke out. It was a Tuesday night [August 14, 1945]. And we didn't hear it until that evening. That's when it was announced to us."

At 7 p.m. in the Eastern Time Zone, President Harry S Truman gathered media at the White House and read an announcement: "I have received this afternoon a message from the Japanese Government in reply to the message forwarded to that Government by the Secretary of State on August 11th. I deem this reply a full acceptance of the Potsdam Declaration which specifies the unconditional surrender of Japan...."[20]

Newspapers rushed to print special editions, and radio networks transmitted the news to the world, initiating a wild celebration unparalleled in the history of mankind. The official surrender took place on September 2 aboard the American battleship USS *Missouri* anchored in Tokyo Bay. But it was the initial news on the evening of August 14 that heralded intense celebrations at McClellan.

"The news was broadcast over the radio that evening," Marie Shay remembered. "The camp was pretty much closed for the day when we heard it. All the offices were closed. But everyone went outside to share the news with anyone you'd come across. You couldn't just sit still. It was too exciting. The phone lines were busy because everyone was trying to call their friends and families back home. We had a car, so we were able to drive and see what was going on. Everyone was honking their horns. And people were milling about and cheering everyone who went by and waving flags. There was traffic, but no one seemed to care.

"Earlier that year, Dad [her husband] was on furlough, and we went to New Orleans to see the Mardi Gras. You would have thought you were back in New Orleans judging from what we saw in Anniston when the war ended."

17

The Closing of the Camp

"You don't just close a facility of that size down overnight."

The end of the war in Europe did not mean immediate liberty for the hundreds of thousands of prisoners held in the United States. Too many logistical and political impediments remained for a swift repatriation.

How do you process the release of all those men? All at once? In staggered increments? Can the nation's trains handle the sheer numbers of men interned all over the country? Can the Virginia and New York ports of embarkation house the men as they await oceanic transportation? Are enough ships available for such transport, considering the ongoing war in the Pacific? To what country do they return? Their country of residence? The country into whose army they were conscripted? Are those countries in any shape to receive them? Will they be returning to cities, towns, and houses utterly destroyed by the ravages of a war whose ferocity has never before been seen on so massive a scale? What about Germany's destruction of parts of France, England, and other countries? Should the POWs be forced to help rebuild those countries first? What about Russia, the least democratic of America's allies, as well as the least trustworthy and most potentially problematic? Will Russia accept responsibility for the rehabilitation of the devastated European mainland and cooperate with its Allied partners in a fair partitioning of the continent? How will the POWs adjust to a resumption of their drastically interrupted lives? Will they work toward establishing democratic principles and capitalist policies? Will they resurrect fascism and try to sabotage any efforts to fashion a new republic from the ashes of the Third Reich? What will the POW exodus mean to American farmers, industrialists, and entrepreneurs who relied on their labor during the war years when America's men were gone?

"When the war in Europe ended, the camp didn't shut down," Staff Sergeant Jack Shay recalled. "The prisoners began leaving one by one in groups, but not right away, not right off the bat. It took a while to get clearance and authorization papers filled out. The army had to arrange for ships to take them back overseas. The pace picked up later on after V-J Day [in August 1945]. But we still had prisoners in '46."[1]

The McClellan CYCLE noted the continued presence of POWs in 1946: "Those siren blasts you've been hearing all week" were "time-to-quit signals for the benefit of stockade prisoners and PWs."[2] However, the exodus had begun the previous year.

Christian Höschle was among the first to leave. "He wrote, 'In July, the rumor went around that the 9th Company, to which I belonged, would be leaving,'" translator Joni Pontius said. "At first, he thought that the Americans wanted to keep him because he was an artist. But that wasn't the case. Captain Dougal gave him his [Dougal's] address and said

177

to keep in touch. His friend, Hubert Maiburg, stayed behind. In the middle of July 1945, Christian left McClellan."[3]

With the war over, the camp relaxed its vigilance. "[W]hile awaiting the completion of arrangements to return home, the prisoners found security conditions somewhat more lax," Bill Plott wrote in the July 14, 1967, issue of *The Anniston Star*. "Col. Macon Hipp, the present commanding officer at Fort McClellan, recalls that when he came here in 1946, the prisoners pretty much wandered around at will, doing the jobs assigned to them."[4]

Because of her job in headquarters, Rita (Johnson) Wells became privy to POW records and paperwork. "We shipped our POWs to Hampton Roads, Virginia, for repatriation," she said. She also recalled several prisoners expressing reluctance to return to Germany, instead attempting to remain in America.

> One of them had an aunt in Boston, and she came down here and pleaded her cause to keep her nephew here in America. She got nowhere in our place [camp headquarters] and had to go to the main post. And they told her she would have to go to Washington.
>
> And one of them played the trumpet, and he had a friend who played the trombone. We heard he was denied.
>
> The Geneva Convention said you had to go back to your country. None of them wanted to go back to the Russian Compound [sector of Germany] and gave us stories like, "Well, my parents moved after I got drafted," and "Please, could they go to a different zone?" At first they'd talk to Lieutenant [Florence] Brownell and then they'd talk to the major [Samuel W. Kendall]. They [POWs] came down to headquarters escorted by our guards. Quite a few did this. I would say more like dozens.

She knew of none who were successful in their petitions.[5]

In a 2010 story in *The Jacksonville News*, reporter David Jennings quoted Mrs. Wells' remembrance of bidding farewell to prisoners she had gotten to know: "That was their going away present to me. They had put a penciled note on a tablet. It said that they would like to stay but they needed to go home and they thanked us for all the kindness we showed them while they were here."[6]

Only a handful of POWs throughout the nation received waivers, and then primarily because they had either previously lived in the United States or held exceptional ties to America.

Those still at McClellan after 1945's year-end holidays received a souvenir booklet to take home. Titled "COMPLIMENTS OF HEADQUARTERS, PRISONER OF WAR CAMP, FORT MCCLELLAN, ALA., JULY 1943–JANUARY 1946," it included 55 black-and-white photographs on 32 pages with English and German text. Designed as a keepsake, it also provided a sobering contrast for the POWs to mull over on the way home. On page 29 of the unnumbered booklet, the text read, "The following pictures were taken at Landsburg Prison, Germany, shortly after the capture of Landsburg by the American 411th Regiment on April 29, 1945. The 411th Regiment was commanded by Colonel Donovan Yeuell, now stationed at Fort McClellan."

The next two pages contained a trio of photographs showing two skeletal, emaciated corpses being carried to the site of their final earthly disposition, as well as a fourth shot of a row of naked and near-naked corpses in a state of rigor mortis, arranged grotesquely, one next to the other on the barren ground, while a detail of (presumably German) civilians dug a huge burial trench in the background. This quartet of photographs presented an unnerving coda to an otherwise-docile remembrance of the prisoners' time in America.

Rita Wells received a copy. She called it "propaganda. Meant for the prisoners to take

COMPLIMENTS OF HEADQUARTERS

PRISONER OF WAR CAMP
FORT McCLELLAN, ALA.
JULY 1943   JANUARY 1946

GEWIDMET VOM HAUPTQUARTIER

PRISONER OF WAR CAMP
FORT McCLELLAN, ALA.
JULI 1943   JANUAR 1946

The souvenir booklet, in both English and German, given to those POWs still in the camp at the beginning of 1946. The dates on the cover are misleading. Though the camp received its first prisoners in July 1943, it did not close in January 1946, as indicated. The POW camp ended operations on April 10, 1946, and the American camp lasted a month longer (author's collection).

back home with them." And Staff Sergeant Shay, who received two copies of the booklet, said, "It showed the difference between how our boys treated the German PWs and how the Nazis treated their prisoners. It probably opened a lot of [POW] eyes, because I don't think they really knew what was going on back in Germany when they came here. It was kind of a poke in the eye for the ones [POWs] just doing their jobs as soldiers. But they [the U.S. Army] did it to show the differences, and it made the point."

Disregarding the last three pages, the booklet became for many POWs the only photographic record of their time in America. The cover showed the current and final camp commander, Major Samuel W. Kendall, in a hip-length military jacket and service cap, standing at the officers' entrance to the camp headquarters building. Another photo of Kendall, this time seated at his desk, with various memoranda and maps of Germany and Japan tacked to a bulletin board in the background, filled the inside front cover. The caption read, "Major Samuel W. Kendall—Camp Commander." An introductory statement bearing Kendall's signature occupied the opposite page:

THE PRISONER OF WAR CAMP, FORT McCLELLAN, ALA., U.S.A., started functioning in July 1943. It consists of three spacy Compounds which lie on the slope of a hill on the West side of the Main Post.

On both sides of the streets in each of the three compounds are rows of well-arranged barracks, comprising 12 companies. In addition there are the kitchens, company orderly rooms, day-rooms, dispensaries, library and reading room. At the compound entrance amidst flowers and shrubbery stands the P. W. Chapel. Under tall trees on a sloping hill is the open-air stage, and scattered through the compounds are wide areas for sports and games.

In their spare time after working hours, the P. Ws. [sic] have beautified their grounds with grass and flowers, and with their handy-work have improved its appearance.

And so the Camp authorities with the assistance of the P. Ws. have together shaped the camp to conform with International agreements, and have made the stay of the Prisoners of War in America such as to send them home with a lasting impression.

Views of the Camp and the life and work of the P. Ws. 'till the end of 1945 is reflected in the pictures on the following pages, which I present to you on Christmas 1945.

Samuel W. Kendall
Major CMP Commanding

The next 25 pages displayed photographs of camp sites familiar to all prisoners, as well as shots of unidentified POWs engaged in various activities either in the camp or on the main post (with the following captions):

- P. W. Camp Headquarters
- Staff of P. W. Camp Headquarters on the job
- Street through middle compound
- Miniature rock garden
- Start of a new day—work details checking through the gate
- P. W. Kitchen crew in messhall of American Personnel
- Radio specialist
- With shovel and wheel-barrow in the coalyard
- A tractor on an unfinished sportfield
- Typewriter repair man at work
- At work in the Q.M. Bakery
- Thousands of loaves of bread baked daily in the Q.M. Bakery

- P. W. personnel section in Camp Headquarters
- Butchers in Hospital Mess No. 1
- Carpenters and upholsterers
- QM carpenter shop
- Steaks for hospital patients
- Repair of broken equipment
- Automechanics in Post Motor Pool
- Keep em rolling
- Tire-shop
- P. W. Canteen Office and staff
- With the bandsaw
- One of the kitchens in the compound
- Messhall, ready to feed 250 P. Ws.
- Business in the P. W. Canteen
- Corner in the reading room
- Course in American History
- Colonel Nielsen—Post Commander
- Awarding of certificates upon completion of course in American History
- P. W. orchestra on stage of indoor theater
- The altar of P. W. Camp Chapel
- P. W. Cemetery
- Greenhouse in the rear of P. W. Camp
- Inspection of the greenhouse area
- P. W. botanical garden
- Dayroom activity
- Grounds around the P. W. Camp
- Partial view of P. W. Camp and surroundings as seen from the greenhouse
- P. W. Camp—Open Air Stage
- P. W. Dentist at work in Compound Dental Clinic
- Typical P. W. Barracks
- Inoculating tree at Officers Club with Vitalife
- Inside the greenhouse
- Setting out shrubs at Ft. McClellan—Officers Club
- Propagating carnations in Greenhouse
- Begonias and Chrysanthemums in Greenhouse
- Chrysanthemum with background of Ferns, in Greenhouse
- Chrysanthemums, Poinsettias, Ferns, Pot Plants in Greenhouse[7]

The souvenir has become a collector's item in recent years because of its presumed scarcity. Back in the 1960s, Staff Sergeant Shay recalled the behind-the-scenes efforts involved in producing it:

Our boys, the U.S. Signal Corps photographers, went around the camp and the post photographing the PWs at work or in class. The idea was to show them doing what they always did. They took more shots than they used. They took one looking up main street through Middle Compound to show what the PW barracks looked like. There was one [shot] of the outdoor stage the PWs built. A lot of shots of the greenhouse and the gardens way up above the camp.

Sergeant Shay's mess hall, spruced up for the cameras (author's collection).

They got a picture of Father Müller saying Mass in the PW Chapel. He was the Catholic chaplain. Major Kendall was in a lot of pictures. They took him up to the post where the PWs were cleaning up around the Officers' Club. Everything had to be spruced up. Just like for an inspection. They took some shots in headquarters of my buddies [Sergeants] Bud Jones and Harry Klein. They'd tell you not to look at the camera—just go about your work as though nothing was happening.

Some of the pictures were action shots, and some were staged. I had to get my mess hall cleaned up for the cameras. They wanted the pictures to look natural, but they had to look neat, too.

Some PWs were in a lot of the shots because they took them in sequence, one after another, using the same guys.

That little book came out around Christmas 1945, early the next year. Some PWs had already shipped out. Not everyone got one. I don't know if all the PWs would have by rights wanted to be reminded of their time in a prisoner of war camp. But it was a nice thing to do. If you had to be a PW, McClellan was a good place to be. It was a nice break in a nasty war.

When released, the POWs took their clothing and toilet articles, any permissible confectionary or smoking items, letters from home, photographs, money earned while interned (in the form of federal checks, not actual cash), reading material (newspapers, the souvenir booklet, issues of *P.o.W. Oase*), and personal items of practical or sentimental value.

Space and weight restrictions, as well as concerns over proper packing for fragile items, limited the amount of artwork or woodwork taken home. That accounted for some of the prisoners' generosity to the GIs. As an example, Sergeant Shay referred to a picture, executed in colored pencil or chalk on a rectangular piece of construction paper a little less than 11 by 8½ inches, depicting an interior view of the camp with a pair of guard towers (along the presumed northeast or northwest angle of the camp). The painting was done by Ober-feldwebel (First Sergeant) Karl Steinmetz, who had intended to mail it to his old address at Kasernenstr. 5, Marburg Lahn, Germany: "He banked on sending it home, and he put an address label on the back. But he changed his mind, and I got it instead."

In *Nazi Prisoners of War in America*, Arnold Krammer wrote of the pace of repatriation picking up in the winter of 1945–1946, with anywhere from 60,000 to 80,000 scheduled to leave each month. Quoting a story from the August 8, 1947, edition of the *New York Times*, he stated that only "24 escapees and 11 hospitalized cases remained" in the country at that date.[8] And in *Men in German Uniform*, Antonio Thompson wrote, "By June 1946, all POWs, with the exception of those sick, injured, and incarcerated, had been repatriated," and "the last left in 1947."[9]

In his 1991 reminiscence, former POW Alfred Arens recounted the gradual reduction in POWs at McClellan and what awaited them before full repatriation (original typescript intact):

In fall 1945 the PW-camp McClellan was dissolved [in fact, this was only one phase of the extended shutting down of the camp] *and we were transferred to Camp Forrest/Tullahooma/Ten-*

Oberfeldwebel Karl Steinmetz's pencil sketch of the rear of the POW camp, depicting two guard towers, POW laundry hanging on lines to dry (lower left), and two soccer fields—one in play with spectators on benches (left center) and another idle (lower center). Intended as a personal souvenir for the artist, the color rendering was instead given to Sergeant Shay (author's collection).

nessy. There we stayed during the winter 1945/46. *In February 1946 we were brought by railway via New York on a ship and we took direction Europe.* Everybody was sure to come straight home to Germany. But what happened? After having landed in Le Havre (France) *we were handed over to the Frenchmen in the notorious PW-camp B o l b e c.* This is the most bitter reproach on the then US–government having sold us like slaves in a modern slave market. And besides: it was a clear offense against the GENEVA convention about the treatment of war-prisoners. The only consosolation was that these activities of the US–government were badly criticized in the American public as we could read it in the newspapers.—The captivity in France was very hard. We had to work in coal-mines *or even dig out hidden mines on the beach of DIEPPE.* With inadiquate tools like sharpened broom-sticks etc. There were many PW's ... who lost her lives a year after the end of the war![10]

Robert Suberg left McClellan after Arens' departure. In a 1987 interview at his home in Solingen, West Germany, he spoke of what awaited him overseas: "In one way we were happy to leave the camp because we could go home to [our] families. But in one way, we were a little unsure. Because we had no knowledge about what our homes would be. There were bombs all over Germany. Destruction. Roads, cities destroyed. What would we go home to find? We ate well at McClellan. But home, people were starving. They were eating potatoes, potatoes we threw out on KP in Alabama because they had mold.

"But we were not permitted to go home. We went on ships to Europe. We had to work in England and France. To build their countries new again. And we stayed there in camps, too. I went to a camp in Belgium. And then to one in England. And then one in Wales. I didn't go home until August 1947. Two years after the war ended! More than two years! And we saw anger from people, from guards. Like we were Hitler. They wanted revenge. We were not given good treatment."

His voice tailed off, as he seemed to grope for words. Finally, the interviewer said, "Robert, was that the worst time in your life?"

He simply nodded his head and softly repeated his questioner's words. "Yes. The worst time in my life."

When Suberg spoke those words to this author, he was 63. And though he vacationed throughout Germany and other parts of Europe in his retirement years, he never returned to the United States. He acknowledged that some POWs, returning home after forced work sojourns in England, France, Belgium, or other rebuilding countries (Czechoslovakia, Greece, the Netherlands, Yugoslavia, among others), became embittered. Their benign memories of McClellan had lost their luster, replaced by darker reflections of a tougher, meaner, grittier sequel.

When the interview ended, the author extended an invitation to host Suberg on a visit to America. Though his wife, Edith, who had never been to the United States, showed great enthusiasm, Robert expressed reservations: "It is not easy to travel with my heart condition and medicines that I must take during the day." His point was valid, but his reluctance seemed as much a reflection of his desire not to rekindle old memories tarnished by their aftermath.[11]

In "Stalag U.S.A.," Staff Sergeant Dan Coberly wrote, "The camp ... officially closed April 10, 1946, according to the *Anniston Star*."[12] Recent attempts to find contemporary confirmation of that date in both *The Anniston Star* and *The McClellan CYCLE*, the two newspapers of local record, came up empty. Tom Mullins, director of the Alabama Room in Anniston's public library, diligently lent time and expertise to the matter. "I checked the paper [*Star*] again and could find nothing," he wrote on December 5, 2012. "Checked 5 days on both sides of April 10 ... online ... they said the POW camp was deactivated on April 10, 1946, but could find nothing in the paper."[13]

But the actual closing of the entire POW complex, including the American military camp, occurred a month later, in May. Staff Sergeant Shay, who witnessed both closings, remarked on the camp's final days:

> It got to where we [the American guards and support staff] didn't have that much to do. The war had ended long ago by that time, and there was no worry that the PWs would make a break for it or do anything out of sorts. As time went by, there were fewer PWs, and conditions became lax. I lost all my PWs [assigned to work details]. They all left. I still had to keep mess operations going for the GIs and our officers. But their numbers went down, too. I had a staff of our own boys and some civilians working on mess hall duty in place of the PWs.
>
> When they [POWs] started leaving at a steady clip, we wondered when we'd get our discharge orders. We knew it was in the cards after V-J Day. But it was some time yet, because you don't just close a facility of that size down overnight. Especially when you've got prisoners of war to guard. And it's always, "Hurry up and wait!" in the army. Even in the best of times. But when the PWs began leaving in bunches, our boys started itching to be released. We knew it would be soon after they [POWs] were gone, but we didn't know when. We heard rumors. Some of the fellas were what we called "lifers." They stayed in and made a career out of the army. But most of us were anxious to finish up our tour of duty and return home to wives or sweethearts or civilian jobs.

An unexpected tornado that struck Anniston with lightning-fast rapidity at 6:30 on the Sunday evening of April 7, 1946, overshadowed the closing of the camp. E. T. Brinkley recorded the fury in pregnant phrases in the following day's *The Anniston Star*:

> Anniston is in shambles today, but miraculously no one is dead or seriously injured after the shell-fire-like tornado and hail storm that lashed the city for thirty minutes last night, causing property damage that will easily mount into millions of dollars.
>
> Not a house nor standing thing here escaped the fury of the storm and today the city resembles the bomb-seared beaches of Normandy and the shell-ripped shore of Okinawa....
>
> Window panes were shot from the northern exposure of virtually every building and dwelling as the hail, driven by a powerful wind that bumped around the mountains ringing this normally serene and beautiful city....
>
> The hail of ice fell with such rapidity that today Anniston looks as though it has been given a going over by some monster threshing machine....
>
> Hundreds of massive trees were either uprooted or broken off by the terrific wind....
>
> The side walls of buildings are pock-marked as though they had been the targets for thousands of machineguns....
>
> Roofs were literally chewed to pieces....
>
> Buildings where the windows were knocked out were flooded by the torrent of rain and hail....
>
> Power and telephone service was paralyzed for hours....
>
> The heavily populated East Side of Anniston was in total darkness from the time the storm struck ... until 4:30 o'clock this morning....
>
> Anniston was totally out of communication with the outside world....
>
> Stores, churches and public buildings suffered tremendously....
>
> [S]everal persons were reported cut and bruised by flying glass and hail....
>
> Near panic prevailed at Anniston Memorial Hospital when the storm hit during visiting hours. A crowd ... milled around the doors, afraid to stay or to venture out into the hell of hail stones....
>
> All highways leading out of Anniston were impassable, due to high water, for several hours....

Buildings, while still standing, are sad sights to behold, hundreds of them being soaked with water and littered with debris....

The storm turned loose on Anniston almost without warning after a beautiful Spring Sabbath. Clouds began gathering in the north in what had been a fleckless sky.

Rolling up in a billowing manner, the greyish mass, illuminated by brilliant flashes of lightning that cut crazy patterns across the Heavens, the cloud formation shifted across the mountains that ring the Model City.

There was a distant rumbling of thunder that sounded like artillery fire playing on the hills. The staccato stepped up, the lightning became more brilliant and there was a hushed rumbling, followed by a terrific flash and a resounding clap of thunder.

Minutes afterward, the skies cut loose, first rain and then a virtual sleet of hail that pounded the city for about 20 minutes, followed by more rain.

The noise was deafening and terrifying. It sounded like millions of machinegun bullets ripping into every surface, and with the city in total darkness the piercing screams of horror-stricken people was audible above the din of the storm....

The hail, many of the pellets big as half dollars, covered the ground for a depth of one foot, was crunched under the wheels of automobiles as they moved with difficulty.

As destructive as the tornado was for Anniston, it largely spared the fort and the POW camp. As Brinkley went on to say:

Fort McClellan reported water did about as much damage as the hail and wind. Window panes in many barracks were broken and some roads on the reservation were blocked by fallen trees. The Fort, however, did not feel the full fury of the storm.

Three soldiers who were believed drowned when they slipped into a ditch on the reservation were later found to be safe. They suffered from exposure and were given treatment at the Regional Hospital on the reservation.[14]

Residing in her duplex house just across Pelham Road from the POW camp, Marie Shay remembered the storm:

It was very scary. It came up all of a sudden. Wind, rain, hail, thunder, lightning all at once. You were afraid to leave wherever you were, but you were afraid to be there, too. It was like the end of the world. I had never seen anything like that before in my life. I felt sorry for the poor people who were trapped outside in that tornado. Well, I guess you just had to run for shelter somewhere and get out of its path. I lit a candle and prayed that it would pass us by. And eventually it did. But until then, it was frightening.

I don't know but what all or most of the PWs were gone by that time, and operations were winding down at the camp. Fort McClellan had some damage but not as much as Anniston. So we were lucky. But I think that for the people still there, well, it sure gave them something to remember for the rest of their lives.

Later on, we drove into Anniston and saw the damage and took pictures of cars that were smashed by fallen trees. You just couldn't believe it. These big, huge trees, taller than houses, just uprooted like they were toothpicks. It was the scariest thing I'd seen in my life.

We were still there a month after the tornado, even after the camp had pretty much shut down. We were there until the 13th [of May] when Dad [her husband] had to be in Fort Dix [New Jersey] for his discharge [May 16]. But we never forgot that tornado.

Rita (Johnson) Wells was in downtown Anniston at the time: "When that tornado struck, I was in church. The First United Methodist Church on Noble Street in Anniston. There were five or six young people in the church with me. We heard the wind. The lights went out. We heard a rumble. We looked up, and we could see the sky. The chimney had come down. It was blown in. My face was streaked by charcoal because the chimney had soot."

The aftermath of the April 7, 1946, Anniston tornado (author's collection).

Dr. Joby Walker also recalled the tornado. According to him, "That tornado damaged houses and buildings in a number of places in Anniston—Wilma, Leighton, Quintard [avenues running north and south in Anniston]. Every window on the north side was knocked out."[15]

The tornado damaged 6,000 homes and uprooted or destroyed hundreds of historic trees, many of them planted along the city's main thoroughfares in the late 1800s by municipal founders. It also temporarily trapped 6,000 GIs, some from the prison camp. As Anne McCarty wrote in the April 9, 1946, issue of *The Anniston Star*, "All Anniston USO Clubs suffered considerable damage.... More than 6,000 soldiers from Fort McClellan were in Anniston Sunday night when the storm hit, and most of that number were sheltered in the city's USO Clubs during and after the storm before the roads were reported clear to the fort."[16]

The tornado provided a definitive exclamation point for those still residing or working in the camp. And when the Fort McClellan complex finally closed a year after the end of combat operations in Europe, it was Alabama's last holding center to be deactivated.

18

Friendships Forged:
Postwar Correspondence

"I will never forget the Christmas 1945
and you Mrs Shay.
you made us feeling like home."

Perhaps the best consequences of interactions between prisoner and prison-keeper were the resultant friendships and correspondence. Despite strict prohibitions against any and all unnecessary social intercourse between the two camps, it happened, and unless such contact was egregious, American authorities often looked the other way.

POW Josef Müller, a Roman Catholic priest who was mentioned anonymously in various inspection reports, left in early 1946. Before going, he gave a photographic postcard of himself to Sergeant and Mrs. Shay, whom he had befriended. Using a standard American manual typewriter lacking German accent marks, he employed the customary "ue" for the German "ü" and typed a message on the back of the card:

To
    Mr. and Mrs.
    J a c k S h a y !!!!!!!
    In
thankful Remembrance !
    God bless Y o u !
Our mother M a r y
    protect Y o u !
I pray for you always!
    Yours sincerely
    Josef Müller, Chaplain. [This line was handwritten.]
PW-Camp Fort Mc Clellan, 1/1/1946.
My home-adress: Father Serenus Mueller
    "Luethenhaus"
    P a d e r b o r n/Westfalen.[1]

Though written and delivered in the camp, this message was the first of dozens of letters, cards, photographs, and so forth that the American couple would receive over the years.

Helmut Engelke, who had surreptitiously passed the note about reduced rations in the POW camp to Sergeant Shay, asking for his intervention, took up pen and personalized stationery to write to the Shays on "January 10, 1947" (actually 1948, as indicated by the Hannover postmark on the envelope):

Dear Mrs. Shay and dear Jack!

Many, many thanks for your Christmas greetings, which I received yesterday.... Now I am very glad, that you haven't forgotten me. Last September Aŭwi was repatriated and we spend a few days together, now he has joint his parents which are now living in the British Zone as well ... bŭt now I will write him today, that yoŭ wrote me. I am fine and I am feeling good as never before, it is nice to be home again. Sometime I remember (and I think I am not the only one) the good days we had as we worked in the Kitchen of the M.P. Department under the sŭpervision of Jack. It was really the best time I had during my captivity. Also I will never forget the Christmas 1945 and you Mrs Shay. you made us feeling like home on those day's. These year I had a nice Christmas and a good start in the New Year. You ask me for a picture. I will send yoŭ a picture of myself as soon as I get one made. You will laugh when you read this, that I even dont have a picture of me. But I am in Germany and not in U.S.A. If yoŭ go to a photograph[er] here in Hannover you have to wait at least 6–8 weeks and if he is short of paper 3–4 month till you get one made. Oh you cant know the difference of living between your people and the german people. But I am optimist it will be better some time. Now I beg you isn't it possible for you to send me a Life" or Post" or Satŭrday Evening" that I can read something of yoŭ back in U.S.A. And now please dont forget your Bell Bottom trousers and write. it don't have to be a large letter, jŭst a few words in a hurry to let me know that you are well. Now good luck for you in 1948.

Very trŭly yours
Helmut

In the 1970s, some 30 years after the exchange of letters had begun, Marie Shay explained the circumstances:

At first we tried to keep in touch with many of the PWs. Dad and I knew dozens of them personally. But a lot of our letters went unanswered, especially those that went to PWs in the Russian part, East Germany, especially after the Berlin Blockade and the Iron Curtain. And

POW Alfons Mildenberger and Sergeant Jack Shay in the American camp with the officers' complex in the background (author's collection).

eventually we surmised that the letters weren't being allowed to go through, because the Russian authorities were intercepting the letters and taking whatever they wanted for themselves. It got to where we didn't even want to send anything of value, particularly money, because you'd always wonder if the person it was intended for ever got it. Some of our other Army buddies [Americans] said the same thing. So eventually we stopped writing since we figured it wouldn't reach the ones we wanted to reach.

I especially remember this one PW. Alfons Mildenberger. We liked him a lot. He was such a nice person, someone you'd take to in a minute. Very gentlemanly, polite. He had such a likable, easy-going manner. Not silly, not loud. We wrote to him, but we never got a response. He probably never got our letters. We never knew if he was alive or dead.[2]

It wasn't until more than a quarter-century after those comments were made, after she had passed away, that her son found some of the letters Marie and her husband had received from former POWs tucked away among her mementos. Too late to ask her questions about what she and her husband had done during the Christmas of 1945 to make the POWs feel as though they were home. She was a good cook and may have made something special for them to take back into their compound or enjoy while they were in the American mess hall. She played the piano and sang at the camp; possibly she serenaded the prisoners with popular American music or German airs. Perhaps she included them in Christmas cards or spoken words—no one can ever know. Whatever made that Christmas so memorable for the POWs went to the grave with her.

On February 23, 1948, Bruno Gross, who remembered Sergeant Shay from the officers' mess hall in the American camp, wrote from Freising in the American Zone:

My dear Fam[ily]. Shay!

...I send you many regards and I hope you feel well and I think you know me still....

It is a long time ago that I leave America. I leave America in 13 May 46 and I been go to England vor [for] 1 year and 3 month. Now I am in the American Zone.... Her[e] is good, but not much to eat ... only 1,300 kalariess [calories] per day....

Now I will close my short letter and I think you know me, which worket in the Offisir Mess in Fort McClellan. Please excuse me when I have made some mistakes in my letter. Many regards from Bruno[.]

Erich Wetzold succeeded in sending several postcards from Lauterbach bei Oelsnitz in the Soviet Occupation Zone in the 1940s. In one he wrote, "I find yоŭr address on a christmas letter wich yоŭr send to me at Christmas 1947. Do yоŭ remember me? I was one of the Boys wich was working in the M.P. Kitchen of the P.o.W. Camp Fort McClellan."

Karl Schardt, newly resettled in Frankfurt in the American Zone, expressed the sentiments of many former POWs in his neatly typed letter of February 18, 1948:

Dear Shays:

A month ago I received your Christmas card for which I will thank you. I really did not expect to hear from you and you can imagine that your letter made me very glad. You are very dear friends to me and I would like to stay in correspondence with you and exchange thoughts about us and the family. I have 2 sisters, father and mother, and we are all well. My older sister works in a bank, and is always looking for a man, but she was never successful to find one. The other one is working for the US Government as a secretary. I'm still at my old firm, a bank. Very often I recall the time I was in the States and I must confess that this time was better than over here. Though I have a very good job here, I would like to be back, as I did not have to care about the food. And this is the biggest question over here. Wouldn't it be fine if you and Mrs. Shay would be in Germany and work in a kitchen and I would be your help. It really was nice in Alabama and I tell you that I can never forget you, you always were good comrades.

In my spare time I'm learning English, and if I should ever have the opportunity I want to go back to the States....

I will attach a picture to this letter, that was taken right after I came home. I hope you do recognize me, the wolf. Is your brother still in Germany, Mrs, Shay?

I will close my letter now hoping to hear from you soon.

With best regards,
I remain [signature]

The Shays were hardly the only Americans corresponding with former POWs.

Karl Hövener, a prisoner who worked under the supervision of civilian contract employee James Byron Wester, Sr., at the post, was also a deft artist who befriended Wester and gave him several paintings and sketches in appreciation of their friendship. Hövener continued sending artwork to Wester even after the war. As Wester's son-in-law, James Bonner (who married Dean Wester), explained, "She [Dean] found out that after Karl returned to Germany he communicated with James [Wester] through letters. Karl wanted to return to the USA with his family. James tried to make arrangements for them to come to the states and offered to let them stay in his home until settled, but the cost for Karl to do this was more than he or James could afford." Dean Bonner was "not sure how long they stayed in touch with each other," but she was told "that after a while letters just stopped coming."

Karl Schardt shortly after repatriation. He found that "the time I was in the States ... was better than over here" (author's collection).

According to an email from James Bonner, Dean's sister "Jean also said the prisoners would write their address back in Germany on notes thrown out [to friendly residents of Anniston from the backs of trucks taking the prisoners on work details] asking them to write letters to them [POWs] when they returned home [to Germany]. Jean did write to some of them but didn't remember any specifics."[3]

The friendship between Gefreiter (PFC) Robert Suberg and Sergeant and Mrs. Shay became one of the most enduring of McClellan's POW legacies. It began during 1944 when the three met in the 1437th mess hall—a German prisoner on a work detail, his American overseer, and the latter's wife.

Born on November 29, 1923, Gefreiter Suberg, called "Robert" by his comrades but the Americanized "Bob" by his American friends, was drafted into the Wehrmacht in 1942, after finishing high school but before he could begin a university education. He went to Tarnowitz (then Silesia, currently Poland) for his basic training. Participating in combat in partisan fighting on the eastern front, he was ordered to the German city of Celle. Sent to Italy, then Sicily, and finally North Africa, he was wounded and captured, eventually being sent to the port of New York for a train to Fort McClellan. He worked for Sergeant Shay in several capacities, including as a "waiter in the American officers' mess."

On January 7, 1946, before leaving McClellan for repatriation, Suberg gave his favorite overseer an engraved photograph of himself, as well as an invitation to correspond. But such was not immediately forthcoming because, against his expectations, the prisoner was not released to Germany but instead sent to Belgium, then England, and later southern Wales. He was finally discharged in August 1947.

Then began the annual Christmas correspondence between the Shays and "Bob" (and Edith Röttgers, whom he met while both were employed in the same mercantile company; they married in 1950). It continued until January 17, 2001, when Robert Suberg died at 77. As of this writing, the correspondence between his widow and the Shays' only son continues.

In between all the letters, cards, postcards, and gift packages going back and forth, Marie Shay and her son visited the Subergs in their Solingen home in August 1987 and September 1988. Despite the main purpose of the visit—reuniting friends from the POW camp—the author took advantage of the opportunity to informally interview Robert Suberg. The questions and answers spread out over several days because, though not reluctant to

In-person reunions between Americans and Germans were scarce, usually occurring when the former POWs returned to visit America. But in 1987 and 1988, Marie Shay and her son reversed the trend, traveling to Europe specifically to see a surviving prisoner. Left to right: the author, Robert Suberg, Edith Suberg, and Marie Shay (Solingen, September 24, 1988) (author's collection).

talk of the past, Robert desperately wanted to take his guests around Solingen and Düssel-dorf and show them everything of interest.[4]

In a November 17, 1987, letter acknowledging Robert's time and generosity with infor-mation, the author wrote, "My father would be so happy to know that my mother and I were able to visit you. From the time I was a little boy, I remember him speaking very fondly of you. Now, after I've met you, I can understand why."[5]

Throughout the author's father's long 20-year decline, Robert Suberg commiserated over the failing health of someone he considered a friend. In his Christmas card of Decem-ber 14, 1982, he wrote, "We are so sorry that Jack is not feeling so good and that he cannot go anywhere. It is a pity that we will not see [him] again." In another letter dated March 6, 1985, he wrote, "We are so sorry that there is no cure for Jack sr. and we can understand that you are feeling bad when you leave him. It is a pity that he cannot come overhere to see us again." And on December 13, 1987, he wrote, "How is Jack sen. doing?? Did anything change in his situation? I wished you could tell him my best greetings and wishes. Please let me know how he is feeling."[6]

19

The POW Cemetery

"We hear the roll of drums
as the mortal remains of a fellow soldier
are brought to this place."

Nothing mortal endures indefinitely.

A good number of McClellan's buildings and structures—barracks, hospitals, PXs, bowling alleys, swimming pools, tailor shops, warehouses, telephone exchanges, mess halls, service clubs, theaters, guest houses, dormitories—no longer survive. Even a cluster of antiquated, World War II–era two-story barracks and nondenominational chapels in the old 24th and 25th Battalion area, still standing in 2007, became flattened rubble heaps, awaiting cleanup and fresh landscaping, just five years later. The street names of the main post have undergone their own metamorphoses: the old 20th Street, slicing diagonally through the heart of the complex, is now Berman Road; 6th Avenue became Castle Avenue; 5th Avenue, losing its linear nature, became split in two—one part Federal Way, the other Care Drive; 3rd Avenue is now Eglin Avenue; and Rocky Hollow Road has morphed into Iron Mountain Road. Most other roads were also recast in new nomenclature: Commandants Drive, Derby Street, Exchange Avenue, Galley Avenue, Halifax Avenue, Langley Avenue, Rota Lane, Town Center Drive, and a couple dozen others.[1]

The POW camp disappeared even faster, its structures dismantled and its terrain scalped. Anything of value, whether lumber or metal, an appliance or a supply, was removed for reuse or appropriate disposition. Other materials of scant intrinsic worth became unsightly scrap heaps destined for oblivion.

An undated, unattributed paper titled "Fort McClellan Prisoner of War Camp, World War II" says, "The buildings that once housed the POWs were removed shortly after the POW camp was deactivated on April 10, 1946. Of the paintings and artistry ... on the walls of the barracks, none remain. Not even the names of the artists and workers...."[2] That paper, neither the first nor the last to use the same or nearly identical words, captured the essence of what happened to the camp.

Nationwide, the army wasted little time in discarding its POW trappings. Some records were destroyed, others mothballed, and a relatively precious few consigned to archival repositories in quick order after the closing of hundreds of major and satellite camps. Prisoner personnel files, reports, rosters, and such found their way to the prisoners' countries when the War Department decided they rightfully belonged there rather than in the nation that had interned the men.

The POW camp buildings, many built by either Civilian Conservation Corps workers beforehand or the Army Corps of Engineers in preparation for the prisoners, met a similar fate. The U.S. government ignored the historic value of maintaining at least some visual residue of the POW experience in America, and wrecking crews came in to remove buildings and flatten landscapes.

In "World War II POW Camps in Alabama," an Internet article, (John) Daniel Hutchinson wrote, "In the decades after World War II, a number of former POWs returned to Alabama to reconnect with their past. Little exists of their sites of imprisonment, however. By 1947 the camps had been dismantled. Today there is scant evidence indicating that the camp ever existed, except for a cemetery at Fort McClellan…."[3]

McClellan actually has a bit more than just the cemetery, though not on the grounds of the former POW camp.

Verbal anecdotes and written narratives through the decades averred that some of the main post masonry (specifically irrigation and drainage) projects reached completion with POW assistance. Prisoners performed pick-and-shovel labor; miscellaneous photographs, written reports, and an occasional tantalizing illustration in *P.o.W. Oase* provide ample evidence of their work. And they lent their muscles and skills to gardening, tree planting and cultivation, weeding and deforestation, and landscaping.

Fort McClellan: A Popular History contended, "*The Fort McClellan News* on April 28, 1980, cited numerous examples of stonework, including stone walls, chimneys, a patio built behind the old Recreation Center, drainage ditches, and landscaping as featuring POW handiwork."[4] Staff Sergeant Dan Coberly, whose "Stalag U.S.A." series in March–May 1980 issues of *The McClellan News* (and reissued, with some changes, in other periodicals) became the basis for much excerpted material in later papers and publications, identified "Many of the chimneys … throughout Ft. McClellan," "Stairs that seem to lead nowhere," "A stone wall … along the bank of a deserted road on post," "the patio built behind the old Recreation Center," "drainage ditches and flood walls," and "the bridge which arches over Cave [Cane] Creek" as the work of POWs. He wrote:

> Most of the stonework throughout post, the drainage ditches, the stone-bridge near the old commissary, the railroad tracks, the paved road through Baines [usually spelled "Bain's" or "Bain"] Gap, and the Duck Pond near the post theater were originally built by POWs.
> The stonework memorial recently reconstructed in front of Noble Army Hospital … was originally built by POWs at the Rod and Gun Club. The fireplace inside the club, as well as several other hearths and chimneys around post are also likely to have been built by the prisoners.[5]

But at this writing, few visible remnants on the main post can be incontrovertibly proven the result of POW labor. Certain sites might be more anecdotal than verifiably documented. Some of the above, either in initial construction or through subsequent reconstruction, most likely resulted from POW labor. But short of finding precise documentation, it would be imprudent to definitively ascribe all such work to prisoner efforts.

The narrow pedestrian bridge across the South Branch of Cane Creek is a case in point. In December 2009, Joan McKinney and Dan Coberly, two of the most energetic champions of McClellan's legacy, exchanged known information and likely hypotheses in a series of emails:

> **McKinney:** Do you have any information about the PWs building the stone bridge over Cane Creek? It's one of those urban legends that I cannot verify. The legend was further enhanced

several years ago when a brass plaque was placed on the bridge that so states ... however, I believe it more likely that the bridge was constructed by the WPA crews who lined Cane Creek with similar rock. I have proof that WPA lined the creek, but I cannot find any information about the bridge.... Another clue that leads me to believe that the bridge was not built by PWs is that the newspaper list[s] all the PW crafts and skills available in the camp ... not a mention of a stone mason or bridge builder.

Coberly: While the WPA work seems similar, we could not find any indication that they built anything on post. However, that does not mean they did not supervise or otherwise provide planning support to Army Engineers who did provide oversight, perhaps using WPA plans which was the style at the time....

It could very well be that the bridge and stonework were built prior to the war in 30s via WPA, and the POWs may have merely repaired them or cleaned up, with correlations made later that POWs "built" them because people saw them working in proximity.

I have a pix of POWs working in or near the ditches....[6]

In recent years, the "brass plaque" referred to above, embossed with the inscription "THIS BRIDGE WAS BUILT BY GERMAN PRISONERS OF WAR DURING WORLD WAR II," was placed on an abutment at the northeastern end of the bridge. But by 2011, it was lying on the paved ground beneath the pillar. It was gone the following year.

In a letter to *The Anniston Star* in 2009, Jacksonville resident Walter E. Wilkerson provided a curious observation:

In the mid–'80s, I was playing golf with John Sellers ... the deputy county extension agent ... at Cane Creek, he picked up a leaf from the tree adjacent to the 18th tee. He said: "Walt, this tree is not native to Alabama. My degree from Auburn is in forestry, and I know every tree in this state." ...

In 1989, I visited my son ... in Germany.... While walking back to the apartment, I noted the same type of leaf.... I picked up some and on my return I met John....

After recalling our encounter on the golf course, we agreed that prisoners of war must have received seeds or seedlings from home to be planted in the area where they were being retained.[7]

In the POW camp itself, nearly everything is gone. Sergeant Coberly aptly summed it up in 1980: "A housing area now stands where the camp once stood. In the woods separating officer and enlisted housing, a few barracks foundations lie crawling with weeds. A stonework well has been filled in. Only a garbage trough remains."[8]

Even the camp's street designations have been changed. Baker Gate, which stood at the intersection of Pelham Road and Baker Road, serving as the main entrance into the POW complex, has been replaced by a traffic light. Baker Road is now called Shipley Road, and Pelham Road is currently the main north-south artery known alternately as McClellan Boulevard and Highway 21. The streets flanking both ends of the POW camp, as well as the inner roads, never had names. Today—altered, widened, blacktopped—they are known, from west to east, as Morton Road, Foxley Road, and Littlebrant Drive. Portions of those same modern roads also pass through what was once the American military camp. The drainage ditch along the northern side of the camp, so familiar to the American personnel who worked on that side, is still there—the only recognizable feature—but now widened and shaped by a concrete lining. The general formation and terrain of both camps can barely be ascertained even by those familiar with the former layout. People revisiting the site remark on how it has changed beyond recognition.

Marie Shay was nearly aghast when she returned in 1985, 39 years after the camp had closed, to see nothing remaining of either the camp or Surrey Hill. "My goodness!" she exclaimed, "It's all changed. It doesn't look anything at all like it used to."⁹ Disappointed by the disappearance of all the buildings in which she had lived, worked, and worshipped, as well as the transformation of Pelham Road, she chose instead to locate friends from the past still living in the area with whom she could share memories.

One memento of the camp was accidentally unearthed in March 1981. Nearly 40 years earlier, members of the 2nd Company in Compound 1 had decided—and apparently received permission—to erect a stone monument commemorating their internment on their company grounds. It survived the razing of all the buildings and subsequent landscaping of the grounds after the camp had closed. Eventually, it became part of the postwar housing development.

On March 12, 1981, Alan Daily, the 11-year-old son of Sergeant Douglas Daily and his wife, who lived on Morton Road, nosed around a rectangular slab that had once stood upright on a concrete base. The piece of fallen concrete, bearing the impression of an outstretched eagle above a large encircled number "2," was noticeably cracked from left to right and through the eagle. More than a generation had passed since the camp had been shut down and irrevocably changed, and anyone who knew of the monument had apparently forgotten or moved away. When the Daily family moved in, they thought the stone odd but not particularly noteworthy.

But then Alan began poking around the exposed base and found a long-discarded Nehi bottle buried within. More curiously, he noticed what appeared to be a paper of some sort within the bottle. Breaking the bottle, he extracted the paper but could not decipher the message written in German. He showed it to his father, who took it to Sergeant Major Richard A. Barth of the German Liaison Department at Fort McClellan, who translated it:

USA, the 3rd September 1943

2nd Company, Prisoner of War Camp
Fort McClellan, Alabama, USA

Early September, 1943 SFC Hoerter, Sgt. Kuther, Sgt. Klose and PFC Buettner created this monument for the

2. Prisoner of War Company in Fort McClellan
Alabama, U.S.A.

It shall serve as a memorial and keep our faith in our beloved German Homeland strong and imperturbable during the time we have to stay here.

Robert Heber
MSG and acting German Company Commander

Sergeant Daily later told the press, "When Alan ran in the house with the letter, I thought it might just be a plain old piece of paper.... But I often wondered about the stone marker.... When Alan told me the bottle and letter were inside it, I knew it had to be some sort of message. Now I'm glad to know what that hunk of cement in my backyard is all about."

The note was given to the federal government, following the appropriate protocol for retrieval of such artifacts on military bases. The monument was later moved to the POW cemetery, where it was placed flat on its back side within a larger, low-to-the-ground cement marker, thus preventing further cracking. It currently reposes, a little less than a half-mile east of where it once stood, enclosed within the cemetery fence and invisible to passing vehicles.¹⁰

The January 10, 1944, *P.o.W. Oase* included an item, apparently submitted by Wm. Gottschlich, describing the layout and events of Company 2. The writer reported the beautification efforts in the company area—porches, gardens of stonework, grass, and shrubbery, as well as attempts to transform a prisoner's barracks into a "Tyrolean farmhouse." He also described an area where the "company symbol," an eagle, was "cast in cement with two garlands."[11]

The only other remaining feature from the POW camp is the cemetery itself, just beyond and southeast of the camp enclosure. It occupies a square, fenced-in section of land atop a small knoll, accessed by a crescent-shaped road off the north side of Shipley Road.

In his 1980 newspaper series, Staff Sergeant Coberly quoted former 382nd Company MP Edward Hooper: "I don't know what happened after 1944. But when I came back in 1946, I heard about the cemetary [*sic*] and just couldn't believe so many had died."[12] However, only a few Germans interred within the grounds have any connection to McClellan. The remainder died of relatively natural (illnesses or accidents) or unnatural (suicides or being slain while attempting to escape) causes elsewhere in Alabama or the South and were brought to the graveyard set aside for POW burials with military honors.

Hutchinson summarized the details as follows: "At Fort McClellan, a POW cemetery was established for ... German and Italian soldiers who died during their captivity in America.... Most camps usually buried the deceased prisoners nearby; later the bodies were exhumed and relocated to Fort McClellan. Although wartime enemies, American authorities permitted the German soldiers the honor of full military funerals."[13]

"They brought the Italians in [for burial] and had a military car interspersed, and they reinterred them from Aliceville," witness Rita (Johnson) Wells said in 2008.[14]

The POW cemetery in 1945, before the war in Europe had ended. It was subsequently enlarged and beautified and today presents an attractive appearance befitting hallowed ground. It is the only recognizable feature of the entire POW complex still intact (author's collection).

The most prominent grave belongs to Brigadier General Hans Schuberth. The high rank on his tombstone commands considerable attention, especially from first-time or novice visitors who mistakenly assume he spent his years of captivity in McClellan's camp.

Speculation about Schuberth has run rampant over the years: he was a dentist; he was a Nazi agitator; he was executed (shot); he was a colonel-general, a rank comparable to brigadier general; his name was actually Hans Schubert. In 2008, Joan McKinney said she had heard all these stories.[15]

In a January 4, 1993, letter, Fort McClellan researcher E. B. Walker wrote:

> The correct name of the place where General Schuberth died was Kennedy General Hospital in Memphis, TN.... The photo of his funeral procession was made at POW Camp Como, Miss., which was a few miles south of Memphis. I believe his only connection with Como is that he was temporarily buried there. No General Officers were normally held at Como. There is nothing to indicate he was ever at POW Camp McClellan.
>
> The U.S. Army had a practice of burying temporarily at the nearest place those who died, and then moving them after the war to permanent graves at National or Post Cemeteries.[16]

The indefatigable Joan McKinney, who relentlessly mines all sources in her efforts to memorialize McClellan, wrote in 2009, "I have a copy of his Bio ... that was obtained from the German archives. According to the records we received, he was born in Bad Elster on Sep 8, 1892. He was promoted to MG on Jul 1, 1942 and captured in Digne France on Aug 19, 1944." The "Bio" she referred to was a February 22, 1983, letter from "Knoll" written on "German Army Liaison Staff US Army Chemical School Fort McClellan" letterhead. It averred that Schuberth was a career veteran holding command posts, including those of battalion commander and chief of staff of the 16th Army, who died on April 4, 1945, in the "Military Hospital, Kennedy, TN" of a brain tumor.[17]

In a February 16, 2013, email, she addressed the continuing paucity of verifiable information:

> There are a couple of "mysteries" about Schuberth.... I don't find any records of him ever being at Ft McClellan, although a letter from the Ft McClellan German Liaison Officer, dated Feb 22, 1983, states at the end of the listing that he was transferred to Ft McClellan. I really think this is a simple error in translation—I think it probably meant that he was transferred to Ft McClellan for burial.
>
> Here comes some more mystery: There are two different records of where he was interned when [he] died. The 1983 letter (and the German Military Records) state Kennedy, TN. Kennedy was a WWII Military Hospital near Memphis that specialized in several acute areas, including neurosurgery and psychiatry. Since his death was a brain tumor, this makes sense.
>
> E. B. Walker's ltr dtd Jan 4, 1993 provides an excellent explanation that I believe has merit. I met with E. B. many times....
>
> E. B. was a retiree who was helping his son with a dissertation of the PWs in Alabama and had amassed an incredible collection on the topic....
>
> [In *Guests Behind the Barbed Wire*, Ruth Beaumont Cook explained, "In 1981, historian E. B. Walker's son Chip chose Camp Aliceville as the subject for a history assignment at Birmingham-Southern College.... When Chip went on to graduate school, he left his Camp Aliceville research materials at home with his father, who remained interested in the subject and began to collect additional information...."[18]]
>
> I really don't think Hans Schuberth was ever a dentist at Camp McClellan. I have never heard, nor have I ever come across any records or indications that he was....
>
> I believe E. B.'s information to be correct—he had documentation for all his writings—and if not, said so.

Yes, I have heard the rumor that Schuberth died of gunshot wounds, but … do not ascribe to it.

In a follow-up email written the next day, McKinney added:

> According to Joachim [Metzner, son of *P.o.W. Oase* editor Paul Metzner], there is no MG Hans Schuberth mentioned in Die Oase. He says there is a "Schubert," first name unknown, discussed as a Chess Player in Apr 1944 and then again in Apr 1945 as a Chess Player. No Hans Schubert….
>   I don't think he was ever at Ft McClellan except as his final resting place.[19]

P.o.W. Oase diligently reported major events at the camp. The paper was still churning out issues when whoever is buried beneath the tombstone marked "Brig. Gen. Hans Schuberth" reportedly died. It seems inconceivable that the paper would not have written about such a high-ranking official. So, at this writing, despite conflicting information and grandiose theories, it seems likely that Schuberth died on April 4, 1945, was originally buried elsewhere, and only considerably later was reinterred at McClellan.

McClellan's annual cemetery tributes are the most visible remnant of the old POW camp. In the July 14, 1967, issue of *The Anniston Star*, PFC Theodore Miller called it "Perhaps the most poignant reminder of years past" and wrote, "A memorial ceremony is traditionally held at the cemetery on the Sunday in November closest to German Memorial Day."[20]

A newspaper fragment, dated November 14, 1977, but otherwise unattributed and bearing the headline "Germans buried at fort honored with services," reposing in the files of the Alabama Room of Anniston's public library, maintained:

> Sunday's ceremony was conducted by a group of German soldiers and airmen stationed at the Redstone Arsenal in Huntsville [Alabama].
>   During the ceremony, the German honor guard and the sergeants major of Ft. McClellan placed a wreath at the Iron Cross in the cemetery….
>   The national anthems of both nations and traditional German songs were played by the 14th U.S. Army band.
>   The Anniston German Club placed flowers on the grave of each German soldier.[21]

In the November 17, 1980, issue of *The Anniston Star*, Marian Uhlman wrote:

> Approximately 100 persons visited the … Cemetery on Sunday afternoon for a brief service to honor these … soldiers. In West Germany, the third Sunday in November is known as "Volkstrauertag"—similar to America's Memorial Day. The day also has acquired a special meaning at Fort McClellan for more than 15 years….
>   [T]he 14th Army Band played "Ich hat einen Kameraden," which translates as "I had a comrade." The band played primarily German music but also performed the U.S. national anthem….
>   Marga Connell from Bynum [Alabama] explained her reason for attending…. Her father, a German, had been a POW in the Soviet Union.
>   "I have no grave to decorate," said the attractive, middle-aged woman who married an American serviceman. "This way I can honor him."
>   She, like other German wives of U.S. military men, helps the Army engineers tend to the cemetery. Mrs. Connell said these graves are "all mine" instead of the one she can't be near.[22]

In *Nazi Prisoners of War in America*, originally published in 1979, Arnold Krammer wrote:

> Each year, the dozen or so German [26 German, 3 Italian] POWs buried there are honored in a bilingual ceremony, presided over by a German liaison officer from Redstone Arsenal, with music supplied by the 14th WAC Army Band, and with decorations provided by both the Ger-

man Consulate General in New Orleans, and the dependent wives who make up the German Club of nearby Anneston [sic], Alabama. The American chaplain recites prayers in English and German, and the WAC Army Band strikes up the national anthems of both countries. "It is," according to Betty J. Kelley, Public Relations Officer at Fort McClellan, "a short but very impressive ceremony." With these exceptions, however, any knowledge that German prisoners had once spent nearly four [actually slightly less than three] years at this base is almost unknown.[23]

That was undoubtedly true when written. But the recent spate of monographs on the POW experience in America has made a considerable number of Annistonians acutely aware of this part of their heritage. In recent years, editors and writers of *The Anniston Star* have provided generous coverage of the annual cemetery observances. And a handful of local survivors from that era, as well as a solid corps of historians and history "buffs," have generated an increasing level of enthusiasm about anything connected to POWs in Anniston.

Longtime Annistonian Margaret Newman has attended several annual observances. Following the November 16, 2008, ceremony, she wrote:

We estimated 75 present. I doubt there were Europeans there. There were 4 Germans in uniform and one Italian in uniform. The Italian [Lieutenant Colonel Ezio Vecchio] helped me over the rough ground. There was no printed program.

The Germans, three abreast, came in carrying a large … wreath. The Italian followed carrying a white, red, green wreath. It looked about the size of a dinner plate in comparison with the German's. He was followed by a woman and 2 children carrying vases of white, red and green flowers. The wreath was placed in front of the Italian graves and the flowers at the individual graves. The German wreath was placed in front of the Iron Cross. The German [Lieutenant Colonel Christian Uhlig] read a short speech in which he said "World War II was the war to end all wars.["] … Then he made reference to Iraq and Israel. Then the Italian read a shorter speech after a moment of silence.…

I anticipated more pomp and ceremony. There was no invocation, benediction, or music. Recorded music would have been fine. It was solemn but not sad. No one was crying.

Afterward there was a reception.… There was a long table loaded with many kinds of goodies.… The room was very crowded.…

The cemetery day was beautiful sunny at 57°.[24]

In his November 21, 2008, column in *The Anniston Star*, Phillip Tutor described the event in emotional terms:

While standing on the McClellan hill, bundled from the November chill, the sights and sounds smacked you squarely between the eyes. It was an inescapable blow.…

There are few apt words that can describe the annual remembrance ceremony.… Held each November, it's an unforgettable, emotional occasion to most who've ever bothered to attend.

Last Sunday's blue-sky gathering represented everything good about the legacy of Anniston's former military post. That it brought citizens …—former war-time combatants—together to remember the dead … was all the better. It's a living, breathing historical classroom that resides in our midst.[25]

In subsequent years, the ceremony has included music and "Taps," and attendance has surpassed 100.

As McKinney said in November 2009:

The cemetery is currently run by the Anniston Army Depot. Probably since about 1999. That was the year that Fort McClellan was officially decommissioned. The depot is the largest tank rebuild center in the world. It goes back to World War II. It's run by the United States Army.

The commander would be a colonel's position, a separate command. It was part of the industrial structure of the army. Fort McClellan was part of the training structure of the army.

The cemetery holds 26 German and three Italian graves. It runs in perpetuity. They contract out to have it cleaned.

A local committee sponsors the Third Sunday in November commemoration in the cemetery: the Society for the Preservation and Memorialization of the POWs. The commemoration began sometime in the 1970s until 1999, when the fort closed. Then there might have been a skip of a couple years before it began again.[26]

On November 16, 2009, journalist Michael A. Bell wrote, "Remembrance ceremonies have been held here for a half-century or longer."[27] A year later, reporter Cameron Steele credited "Jacksonville resident Klaus Duncan, a member of the [Fort McClellan] POW society," as the "man responsible for organizing the annual remembrance ceremony."[28] And in 2011, Laura Johnson wrote, "The event is organized by the Fort McClellan Memorial Association."[29]

A photocopied newspaper clipping, with no attribution or date save Paige Rentz's byline and the handwritten notation "NOV. 2012," was sent to the author. It indicated:

> The ceremony is scheduled each year to coincide with the German national day of remembrance that falls each year on the third Sunday of November and which aligns closely with the Italian holiday to honor the military, which falls earlier in the month.
>
> The Fort McClellan POW Association, led by Rita Wells, Joan McKinney and Klaus Duncan, have organized the ceremony since McClellan closed.
>
> Duncan said the Anniston Army Depot takes care of the upkeep at the cemetery, and all funding for the event comes through donations.[30]

The cemetery is small but spacious for its 29 graves. Its most noticeable feature, appropriate for the memories of those interred but jarring for unwary passersby, is a large Iron Cross, nearly as familiar—and notorious—as the German swastika.

The 29 stones carry the names, ranks, and death dates of those interred. The inscribed information and name spellings are only as accurate as the records from which they were procured at the time of burial. Several misspellings exist, as well as a curious, almost cavalier alternation of English and German for the POWs' ranks. At this writing, no modern monuments, correcting the errors, have been placed. The 26 Germans and three Italians are as follows:

Alfred Adler	Cpl.	11–11–44
Albert Heinrich Barthelmess	Sgt.	12–4–44
Marcel Beck	Corporal	11–14–43
Paul Bornmann	Gefreiter	7–26–44
Alfred Christoph	Obergefreiter	9–28–44
Fritz Clemens	Gefreiter	2–7–44
Werner Elflein	Gefreiter	7–18–44
Willy Fischer	1 Lieut.	1–31–45
Karl Frank	Cpl.	8–21–45
Peter Gnau	Cpl.	11–11–44
Gunter Hoever	L. Cpl.	8–25–43
Otto Jaeckel	Soldat.	9–16–45
Richard Jaeckel	Obergefreiter	11–3–45
Kurt Knopf	Sgt.	5–1–45
Josef Kohl	Gefreiter	1–25–44
Karl Krause	Hilfszoll Assistant	6–8–45

Walter Lienert	Cpl.	4–30–44
Erich Nachtigall	Cpl.	2–20–46
Waldemar Ott	Ober-Gefreiter	7–20–44
Friedrich Rauschenberg	Pvt.	8–18–43
Heinz Reinke	Pvt. 1 Cl.	9–13–44
Rolf Schneider	Sgt.	8–6–43
Heinrich Schorr	Pvt.	5–28–45
Hans Schuberth	Brig. Gen.	4–4–45
Otto F. Ulrich	L. Corp.	9–12–43
Willi Waechter	Obergefreiter	7–29–43
Giuseppe Iacoboni	Capt.	3–4–44
Resorie Spera	Pvt.	8–24–43
Vincenzo Vernacchio	Pvt.	2–17–44[31]

Willi Waechter was the first to die (July 29, 1943), and Erich Nachtigall (also spelled Nachtingall) was the last (February 20, 1946—almost a year after the war in Europe had ended). Most deaths occurred elsewhere, chiefly Camp Aliceville in Alabama ("We have 14 Germans from Aliceville that were reburied at McClellan," wrote Joan McKinney in August 2013[32]) and Camps Como and McCain in Mississippi.

In his paper translating highlights of several issues of *P.o.W. Oase*, Klaus Duncan wrote:

> August 1, 1943, Rolf Schneider (24) was shot by machinegun fire. He died August 6, 1943.
> August 17, 1943, Friedrich-Karl Rauschenburg (19) was shot while working at a camp sawmill and died August 17. He had been trying to escape or had a fight with a guard.

Neither death occurred at McClellan. In the same paper, he added, "Seven POWs died and were buried in Aliceville. Following the de-activation of Camp Aliceville in 1945, the U.S. Army moved the Bodies to … Ft. McClellan."[33]

In the July 27, 1944, issue of *P.o.W. Oase*, Paul Metzner waxed sentimental over the burial of two other German soldiers, "members of the Camp Aliceville … and admitted because of illness to the General Hospital in Atlanta, in the vain hope to recover." His son translated a portion of the heartfelt eulogy:

> From the little hill in the neighborhood of our camp where the prisoners pass on their way to their daily workplaces … a somber wooden sign overlooks the street. POW-CEMETERY is the inscription. It is the cemetery of the POW-camp of Fort McClellan.
> It is a bitter, serious transition every time when we hear the roll of drums as the mortal remains of a fellow soldier are brought to this place…. And so in the past few days, we carried two German soldiers to their graves, two German men who were just beginning their lives, 20-year-old Gefreiter W. Elflein and 23-year-old OGefr. Waldemar Ott….
> Two new soldiers' graves lie in the soil of Alabama.[34]

Only four of those buried in the cemetery actually died at McClellan:

• Willi Waechter, who died of a skull fracture, severe brain laceration, and severe subdural hemorrhage when a truck he was riding in overturned on July 29, 1943.

• Josef Kohl, who died of a "probable barbiturate poisoning" on January 25, 1944.

• Fritz Clemens, who died of "cardiac dilation with congestive heart failure" on February 7, 1944.

• Karl Krause, who strangled himself on June 8, 1945.[35]

Remembering the
Fort McClellan POW Camp

"There has developed a kind of home-sickness in me
when I see this region."

People often memorialize what they esteem by erecting statues or monuments and transferring names to topographical features or manmade constructions.

McClellan commissioned no statues or monuments. But plaques have been posted, buildings christened, and streets renamed.

Today's Morton Road comes from Major General Charles Gould Morton, the commander of the 29th Infantry Division of the New York National Guard, the first commandant of Camp McClellan.

Summerall Gate and Summerall Gate Road honor the memory of General Charles P. Summerall, informally known as the "Father of Fort McClellan," a man instrumental in its formation and transition to a full-fledged fort.

Littlebrant Drive takes its name from Colonel William T. Littlebrant, the commander in 1919, while Baltzell Gate and Baltzell Gate Road pay tribute to Colonel George Franklin Baltzell, commander from 1934 to 1936, when many of the permanent buildings were built in the Spanish architectural style.

Buckner Hall (the main headquarters edifice), the thumb-shaped Buckner Circle (which hosts most of the Spanish-style buildings, both residential and administrative), and Buckner Drive all salute Lieutenant General Simon Bolivar Buckner Jr., a McClellan commander during 1938–1939 who was killed on June 18, 1945, along with some of his 10th Army soldiers, by Japanese artillery shelling on Okinawa during the final weeks of the War in the Pacific.

Galloway Gate and Galloway Road call to mind Colonel Irene O. Galloway, the fourth director of the Women's Army Corps (WAC), who oversaw the complete integration of the corps within the army, as well as the establishment of McClellan as its first permanent home during her term (1953–1957).

Both Hutchinson Hall and Remington Hall, atop the "Headquarters Hill" section of the main post, identify two men active in the long-forgotten Datu Ali Expedition on Mindanao, the large southern island in the Philippine chain, in October 1905. William R. Hutchinson was a private in Company K of the 22nd Infantry Regiment who received a citation for "bravery in action on the Malaia River." Philip Remington was a second lieutenant in the same regiment who, according to a plaque on the outer wall just right of the hall's entrance, "killed Datu Ali and led the advance guard detachment which captured his cotta and killed his followers."

Silver Chapel, the main post house of worship, memorializes Horace Percy Silver, a well-known army chaplain, and Monteith Amphitheater commemorates First Lieutenant Jimmie W. Monteith Jr., of the 15th Battalion, 5th Regiment IRTC, who died on June 6, 1944, near Colleville-sur-Mer, France, in the horrific engagement that history has termed D–Day.

Pelham Road, the current McClellan Boulevard/Highway 21, for years kept alive the name of John Pelham, a near–West Point graduate who left the academy weeks before graduation to join his native Alabama in the action against the North in the Civil War. Competent, dashing, and handsome, the artillery officer earned recognition from his superiors in the engagements at Manassas (or First Bull Run), Second Bull Run, Sharpsburg (or Antietam), and Fredericksburg. After the last conflict, General Robert E. Lee, commanding the Army of Northern Virginia, referred to him as the "Gallant Pelham." While leading a detachment of General James Ewell Brown ("Jeb") Stuart's mounted artillery on March 17, 1863, during the battle of Kelly's Ford, Virginia, the 24-year-old, just two weeks commissioned a lieutenant colonel, was struck in the head by an enemy shell as he urged his men onward with the shout, "Forward, boys! Forward to victory and glory!" He lingered throughout the day and died shortly after midnight. Pelham was buried in Jacksonville, north of Anniston. The current Pelham Range, on the west side of the former Pelham Road, is named for him.

And various streets winding through the complex that once was Fort McClellan bear names associated with former military luminaries: Nielsen Street (also spelled Neilsen and Nielson in various maps and signs), for Colonel George Clarence Nielsen, who was in charge of McClellan during the pivotal year of 1945, when World War II ended; Drennan Drive (also spelled Drennen), for Major William A. Drennan, a onetime post adjutant; and so forth.[1]

However, in recent years, much of the attention given McClellan has focused not on the main post, but rather on its POW camp, now alive primarily in memory. Fostered by the popularity of classic World War II films like *The Great Escape* and intensified interest in the war, an undeniable romanticism clings to the aura of America's POW camps, ennobling them as paragons of hospitality, particularly when juxtaposed with the images of Europe's notorious concentration camps.

Any German who survived the war as a POW is today viewed heroically as someone who had the misfortune of being captured while taking up arms on behalf of his country. And the American GI guarding the camp, once considered less courageous than the combat veteran, perhaps even a goldbrick, now claims his rightful place as one who served his country in the capacity in which he was placed.

Whenever people asked Jack Shay what he did during the war, he answered, "I served in Alabama. Fort McClellan. Prisoner of war camp. We guarded the German prisoners."[2] And in comments made to his son nearly half a century ago, remarks he never thought would be recorded in a book, he said, "None of us knew going in where we'd end up. We were prepared to fight and die. It was just a roll of the dice that determined where you'd go. It wasn't how strong you were or how big you were. I played sports when I was young. I knew how to fight. But I got an infection and wound up on the home front. Some guys were smaller than me. Pipsqueaks. And they wound up decorated war heroes in combat. We all did our duty, the same as the other guy."[3]

Today, there is a palpable luster to America's POW camps. Upon hearing of this project, one person exclaimed, "Ooh, your father actually served in a prisoner of war camp? I didn't even know we had prison camps here in America!"[4]

Margaret Newman, an Annistonian who served in World War II as a Navy WAVE (Women Accepted for Volunteer Emergency Service), returned home on furlough and visited the American military camp. She later became a career educator, teaching at schools throughout Alabama, and wrote several biographical and genealogical books. She spoke for many when she wrote on June 16, 2011, "Many in Anniston did or do not know it [the camp] was there."[5]

Across the state from Anniston, and with a population only a tenth as large, Aliceville holds a museum and various collections devoted to the POW experience. As a rack card explains:

> At Camp Aliceville, the U.S. Army housed more than 6,100 German POWs and employed more than 1,000 American military and civilian personnel....
> Exhibited are the artistic expressions of these POWs as seen through their paintings, musical instruments, sculpture, photographs, and furniture. Former POWs donated many items including Afrika Korps military equipment and Camp Aliceville publications.
> A fifteen-minute video introduces the visitor to the Camp Aliceville experience through eyewitness accounts by former POWs, military guards and civilian employees.[6]

Mary Bess Paluzzi, the museum's former executive director, wrote, "During an average year, the museum welcomes more than 3,000 visitors, including military history enthusiasts and descendants of former POWs. The museum provides them with an increased appreciation of German culture, as it was cherished and preserved by the POWs, and a renewed appreciation for the humane treatment of prisoners...."[7]

And *Nazi POWs in America*, a 2002 documentary on the History Channel, in focusing on a general treatment of its subject with special segments on Aliceville, included some photographs of McClellan's camp and cemetery, but with nary a word of identification.

It remains to be seen whether McClellan will ever possess the same resources and receive the same attention as Aliceville. There has been some interest in preserving the murals in Remington Hall as a unique representation of German creativity while robed in POW uniforms. But at this writing, Remington Hall, with its outer grounds sprouting wild and unsightly vegetation, needs attention.

So how is McClellan's POW camp remembered?

On the surface, life in McClellan was little different from life in any other camp. Prisoners experienced relatively spacious barracks; buildings for artistic, hobby, and craft activities; entertainment facilities and sports fields; libraries; canteens; and leisure rooms in which to pursue the same interests they indulged before the bullets and bombs began flying. The POW camps' work details allowed prisoners to utilize specific skills or tasks and make money. They had produce and flower gardens, greenhouses, education classes, history lessons, studies in the English language, newspapers in their own language, music, and good and plentiful food.

Perhaps the most difficult affliction affecting the prisoners was not even the much-trumpeted boredom of life in camp, but rather the loneliness born of isolation from one's homeland and loved ones. "When you first arrived in camp, whether you were a German PW or a GI, you felt homesick," Jack Shay remarked. "You felt like crying, but you braced up. You prayed for your family back home. You wrote whenever you could. And you made buddies real fast."

But apart from the nagging loneliness experienced by soldiers on both sides—and, for the prisoners, the uncertainty of conditions back home—life in most camps was fairly carefree, a safe respite from the weary worries of war.

But still, there was something special about McClellan.

It received accolades from military officials and civilian contractors for its physical beauty—for Cane Creek, its scenic pond, two decorative pedestrian bridges, swimming pools, bowling alleys, an outdoor amphitheater carved within a sloping hillside, and the mix of new architectural buildings in the Spanish style among the older wooden barracks. Even the POW camp, rising from a wooded hill, presented a not unpleasant sight, despite the looming guard towers and lack of stuccoed and tiled architectural gems.

When Colonel George C. Nielsen arrived in early January 1945 to assume his duties as commander of Fort McClellan, he expressed pride in the post's beauty and spotless condition. As a reporter wrote:

> …Colonel Nielsen declared that he believed Ft. McClellan to be far in advance of the average high standard. He expressed gratification over the extensive facilities … and said he believed "this in part is a factor accounting for the outstanding performances noted thus far." …
>
> The colonel declared … the one [mess hall] he did visit is "the cleanest I've ever seen in the Army."[8]

Similar comments through the years helped McClellan achieve its reputation as a model fort. The POW camp became a natural extension of the fort itself, collecting the same approbation.

Camp administrators did not stint on amenities to make POW incarceration as pleasant as possible, considering the unavoidable strictures the war forced upon the "guests."

McClellan's camp saw few strikes, protests, and escape attempts (none successful), and palpably little discontent or agitation. McClellan was a "safe" camp, unlike others in which either virulent Nazism or anti–Nazism threatened lives and tranquility. It routinely received favorable reviews from the International Red Cross, International YMCA, and other inspection teams.

McClellan had, proportionally, a high percentage of talented prisoners—gifted writers, artists, and craftsmen. And it was a large camp—with a capacity of over 3,000 (although far more than 3,000 different prisoners cycled through at one time or other)—even if not as large as some of the mammoth camps several times that number. Those larger camps and the "political" ones, because of their size and philosophical milieu, could expect (and often exhibited) less homogeneity and a greater rate of incidents.

For these reasons, Fort McClellan and its POW appendage enjoyed the reputation of being a model installation.

In the 1960s, Jack Shay explained McClellan's singularity:

> McClellan was one of the best PW camps in the country. We treated our PWs very fairly all over America. But McClellan was something special. That's not just me. We heard it from the military brass when they were visiting and from all the inspectors who sized up the place to see if we were up to snuff as far as the Geneva Convention went.

PW camps were like anything else in life—very personal. Look, if you have a good experience anywhere, you're gonna come away with a good opinion. If you have a bad experience, you're gonna hate it. It's as simple as that.

But when you have PWs and staff coming in from other camps, whether it's Aliceville or Opelika or Rucker, and they tell you they like McClellan best, then you start believing that it's not just you.

There was good and bad in all camps, I don't care what anyone says. But McClellan was a good one, maybe the best. That's why they called it the "model camp." That's what we heard from others.

Of the several thousand internees and American GIs stationed at the camp from 1943 to 1946, only a few ever returned to see the site. Time, geography, disinterest, and new commitments in life all played a role.

One POW who returned was Alfred Arens, who wrote a personal reminiscence (original typescript intact):

> And now my *fourth visit,* and it leads me again to *McClellan.* Why have I come? Why have I undertaken the stress of crossing 5.000 miles over the sea? Well, if I think it over the stay in McClellan was—after the years in my parents' house—the longest coherent period of staying in the same place in my life. Therefore there has developed a kind of home-sickness in me when I see this region, these streets and these old trees which stood already here during my time nearly 50 years ago.[9]

Today, even those not alive during the camp's existence recall it. They find the whole POW experience at McClellan fascinating, riveting, and timeless. They stroll its grounds, irrevocably changed for all time. They drive by the places where once polyglot prisoners lived out their lives in captivity. They collect every scrap of paper their revered ancestors might have saved from their POW years.

One of these is Anniston resident Thom Cole, a military historian and collector, who was pleased to acquire a POW shirt presumably worn by someone at McClellan. "Sam Walker ran a surplus store in Bynum, Alabama," he explained. "And I met him about 1980. Sam was a marine wounded in Korea and collected old military uniforms and equipment. Sam had some old uniforms hanging from the wall of his storeroom. One of them was an old white shirt with 'PW' stenciled on it. I asked Sam what that was, and he said it was a prisoner of war shirt from Fort McClellan. I asked him how he got it. He said it came in a bundle of about 500 from Fort McClellan which he bought in the 1970s to be cut up as rags. He was told by Fort McClellan what they were, so he kept one as a historical souvenir and cut up all the rest for rags. I got the shirt from Sam because he was like a dad to me."

Cole went on to say, "Kimberly O'Dell once told me she was writing a book of the Fort McClellan POW Camp. And the number inside the collar identified the year and corps area the prisoner was captured in. This one has 'PW-CRA 4401.' She said it meant he was captured in 1944, 1st Corps area."[10] (However, most of the numbers assigned to McClellan's POWs that this author was able to verify had a different marking system, with up to eight characters, including designation of the pertinent U.S. Service Command and prisoner's home country. For example, Robert Suberg's number was 4WG-29728. This meant "4"th Service Command, "W"ar Department, "G"ermany, and prisoner number "29,728.") The shirt is among Cole's favorite and most personal acquisitions.

Though bereft of nearly everything it once held, the McClellan camp site is still a magnet for those who cannot forget its quondam purpose. Not as haunting as the sunken hulk of the U.S.S. *Arizona* forever interred beneath the waters of Pearl Harbor, not as emotional as the rows of graves at Normandy, it still tugs at the sentiments of anyone who knows its history.

In October 2010, Peter Gölzhäuser of Marburg, Germany, journeyed to the old POW site, intent on visiting the grave of Peter Gnau, his grandfather, who perished with fellow POW Alfred Adler on November 11, 1944, in a "traffic accident" in Camp McCain, Mississippi, and was interred in McClellan's cemetery. It was Gölzhäuser's third pilgrimage to the burial site of the grandfather he never knew. He presented Annistonian Joan McKinney with copies of documents and letters pertaining to Gnau, including a notice of his death that the American Red Cross sent to the POW's family in May 1946. According to the *Calhoun Community Press*, the grandson visited the cemetery twice on October 14, remarking, "I was astonished that the cemetery was in such good order 17 years ago and it is still in good order."[11]

McClellan's POW camp has no museum, no historical marker.

It yields only memories.

Epilogue

"Do you remember,
back in the days of McClellan?"

Most of the people who populated both sides of the POW camp have now passed from the scene.

In 2013, "Stalag U.S.A." author Dan Coberly, retired from the army and working for the federal Environmental Protection Agency, addressed the possibility of any of his interviewees from the late 1970s still being alive: "Haven't heard from any of the people quoted since the 80s, they were in their 60s or 70s then, so I have no idea who still lives...."[1]

The Newmans, who rented a room in their Surrey Hill house to a GI from New York and his wife, have both passed away: Bessie Mae Keelen Newman on Good Friday, April 19, 1946, at age 53; and Jesse James Newman on the Fourth of July 1981, at 93.[2]

Sergeant Albert A. "Bud" Jones, who worked in the POW camp headquarters building, resumed a career in food retail management in York County, Pennsylvania, after the war. He died May 6, 1976, at 59. His wife, Evelyn, died January 24, 1983, at 72.[3]

Tennessean Otto Haskell King, of the 1437th Service Command Unit, the POW camp's chief telephone switchboard operator, died at 82 on March 27, 1981, at his home in Columbia. He had retired from his position as a salesman for Raleigh Products. His obituary in the *Columbia Daily Herald* identified him as an "active member of the Central Christian Church" but a man with "no immediate survivors." The "new star in his love-life that is burning right brightly," as *The McClellan CYCLE* reported on November 26, 1943, had apparently long since burned out.[4]

Alabamian Essie L. Woodward, who served as the manager of the PX in the American military camp, lived in Jacksonville after the war. She never married and in her later years became a seamstress. She died on January 26, 1988, at 81.[5]

Jack Shay utilized the knowledge gained as a mess sergeant in his postwar restaurant management career. He owned and operated several food businesses, including "Danceland," a live entertainment pavilion and restaurant in New York. Friends and relatives often looked to him for proper food preparation and presentation, and they listened to him expound on the nuances of porterhouse and T-bone steaks and other meats. Old habits died hard; when crafting his own sauces and fudges, he used multi-gallon kettles—"enough to feed an army," according to his wife. He also became active in the American Legion, the Disabled American Veterans, and church organizations.

The illness that would claim his life first appeared in 1971. His wife and son cared for him as he gradually lost all ability to live independently. Unable to walk, talk, eat, or communicate, he died in a fetal position, a feeding tube hooked to his stomach, on April 2, 1991, at 79.[6]

Massachusetts native John J. George, a master sergeant who worked at the camp and served as a correspondent for *The McClellan CYCLE*, became a career military man, serving in World War II, the Korean War, and the Vietnam War, retiring in 1966 after 24 years of continuous duty. After the death of his first wife, Loretta, he remarried, became a widower for a second time, and remarried for the final time in the latter part of the 1980s. A gentle, soft-spoken man devoted to his four children and five grandchildren, he kept in touch with Staff Sergeant Shay (who served as best man at his November 1944 Anniston wedding) and his wife. During one of several visits with the Shays, he spoke of the loneliness inherent in losing a spouse: "I got married again, but it wasn't for passionate love. It was for companionship. I was so lonely after Loretta died." His second and third wives also had children from previous marriages, and they married him to relieve the same sense of solitude they experienced.

He visited Jack Shay for the last time on October 26, 1985, when the latter was suffering from a nearly 20-year debilitating illness that gradually robbed him of every physiological capability. He beamed his customary smile. "Hi, Jack. You remember me, Jack? From Fort McClellan. The POW camp. You were my best man."

But there was no sign of recognition. And John George's effervescent smile disappeared. "I was so sure he would remember me," he sighed in disappointment.

His last Christmas card bore only a "Dear Marie" salutation: "[W]e've had our spells of heart problems in and out of the hospital but we're hanging in there. Hope Jack is doing better and wished I could write to him."

A member of the American Legion, Disabled American Veterans, Knights of Columbus, and Loyal Order of Moose, George died at 78 in the Walter Reed Medical Center in Washington, D.C., on April 12, 1991—ironically 10 days after his best man had died. Neither McClellan buddy knew of the other's passing.[7]

Sergeant Joseph A. Spinelli, whose injury while in the 82nd Airborne kept him out of combat and detoured him to McClellan, returned to his Johnstown-area home in Pennsylvania after the war and immersed himself in raising a family and working in a number of fields, including cuisine and architecture. As his brother, Patrick, wrote, "Joe was the kindest most giving man and best brother" who "shared his knowledge.... My four boys were ... amazed how they learned from him. Joe gave his time to his Church as a ... carpenter.... He built a pantry kitchen for the St. Vincent DePaul Society. He designed and built a house for our parents."[8]

In his postwar years, Joe Spinelli often joked with his family about the injury that had derailed his airborne career and sent him to McClellan. "He'd always say, 'Oh, my old army injury is acting up' or 'Oh, my back!' and he'd grab his back, pretending like he wanted to get out of work," daughter Mary Jo Berardone explained.

A deeply religious man devoted to St. Anthony of Padua Church, Spinelli died at 80 on March 17, 1998, nearly 18 years after his wife, Mim, and is buried in the same church cemetery in Windber, a few dozen yards from the central bell pavilion he designed and built. "He was born on Groundhog Day and died on St. Patrick's Day," his daughter remembered.[9]

Oklahoma native Jack S. Steward, another permanent party veteran, returned to his home in Colorado after his discharge, along with his wife, Tulsa, and toddler son, Jack E. He operated his own business, sold it, and then became a realtor. He gave full rein to his passionate pastimes, indulging in annual fishing, hunting (elk, antelope, deer, pheasant, etc.), hiking, and camping excursions. He acquired a fleet of vehicles (jeeps, RVs, trailers, SUVs) and traveled extensively throughout North America.

Over the years, the Stewards had four reunions with their next-door neighbors who shared the same duplex on Surrey Hill across from the POW camp. Upon Jack's retirement in the mid–1970s, they moved to Arizona. Tulsa's last letter to their onetime neighbors was postmarked July 2, 1981. She ended with the words, "So Dear Friend—again I … only hope we can continue to keep in touch. Much love to all of you." She died January 3, 1986, at 75. Her husband scattered her ashes from one of his hiking trails in the Tucson Mountains, west of the city of the same name. He later told Marie Shay, "When I hike in those mountains, I stop at the place where I threw her ashes, and I say, 'Hi, Ma.'" When Jack died in his early 90s in 2000, his ashes symbolically joined hers in the same mountain range.[10]

And they continued to die—the Americans and Germans from the camp—with increasing frequency each passing year.

In a letter dated January 18, 1996, Harry L. Springer, who had lost his wife, Ruth, in 1994, alluded to McClellan when he wrote to Marie Shay: "I reminisce about the past and think of the good days we had. As you wrote, we must keep the good thoughts. We had a wonderful friendship."

His last letter to her, written on January 12, 1998, spoke of a hip surgery, numerous chiropractic appointments, removal of a facial tumor, and 33 resultant radiation treatments. He closed by writing, "Stay in good health—that's the most precious asset anybody can have. Again, thanks for thinking of me." Her last card to him, postmarked December 16, 2000, came back marked "Returned to Sender."[11]

Christian Höschle, whose autobiography, *Hast du nichts so bist du nichts* (translated by Joachim Metzner as "If You Have Nothing, You Are Nothing"), provided an intimate glimpse into the POW camp, left McClellan in July 1945, but not for home. According to Metzner's translation, "he was moved to a camp in the woods of South Carolina," where his "Main task … was timber" and where the conditions "were really bad." That camp closed in March 1946, and he left America on April 6. "Another year of captivity in London" followed, but it "was not that bad, because … Höschle could do his favorite work, mainly painting portraits or landscapes for the British Officers." He arrived in Cuxhaven, Germany, on March 15, 1947. But he had to stay in "2 more Camps, first for around 2 weeks [in] Munsterlager, run by the British and then Dachau near Munich, run by the Americans…. Then the official discharge took place on April 3 and Höschle travelled by train to his sister living near Stuttgart and then back in his little home village."

He married in 1948 and became a successful businessman, once employing "100 workers." He sold the company in 1961, moved to Switzerland, started another company, and finally retired in 1980 "to concentrate on his old passion to paint and draw." Höschle died in 2001 at 82.[12]

Robert Suberg, interned at the camp from 1943 to 1946, never again visited America. Marie Shay extended countless invitations for him to come back and reminisce, but health was always a problem. As he explained in a March 6, 1985, letter, "You think it is the right idea to travel. But for me it is not so easy to find the hotel we need. As you know I have to

eat [a special] diet and I am not allowed to eat anything with sugar." Following an unexpected retirement at age 59, his health became even more precarious. "I don't trust to come
over there," he wrote on February 4, 1993. "I am afraid of the long flight, then the difficulties
with my heart and further my diabetes." Multiple hospitalizations, bouts of apoplexy, heart
surgery, a sextuple-bypass operation, and other ailments plagued him for the rest of his
days.

Traveling through Europe by car and train proved easier than a trans-Atlantic trip,
and Suberg spent much of his retirement years off on numerous short holiday jaunts. He
also became a consummate hobbyist, collecting stamps and postcards, building model
ships, and constructing train sets, including a small-scale facsimile of Europe's largest railroad bridge (107 meters high, the "Schwebebahn in Wuppertal"), connecting Solingen and
Remscheid.[13]

He died at 77 on January 17, 2001, having suffered an apparent stroke sometime earlier.
As his widow, Edith, explained, "Robert could think but unfortunately not talk. He would
have remained a severe case for nursing if the heart would have gone on." And his friends
from the war years, inevitably, died apace. According to Edith, "One of his comrades was
from Thüringen … and another one was from the Lower Rhine. They are both dead now.
Mr. [Karl] Merbold is dead also."[14]

Marie Shay capitalized on her experience in the camp and main post headquarters
during a postwar 35-year clerical career in corporations and hospitals. A member and
officer in six organizations, she also volunteered for the Veterans Administration. A tuber-
culosis survivor who spent her late-teen years at the Trudeau Sanitorium in the Adirondack
Mountains, she accepted an on-camera speaking role in a 1990s Florentine Films documentary on the disease.

Having survived pneumonia, an aortic aneurysm and emergency surgery, a heart
attack and open-heart operation, diabetes, chronic arthritis, renal failure, and melanoma,
she eventually succumbed to congestive heart failure. As a teen in the sanitorium, surrounded by older patients (some of whom perished) and expecting to die, she once said,
"If I can just live to be 45," her mother's age at the time. She had nearly doubled it when
she died on March 15, 2005 (fittingly, her mother's birthday).[15]

Widowed since 2009 and entrusted with caring for her accomplished adult son, Steve,
who had valiantly battled physical adversity all his life, Ruth Allen, who worked in the GI
PX, still kept treasured souvenirs from her days in McClellan. "I have pay statements and
Ray's [her husband's] purchase card from Fort McClellan, dated March 8, 1944. We could
buy things in the PX with that. And I have all the photographs that we took there." Then
she added softly, "This will all disappear when I go."[16]

Eugene Steppe, a corporal in the 382nd Military Police Escort Guard Company, who
sat down with the author in October 2008 and pinpointed the location of several buildings
in the camp, passed away three years after that interview. Tom Mullins, the director of the
Alabama Room at Anniston's public library and the person who arranged the interview,
sent an email in November 2012 with the terse phrase, "Sorry to tell you, but he died last
year."[17]

Dr. Joseph (Joby) Walker, whose father constructed housing for GIs on Surrey Hill
across from the POW camp, and who, as a teenager, saw POWs on a daily basis, died on
January 10, 2013, at 85.[18]

Soon McClellan will exist only in fragmented images summoned in the minds of newer generations who can only imagine what it was once like for the people in the old black-and-white photographs—the people who wrote those old letters and reminiscences.

Jack E. Steward, who, as a toddler, moved to Anniston with his parents, was too young to remember anything about the camp and his parents' house on Surrey Hill—too young to remember Sergeant and Mrs. Shay, his neighbors, taking pictures of him running through the grass. Though he would have seen MPs and POWs alike as a two-year-old, he only remembers that "my father was in the army in Alabama, at the POW camp. He was a camp guard, an MP, and I'm sure he was a sergeant."[19]

In an email to the author, Rodney George, born after the camp closed to Master Sergeant John and Loretta George, fondly remembered his father:

Proud to say I am John George's son. Thank you for what you are doing.

I have a bayonet that I believe my Dad obtained when he was at Ft McClellan. I seem to recall one or two other memorabilia items from Ft McClellan.... I recall his sharing with me some brief stories about the prisoners and their handiwork.[20]

And Paul Metzner, who, more than anyone else on either side of the road separating German from American, memorialized the camp in the 75 issues of his invaluable newspaper, left a priceless legacy not lost on his surviving son. As Joachim Metzner commented to the author, "More than once he called himself a conscientious chronicler. To preserve history for the future was obviously his intention and we have the benefit today. Articles in POW-Oase had often many details ... and a lot of other information that helped you and me now exploring the past. Jack, if you can point at this, I think he will be honored in a fair way."[21]

Though not a poet by profession, Paul Metzner often used sublime phrasing to portray emotions that pulsed from the heart. In the January 1, 1944, issue, intended to lift the morale of fellow prisoners and instill a sense of normality in an alien land, he crafted timeless sentiments known to all men, whenever the present recedes into the past, and the future bestows an ineffable yearning. He could have been speaking for himself or for Hermann Haugg ... for Father Josef Müller or Robert Suberg ... for Christian Höschle or Helmut "Bell-Bottom Trousers" Engelke ... for Eugene Steppe or Otto King ... for Sergeants Joe Spinelli or John George ... for Ruth Allen or Rita (Johnson) Wells ... or anyone who shared the days and breathed the air of McClellan so long ago:

And when the chess pieces, the small articles of daily life, the ashtrays ... the cigarette cases, the writing materials ... and so on have their honored places in your homes as the best memories of your unexpected sojourn in America, then you who created them can ponder those memories and hear their quiet voices as they seem to say, Do you remember how it was back in Fort McClellan when you crafted me...?

And it will be as if you are talking to a friend who knows the deepest recesses of your heart.... Do you remember, back in the days of McClellan...[?][22]

No poet could have expressed it more touchingly.

And now, as the last of the thousands of people who once shared those moments pass into history, it is only for us—born too late in time or living too far away in place—to remember. As we strain to hear those faint voices from the grave ... now just silent echoes of the past.

Appendix A

The Alfred Arens Reminiscence

[Alfred Arens was a POW at Fort McClellan who later returned to the site of his former internment a number of times. He left behind a letter on the occasion of his 1991 visit. It was included in the collection of E. B. Walker, a copy of which resides in the current collections of Joan McKinney, for many years the protocol director and public affairs office community outreach coordinator for Fort McClellan. A card, containing explanatory background by E. B. Walker and dated 1993, was attached to the letter. To maintain fidelity to the phrasing and highly personal sentiments of the author, the entire document is presented in its original typescript, including misspellings and mistakes.]

4-14-93

Dr. Arens was am invited guest of the 305th MP Escort Guard Company at the reunion there in 1991. He prepared this for for [*sic*] his hosts and friends. Somehow, I got the feeling that he was sort of telling me that this was sort of a farewell message, and sure enough, within a year he was near death with heart trouble. He had surgery and I think doing ok now.

The reference to the Lt. Col. in the Alabama Militia is due to one of the fancy certificates (Commission) which the governor's office gives out. During the '89 reunion I got a friend to secure a number of these for friends and visitors, including some of the Germans. They seemed impressed, and we all had fun referring to each other as "Colonel."

EB

* * *

Dr. Alfred ARENS
Schattbach 38
D-463 Bochum
Germany

Sept. 1991

Dear American friends!

If I had had to address you 50 years ago I would have said: "My dear ennemies!" That would have been correct in a double way of meaning: you formally were then my so-called "ennemies," but otherwise you were "dear ennemies," because mentally there was no difference between us regarding the fact that we all were members of the same mental community, namely the western culture. In that time our real ennemies were the Russians because we felt that Bolshevics were threatening our border and our culture. Despite that fact I am lucky to say that I had to kill only one Russian,—and that was a shot of mercy. In those days, in the hot summer 1941 during our attack on Russia I found a badly injured Russian soldier. He was unconscious and more dead than alive. He layed under the burning sun and there was fight around me. He couldn't be helped by anybody and in consequence I did what I thought—and think today—was necessary. But believe me that situation has pursued me lifelong. My consolation is the thought: if it had been possible to ask the man: "What do you want me to do?" he would have said: "Do it! Release me!" So I did it, but I could never forget, that I had to send a human beeing into the eternity. Contrarily to that I was never obliged to shoot on British or Americans in Africa due to the fact that I drove here a motocycle for transporting messages from one military unit to the other, and that excluded shooting activities. Sometimes I had to escort British or American prisoners to the assembling points and I prayed that the would not try to escape. They didn't. And I treated them fairly hoping that they would do so with myself if…. They did! You see, dear members of the 305., we were companions and brothers in this way of military activities as well.

217

I was *born in 1920* as son of a merchant in *Bochum*, that is a town of about 400.000 inhabitants on the river Ruhr in the biggest industrial region of Germany and Europe. There I live still today. After 4 years elementary school and 9 years high-school I was *drafted to the German obligatory* "Arbeitsdienst," that means labor service in which I worked on the so-called "Westwall" (=western wall) In that time the war against Poland France and Englang broke out sept. 1 1939. As we built the concrete fortifications in view of the Frenchmen it was necessary to do the work during the night. But obviously the French could hear us and fired some shots of artillery in our direction so we experienced the first losses: 2 dead and some injured men. I was released at the beginning of *1940* so I could enter the *university of Göttingen* (in Lower-Saxonia) for stydying the law. But for half a year only, then I was drafted again, this time to the German Army ("Wehrmacht"). After having been trained as a motocyclist for ¾ of a year I was sent to my later military unit, "the 10.Panzer-Division." *That was in mai 1941*, one month before we invaded Russia. The division was placed in Poland near the Russian border, that means in the midst of the later front of about 2.000 miles. The *attack began June 22, 1941, and we took the direction Moscow.* Accompanied by heavy losses we passed within 5 month 1.500 miles and stood in November/December 1941 about *10 miles in front of Moscow,*—so near that we could see the Russian anti-aircraft-fire when the German planes attacked Moscow. It was an extremely hard situation. The Russians got stronger and stronger since they knew by a German traitor-spy in the Tokyo-ambassady, that the Japanese would not attack them from rear so they could throw all their eastern troops toward west against us. It was extremely cold, more than 45* Celsius (I don't know what it is in Fahrenheit), anyway so cold that our machine-guns stopped firing and the skin of a non-glove-protected hand would hang on any metallic material when touching it. 1 meter snow and so on. In this extremely dangerous situation—1 day after the Japanese attack on Pearl harbour—*the 7.dec.1941 Hitler declared war to the US.* You may understand that we were shocked. Not that we were able to criticise him, but we thought how to manage a new big ennemy when we are not able to get superiority over the Russians? *In april* 1942 we were taken out of Russia and *turned to France* because it seemed impossible to reorganize a badly damaged, high-technical tank-division in Russia. In France we stayed until fall 1942 after participated in *repelling the Britisch attack on Dieppe in august 1942.* Just before probably going back to Russia *the Americans landed in North-Africa Nov. 1942 and we went in a hurry through France and Italy to Tunisia,* where I arrived by airplane (JU 52) dec. 19. 1942. Already 6 days later on Christmas 1942 we were engaged in bitter fights against the British in the mountains about 20 miles west of the city of Tunis,—finally we hold the hights otherwise Tunis would have fallen in the hands of the allies already in 1942. Therfore the British call the mountain "the long stop hill" and built there after the war a monument which I saw when I visited Tunisia in 1961 and 1966. In consequence of the overwhelming allied superiority in men and material we had to surrender in the first days of may 1943. I was captured by soldiers of the British 8.army near the town of Tunis—and my 3-years captivity began. We were transported by railway to the harbour of Oran in Marocco[.] There we entered a ship direction England. When we approached the street of Gibraltar some of us planned to spring over bord and swim to Spanish Marocco. But the British were as prudent as we were and locked us for some hours under deck.

We arrived in England in the *last days of may 1943* and remained there 2 or three weeks. It was *in Oldham near Manchester* in an old machine hall. One day we were guided again on a ship named the "Empress of Scotland" and we thought we would driven perhaps to Scotland itself. But after 3 days on sea suddenly appeared a couple of American officers breaking a sealed letter in front of us and reading that *from now on we were American PW's* according to an agreement between the goverments of UK and USA. The obvious reason was that the British were not able to feed themselves let alone some 100.000 prisoners. It has remained in my mind that during the voyage we had alarm because of a German submarine, but after having been informed about the prisoners on board by an open wireless message it went—thanks to God—away.—*We landed in Newport News/Virginia* where a train was waiting for us which drove us southbound. I won't forget that when passing Washington DC by night we saw the illuminated Capitol and were astonished about that because in all Europe the lights went off Sept. 1, 1939.—*On july 3., 1943 we entered Fort McClellan.* The first impression was excellent. Get in your mind: we were tired, exhausted soldiers who were hunted in the last days in Tunisia like hares by spitfires and thunderbolds, day and night. And now new, clean barracks. The highlight in this evening was a meal of turkeys big like eagles served by men in white jackets: we thought we had arrived in paradise. Naturally, in the following days and month the life got more normal, the normal life of a PW. As a corporal I was not obliged to work but I—and most of the others—worked voluntarily because of the payment of 80 cts instead of 10 cts for non-workers. In this way I baked bread in the Fort McClellan's bakery, learned to harvest cotton and peanuts and to discern black-snakes from rattle-snakes (what some inhabitants did never achieve). In the springtime 1945 we built imitated Japanese villages for training purposes of the GI's, since—before Pearl Harbour—

the US was planning to invade Japan. During these years we came during the harvest-time also to Georgia, Mississippi, Florida and Tennessy.

When the war in Europe came to an end, in springtime 1945, *the life got worse in the camp.* One night trucks drove to our canteens and took away the finer objekts which are able to make the life livingworth, chocolate, beer and so on. And we had to suffer a little bit hunger as well. That throws a shadow on the former US-PW-politics beeing suspicious of having treatened the PW correctly as long only as they had to fear retaliation on American PW's in Germany. In the last days of the war when informations came in that the Russians had invaded eastern Germany one or two PW'S committed suicide hanging one morning in the tree of the camp. They are buried now on Fort McClellans' cemetary. *In fall 1945 the PW-camp McClellan was dissolved and we were transferred to Camp Forrest/Tullahooma/Tennessy.* There we stayed during the winter 1945/46. *In February 1946 we were brought by railway via New York on a ship and we took direction Europe.* Everbody was sure to come straight home to Germany. But what happened? After having landed in Le Havre (France) *we were handed over to the Frenchmen in the notorious PW-camp B o l b e c.* This is the most bitter reproach on the then US–government having sold us like slaves in a modern slave market. And besides: it was a clear offense against the GENEVA convention about the treatment of war-prisoners. The only consonsolation was that these activities of the US–government were badly criticized in the American public as we could read it in the newspapers.—The captivity in France was very hard. We had to work in coal-mines *or even dig out hidden mines on the beach of DIEPPE.* With inadiquate tools like sharpened broom-sticks etc. There were many PW's (in french: PG) who lost her lives a year after the end of the war! In my releasing transport was a comrade who had lost both eyes by an exploding mine.

By an incredible luck *I was released* from french captivity already *in june 1946* two years earlier than my poor fellow-prisoners who had to stay until 1948. Back home I returned to my studies of law *at the university of Münster/Westphalia.* I passed the 2 obligatory German examens in 1949 and 1953. In *1956 I was promoted a doctor of law* by writing a dissertation entitled: "Die künstliche Befruchtung beim Menschen im gegenwärtigen und künftigen deutschen Strafrecht." (The artificial insemination with human beeings in actual and future German penal law).—I began my professional career as an official in the German financial administration. Then—in 1963—*I became a judge,* first of all for all civil and penal matters (claims, divorces, convictions), later for the special branche of finances and taxes: If a citizen in Germany believes that the state demands to high taxes from him he can go to an independent judge who has to check the case according to the law only.—*I am married since 1951 and we have 4 children and 4 grandchildren.* Now I am 71 years old and retired. I feel mentally o.k., by my physis is not satisfying, especially my walking and climbing is very restricted. But who in my age is without any health problems?

Let me say some last words: That is now the fourth time that I visit the US after the war. The first time was *in 1984* when we did a trip along the east-coast from Boston to Niagara falls to Washington to New Orleans to Florida. During that voyage I returned the first time here to McClellan and I was deeply impressed to see this place again.—The second time was *in 1987* for visiting the east-coast from Los Angeles to San Francisco where we experienced an earthquake 5.8, then to Grand Canyon, Salt Lake City, Las Vegas and finally Hawai. When in Pearl Harbour I stood on the Memorial above the sunken battleship "Arizona" whose outlines could be seen under water, and when I was aware that under me were buried in the hull the bodies of 1.100 Americans marines I was deeply sad having the impression that under me were laying my own brothers, soldiers like me in the last war.—The third time was *in 1989 in Aliceville* for celebrating the foundation of the former PW-Camp there in the neighborhood of McClellan which I visited then as well. You remember that I met some of you guys two years ago in Aliceville.

And now my *fourth visit,* and it leads me again to *McClellan.* Why have I come? Why have I undertaken the stress of crossing 5.000 miles over the sea? Well, if I think it over the stay in McClellan was—after the years in my parents' house—the longest coherent period of staying in the same place in my life. Therefore there has developed a kind of home-sickness in me when I see this region, these streets and these old trees which stood already here during my time nearly 50 years ago.

At the end forgive my rather bad English. I never learned it at school,—it is all self-made without any practice. Thank you for your kind invitation but in a certain sense I was really obliged to come viewing the fact that *I am since 1989 Honorary Lieutenant Colonel of the Alabama Militia* (Please keep your seat, you needn't fall in line!)

And the last sentence: all the best for you and the 305. military unit. May it proceed into a successful but peaceful future!

McClellan, sept. 1991
Alfred ARENS

Appendix B

The Erhard Eifler
Reminiscence

[The following is a reminiscence from Erhard Peter Richard Eifler, a former POW at Fort McClellan, sent to a student working on a "history project." It was written in 1991 and also includes a letter of introduction by Erhard's son, Norbert. It provides a look into the typical activities experienced by common POWs while interned at McClellan. A copy is in the possession of Annistonian Joan McKinney, who has amassed a large body of McClellan documents and lectured on various aspects of the fort and POW camp. To maintain the flavor of the original thoughts, the entire text is presented with original syntax intact.]

Bausendorf, 08.02.1991

Dear Richard!

At first a few words in advance. My father is not able to write the letter in English, so I have to translate his story from German into your language. And as you can expect, I am also not totally free in writing mistakes.

My father is very pleased to hear from you that the young americain generation is so interested in the WWII history. And somehow he is even proud to give his contribution as a former prisoner of War and as a german citizen to your history project.

We hope that you will receive our letter just in time for your history fair.

I also included two copies of a picture of my father Erhard Eifler and my uncle Oswald Pauli, who was also at Ft McClellan as a prisoner of WWII, but died last year, and a photo of a barrack.

The extract of my fathers life at Ft McClellan from 11th May 1943, when he was captured in Tunis (Africa) by the 8th British Army, until April 1946, when he left Ft McClellan to Fort Benning, will follow on the seperate letter, which is included, too.

Much fun with his story and maybe

your and my generation will keep in mind
that not all prisoners of War from 1939–1947/48
had to suffer very much.

Thank you again for your letter which gave me and my father the incentive again to reflect former times. Best wishes to you and also to Dr. Dan Spector, sincerely Norbert Eifler

Buhlenberg, 08th Febr. 1991

Dear Richard!

My name is *Erhard* Peter Richard Eifler and I am 68 years now. I live in a rural area in the west of Germany, close to the French border.

It is true that I was a POW at Ft McClellan.

My life as a POW started in Africa, when I was captured as a german soldier close to Tunis by the 8th British Army. They brought us to Algir, where the Americans travelled with us for 4 days on trucks to Casablanca. There, we had to spend about four weeks in tents under a very hot african sun. So from the 11th May 1943, when I was captured until early August, I saw already parts of Africa, some European tourists would wonder now.

From Casablanca we "sailed" with Liberty ships in a convoy to New York. It lasted about two weeks. After our arrival we had to wash our really dirty body and I still remember this soft and white towel we got. I hadn't seen such a marvelous towel before. My first impression was already very good.

Then we travelled about 4 days by train through Virginia, North Carolina to Alabama, Ft McClellan.

At the 18th of August probably, I arrived at the Camp. Even it was hot and sultry, I felt great, because I knew that this bad war was over for me.

I was ordered to go to Camp 3, 3rd Btl. Our boss was Capt. Welles, I believe. We were about three thousand german POWs, one thousand in a camp, as far as I remember. 12 POWs slept in one of the barracks that is shown on the drawing. The barracks had round windows, like portholes. In the middle of the building stood the big oven that we could feed with wood or coal, if necessary.

We really got enough to eat, especially this unforgetable white bread which we never saw before in Germany. And the food during wartime in Africa was quite bad. The kitchen in the camp was of course a main institution for us. The POWs themselves prepared and cooked the meals. We had a lot of fruits, like apples, oranges and pears. Besides water we had the possibility to drink tea, coffee, and to buy milk or even "Redcap" beer. 200 cigarrettes costed 1,20$ in the cantine, a beer 20 cents, I think or even less.

During the first year I worked outside the camp on a farm near Anniston. The farmers name was Wiley, I think. We harvested peanuts, cotton and millet. I got 80 Cents for 80 pounds of cotton. The work was o.k. and we could earn some extra money, to buy special things in the cantine. As a non-smoker I dealt the cigarettes with Oswald Pauli for food or beer or other beverages.

After one year I had to work as a fireman or stoker. For a twelve hour shift I had to take care of the heating of officers homes. Therefore I got a bicycle to tour around at Ft McClellan. I did this job also about a year.

Then I had to change my duty-work again and helped in the hospital kitchen starting at 06 p.m. until 01 a.m. There I baked thousands of pies. This job lasted about 5–6 months.

Between our duty hours we had of course also time for some hobbies. The POWs had built their own soccer fields and a theatre stage. We played table tennis and a kind of punch-ball game. I think we had about seven soccer teams that played in tournaments. And one special thing was our Camp news-paper, where you could read the camp news, poems and sport events, sometimes also from abroad. I still have a collection of the news and I will send a copy of it to the historian of Ft McClellan soon.

But we also destilled brandy in our barrack which was forbidden. It tasted awful, but we got drunk, which was helpful once in a while, when we got homesick. We didn't have connections outside of the camp other than with the work. With the monthly 3$ salary we could earn another 20$ per month with our work.

I also remember my last job in Ft McClellan, when I worked at the post motor pool and as a mechanist I fixed cars. Each POW had an american civilian aside. My colleague was Mr. Bowman. He gave me once a very nice golden fountain-pen. I still keep it as a souvenir. My friend Oswald and I also made rings out of spoons. We bended the upper edge of the spoon and put a five cent coin on top and grinded and polished the coin. Then we sold those rings to Americans in the Camp. That was some extra money for us. I also have to add, that I built the destillery in the motor pool.

But after some weeks the american guards realized the smell in our barrack and discovered the hole in the bottom of our barrack. So we had to give up our "Black forest" destillery.

I really could tell you more stories about our camp live but at the moment I think, I have to finish otherwise you wouldn't get your letter in time.

I left Ft McClellan in April 1946 to Fort Benning. From there to Camp Shanks in New York where we were shipped over again to Scotland. They didn't have that much to eat and drink for us, so I arrived rather skinny at home on the 31st of october 1946, just one day before my 24th anniversary.

Because I met Oswald Pauli in Ft McClellan, I got in touch with his sister in Germany and we married in 1950. My son Norbert is therefore more or less originated by the lucky chance that Oswald and I met in Ft McClellan.

I hope that my little story helps you to get a good grade for your history project. I wish you and your parents a peaceful and happy life. If you are interested in seeing us, come along. We are happy to tell you more.

Best wishes to all of you

E. Eifler

[Erhard Eifler, born November 1, 1922, died in Buhlenberg on April 23, 2012, at age 89.]

Appendix C

The Rita Wells Memoir

[The following was written by Rita Wells, a civilian employee stationed in the headquarters building just outside and west of the POW camp. She wrote it more than 60 years after her war service. It is published as written. She told the author during interviews in 2008 and 2009 that she had purposely inked out one section because it included a "promise" she had made to an American officer in the 1940s. But she added, "I suppose maybe it should now be told because it is more important for posterity and the historical record." The unexpurgated version follows exactly as typed, allowing for commonly made spelling mistakes, with only six corrections inserted in brackets.]

The Prisoner of War Camp
Fort McClellan, Alabama, U.S.A.

The Prisoner of War Camp at Fort McClellan, Alabama, began functioning in July, 1943, for the purpose of housing German prisoners of war (PWs) during World War II. There were three compounds which lay on the slope of a hill on the west side of the Main Post. On both sides of the streets in each of the compounds were rows of barracks, comprising twelve companies. In addition, there were the kitchens, company orderly rooms, day-rooms, dispensaries, a library and a reading room. At the compound entrance was the PW Chapel surrounded by flowers and shrubbery. There was an open-air stage as well as wide area for sports and games. After work hours the POWs beautified their grounds with grass, flowers and their handy-work. Camp authorities and PWs worked together to conform to international agreements to make the PWs stay in American [America] one that would make a lasting impression they would take home with them later.

The previous description was a paraphrase of the Camp Commander, Major Samuel W. Kendall in December, 1945, excerpted from an untitled book complete with pictures and description of PW life at the military installation.

At its peak, the camp housed approximately 3,000 German prisoners captured by the Allies during World War II. It opened in July, 1943, with the opening of the Baker Gate. Before that, there was only one entrance to Fort McClellan—Baltzell Gate. The PW Camp was a completely separate entity from the Main Post. It had its own Commanding Officer, Executive Officer, Adjutant, Security and Intelligence Officer and Administrative staff. It was under the jurisdiction of the Post Commander.

As a young lady, Miss Rita Johnson (later Mrs. Hoyt Wells) began working at the PW Camp in November, 1944, in the Administrative Division in Headquarters Building located just inside baker gate on the left. The following is an account of her memories of working at the PW Camp:

The area to the right, just inside the gate, held rows of buildings containing a motor pool, automotive repair shop, storage warehouses, typewriter repair shop, carpenter shop and clothing warehouses. All these were manned by our troops and/or a civilian foreman, aided by some of the more cooperative and competent prisoners. Further into the base, on the right, were barracks housing U.S. soldiers who were assigned to perform operations needed in the PW activities. The kitchen or mess hall was also in that area. Civilian employees were allowed to eat lunches in the mess hall at a large corner table for the cost of a quarter ($.25) per meal. The food was good, especially the crumb cake. Most of the cooks in this kitchen, under the supervision of the mess sergeant, were prisoners who chose to cook. On the left, just past the headquarters building was the fence around the entire area where prisoners were housed. This was the compound area with several tall towers topped by armed guards stationed around the clock. Inside the compound, on both sides of the street were neat rows of barracks where the prisoners lived. They were exactly the same as the barracks occupied by U.S. troops. Each of the compounds housed twelve [four] companies of prisoners. There were various other buildings for activities for the prisoners such as orderly rooms, day rooms, dis-

222

pensaries, a library and reading room, a hobby shop and a canteen. At the main entrance, the chapel was surrounded by flowers and shrubbery grown in the PW greenhouse. The open air stage and areas for sports and games was available for PWs also.

The treatment of prisoners included a basic allowance of $.10 per day or $3.00 per month. A prisoner could choose to work or not work. If he worked he was paid $.10 per hour or $.80 per day plus the basic allowance, and he was paid monthly. This was 1943, and what seems like a paltry sum was spent mostly at the canteen inside the compound to buy sodas and candy bars for $.05-$.10 or toothpaste for $.15. Shaving cream, cigarettes, and writing tablets were also available. Many of the prisoners maintained the huge greenhouse and were excellent gardeners. Their plants and shrubs were always healthy and sturdy and were used to landscape and beautify areas all over the post. Other prisoners chose to work in the various repair shops and warehouses in the PW camp area, and outside the compound such as the quartermaster bakery, hospital kitchen or dental clinic. Others were accomplished artists painting portraits of some of the officers' wives. Remington Hall contains several gorgeous murals on the walls painted by PWs. At this writing the murals have endured over sixty years.

In addition to working on-post, PWs also worked off-post. The government had contracts with civilian companies to provide them with laborers. Logging companies and cotton farms needed healthy men because many American men had been drafted into the armed forces. Though most of the PWs were well disciplined, strict procedures were followed to prevent their escape. They were transported to and from work sites by army trucks, each containing two armed guards, one in back with PWs and one in front with the American driver. Procedure was a roll call upon loading with a head count at the compound gate. Roll call happened again at Baker Gate and upon reaching the work site. The same routine took place upon the return trip.

One day in September, a work detail was sent south, to Clanton, Alabama, to work with a logging company. All procedures were followed as usual, but around 2:00 a.m. the post commanding officer (CO) received a call from the Chilton County sheriff stating they had two PWs in custody. The CO said, "You must be mistaken, no one here is missing." Upon further discussion and convincing facts given by the sheriff, the CO woke the PW camp CO who hurriedly put together a team that travelled to Clanton to check the situation. Sure enough, the two men were PWs from Fort McClellan. After a few days in interrogation, the PWs confessed that they had received a message that Hitler was to have a ship in Argentina the following February 2, to transport back to Germany anyone who could escape and board the ship. These two PW's had devised a plan of escape. While two or three of their buddies created a loud confrontation with each other, these two sneaked away into the woods. Their friends would gruffly answer roll call for them so they would not be missed immediately. They thought all was well, but that night a severe electrical storm came with heavy rain and hail. The PWs took cover on the front porch of a little, old, unpainted farm house they thought was empty since they saw no lights. However, the farmer and his wife were in bed, asleep. When they heard noise and voices, the farmer met them with a shotgun and asked them what they were doing. Speaking no English, the PWs could not communicate. So, the farmer sent his wife walking to the nearest phone, one and a half miles away to call the sheriff while he held the two at gunpoint. The sheriff quickly was there to handcuff the PWs and take them to jail. He found large, home-made kitchen knives with wooden handles, made in the Hobby Shop of the PW Camp. Each knife had a hole bored in the handle with a leather string run through and tied around each PWs leg, just below the knee. The body search which normally starts under the arms and ends at the knee had not discovered the knives earlier. Punishment was the standard two weeks solitary confinement on bread and water. According to the Geneva Convention, confinement on bread and water can only last one week without a break. One day, providing three good meals, is the break that allows the second week to complete the sentence of two weeks on bread and water. Two weeks is the maximum.

Self improvement was another pastime for many PWs. Religious classes were taught at night by the post chaplain, and American government, history and English classes were taught by instructors. Many PWs had some English skills just by hearing it spoken at the PW Camp. Others had studied English in high school in Germany. Two of these PWs worked in our office as typists. Very polite and nice, their names were Alfred and Freitag. Both spoke and understood English fairly well but Alfred had a lisp. His "s" came out as "th." To him I was "Mith Johnthon." One morning I went to work a bit earlier than usual and heard the small radio playing in our office. He didn't know I was there but Alfred was reciting the Stanback Headache Powder commercial–"Snap back with Stanback." His version was "Thap back with Thanback." Since he volunteered to teach English at night to other PWs, I wondered how many men went back to Germany speaking English with a lisp.

Many of the PWs were master craftsmen. I have two beautiful pieces—a jewelry box and a handkerchief box—made in the hobby shop and given to me by Alfred and Freitag. They contained notes of appreciation for the kindness they had received. Neither of them showed any bitterness when they returned to Germany.

PWs were allowed to receive mail and send it to their home about twice a month. Both were censored and anything considered dangerous to the war effort was blocked. Sometimes things were in code. Interpreters caught things like the first and last letters on each line moving down the page to spell out words. PWs were very clever in attempting to communicate secretly. In addition to letters, packages were received by the PW's, but everything was closely inspected by security. One time a PW received an innocent-looking pair of work shoes from his family. They almost passed inspection but were found to contain a note under the insole that contained forbidden information. After that some items were exchanged at the Post Exchange (PX) for like items. Even a writing tablet sent from Germany might contain invisible ink. So no chances were taken.

PWs had recreational facilities and activities. Those who were musically talented formed a very good, almost professional orchestra. Two of the musicians filed applications to remain in America to play with an orchestra in Boston after the war was over. One had an aunt there and had secured a job for each of them, a trumpeter and trombonist. The aunt pleaded their cases at the PW Camp and in Washington, but their requests were denied.

The rules of the Geneva Convention state that all prisoners of war, upon the cessation of hostilities, must be returned to their own country and place of residence at the time he entered the armed forces. After the truce was signed, many prisoners wanted to change their addresses. None wanted to return to the East Zone as they did not trust the Russians. Many gave addresses in the West Zone saying their families had moved there. This was questionable and not approved.

My original job was a typist in the administrative branch, typing payrolls for the PWs and updating information in their personnel files. But the job I liked best was substituting as secretary to the security and intelligence officer. I was given access to information classified as "secret." I had to take an oath not to reveal a single detail of anything I saw or learned that was secret. I have honored that oath until recently. I doubt is [if] there is anyone alive who is not in the same senile state as I that would even be able to prosecute me. Now after sixty years I consider this information to be history. So, I will share some of my secrets below:

Many of the PWs were very Pro-Nazi. They were very proud of their uniforms and the medals on them. These were taken from them after their capture. But they were quite clever at improvising. American guards periodically conducted unannounced inspections which they called "shake downs." The contents of their barracks, including the small chests which held their clothing were closely examined. During one of the shake downs the inspectors found homemade medals. PWs had taken plain wood and carved the intricate designs which were the impressions of their medals to use as molds. Somehow they acquired lead, melted it and poured it into these hand carved molds making replicas of their precious German war medals. The details were almost perfect, proving that many hours were spent in this venture. However, these "fake" medals were taken from the PWs and almost all of them were destroyed also.

One day as I was straightening some files in our office I came across the "fake" medals mentioned above that were supposed to be destroyed. The security and Intelligence officer wanted to appear a tough and grumpy bear, but after getting to know him, he was really a teddy bear. He was especially nice to me and the other secretary. When I asked him about the medals he said, "Oh, I just haven't gotten around to destroying them yet." So, I asked if I could have a couple of them. He said he could not legally say "yes," but if some just happened to fall into my purse when he was out of the office, he would never know it. However, if that should happen, I could not show them to anyone, nor let it be known that I had them. So, after all these years, I am telling you that I have those medals. They have been in an old envelope, yellow with age, in the back of a dresser drawer all these years. I recently had them framed in a shadow box to display at a civic club and tell this story that I had not told until then.

I remember typing the report for another interesting incident. During a random body search a guard found on a PW a very expensive silver fox fur kolinsky. It was wrapped around his waist just above his belt. His shirt was tucked loosely into his pants creating a natural looking bulge. After extensive questioning, he never told how he acquired it and was given solitary confinement for two weeks and still refused to cooperate. The fur was taken to Ullman's, an exclusive department store in town. They did not sell that type of fur, nor could they trace its origin. After checking back on the PW's recent work detail, they determined he had done janitorial work in Remington Hall, the commissioned officer's club where officer's [sic] entertained each other and their guests. After some detective work the final conclusion was that some officer had taken someone other than his wife to the club one night and left inebriated, forgetting the fur. It was never claimed due to the embarrassment that it would have caused.

PWs were not allowed to fraternize with American women, which, of course made it even more tempting to see if they could get away with it. One such PW worked at the main PX and was attracted to a young American girl who worked there. They must have been very discreet because only two or three people working there were aware of the hanky-panky going on. A note passed by the PW to the girl was intercepted by the guard, and there was quite a scene. I typed the report and found it amusing that the German man's English was somewhat limited as he wrote, "I see you, Fraulein, und sends my blood cooking, mad, insane in my veins." He received the usual solitary confinement and could no long work around women. The girl was fired from the PX.

One thing I have not touched on is the PW cemetery. It is the only thing that has survived all these years. No one in our office ever attended a burial there, but I was told that the post chaplain conducted graveside rites at each one, with only a very few friends of the deceased and some of the military personnel attending. Some Italian prisoners are also buried there. They were originally buried in Aliceville, Alabama, where a small group of PWs were temporarily housed at one time. When that facility closed, the bodies were exhumed and moved to Fort McClellan. This was done in a very reverent and respectful manner. I remember some of us stood at the office window and watched the five black hearses carrying the caskets, with army vehicles interspersed between each hearse as the bodies were brought to Ft. McClellan for re-burial. According to the Anniston Star, a memorial service is still held in this cemetery each spring [actually fall] with family and friends who live in the U.S. attending.

The last thing I want to mention is the book I have that contains pictures and some documentation about the PW Camp. This book that was mentioned in the second paragraph was the one given to PWs to take home with them when they returned to Germany. The pictures in the book were made at the PW Camp at Ft. McClellan but also contained cruel photos of the concentration and inter[n]ment camps under German rule. The book was a courteous gesture and souvenir for the German PWs, but also a piece of propaganda, as it contained pictures revealing the inhumane way Germans treated their prisoners in contrast to the humane practices of American PW camps.

By: Rita Johnson Wells
Edited and typed by: Elaine Morris Heath (her niece)
July 27, 2008

Chapter Notes

Chapter 1

1. The background information on World War II is intended only to present a brief exposition of a very complex subject in order to aid the reader in understanding how and why German prisoners came to the United States. It is distilled from the following sources: C. L. Sulzberger and the editors of *American Heritage*, *The American Heritage Picture History of World War II* (New York: American Heritage/Bonanza Books, 1966), 216–47; B. H. Liddell Hart, *History of the Second World War* (New York: Perigee Books, 1982), 109–27, 171–98, 266–309, 334–42, and 397–432; "King & Country's Rommel in Afrika" [brochure] (Hong Kong: King & Country, 2011); *National Geographic Atlas of the World* (Washington, DC: National Geographic Society, 1992), plate 92; Arnold Krammer, *Nazi Prisoners of War in America* (Lanham, MD: Scarborough House, 1996), 3–4; "Richfield World-Wide News Map" (Chicago: Rand McNally, 1941); and William L. Shirer, *The Rise and Fall of the Third Reich* (New York: Fawcett Crest, 1960), 1084, 1191–93, and 1201–6.

2. Shay family memoirs. See Note C in bibliography.

Chapter 2

1. Patricia Hoskins Morton, "Calhoun County," *Encyclopedia of Alabama* [Internet] (http://www.encyclopediaofalabama.org/face/Article.jsp?id=h-1198), 2.

2. The background information on Anniston's development and history is from Morton, "Calhoun County," 1–3; "Fort McClellan, Anniston, Alabama, Guide for Service Personnel" [flyer]; and "Historic Driving Tour of Calhoun County" [brochure] (Anniston, AL: Calhoun County Chamber of Commerce), 1–12.

3. Thomas J. Watson Jr. and Peter Petre, *Father, Son & Co.* (New York: Bantam Books, 1990), 87–89.

4. All information on Fort McClellan and its predecessors, as well as the current status of the former fort, is in "Information Hand Book for the Soldier" [booklet] (Headquarters Infantry Replacement Training Center, Fort McClellan, 1944), 5; Morton, "Calhoun County," 3; *Fort McClellan News*, July 18, 1967, pp. 1, 3, 5, and 7; *Transition Force: United States Army Garrison—Fort McClellan, Alabama* [Internet] (http://www.mcclellan.army.mil/Info.asp), 1–3; and

Wikipedia, "Fort McClellan" (http://en.wikipedia.org/wiki/Fort_McClellan), 1–7.

5. The information on George B. McClellan is from "General George B. McClellan: Controversial Union Commander," *Fort McClellan News*, July 12, 1968, p. 3; "The Civil War at a Glance" [brochure] (Washington, DC: Government Printing Office, 1991); and William A. DeGregorio, *The Complete Book of U.S. Presidents* (New York: Wings Books, 1993), 235–36.

6. McKinney, interview, June 23, 2008.

Chapter 3

1. *Transition Force: United States Army Garrison—Fort McClellan, Alabama* [Internet] (http://www.mcclellan.army.mil/Info.asp), 5.

2. Arnold Krammer, *Nazi Prisoners of War in America* (Lanham, MD: Scarborough House, 1996), iii.

3. Antonio Thompson, *Men in German Uniform* (Knoxville: University of Tennessee Press, 2010), 1.

4. Glenn A. Sytko, *German POWs in North America* [Internet] (http://www.uboat.net/men/pow/pow_in_america.htm), 1.

5. Krammer, *Nazi Prisoners of War in America*, 88.

6. Thompson, *Men in German Uniform*, 15 and 130.

7. Mary Beth Reed, William R. Henry Jr., and J. W. Joseph, *"The Military Showplace of the South": Fort McClellan, Alabama, a Historic Building Inventory* (Mobile, AL: U.S. Army Corps of Engineers, 1993), 59.

8. "M'CLELLAN RECEIVES NEW WAR PRISONERS," *The Anniston Star*, July 6, 1943, p. 6.

9. "Axis Prisoners of War Arrive," *The McClellan CYCLE*, July 9, 1943, p. 1.

10. *History of the Prisoner of War Camp, Fort McClellan, Alabama*, E. B. Walker Collection, copy in files of Joan McKinney.

11. J. Metzner, April 1, 2013, email.

12. Dan Coberly, "Stalag U.S.A. Part Seven: Locals recall camp years," *The McClellan News*, May 7, 1980, p. 2.

13. Allen, interviews, January 19 and February 18, 2013.

14. Published in the October 17, 1943, issue of *P.o.W. Oase* and contained in a large collection of doc-

uments sent via email by Joachim Metzner, Paul's son, on October 6, 2011. The translation was done on November 25, 2012, by Joni L. Pontius, who provided a brief preface: "A nicely poetic description of their journey in the dark on the train…. Nice turns of phrase; admittedly better in the German, but rendered somewhere between accurate and comprehensible into English. It's always a balancing act."

15. Alfred Arens, "Dear American friends!" letter (written as presentation for reunion), 1991, p. 3, E. B. Walker Collection, copy in files of Joan McKinney.

16. Erhard Eifler, handwritten letter of reminiscences, February 8, 1991, p. 1, copy in files of Joan McKinney.

17. Paul Metzner's diary comments, *Teil 3 August 1943–Frühling 1944*, edited and annotated by Joachim Metzner, sent in October 6, 2011, email; translated by Joni L. Pontius, November 17, 2012.

18. Christian Höschle, *Hast du nichts so bist du nichts* (Irdning/Steiermark, Austria: Stieglitz Verlag, 1992); translations of portions of his book by J. Metzner, September 2013 emails.

19. Höschle, *Hast du nichts so bist du nichts*, 156–60, translated by Joni L. Pontius, September 28, 2013.

Note on Rank: The American equivalents of various German ranks are found in several sources, including a World War II dictionary by Hans Günther, as well as German Internet sites supplied by Joachim Metzner in July 4, 28, and 31, 2013, emails. However, these sources do not always agree. For example, *Gefreiter* is variously listed as both PFC and Private E2; *Obergefreiter* as Corporal and PFC; *Unterfeldwebel* as Staff Sergeant and Sergeant; *Feldwebel* as Technical Sergeant and Staff Sergeant; *Oberfeldwebel* as First Sergeant, Technical Sergeant, and Staff Sergeant; and *Hauptfeldwebel* as Master Sergeant and First Sergeant. When sources diverged, the likeliest equivalent rank inferred from the quoted source material was used. When that was impossible to ascertain, Günther's dictionary, compiled for soldiers during the war, was used.

Chapter 4

1. Antonio Thompson, *Men in German Uniform* (Knoxville: University of Tennessee Press, 2010), 10.

2. Estimates, based on existing topographical maps.

3. Author's collection. See Note A in bibliography.

4. Mary Beth Reed, William R. Henry Jr., and J. W. Joseph, *"The Military Showplace of the South": Fort McClellan, Alabama, a Historic Building Inventory* (Mobile, AL: U.S. Army Corps of Engineers, 1993), figure 15 and 59–61.

5. J. Metzner, August 16, 2012, email.

6. Christian Höschle, *Hast du nichts so bist du nichts* (Irdning/Steiermark, Austria: Stieglitz Verlag, 1992), 160, translated by Joni L. Pontius, September 28, 2013.

7. Reed et al., *"The Military Showplace of the South,"* 59–61.

8. Erhard Eifler, handwritten letter of reminiscences, February 8, 1991, p. 2, copy in files of Joan McKinney.

9. Author's collection.

10. Ibid.

11. J. Metzner, October 21, 2012, email.

12. J. Metzner, October 24, 2012, email.

13. J. Metzner, April 20, 2013, email.

14. Cpl. William R. Frye, "Inside the PW Camp: Pin-Up Girls, PXs, Nazi 'Heils' Found Behind Grim Stockade," *The McClellan CYCLE*, May 12, 1944, p. 3.

15. Wells, interviews, October 1, 2008, and November 30, 2009.

16. Information on guard towers is from the Shay family memoirs and photographs. See Note C in bibliography.

17. Private Clifford Prior letters, in collection of Thom Cole.

18. Dan Coberly, "Stalag U.S.A. Part Seven: Locals recall camp years," *The McClellan News*, May 7, 1980, p. 2.

19. J. Metzner, July 20, 2012, email.

20. Shay family memoirs.

21. J. Metzner, July 18, 2012, email.

Chapter 5

1. *History of the Prisoner of War Camp, Fort McClellan, Alabama*, E. B. Walker Collection, copy in files of Joan McKinney.

2. Author's collection. See Note A in bibliography.

3. *History of the Prisoner of War Camp, Fort McClellan, Alabama*.

4. J. Metzner, July 10, 2012, and March 21, 2013, emails.

5. J. Metzner, October 24, 2011, email.

6. J. Metzner, April 9, 2012, email.

7. J. Metzner, October 28, 2012, email.

8. Shay family memoirs. See Note C in bibliography.

9. Author's collection.

10. Ibid.

11. Willi Utz, *P.o.W. Oase*, translated by Joni L. Pontius, November 17, 2012.

12. J. Metzner, December 9, 2012, email.

13. Christian Höschle, *Hast du nichts so bist du nichts* (Irdning/Steiermark, Austria: Stieglitz Verlag, 1992), 161, translated by Joni L. Pontius, September 28, 2013.

14. Author's collection.

15. J. Metzner, March 3, 2014, email.

16. Cpl. William R. Frye, "Inside PW Camp: Bomb Stories Bunk, Nazi Prisoners Say; Call War News 'Lies,'" *The McClellan CYCLE*, May 19, 1944, pp. 3 and 5.

17. Author's collection.

18. Ibid.

19. J. Metzner, February 18, 2013, email.

20. Chania Stymacks' translations of *P.o.W. Oase*, November 17, 2011.

21. Author's collection.

22. Ibid.

23. The corrected or probable German spelling is from Joachim Metzner's March 2 and 3, 2014, emails.

24. Author's collection.

25. Shay family memoirs.

26. Pontius, interview, November 17, 2012.

27. Author's collection.

28. Ibid.

29. Ibid.

30. Erhard Eifler, handwritten letter of reminiscences, February 8, 1991, p. 2, copy in files of Joan McKinney.

31. Höschle, *Hast du nichts so bist du nichts*, 160 and 162–63, translated by Pontius, September 28, 2013.

32. Eifler, February 8, 1991, letter, 3–4.

33. Höschle, *Hast du nichts so bist du nichts*, 177, translated by Pontius, September 28, 2013.

34. J. Metzner, July 10, 2012, email.

35. J. Metzner, April 19, 2013, email.

36. J. Metzner, March 23, 2013, email.

37. Wells, interview, October 1, 2008.

38. Bakke and Cole, interviews, April 2, 2011.

39. Suberg, interview, August 28, 1987.

40. Author's collection.

41. Ibid.

42. Wells, interviews, October 1, 2008, and November 30, 2009.

43. J. Walker, interview, December 1, 2009.

44. McKinney, interview, November 29, 2009.

45. Klaus W. Duncan, *The Oase* (private paper, undated), 4–5 (copy in author's collection).

46. Miller, interview, June 30, 2010.

47. J. Metzner, April 1, 2013, email.

48. Google translation with corrections by J. Metzner.

49. Suberg, interviews, August 28 and 29, 1987.

Chapter 6

1. Bill Plott, "For 3000 Nazis, WWII Ended at Fort," *The Anniston Star*, July 14, 1967, p. 7-C.

2. Dan Coberly, "Stalag U.S.A. Part Six: The Camp McClellan Story," *The McClellan News*, May 2, 1980, p. 2.

3. Bakke, interview, April 2, 2011.

4. Author's collection. See Note A in bibliography.

5. Christian Höschle, *Hast du nichts so bist du nichts* (Irdning/Steiermark, Austria: Stieglitz Verlag, 1992), 160–61, translated by Joni L. Pontius, September 28, 2013.

6. J. Metzner, December 5, 2012, email.

7. J. Metzner, December 9, 2012; December 23, 2013; and March 6, 2014, emails.

8. The names of these POWs contained in *P.o.W. Oase*, as well as why they were recorded, are taken from a series of emails from J. Metzner: October 20, 2011; April 3, 4, 9, and 12, and December 3, 2012; and March 3, 2014.

9. Höschle, *Hast du nichts so bist du nichts*, 174–75, translated by Pontius, September 28, 2013.

10. Suberg, interview, August 29, 1987.

11. Höschle, *Hast du nichts so bist du nichts*, 176–78, translated by Pontius, September 28, 2013.

12. Cpl. William R. Frye, "Inside the PW Camp: Pin-Up Girls, PXs, Nazi 'Heils' Found Behind Grim Stockade," *The McClellan CYCLE*, May 12, 1944, p. 3.

13. McKinney, November 30, 2012, email.

Chapter 7

1. Arnold Krammer, *Nazi Prisoners of War in America* (Lanham, MD: Scarborough House, 1996), 47–48.

2. Klaus W. Duncan, *The Oase* (private paper, undated), 4 (copy in author's collection).

3. Christian Höschle, *Hast du nichts so bist du nichts* (Irdning/Steiermark, Austria: Stieglitz Verlag, 1992), 160, 162, and 170, translated by Joni L. Pontius, September 28, 2013.

4. J. Metzner, September 4, 2012, email.

5. Major Mary C. Lane, WAC, compiler, *The History of Fort McClellan*, July 14, 1955 ("Reproduced December 1958—Brought up to date by Annex K"), 28, in McClellan files, Alabama Room, Public Library of Anniston and Calhoun County, Anniston.

6. Author's collection. See Note A in bibliography.

7. Ibid.

8. Ibid.

9. Ibid.

10. Ibid.

11. Ibid.

12. Ibid.

13. Ibid.

14. Alfred Arens, "Dear American friends!" letter (written as presentation for reunion), 1991, p. 3, E. B. Walker Collection, copy in files of Joan McKinney.

15. Erhard Eifler, handwritten letter of reminiscences, February 8, 1991, p. 2–3, copy in files of Joan McKinney.

16. Stymacks, translations, November 17, 2011.

17. Dan Coberly, "Stalag U.S.A. Part Seven: Locals recall camp years," *The McClellan News*, May 7, 1980, p. 2.

18. J. Walker, interviews, June 24, 2008, and December 1, 2009.

19. Wells, interviews, October 1, 2008, and November 30, 2009.

20. Newman, interview, November 30, 2009; and letter, April 21, 2009.

21. Bakke, interview, April 2, 2011.

22. Aderholdt, interview, November 30, 2009.

23. Bonner (James and Dean), interviews, December 1, 2009.

24. Miller, interview, June 30, 2010.

25. From 1945 and 1946 POW duty rosters in the author's collection. Joachim Metzner corroborated correct or likely spellings of names.

26. McKinney, interview, November 29, 2009.

27. J. Metzner, August 19, 2012, email.

28. J. Metzner, December 23, 2012, email.

29. J. Metzner, January 5, 2013, email.

30. J. Metzner, October 11, 2012, email.

Chapter 8

1. McKinney, interview, November 29, 2009.

2. Author's collection. See Note A in bibliography.

3. Christian Höschle, *Hast du nichts so bist du nichts* (Irdning/Steiermark, Austria: Stieglitz Verlag, 1992), 171, translated by Joni L. Pontius, September 28, 2013.

4. Ibid., 161, 164, 166, and 183.

5. Mary Beth Reed, William R. Henry Jr., and J. W. Joseph, *"The Military Showplace of the South": Fort McClellan, Alabama, a Historic Building Inventory* (Mobile, AL: U.S. Army Corps of Engineers, 1993), 113, 119, and 125.

6. Laura Ann Freeman, "POW art: Vibrant, sometimes masterful, work of German soldiers uncovered at Fort McClellan," *The Anniston Star*, September 16, 1979, pp. 1–2C.

7. Mike Oliver, "German POWs painted murals of chaos, despair," *The Birmingham News*, May 30, 1982, Sunday Spotlight section.

8. Catherine Gambrell Rogers, *Conservation of Decorative Murals at Fort McClellan, Anniston, Alabama: Condition Report and Treatment Proposal* (report submitted to Tim Rice, director of environment, Fort McClellan, March 5, 1998), 2 and 4 (copy in files of Joan McKinney).

9. Aamer Madhani, "POW murals at officers' club to be cleaned, stabilized," *The Anniston Star*, September 26, 1998, p. 1B.

10. Rose Livingston, "POW murals get brush up," *The Birmingham News*, November 10, 1998, pp. 1Bff.

11. Tim Lockette, "Meaning behind murals remains a mystery," *Gadsden Times*, May 13, 1999, p. 1A.

12. Joan McKinney, "Fort McClellan's Diverse Mission: Lingering Memories—Lasting Heritage," *Alabama Historical Association Newsletter* (Fall 2007), 10.

13. Author's collection.

14. McKinney, interview, November 29, 2009.

15. McKinney, December 12, 2012, email.

16. Author's collection.

17. Meta Kordiš, August 28, 2012, email to J. Metzner.

18. Richelle Turner-Collins, "Late German POW lives on through his restored murals," *Stars and Stripes*, January 7, 2000, p. 5.

19. Susanne Belau, April 14, 2013, email to J. Metzner.

20. J. Metzner, November 6, 2012, email.

21. J. Metzner, April 17, 2013, email.

22. Springer, interview, November 30, 2009.

23. Johnson, interview, December 1, 2009.

24. "Remington Hall Meeting Center" [brochure].

25. Joan McKinney, "The POW Murals: Anniston's Hidden Treasure," *Alabama Heritage* (Fall 2009), 6.

26. McKinney, November 15, 2013, email.

27. Author's collection.

28. Stymacks, translations, November 17, 2011.

29. Klaus W. Duncan, *The Oase* (private paper, undated), 3 (copy in author's collection).

30. Stymacks, interview, November 17, 2011.

31. Lockette, "Meaning behind murals remains a mystery," 1A.

32. Author's collection.

33. Wells, interview, November 30, 2009.

34. Author's collection.

35. Stymacks, translations, November 17, 2011.

36. J. Metzner, March 21, 2013, email.

37. J. Metzner, December 9, 2012, email.

38. Höschle, *Hast du nichts so bist du nichts*, 167, translated by Pontius, September 28, 2013.

39. Wells, interview, November 30, 2009.

Chapter 9

1. Arnold Krammer, *Nazi Prisoners of War in America* (Lanham, MD: Scarborough House, 1996), 61.

2. J. Metzner, April 14, 2012, email.

3. Klaus W. Duncan, *The Oase* (private paper, undated), 1–2 (copy in author's collection).

4. J. Metzner, October 24, 2012, email.

5. J. Metzner, October 6, 2011, and October 28, 2012, emails.

6. J. Metzner, March 27, 2013, email.

7. Phillip Tutor, "Quiet Synthesis," *The Anniston Star*, May 3, 2009, p. 1E.

8. Pontius, translations, November 22, 2012.

9. Pontius, translations, November 20, 2012.

10. Pontius, interview, November 17, 2012.

11. Pontius, translations, November 18, 2012.

12. J. Metzner, August 19, 2012, email.

13. J. Metzner, November 26, 2012, email.

14. J. Metzner, December 5, 2012, email.

15. J. Metzner, November 21, 2011; April 4 and 12, 2012; and March 27 and October 3, 2013, emails.

16. J. Metzner, March 24, 2014, email.

17. Pontius, translations, undated but from late November 2012.

18. Pontius, interview, November 17, 2012.

19. Ibid.

20. Stymacks, translations and interview, November 17, 2011.

21. J. Metzner, March 23, 2013, email.

22. J. Metzner, July 10, 2012, email.

23. J. Metzner, December 23, 2012, email.

24. J. Metzner, August 3, 2012, email.

25. J. Metzner, April 23, 2013, email.

26. J. Metzner, April 19, 2013, email.

27. J. Metzner, May 2, 2012, email.

28. J. Metzner, March 27, 2013, email.

29. Author's collection. See Note A in bibliography.

30. Daniel Hutchinson, "The Oasis: German POWs at Fort McClellan," *Alabama Heritage* (Summer 2008), 48.

31. Dan Coberly, "Stalag U.S.A. Part Six: The Camp McClellan Story," *The McClellan News*, May 2, 1980, p. 2.

32. Author's and J. Metzner's collections.
33. Erhard Eifler, handwritten letter of reminiscences, February 8, 1991, p. 3, copy in files of Joan McKinney.
34. J. Metzner, December 18, 2011, email.
35. Phillip Tutor, "Hear the voices at McClellan," *The Anniston Star*, November 21, 2008, p. 7A.
36. J. Metzner, October 28, 2012, email.
37. J. Metzner, November 4, 2012, email.
38. J. Metzner, December 20, 2012, email.
39. J. Metzner, April 13, 2013, email.
40. J. Metzner, April 1 and October 3, 2013, emails.

Chapter 10

1. The probable spellings of German names, differing from the U.S. spellings because American typewriters did not have characters with umlauts, are from a March 16, 2014, email from Joachim Metzner.
2. Author's collection. See Note A in bibliography.
3. Ibid.
4. Ibid.
5. Ibid.
6. Ibid.
7. Ibid.
8. Ibid.
9. Ibid.
10. Ibid.
11. Bill Plott, "For 3000 Nazis, WWII Ended At Fort," *The Anniston Star*, July 14, 1967, p. 7-C.
12. Dan Coberly, "Stalag U.S.A. Part Six: The Camp McClellan Story," *The McClellan News*, May 2, 1980, p. 2.
13. Dan Coberly, "Stalag U.S.A. Part Seven: Locals recall camp years," *The McClellan News*, May 7, 1980, p. 2.
14. The information on Willi Waechter's death is from *The Anniston Star* (a clipping on a photocopied sheet hand-dated "Aug 1, 1943") and also Certificate of Death 12691 (Center of Health Statistics, Alabama Department of Public Health), copies in files of Joan McKinney.
15. From material compiled and annotated by J. Metzner (List: "9.11. Fallen memorial Utz"), translated by Pontius, November 24, 2012.
16. Bakke, interview, April 2, 2011.
17. Newman, November 5, 2011, letter.
18. Wells, interview, October 1, 2008.
19. Antonio Thompson, *Men in German Uniform* (Knoxville: University of Tennessee Press, 2010), 97.
20. Wells, interview, October 1, 2008.
21. David Jennings, "WWII prisoner of war camp holds history, memories for base typist Rita Wells," *The Jacksonville News*, undated copy (probably August 11, 2010).
22. Arnold Krammer, *Nazi Prisoners of War in America* (Lanham, MD: Scarborough House, 1996), 136.
23. Private Clifford Prior letter, in collection of Thom Cole.

24. Alfred Arens, "Dear American friends!" letter (written as presentation for reunion), 1991, p. 3, E. B. Walker Collection, copy in files of Joan McKinney.
25. Standard Certificate of Death, State File No. 00125 (Center of Health Statistics, Alabama Department of Public Health), copy in files of Joan McKinney. See also Report of Autopsy; Clinical Abstract; Clinical History; and Autopsy Protocol (Laboratory Station Hospital, Fort McClellan), copy in collection of Thom Cole.
26. Translated by Pontius, November 28, 2012.
27. Standard Certificate of Death, State File No. 18060 (Center of Health Statistics, Alabama Department of Public Health), and clipping from *P.o.W. Oase*, copies (along with her annotations) in files of Joan McKinney.
28. Christian Höschle, *Hast du nichts so bist du nichts* (Irdning/Steiermark, Austria: Stieglitz Verlag, 1992), 169, translated by Joni L. Pontius, September 28, 2013.
29. J. Metzner, September 5, 2013, email to McKinney (forwarded to author on the same date).
30. Clinical Abstract (Laboratory Station Hospital, Fort McClellan), copy in collection of Thom Cole; Report of Autopsy (Laboratory Station Hospital, Fort McClellan), copy in files of Joan McKinney; Standard Certificate of Death, State File No. 4461 (Center of Health Statistics, Alabama Department of Public Health), copy in files of Joan McKinney.
31. J. Metzner, December 9, 2012, email.

Chapter 11

1. Antonio Thompson, *Men in German Uniform* (Knoxville: University of Tennessee Press, 2010), 10.
2. Major Mary C. Lane, WAC, compiler, *The History of Fort McClellan*, July 14, 1955 ("Reproduced December 1958—Brought up to date by Annex K"), 28, in McClellan files, Alabama Room, Public Library of Anniston and Calhoun County, Anniston; *History of the Prisoner of War Camp, Fort McClellan, Alabama*, E. B. Walker Collection, copy in files of Joan McKinney.
3. Mary Diskin Brown, "Col. Martin H. Meaney Prison Camp Commander," McClellan files, Alabama Room, Public Library of Anniston and Calhoun County, Anniston.
4. Author's collection. See Note A in bibliography.
5. J. Metzner, October 24, 2011, email.
6. J. Metzner, April 14, 2012, email.
7. The quotes from Rita (Johnson) Wells throughout this chapter, unless otherwise noted, are from interviews by phone (August 15, 2008) and in person (October 1, 2008, and November 30, 2009).
8. Sergeant John J. George, "PW Camp News," *The McClellan CYCLE*, March 24, 1944, p. 6.
9. Shay family memoirs. See Note C in bibliography.
10. Wells, August 27, 2008, letter.
11. Steppe, interview, October 2, 2008.
12. RESTRICTED SPECIAL ORDERS, Headquar-

ters Infantry Replacement Training Center, Fort Mc-Clellan, May 27, 1944 (copy in author's collection).

13. RESTRICTED SPECIAL ORDERS, Army Service Forces, Fourth Service Command, Fort Mc-Clellan, April 30, 1945 (copy in author's collection).

14. Author's collection.

15. Ibid.

16. Joseph A. Walker Sr., "Across the Brick Pike: Growing Up in the Shadow of Fort McClellan," a reminiscence presented to the Calhoun County Historical Society, January 15, 2008.

17. J. Walker, interview, December 1, 2009.

Chapter 12

1. Arnold Krammer, *Nazi Prisoners of War in America* (Lanham, MD: Scarborough House, 1996), 6 and 39.

2. All quoted information from Jack and Marie Shay throughout this chapter is from the Shay family memoirs. See Note C in bibliography.

3. Patrick D. Spinelli, July 17, 2013, email.

4. Berardone, interviews, May 1 and July 20, 2013.

5. "Former McClellan Trainee, Captured by Nazis in ETO, Now Cooks at Fort PW Camp," *The McClellan CYCLE*, November 9, 1945, p. 2.

6. Mess hall menus are in the author's collection.

7. "300 Fort Jobs Open to Army Wives Here," *The McClellan CYCLE*, March 10, 1944, p. 3.

8. Allen, interviews, January 19, February 18, and April 18, 2013.

9. Cpl. Harry Sloan, "PW Camp News," *The McClellan CYCLE*, October 15, 1943, p. 6.

10. Cpl. Harry Sloan, "PW Camp News," *The McClellan CYCLE*, October 29, 1943, p. 6.

11. Cpl. Harry Sloan, "PW Camp News," *The McClellan CYCLE*, November 5, 1943, p. 6.

12. Cpl. Harry Sloan, "PW Camp News," *The McClellan CYCLE*, November 19, 1943, p. 6.

13. Cpl. Howard Cope, "PW Camp News," *The McClellan CYCLE*, November 26, 1943, p. 6.

14. Cpl. Howard Cope, "PW Camp News," *The McClellan CYCLE*, January 7, 1944, p. 10.

15. Cpl. John J. George, "PW Camp News," *The McClellan CYCLE*, February 4, 1944, p. 6.

16. Cpl. Howard Cope, "PW Camp News," *The McClellan CYCLE*, February 18, 1944, p. 6.

17. Cpl. John J. George, "POW Camp News," *The McClellan CYCLE*, February 25, 1944, p. 6.

18. Sgt. John J. George, "PW Camp News," *The McClellan CYCLE*, March 17, 1944, p. 6.

19. Sgt. John J. George, "PW Camp News," *The McClellan CYCLE*, March 24, 1944, p. 6.

20. Sgt. John J. George, "PW Camp News," *The McClellan CYCLE*, March 31, 1944, p. 6.

21. Sgt. John J. George, "PW Camp News," *The McClellan CYCLE*, April 14, 1944, p. 7.

22. Sgt. John J. George, "PW Camp News," *The McClellan CYCLE*, April 21, 1944, p. 7.

23. Sgt. J. J. George, "PW Camp News," *The McClellan CYCLE*, May 12, 1944, p. 7.

24. Sgt. John J. George, "PW Camp," *The McClellan CYCLE*, May 19, 1944, p. 7.

25. Sgt. J. J. George, "PW Camp," *The McClellan CYCLE*, May 26, 1944, p. 7.

26. Sgt. John J. George, "PW Camp," *The McClellan CYCLE*, June 2, 1944, p. 7.

27. "PW Camp," *The McClellan CYCLE*, June 23, 1944, p. 7.

28. "PW Camp," *The McClellan CYCLE*, December 15, 1944, p. 9.

29. S/Sgt. John J. George, "PW Camp," *The McClellan CYCLE*, December 29, 1944, p. 9.

30. "PW Camp," *The McClellan CYCLE*, December 8, 1944, p. 11.

31. "It's McClellan's First New Year's Baby," *The McClellan CYCLE*, January 11, 1946, p. 3.

32. Berardone, interview, July 20, 2013.

33. "PW Camp," *The McClellan CYCLE*, February 16, 1945, p. 9.

34. Jack Shay, undated June 1971 letter.

Chapter 13

1. Mabry, interview, November 30, 2009.

2. Springer, interview, November 30, 2009.

3. Allen, interviews, February 18 and April 18, 2013.

4. Marie Shay's quotes are from the Shay family memoirs. See Note C in bibliography.

5. All quotations from Dr. Joby Walker from interviews on June 24 and October 2, 2008, and November 29 and December 1, 2009; as well as October 16, 2008, letter and map.

6. Margaret Keelen Newman, *Walter Newman and some of his descendants, 1683–1974* (Talladega, AL: Margaret Newman, 1974), 68–69; Newman, letters (July 25, 2008; undated but postmarked September 4, 2008; and March 26, 2010).

7. M. Walker, interview, November 29, 2009.

Chapter 14

1. Author's collection. See Note A in bibliography.

2. Ibid.

3. Ibid.

4. Ibid.

5. Ibid.

6. Dan Coberly, "Stalag U.S.A. Part Seven: Locals recall camp years," *The McClellan News*, May 7, 1980, p. 2.

7. Arnold Krammer, *Nazi Prisoners of War in America* (Lanham, MD: Scarborough House, 1996), 150.

8. Jack and Marie Shay's quotes are from the Shay family memoirs. See Note C in bibliography.

9. His probable name is from J. Metzner, March 24, 2014, email.

10. Wells, interviews, October 1, 2008, and November 30, 2009.

11. Erhard Eifler, handwritten letter of reminiscences, February 8, 1991, p. 3, copy in files of Joan McKinney.

12. Christian Höschle, *Hast du nichts so bist du nichts* (Irdning/Steiermark, Austria: Stieglitz Verlag, 1992), 160–61, 167, 181–82, and 184, translated by Joni L. Pontius, September 28, 2013.

13. Laura Ann Freeman, "POW art: Vibrant, sometimes masterful, work of German soldiers uncovered at Fort McClellan," *The Anniston Star*, September 16, 1979, p. 2C.

14. Bill Brownell, May 24, 2009, email.

15. Aderholdt, interview, November 30, 2009.

16. The information on Karl Hövener and James Byron Wester is from James Bonner, 2009, emails; and James and Dean Bonner, interview, December 1, 2009.

17. Janice Erfle, April 28, 2010, and September 28, 2011, emails.

18. Cole, interview, April 2, 2011.

19. Berardone, interviews, May 1 and July 20, 2013.

20. Spinelli, July 17, 2013, email.

21. Berardone, interview, July 20, 2013.

22. Coberly, "Stalag U.S.A. Part Seven," p. 2.

23. James Hamilton, handwritten reminiscence, dated March 18, 2009, in collection of Klaus W. Duncan.

Chapter 15

1. All Jack Shay quotes are from the Shay family memoirs. See Note C in bibliography.

2. Arnold Krammer, *Nazi Prisoners of War in America* (Lanham, MD: Scarborough House, 1996), 305, fn. 55.

3. Suberg, interviews, August 28 and 29, 1987.

4. John Daniel Hutchinson, "Guests Behind Barbed Wire: German Prisoner of War Camps in Alabama during World War Two," Master of Arts thesis (University of Alabama at Birmingham, 2005), 164.

5. Alfred Arens, "Dear American friends!" letter (written as presentation for reunion), 1991, p. 3, E. B. Walker Collection, copy in files of Joan McKinney.

6. Christian Höschle, *Hast du nichts so bist du nichts* (Irdning/Steiermark, Austria: Stieglitz Verlag, 1992), 180–81 and 184, translated by Joni L. Pontius, September 28, 2013.

7. J. Metzner, April 13, 2013, email.

8. Hutchinson, "Guests Behind Barbed Wire," 164.

9. Krammer, *Nazi Prisoners of War in America*, 240 and fn. 48 on 312, in which he credits a number of War Department, army, and newspaper sources.

10. Helmut Engelke, undated note to Staff Sergeant Jack Shay.

11. The Annistonians skeptical of anything resembling a vendetta at McClellan expressed their doubts to the author in separate interviews taking place on several occasions beginning in 2008. As of this writing, they are still alive, and their identities are being withheld.

Chapter 16

1. Google translation with corrections by Joni L. Pontius, November 17, 2012.

2. Christian Höschle, *Hast du nichts so bist du nichts* (Irdning/Steiermark, Austria: Stieglitz Verlag, 1992), 167–68, translated by Joni L. Pontius, September 28, 2013.

3. "Newspaper Party Inspects PW Camp," *The McClellan CYCLE*, April 14, 1944, p. 2.

4. Stymacks, interview, November 17, 2011.

5. Ibid.

6. Klaus W. Duncan, *The Oase* (private paper, undated), 2 (copy in author's collection).

7. Stymacks, interview, November 17, 2011.

8. J. Metzner, April 20, 2013, email.

9. J. Metzner, April 23, 2013, email.

10. Paul Metzner, *Teil 3 August 1943–Frühling 1944*, October 4 entry, edited and annotated by Joachim Metzner, sent in October 6, 2011, email; translated by Joni L. Pontius, November 17, 2012.

11. Robert Suberg's remarks throughout this chapter are from interviews in August 1987 and September 1988.

12. Höschle, *Hast du nichts so bist du nichts*, 163, 172, and 174, translated by Pontius, September 28, 2013.

13. All Marie Shay quotes are from the Shay family memoirs. See Note C in bibliography.

14. "ROOSEVELT DEAD" and "OUR COMMANDER-IN-CHIEF," *The McClellan CYCLE*, April 13, 1945, pp. 1 and 11.

15. Heike B. Görtemaker, *Eva Braun*, translated by Damion Searls (New York: Alfred A. Knopf, 2011), 240–41.

16. Höschle, *Hast du nichts so bist du nichts*, 178–79, translated by Pontius, September 28, 2013.

17. J. Metzner, April 13, 2013, email (his translations).

18. Google translation, enhanced by J. Metzner, April 17, 2013, email.

19. Google translation "corrected by hand" from J. Metzner, April 23, 2013, email.

20. C. L. Sulzberger and the editors of *American Heritage*, *The American Heritage Picture History of World War II* (New York: American Heritage/Bonanza Books, 1966), 617 and 620.

Chapter 17

1. All Jack and Marie Shay quotes are from the Shay family memoirs. See Note C in bibliography.

2. "Siren Sounds Time Signal for Prisoners," *The McClellan CYCLE*, February 8, 1946, p. 3.

3. Christian Höschle, *Hast du nichts so bist du nichts* (Irdning/Steiermark, Austria: Stieglitz Verlag, 1992), 184–85, translated by Joni L. Pontius, September 28, 2013.

4. Bill Plott, "For 3000 Nazis, WWII Ended at Fort," *The Anniston Star*, July 14, 1967, p. 7-C.

5. Rita Wells' memories throughout this chapter

are from interviews on October 1, 2008, and November 30, 2009.

6. David Jennings, "WWII prisoner of war camp holds history, memories for base typist Rita Wells," *The Jacksonville News*, undated copy (probably August 11, 2010).

7. Author's collection.

8. Arnold Krammer, *Nazi Prisoners of War in America* (Lanham, MD: Scarborough House, 1996), 237–38 and fn. 94 on 315.

9. Antonio Thompson, *Men in German Uniform* (Knoxville: University of Tennessee Press, 2010), 102–3.

10. Alfred Arens, "Dear American friends!" letter (written as presentation for reunion), 1991, p. 3, E. B. Walker Collection, copy in files of Joan McKinney.

11. Suberg, interviews, August 28 and 29, 1987.

12. Dan Coberly, "Stalag U.S.A. Part Six: The Camp McClellan Story," *The McClellan News*, May 2, 1980, p. 2.

13. Tom Mullins, December 5, 2012, email.

14. E. T. Brinkley, "Damage to Property Runs into Millions; No Fatalities Occur," *The Anniston Star*, April 8, 1946, pp. 1–2.

15. J. Walker, interview, October 2, 2008.

16. "City's Trees Hit Hard Blow by Wind, Hail," 1 and 6; Anne McCarty, "Anniston Begins Rehabilitation," 1 and 6; and Jack Scott, "6000 Homes Are Damaged by Tornado," 1. All articles are from *The Anniston Star*, April 9, 1946.

Chapter 18

1. All quoted letters/postcards to Jack and Marie Shay are from the author's collection.

2. Shay family memoirs. See Note C in bibliography.

3. James Bonner, May 11, 2011, email.

4. Robert Suberg, interviews, 1987 and 1988; and Edith Suberg, April 23, 2010, letter.

5. Author's November 17, 1987, letter to Robert Suberg.

6. Robert Suberg, December 14, 1982; March 6, 1985; and December 13, 1987, letters.

Chapter 19

1. Various maps: author's collection, and McClellan files, Alabama Room, Public Library of Anniston and Calhoun County, Anniston.

2. McClellan files, Alabama Room.

3. Daniel Hutchinson, "World War II POW Camps in Alabama," *Encyclopedia of Alabama* [Internet] (http://encyclopediaofalabama.org/face/Article.jsp?id=h-1418), 4.

4. Mary Beth Reed, Charles E. Cantley, and J. W. Joseph, *Fort McClellan: A Popular History* (Mobile, AL: U.S. Army Corps of Engineers), 104–5 (in McClellan files, Alabama Room).

5. Dan Coberly, "Stalag U.S.A. What they left behind…," *The McClellan News*, May 16, 1980, p. 7.

6. McKinney and Coberly, December 1, 2009, emails.

7. Walter E. Wilkerson, "The trees at McClellan," *The Anniston Star*, June 20, 2009.

8. Coberly, "Stalag U.S.A. What they left behind…," 7.

9. Author's observation, August 27, 1985.

10. Photocopies of articles: Dan Coberly, "Discovered bottle tells story of POW's faith, pride"; "Time Capsule Found," *MIDWEEK*, March 25, 1981; "Nazi POW capsule found by youth at fort," *The Anniston Star*, March 25, 1981; and other typed sheets bearing no attribution. All can be found in the McClellan files, Alabama Room (also in files of Joan McKinney).

11. Author's collection; provided translation.

12. Dan Coberly, "Stalag U.S.A. Part Seven: Locals recall camp years," *The McClellan News*, May 7, 1980, p. 2.

13. John Daniel Hutchinson, "Guests Behind Barbed Wire: German Prisoner of War Camps in Alabama during World War Two," Master of Arts thesis (University of Alabama at Birmingham, 2005), 189.

14. Wells, interview, October 1, 2008.

15. McKinney, interview, June 23, 2008.

16. E. B. Walker, January 4, 1993, letter to LTC Friedrich Ebberfeld, Fort McClellan's German Army Liason [sic] Staff.

17. McKinney, November 30, 2009, email to author, and November 30, 2009, email to Coberly.

18. Ruth Beaumont Cook, *Guests Behind the Barbed Wire* (Birmingham, AL: Crane Hill, 2006), 517.

19. McKinney, February 16 and 17, 2013, emails to author.

20. PFC Theodore Miller, "Fort's 50 Years Live in the Names of Its Buildings," *The Anniston Star*, July 14, 1967.

21. "Germans Buried at fort honored with services," newspaper scrap, McClellan files, Alabama Room.

22. Marian Uhlman, "Fort's POW memorial gives 'sense of heritage,'" *The Anniston Star*, November 17, 1980.

23. Arnold Krammer, *Nazi Prisoners of War in America* (Lanham, MD: Scarborough House, 1996), 261.

24. Newman, November 21, 2008, letter.

25. Phillip Tutor, "Hear the voices at McClellan," *The Anniston Star*, November 21, 2008, p. 7A.

26. McKinney, interview, November 29, 2009.

27. Michael A. Bell, "NOT FORGOTTEN," *The Anniston Star*, November 16, 2009, p. 1A.

28. Cameron Steele, "Somber respect," *The Anniston Star*, November 15, 2010, p. 1A.

29. Laura Johnson, "'Keep the history alive,'" *The Anniston Star*, November 14, 2011, p. 8A.

30. Paige Rentz, "Italian, German program planned," November 2012, in collection of Klaus W. Duncan.

31. Author's inspection cross-checked with list in files of Joan McKinney.

32. McKinney, August 5, 2013, email.

33. Klaus W. Duncan, *The Oase* (private paper, undated), 1–2 (copy in author's collection).

34. J. Metzner, September 5, 2012, email.

35. Dates and causes of death are in death certificates and medical reports. See "Papers, Reports, and Documents" in bibliography.

Chapter 20

1. The information on the eponyms of Fort McClellan are in "Efficiency Marks Post Commanders," "Range Named for 'Gallant Pelham,'" "Gate Memorializes 4th WAC Director," and "Traditions in Buildings, Landmarks," included within the stories commemorating the 50th anniversary of McClellan clipped from the July 18, 1967, edition of *Fort McClellan News* and compiled in "Fort Marks Its 50th Anniversary Today," a copy of which is in McClellan files, Alabama Room, Public Library of Anniston and Calhoun County, Anniston; Major Mary C. Lane, WAC, compiler, *The History of Fort McClellan*, July 14, 1955 ("Reproduced December 1958—Brought up to date by Annex K"), 44–49, 57, and 67–69, in McClellan files, Alabama Room; PFC Theodore Miller, "Fort's 50 Years Live in the Names of Its Buildings," *The Anniston Star*, July 14, 1967; and Betty Kelley, "Streets Named for Individuals," *The Anniston Star*, July 14, 1967, p. 7-C.

2. Author's observation.

3. All Jack Shay quotes are from the Shay family memoirs. See Note C in bibliography.

4. Author's observation.

5. Newman, interviews, June 25, 2008, and November 30, 2009; George Smith, "For Gay, Nestor 'n Newman," *The Anniston Star*, April 10, 2011; and Newman, June 16, 2011, letter.

6. "Aliceville Museum" [rack card] (Greater Tuscaloosa Convention & Visitors Bureau).

7. Mary Bess Paluzzi, "Aliceville Museum and Cultural Arts Center," *Encyclopedia of Alabama* [Internet] (http://encyclopediaofalabama.org/face/Article.jsp?id=h-2322).

8. "Col. Geo. C. Nielsen Post Commander," *The McClellan CYCLE*, January 19, 1945, p. 2.

9. Alfred Arens, "Dear American friends!" letter (written as presentation for reunion), 1991, p. 4, E. B. Walker Collection, copy in files of Joan McKinney.

10. Cole, interview, April 2, 2011.

11. "German Family Visits POW Cemetery," *Calhoun Community Press*, November 2010, p. 1.

Epilogue

1. Coberly, January 7, 2013, email.

2. Margaret Keelen Newman, *Walter Newman and some of his descendants, 1683–1974* (Talladega, AL: Margaret Newman, 1974), 68; and Newman, interview, November 30, 2009.

3. "A. A. Jones Dies; Managed Food Chain Store," *York Daily Record*, May 8, 1976, p. 11; and "Mrs. Evelyn I. Jones," *York Dispatch*, January 26, 1983.

4. "Obituaries: O. H. King," *Columbia Daily Herald*, March 27, 1981; and Virginia W. Alexander, ed., *Maury County Remembers World War II, Part One* (Columbia, TN: Maury County Historical Society, 1991), 164.

5. Author's observations.

6. Author's observations.

7. Personal visits with author; undated Christmas card from John George sent in late 1980s; and Shannon Kraushaar, May 26, 2007, email.

8. Spinelli, July 17, 2013, email.

9. Berardone, interview, July 20, 2013; "SPINELLI—Mary Ann," *Tribune Democrat*, April 22, 1980, p. 16; and "SPINELLI—Joseph A. Sr.," *Tribune Democrat*, March 19, 1998, p. D7.

10. Author's observations; Tulsa Steward, July 2, 1981, letter; Shay family memoirs; and Jack E. Steward, interview, July 15, 2012.

11. Harry Springer, December 29, 1994; January 18, 1996; and January 12, 1998, letters.

12. J. Metzner, September 10 and 14, 2013, emails.

13. Robert Suberg, March 6, 1985; March 18, 1988; February 15, 1989; February 4, 1993; and April 19, 1995, letters.

14. Edith Suberg, March 4 and July 30, 2001, and April 23, 2010, letters.

15. Author's observations.

16. Allen, interviews, February 18 and March 23, 2013.

17. Mullins, November 2, 2012, email.

18. Newman, April 11, 2013, letter.

19. Steward, interview, July 15, 2012.

20. R. George, September 29, 2011, email.

21. J. Metzner, April 3, 2013, email.

22. J. Metzner, November 14, 2012, email.

Bibliography

A Note on Camp Records

Only a small number of records once maintained by the Fort McClellan POW Camp are currently known to exist. As federal archivist Ken Schlessinger (AII Reference Section, National Archives at College Park, Maryland) explained in a September 10, 2008, email:

> During the 1950s the Department of Defense decided it was a good idea to destroy records of World War II camps, forts, and airfields, including records of POW camps. Record Group 389, Records of the Office of the Provost Marshal General, does contain several series of headquarters-level files arranged in whole or in part by specific POW camp. I have attached box and file lists for three relevant RG 389 series (Entries 457, 459-A, and 461).

> Please note, that while Entry 457 contains records about camp construction, the quality of the files in this particular series is spotty at best. Attachments and enclosures don't seem to have made it into this series. Consequently, I have also attached a box and file list for a series of Army Corps of Engineer construction completion reports (RG 77, Records of the Chief of Engineers, Entry 391). This series contains a number of files about Fort McClellan, although it is not clear how much of the material, if any, relates to the POW camp.

The National Archives holds these records:

Record Group 77, Records of the Office of the Chief of Engineers; Entry 391, Construction Completion Reports, 1917–1943, Boxes 184–187.

Record Group 389, Records of the Office of the Provost Marshal General, Prisoner of War Operations Division, Operations Branch; Entry 457 (A1), Subject Correspondence Files Relating to the Construction of and Conditions in Prisoner of War Camps, 1942–1947, Box 1424.

Record Group 389, Records of the Office of the Provost Marshal General, Special Projects Division; Entry 459-A (A1), Decimal Files, 1943–1946, Box 1617.

Record Group 389, Records of the Office of the Adjutant General, Enemy Prisoner of War Information Bureau; Entry 461 (A1), Subject Files, 1942–1946, Boxes 2482, 2513, 2518, 2579, 2604, 2666, 2691, 2692, and 2714.

Not all the files are equally helpful. And some duplication and misfiling occurred during the author's September 2008 visits; the existence of an airfield in California with the McClellan name did not help matters either.

The author's parents, who worked in the POW camp and fort headquarters, had access to copies of paper files, many of which were discarded at the camp's closing. Because of their interest in historical legacy, they diverted some documents and/or copies, including attached carbons, from the scrap heap. When the author checked the requisite files in the National Archives, he found many, but not all, of the documents that his parents had saved.

Many of these same papers concurrently reside in the collection of Joan McKinney of Anniston, Alabama, the retired director of protocol and public affairs coordinator of Fort McClellan, as well as in the McClellan files in the Alabama Room of the Public Library of Anniston and Calhoun County (also in Anniston). In addition, the author has located many of these papers in the collections of various veterans' families, leading him to conclude that probable sharing with like-minded individuals occurred over the years.

The specific documents reposing in these multiple locations include the following:

- letters dealing with POW transfers (September 7, 18, and 23, 1943; October 5, 12, 18, and 25, 1943; December 30, 1943; and January 5 and 19, 1944);
- post-visit reports filed by various inspectors/officers (Karl Gustaf Almquist; Captain W. J. Bridges Jr.; Parker W. Buhrman; A. Cardinaux; Lieutenant A. G. McCaughrin; Eldon F. Nelson; Paul A. Neuland; Edouard Patte; Maurice Ed. Perret; and Captain Edward C. Shannahan);
- POW educational class offerings, participation, and teachers (February 23–24 and March 1, 1945);
- POW occupational summaries (December 1, 1943) and work schedules (December 13, 1943); and
- U.S. officers stationed at the POW camp (December 14, 1943).

A Note on Local Published Sources

Copies of *The McClellan CYCLE*, published during the war at Fort McClellan, exist today in three bound volumes in the Alabama Department of Archives and History in Montgomery, Alabama. The volumes are numbered MIL.0008 (September 1, 1942–September 1, 1943), MIL.0007 (September 11, 1943–September 3, 1944), and MIL.0009 (September 8, 1944–April 7, 1947). Additionally, the author's parents retained some copies of the newspaper from their time in the POW camp; today these copies are part of the author's collection.

The Anniston Star is currently available on microfilm in the Alabama Room of the Public Library of Anniston and Calhoun County.

Original copies of the complete collection of *P.o.W. Oase*, as edited and published by Paul Metzner, are among the possessions of his son, Joachim Metzner, of Wolfsburg, Germany. Additionally, several people (including Joan McKinney) in the Anniston area have photocopies of various issues. The author also holds photocopies of many editions, as well as some originals. For information from *P.o.W. Oase* contained in this book, the author used translations by Klaus W. Duncan, Joachim Metzner, Joni L. Pontius, Chania Stymacks, and (when appropriate) Google.

A Note on the Shays' Reminiscences

The substantial information and quotes from Staff Sergeant Jack E. Shay and Marie B. Shay (the author's parents) was drawn from their informal reminiscences and anecdotes from the early 1960s to the 1980s (with only a few as recent as 1993). Some comments were written; others were spoken to the author and transcribed, but never with this project in mind. Consequently, dates were seldom recorded and follow-up questions seeking more amplification never occurred. These reflections were found later—sometimes alone, sometimes commingled with other written family memories. The words were theirs and are presented in this book in unvarnished form. However, it would be pure guesswork to attempt to reconstruct the actual dates at this point.

Interviews

Aderholdt, Meredith. November 30, 2009. Jacksonville, AL.

Allen, Ruth. January 19, February 18, March 23, and April 18, 2013. Telephone.

Bakke, Steve. April 2, 2011. Anniston, AL.

Berardone, Mary Jo. May 1, 2013 (telephone). July 20, 2013 (Johnstown, PA).

Bonner, Dean. December 1, 2009. Anniston, AL.

Bonner, James. December 1, 2009. Anniston, AL.

Cole, Thom. April 2, 2011. Anniston, AL.

Johnson, Mary Elizabeth. December 1, 2009. Anniston, AL.

Mabry, Betty. November 30, 2009. Anniston, AL.

McKinney, Joan. June 23, 2008; November 29, 2009. Anniston, AL.

Miller, Clark J. June 30, 2010. Hollidaysburg, PA.

Newman, Margaret. June 25, 2008; November 30, 2009. Anniston, AL.

Poindexter, Ann. June 24, 2008. Anniston, AL.

Poindexter, Thomas G. June 24, 2008. Anniston, AL.

Pontius, Joni L. November 17, 2012; September 28, 2013. Seneca Falls, NY.

Springer, Rita. November 30, 2009. Anniston, AL.

Steppe, Eugene. October 2, 2008. Anniston, AL.

Steward, Jack E. July 15, 2012. Telephone.

Stymacks, Chania. November 17, 2011. Binghamton, NY.

Suberg, Robert. August 28 and 29, 1987; September 23, 1988. Solingen, West Germany.

Tutor, Phillip. December 2, 2009. Anniston, AL.

Walker, Dr. Joseph "Joby." June 24 and October 2, 2008; November 29 and December 1, 2009. Anniston, AL.

Walker, Mary Beth. June 24 and October 2, 2008; November 29, 2009. Anniston, AL.

Wells, Rita. August 15, 2008 (telephone). October 1, 2008; November 30, 2009 (Anniston, AL).

Papers, Reports and Documents

Certificate of Death 12691 [Willi Waechter]. Center of Health Statistics, Alabama Department of Public Health, Montgomery. Copy in files of Joan McKinney, Anniston, AL.

Clinical Abstract [Fritz Clemmens (Clemens)]. Laboratory Station Hospital, Fort McClellan, AL. Copy in collection of Thom Cole, Anniston, AL.

Duncan, Klaus W. *The Oase*. Private paper, undated, unpaged. Copy in author's collection.

"Fort McClellan Prisoner of War Camp, World War II." McClellan files, Alabama Room, Public Library of Anniston and Calhoun County, Anniston, AL.

"HEADQUARTERS DETACHMENT SERVICE COMMAND UNIT 1463 Prisoner of War Camp Military Police, Fort McClellan, Alabama." Menu, May 4, 1945. Author's collection.

History of the Prisoner of War Camp, Fort McClellan, Alabama. E. B. Walker Collection. Copy in files of Joan McKinney, Anniston, AL.

Hutchinson, John Daniel. "Guests Behind Barbed Wire: German Prisoner of War Camps in Alabama during World War Two." Master of Arts thesis, University of Alabama at Birmingham, 2005.

Interments in the German-Italian POW Cemetery, Fort McClellan, Alabama. E. B. Walker Collection. Copy in files of Joan McKinney, Anniston, AL.

Lane, Major Mary C., WAC, compiler. *The History of Fort McClellan.* July 14, 1955. "Reproduced December 1958—Brought up to date by Annex K." In McClellan files, Alabama Room, Public Library of Anniston and Calhoun County, Anniston, AL.

"MERRY CHRISYMAS [sic] AND HAPPY NEW YEAR." Fort McClellan, AL. Christmas 1945 dinner menu. Author's collection.

"1437th SERVICE COMMAND UNIT Prisoner of War Camp Fort McClellan, Alabama." Menus, December 25, 1944, and January 17, 1945. Author's collection.

Reed, Mary Beth, Charles E. Cantley, and J. W. Joseph. *Fort McClellan: A Popular History.* Mobile, AL: U.S. Army Corps of Engineers, Mobile District. Prepared by New South Associates, Stone Mountain, GA. Contract No. DACA01–93-D-0033. In McClellan files, Alabama Room, Public Library of Anniston and Calhoun County, Anniston, AL.

Reed, Mary Beth, William R. Henry Jr., and J. W. Joseph. *"The Military Showplace of the South": Fort McClellan, Alabama, a Historic Building Inventory.* Mobile, AL: U.S. Army Corps of Engineers, Mobile District, June 15, 1993. Report submitted by New South Associates (Stone Mountain, GA) and ERC Environmental and Energy Services Co., Inc. (Knoxville, TN). New South Associates Technical Report 61. Copy in files of Joan McKinney, Anniston, AL.

Report of Autopsy [Fritz Clemmens (Clemens)]. Laboratory Station Hospital, Fort McClellan, AL. Copy in files of Joan McKinney, Anniston, AL.

Report of Autopsy; Clinical Abstract; Clinical History; and Autopsy Protocol [Joseph Kohl]. Laboratory Station Hospital, Fort McClellan, AL. Copy in collection of Thom Cole, Anniston, AL.

RESTRICTED SPECIAL ORDERS. Army Service Forces, Fourth Service Command, Fort McClellan, AL. April 30, 1945. Author's collection.

RESTRICTED SPECIAL ORDERS. Headquarters Infantry Replacement Training Center, Fort McClellan, AL. May 27, 1944. Author's collection.

Rogers, Catherine Gambrell. *Conservation of Decorative Murals at Fort McClellan, Anniston, Alabama: Condition Report and Treatment Proposal.* Report submitted to Tim Rice, director of environment, Fort McClellan, March 5, 1998. Copy in files of Joan McKinney, Anniston, AL.

Standard Certificate of Death, State File No. 00125 [Joseph Kohl]. Center of Health Statistics, Alabama Department of Public Health, Montgomery. Copy in files of Joan McKinney, Anniston, AL.

Standard Certificate of Death, State File No. 18060 [Karl Krause]. Center of Health Statistics, Alabama Department of Public Health, Montgomery. Copy in files of Joan McKinney, Anniston, AL.

Standard Certificate of Death, State File No. 4461 [Fritz Clemens]. Center of Health Statistics, Alabama Department of Public Health, Montgomery. Copy in files of Joan McKinney, Anniston, AL.

Newspapers and Magazines

Some of the following are clippings in files or scrapbooks and bear incomplete source attribution.

"A. A. Jones Dies; Managed Food Chain Store." *York Daily Record* (York, PA), May 8, 1976, p. 11.

"Axis Prisoners of War Arrive." *The McClellan CYCLE* (Fort McClellan, AL), July 9, 1943, p. 1.

Bell, Michael A. "NOT FORGOTTEN." *The Anniston Star* (Anniston, AL), November 16, 2009, p. 1A.

Brinkley, E. T. "Damage to Property Runs into Millions; No Fatalities Occur." *The Anniston Star* (Anniston, AL), April 8, 1946, pp. 1–2.

Brown, Mary Diskin. "Col. Martin H. Meaney Prison Camp Commander." McClellan files, Alabama Room, Public Library of Anniston and Calhoun County, Anniston, AL.

"City's Trees Hit Hard Blow by Wind, Hail." *The Anniston Star* (Anniston, AL), April 9, 1946, pp. 1 and 6.

Coberly, Dan. "Discovered bottle tells story of POW's faith, pride." Photocopy in McClellan files, Alabama Room, Public Library of Anniston and Calhoun County, Anniston, AL, and the files of Joan McKinney of Anniston, AL.

_____. "Stalag U.S.A. Part Seven: Locals recall camp years." *The McClellan News* (Fort McClellan, AL), May 7, 1980, p. 2.

_____. "Stalag U.S.A. Part Six: The Camp McClellan Story." *The McClellan News* (Fort McClellan, AL), May 2, 1980, p. 2.

_____. "Stalag U.S.A. What they left behind…" *The McClellan News* (Fort McClellan, AL), May 16, 1980, pp. 6–7.

"Col. Geo. C. Nielsen Post Commander." *The McClellan CYCLE* (Fort McClellan, AL), January 19, 1945, p. 2.

Cope, Cpl. Howard. "PW Camp News." *The McClellan CYCLE* (Fort McClellan, AL), November 26, 1943, p. 6.

_____. "PW Camp News." *The McClellan CYCLE* (Fort McClellan, AL), January 7, 1944, p. 10.

_____. "PW Camp News." *The McClellan CYCLE* (Fort McClellan, AL), February 18, 1944, p. 6.

"Former McClellan Trainee, Captured by Nazis in ETO, Now Cooks at Fort PW Camp." *The McClellan CYCLE* (Fort McClellan, AL), November 9, 1945, p. 2.

"Fort Marks Its 50th Anniversary Today." *Fort McClellan News* (Fort McClellan, AL), July 18, 1967.

Freeman, Laura Ann. "POW art: Vibrant, sometimes masterful, work of German soldiers uncovered at Fort McClellan." *The Anniston Star* (Anniston, AL), September 16, 1979, pp. 1–2C.

Frye, Cpl. William R. "Inside PW Camp: Bomb Stories Bunk, Nazi Prisoners Say; Call War News 'Lies.'" *The McClellan CYCLE* (Fort McClellan, AL), May 19, 1944, pp. 3 and 5.

_____. "Inside the PW Camp: Pin-Up Girls, PXs, Nazi 'Heils' Found Behind Grim Stockade." *The McClellan CYCLE* (Fort McClellan, AL), May 12, 1944, p. 3.

"General George B. McClellan: Controversial Union Commander." *Fort McClellan News* (Fort McClellan, AL), July 12, 1968, p. 3.

George, Sgt. J. J. "PW Camp." *The McClellan CYCLE* (Fort McClellan, AL), May 26, 1944, p. 7.

_____. "PW Camp News." *The McClellan CYCLE* (Fort McClellan, AL), May 12, 1944, p. 7.

George, Cpl. John J. "POW Camp News." *The McClellan CYCLE* (Fort McClellan, AL), February 25, 1944, p. 6.

_____. "PW Camp News." *The McClellan CYCLE* (Fort McClellan, AL), February 4, 1944, p. 6.

George, Sgt. John J. "PW Camp." *The McClellan CYCLE* (Fort McClellan, AL), May 19, 1944, p. 7.

_____. "PW Camp." *The McClellan CYCLE* (Fort McClellan, AL), June 2, 1944, p. 7.

_____. "PW Camp News." *The McClellan CYCLE* (Fort McClellan, AL), March 17, 1944, p. 6.

_____. "PW Camp News." *The McClellan CYCLE* (Fort McClellan, AL), March 24, 1944, p. 6.

_____. "PW Camp News." *The McClellan CYCLE* (Fort McClellan, AL), March 31, 1944, p. 6.

_____. "PW Camp News." *The McClellan CYCLE* (Fort McClellan, AL), April 14, 1944, p. 7.

_____. "PW Camp News." *The McClellan CYCLE* (Fort McClellan, AL), April 21, 1944, p. 7.

George, S/Sgt. John J. "PW Camp." *The McClellan CYCLE* (Fort McClellan, AL), December 29, 1944, p. 9.

"German Family Visits POW Cemetery." *Calhoun Community Press* (Anniston, AL), November 2010, p. 1.

"Germans buried at fort honored with services." Newspaper fragment dated November 14, 1977; no other attribution. McClellan files, Alabama Room, Public Library of Anniston and Calhoun County, Anniston, AL.

Hutchinson, Daniel. "The Oasis: German POWs at Fort McClellan." *Alabama Heritage* (Summer 2008): 40–49.

"It's McClellan's First New Year's Baby." *The McClellan CYCLE* (Fort McClellan, AL), January 11, 1946, p. 3.

Jennings, David. "WWII prisoner of war camp holds history, memories for base typist Rita Wells." *The Jacksonville News* (Anniston, AL), undated Internet copy but probably August 11, 2010.

Johnson, Laura. "'Keep the history alive.'" *The Anniston Star* (Anniston, AL), November 14, 2011, pp. 1 and 8A.

Kelley, Betty. "Streets Named for Individuals." *The Anniston Star* (Anniston, AL), July 14, 1967, p. 7-C.

Livingston, Rose. "POW murals get brush up." *The Birmingham News* (Birmingham, AL), November 10, 1998, pp. 1Bff.

Lockette, Tim. "Meaning behind murals remains a mystery." *Gadsden Times* (Gadsden, AL), May 13, 1999, p. 1A.

Madhani, Aamer. "POW murals at officers' club to be cleaned, stabilized." *The Anniston Star* (Anniston, AL), September 26, 1998, p. 1B.

McCarty, Anne. "Anniston Begins Rehabilitation." *The Anniston Star* (Anniston, AL), April 9, 1946, pp. 1 and 6.

"M'CLELLAN RECEIVES NEW WAR PRISONERS." *The Anniston Star* (Anniston, AL), July 6, 1943, p. 6.

McKinney, Joan. "Fort McClellan's Diverse Mission: Lingering Memories—Lasting Heritage." *Alabama Historical Association Newsletter* (Fall 2007): 4–10.

_____. "The POW Murals: Anniston's Hidden Treasure." *Alabama Heritage* (Fall 2009): 4–6.

Miller, PFC Theodore. "Fort's 50 Years Live in the Names of Its Buildings." *The Anniston Star* (Anniston, AL), July 14, 1967.

"Mrs. Evelyn I. Jones" [obituary]. *York Dispatch* (York, PA), January 26, 1983.

"Nazi POW capsule found by youth at fort." *The Anniston Star* (Anniston, AL), March 25, 1981, p. 8D.

"Newspaper Party Inspects PW Camp." *The McClellan CYCLE* (Fort McClellan, AL), April 14, 1944, p. 2.

"Obituaries: O. H. King." *Columbia Daily Herald* (Columbia, TN), March 27, 1981.

Oliver, Mike. "German POWs painted murals of chaos, despair." *The Birmingham News* (Birmingham, AL), May 30, 1982, Sunday SPOTLIGHT section.

"OUR COMMANDER-IN-CHIEF." *The McClellan CYCLE* (Fort McClellan, AL), April 13, 1945, p. 11.

Plott, Bill. "For 3000 Nazis, WWII Ended at Fort." *The Anniston Star* (Anniston, AL), July 14, 1967, p. 7-C.

"PW Camp." *The McClellan CYCLE* (Fort McClellan, AL), June 23, 1944, p. 7.

"PW Camp." *The McClellan CYCLE* (Fort McClellan, AL), December 8, 1944, p. 11.

"PW Camp." *The McClellan CYCLE* (Fort McClellan, AL), December 15, 1944, p. 9.

"PW Camp." *The McClellan CYCLE* (Fort McClellan, AL), February 16, 1945, p. 9.

Rentz, Paige. "Italian, German program planned." Newspaper clipping bearing handwritten note "NOV. 2012," in collection of Klaus W. Duncan, Jacksonville, AL.

"Review to Mark McClellan's 51st Anniversary." *Fort McClellan News* (Fort McClellan, AL), July 12, 1968, pp. 1 and 3.

"ROOSEVELT DEAD." *The McClellan CYCLE* (Fort McClellan, AL), April 13, 1945, p. 1.

Scott, Jack. "6000 Homes Are Damaged by Tornado." *The Anniston Star* (Anniston, AL), April 9, 1946, p. 1.

"Siren Sounds Time Signal for Prisoners." *The McClellan CYCLE* (Fort McClellan, AL), February 8, 1946, p. 3.

Sloan, Cpl. Harry. "PW Camp News." *The McClellan CYCLE* (Fort McClellan, AL), October 15, 1943, p. 6.

_____. "PW Camp News." *The McClellan CYCLE* (Fort McClellan, AL), October 29, 1943, p. 6.

_____. "PW Camp News." *The McClellan CYCLE* (Fort McClellan, AL), November 5, 1943, p. 6.

_____. "PW Camp News." *The McClellan CYCLE* (Fort McClellan, AL), November 19, 1943, p. 6.

Smith, George. "For Gay, Nestor 'n Newman." *The Anniston Star* (Anniston, AL), April 10, 2011.

"SPINELLI—Joseph A. Sr." [obituary]. *Tribune Democrat* (Johnstown, PA), March 19, 1998, p. D7.

"SPINELLI—Mary Ann" [obituary]. *Tribune Democrat* (Johnstown, PA), April 22, 1980, p. 16.

Steele, Cameron. "Somber Respect." *The Anniston Star* (Anniston, AL), November 15, 2010, pp. 1 and 7A.

"300 Fort Jobs Open to Army Wives Here." *The McClellan CYCLE* (Fort McClellan, AL), March 10, 1944, p. 3.

"Time Capsule Found." *MIDWEEK* (photocopy, presumably Anniston, AL), March 25, 1981.

Turner-Collins, Richelle. "Late German POW lives on through his restored murals." *Stars and Stripes*, January 7, 2000, p. 5.

Tutor, Phillip. "Hear the voices at McClellan." *The Anniston Star* (Anniston, AL), November 21, 2008, p. 7A.

_____. "Quiet Synthesis." *The Anniston Star* (Anniston, AL), May 3, 2009, p. 1E.

Uhlman, Marian. "Fort's POW memorial gives 'sense of heritage.'" *The Anniston Star* (Anniston, AL), November 17, 1980.

"WAR PRISONER DIES IN ACCIDENT AT FORT: Six Other Prisoners Hurt When Truck Overturns." *The Anniston Star* (Anniston, AL), August 1, 1943. Hand-dated clipping in files of Joan McKinney, Anniston, AL.

Wilkerson, Walter E. "The trees at McClellan." *The Anniston Star* (Anniston, AL), June 20, 2009.

Books

Alexander, Virginia W., ed. *Maury County Remembers World War II, Part One*. Columbia, TN: Maury County Historical Society, 1991.

Castell, Ron, ed. *Blockbuster Video Guide to Movies and Videos, 1996*. New York: Island Books, 1995.

Cook, Ruth Beaumont. *Guests Behind the Barbed Wire*. Birmingham, AL: Crane Hill, 2006.

DeGregorio, William A. *The Complete Book of U.S. Presidents*. New York: Wings Books, 1993.

Görtemaker, Heike B. *Eva Braun*. Translated by Damion Searls. New York: Alfred A. Knopf, 2011.

Günther, Hans. *Wie sagt man's Englisch?* Heidenheim/Brenz: Carl Edelmann G.m.b.H., 1945.

Höschle, Christian. *Hast du nichts so bist du nichts*. Irdning/Steiermark, Austria: Stieglitz Verlag, 1992.

Klatt, Prof. E., and G. Golze. *Langenscheidt's German-English English-German Dictionary*. New York: Washington Square Press, 1966.

Krammer, Arnold. *Nazi Prisoners of War in America*. Lanham, MD: Scarborough House, 1996.

Liddell Hart, B. H. *History of the Second World War*. New York: Perigee Books, 1982.

National Geographic Atlas of the World. Washington, DC: National Geographic Society, 1992.

Newman, Margaret Keelen. *Walter Newman and Some of His Descendants, 1683–1974*. Talladega, AL: Margaret Newman, 1974.

Shirer, William L. *The Rise and Fall of the Third Reich*. New York: Fawcett Crest, 1960.

Sulzberger, C. L., and the editors of *American Heritage*. *The American Heritage Picture History of World War II*. New York: American Heritage/Bonanza Books, 1966.

Thompson, Antonio. *Men in German Uniform*. Knoxville: University of Tennessee Press, 2010.

Watson, Thomas J., Jr., and Peter Petre. *Father, Son & Co*. New York: Bantam Books, 1990.

Booklets, Brochures, Pamphlets, Flyers and Rack Cards

"Aliceville Museum." Greater Tuscaloosa Convention & Visitors Bureau, AL.

"The Civil War at a Glance." Washington, DC: Government Printing Office, 1991.

"COMPLIMENTS OF HEADQUARTERS, PRISONER OF WAR CAMP, FORT MCCLELLAN, ALA., JULY 1943–JANUARY 1946." No further information.

"Fort McClellan, Anniston, Alabama, Guide for Service Personnel." No further information.

"Historic Driving Tour of Calhoun County." Anniston, AL: Calhoun County Chamber of Commerce.

"Information Hand Book for the Soldier." Infantry Replacement Training Center, Fort McClellan, AL, 1944.

"King & Country's Rommel in Afrika." Hong Kong: King & Country, 2011.

"Remington Hall Meeting Center." No further information.

"Richfield World-Wide News Map." Chicago: Rand McNally, 1941.

Reminiscences

Arens, Alfred. "Dear American friends!" Personal reminiscence in the form of a letter. Written as a presentation for a 1991 Alabama reunion and acquired by E. B. Walker. Author's copy, courtesy of Joan McKinney, Anniston, AL.

Eifler, Norbert, and Erhard. Untitled personal reminiscence in the form of a letter. February 8, 1991. Author's copy, courtesy of Joan McKinney, Anniston, AL.

Hamilton, James (Jimmy). Untitled personal reminiscence. March 18, 2009. Author's copy, courtesy of Klaus W. Duncan, Jacksonville, AL.

Metzner, Paul. *Teil 3 August 1943–Frühling 1944*. Original journal entries edited and annotated by Joachim Metzner. Copy sent to author, October 6, 2011.

Walker, Joseph A., Sr. "Across the Brick Pike: Growing Up in the Shadow of Fort McClellan." Memoirs of Joseph A. Walker Sr., presented to Calhoun County Historical Society, January 15, 2008. Author's copy, courtesy of Joseph A. Walker Sr., Anniston, AL.

Wells, Rita. *The Prisoner of War Camp, Fort McClellan, Alabama, U.S.A.* Edited by Elaine Morris Heath, July 27, 2008. Author's copy, courtesy of Rita Wells, Anniston, AL.

Letters/Emails

Belau, Susanne. Email to Joachim Metzner, April 14, 2013; forwarded to author, April 16, 2013.

Bonner, James. Emails to author. May 24 and June 23, 2009; and May 11, 2011.

Brownell, Bill. Email to author. May 24, 2009.

Coberly, Dan. Email to author. January 7, 2013.

_____. Emails to Joan McKinney. November 30 and December 1, 2009. Forwarded to author.

Engelke, Helmut. "Dear Jack.!" Undated note to Sergeant Jack Shay.

_____. Letter to Mr. and Mrs. Shay. January 10, 1947 [1948].

Erfle, Janice. Emails to author. April 28, 2010; and September 28, 2011.

George, John. Christmas card to Marie Shay. Undated, late 1980s.

George, Rodney. Email to author. September 29, 2011.

Gross, Bruno. Letter to Jac [*sic*] Shay. February 23, 1948.

"Knoll." Letter to General Nord, Commandant, US Army Chemical School, Fort McClellan. February 22, 1983. In files of Joan McKinney, Anniston, AL.

Kordiš, Meta. Email to Joachim Metzner. August 28, 2012. Forwarded to author.

Kraushaar, Shannon. Email to author. May 26, 2007.

McKinney, Joan. Emails to author. November 30 and December 12, 2012; February 16 and 17, May 2, August 5, September 5, and November 15, 2013.

_____. Emails to Dan Coberly. November 30 and December 1, 2009. Forwarded to author.

Metzner, Joachim. Emails to author. October 6, 20, and 24, November 21, and December 18, 2011; April 3, 4, 9, 12, and 14, May 2, July 10, 18, 20, and 31, August 3, 9, 16, and 19, September 4 and 5, October 10, 11, 21, 24, 26, and 28, November 4, 6, 14, and 26, and December 3, 5, 9, 20, and 23, 2012; January 5, February 18, March 21, 23, and 27, April 1, 3, 13, 17, 19, 20, and 23, July 4, 28, and 31, August 22, September 1, 9, 10, and 14, October 3 and 16, and December 23, 2013; March 2, 3, 6, 12, 14, 16, 24, and 27, and April 10, 2014.

_____. Email to Joan McKinney. September 5, 2013. Forwarded to author.

Müller, Josef. Postcard to Mr. and Mrs. Jack Shay. January 1, 1946.

Mullins, Tom. Emails to author. November 2 and December 5, 2012.

Neville, C. P. Letter to "Whom It May Concern." June 18, 1947. In collection of Meredith Aderholdt, Jacksonville, AL.

Newman, Margaret. Letters to author. July 25, undated but postmarked September 4, and November 21, 2008; February 18 and April 21, 2009; March 26, 2010; June 16 and November 5, 2011; December 10, 2012; and April 11, 2013.

Pontius, Joni L. Package to author of translations of *P.o.W. Oase* excerpts dated November 20, 22, 24, 25, and 28, 2012, and postmarked December 1, 2012.

_____. Undated letter to author postmarked May 21, 2013.

Prior, Pvt. Clifford. Letters to Mrs. Goldie M. Terry. October 22 and 29, November 2, and December 16, 1943. In collection of Thom Cole, Anniston, AL.

Schardt, Karl. Letter to Mr. and Mrs. Jack Shay. February 18, 1948.

Schlessinger, Ken. Email to author. August 12, 2008.

Shay, Jack [author]. Email to Joachim Metzner. October 16, 2013.

_____. Letter to Robert and Edith Suberg. November 17, 1987.

Shay, Jack E. Letter to Jack Shay [author]. June 1971.

Smith, LTC C. F. Letter to Ferrol Aderholdt. June 26, 1947. In collection of Meredith Aderholdt, Jacksonville, AL.

Spinelli, Patrick D. Email to author. July 17, 2013.

Springer, Harry. Letters to Marie Shay. December 29, 1994; January 18, 1996; and January 12, 1998.

Steward, Tulsa. Letter to the Shays (Jack–Marie–Jack Jr.). Postmarked July 2, 1981.

Suberg, Edith. Letters to author. February 15 and April 23, 2010.

_____. Letters to the Shay family. March 4 and July 30, 2001.

Suberg, Edith, and Robert (Bob). Letters and cards to the Shay family. December 14, 1982; March 6, 1985; December 13, 1987; March 18, 1988; February 15, 1989; February 4, 1993; and April 19, 1995.

Walker, E. B. Letter to LTC Friedrich Ebberfeld, German Army Liason [*sic*] Staff, Fort McClellan, AL. January 4, 1993. Copy in files of Joan McKinney, Anniston, AL.

Walker, Dr. Joseph "Joby." Letter to author. October 16, 2008.

Weber, Steven. Letter to author. October 10, 2013.

Wells, Rita. Letters to author. August 27 and October 4, 2008.

Wetzold, Erich. Postcards to Mr. Jack Shey [*sic*]. December 9, 1947, and undated.

Internet Sites (and Dates Accessed)

Folgende Dateien oder Links können jetzt als Anlage mit Ihrer Nachricht gesendet werden: Ranks.pdf. Accessed July 4, 28, and 31, 2013.

Hutchinson, Daniel (Florida State University). "World War II POW Camps in Alabama." *Encyclopedia of Alabama.* http://encyclopediaofalabama.org/face/Article.jsp?id=h-1418. Accessed June 14, 2012.

Morton, Patricia Hoskins (Auburn University). "Calhoun County." *Encyclopedia of Alabama.* http://www.encyclopediaofalabama.org/face/Article.jsp?id=h-1198. Accessed October 27, 2011.

Paluzzi, Mary Bess. "Aliceville Museum and Cultural Arts Center." *Encyclopedia of Alabama.* http://encyclopediaofalabama.org/face/Article.jsp?id=h-2322. Accessed June 14, 2012.

Sytko, Glenn A., compiler. *German POWs in North America.* http://www.uboat.net/men/pow/pow_in_america.htm. Accessed June 14, 2012.

Transition Force: United States Army Garrison—Fort McClellan, Alabama. http://www.mcclellan.army.mil/Info.asp. June 14, 2012.

Wikipedia. "Fort McClellan." http://en.wikipedia.org/wiki/Fort_McClellan. Accessed October 7, 2011.

Miscellaneous

"Goodbye to a comrade." Typed translation of a clipping from *P.o.W. Oase*, hand-dated June 6 [16], 1945, along with annotations. In files of Joan McKinney, Anniston, AL.
Nazi POWs in America. History Channel, A&E Television Networks. 2002.

Additional Assistance

The following people, whether in person or via telephone, email, or U.S. mail, provided direction and suggestions, granted access, made referrals, presented sound historical speculation, or otherwise assisted in gathering information that provided the bedrock material or ancillary subject matter included in this book. Their help, whether rendered in a single instance or stretching out over hours (and numerous occasions, as in the case of archivist extraordinaire Tom Mullins), helped either open doors to welcome information or close portals that would have led to dead ends. Their titles and addresses are relevant to the time assistance was given.

Finally, after the manuscript was completed, Betty Casey took up the laborious chore of converting prose and photographs into the electronic format necessary for publication.

Darryl Bottoms, National Archives and Records Administration, College Park, MD.
Steve Brueckner, librarian, King Public Library, King, NC.
Michelle Cannon, archivist, Maury County Archives, Columbia, TN.
Lawrence R. Carter, Center United Methodist Church, W. Mocksville, NC.
Betty Casey, media consultant and interview assistant, Endicott, NY.
Dan W. Cleckler, executive director, Anniston–Calhoun County Fort McClellan Development Joint Powers Authority, Anniston, AL.
William R. Divelbiss Sr., executive vice president of Rose Hill Cemetery, Hagerstown, MD.
Nancy Dupree, archivist, Alabama Department of Archives and History, Montgomery, AL.
Kurt M. Eschbach, German Club, Binghamton, NY.
Amanda Eveler, assistant director of library and archives, York City Heritage Trust, York, PA.
David Ford, business development coordinator, Berman Museum of World History, Anniston, AL.
Shannon Kraushaar, adult reference librarian, Washington County Free Library, Hagerstown, MD.
Hayes Ledford, Chamber of Commerce, Chattanooga, TN.
Beth Lipford, National Archives and Records Administration, College Park, MD.
Linda L. Mann, executive secretary/office manager,

Anniston–Calhoun County Fort McClellan Development Joint Powers Authority, Anniston, AL.
Gedra Martin, National Archives and Records Administration, College Park, MD.
Shannon Mathew, professional photo and copy specialist, Binghamton, NY.
Randy Messing, German Club, Binghamton, NY.
Connie Morningstar, volunteer, York City Heritage Trust, York, PA.
Tom Mullins, director, Alabama Room, Public Library of Anniston and Calhoun County, Anniston, AL.
Jennifer Pruchnic, reference librarian, Cambria County Library, Johnstown, PA.
Ken Schlessinger, National Archives and Records Administration, College Park, MD.
Don Singer, National Archives and Records Administration, College Park, MD.
Ray Tutterow, *Davie County Enterprise Record*, Mocksville, NC.
Major General (Retired) Gerald G. Watson, Jacksonville, AL.
Steven Weber, archives technician, National Personnel Records Center, National Archives, St. Louis, MO.
Elmer Wheatley, deputy director, Calhoun County Economic Development Council, Anniston, AL.
Patricia Wilson, archivist, Alabama Department of Archives and History, Montgomery, AL.
Jerry York, Fort McClellan enthusiast and memorabilia collector, Oxford, AL.

Translators

A considerable amount of material, including various letters and the entire content of *P.o.W. Oase*, was written in German and required translation. The following people, most neither requesting nor accepting remuneration, translated significant portions of the information included in this book:
Richard "Burt" Burtless, Seneca Falls, NY. Letters.
Klaus W. Duncan, Jacksonville, AL. *P.o.W. Oase*.
Leon Horwitz, Binghamton, NY. Letters.
Joachim Metzner, Wolfsburg, Germany. *P.o.W. Oase*.
Joni L. Pontius, Syracuse and Seneca Falls, NY. *Hast du nichts so bist du nichts*; *P.o.W. Oase*; *Teil 3 August 1943–Frühling 1944*; and letters.
Chania Stymacks, Binghamton, NY. *P.o.W. Oase*.
A word about translating German into English: A strict translation (or transliteration) is impossible without losing the original sense of meaning. Joni Pontius, who holds a B.A. in German from the University of Oregon, an M.A. in German from the State University of New York at Buffalo, and an A.B.D. in German language and literature from the latter university, enumerated the pitfalls inherent in a strictly linear translation. In a note dated November 24, 2012, using part of this sample excerpt from the original German:

Zum Frieden! Vielleicht kommt er schneller, als die meisten zu hoffen wagen.... Die auf hohem Bergeshange über der Straße zwischen dem Grün der Bäume hervorlugende Tafel mit der Aufschrift

P.W.-Cementary lässt uns auf solche Gedanken kommen: dort ruht ein Kamerad für immer von den Schrecknissen des Krieges, den er glücklich überstand, aus: kurz nach seiner Ankunft im Lager McClellan fand er bei einem Autounfall den Tod.

she began translating:

To peace!

Perhaps it will come faster than most dare to hope.... On the high mountain slope above the road, peeping out between the green of the trees, the plaque with the inscription P.o.W. Cemetery allows us to arrive at such thoughts....

(My note [Joni Pontius]—I've rearranged the sentence word order so it makes sense to an English speaker. You can further modify the above by making a few substitutions, if you like: instead of "*such thoughts*" you could use "*these.*" I included the "*to peace*" part because it leads into the next paragraph. Without it, it would make less sense to what is the "*it*" otherwise?)

(The last sentence shows ... why an on-line translator can't work:

"The on the high mountainslope over the road between the green of the trees peeping out plaque...")

And as Chania Stymacks said on November 17, 2011, with dozens of pages of *P.o.W. Oase* spread out on the table before her, "The newspaper was typed on an American typewriter. There were no umlauts. They used an 'e' in place of an umlaut. That distorts the meaning. Parts of the newspaper would have been difficult even for the German POWs to understand. Some of the Germans and other prisoners who were not from Germany but from other parts of Europe would have had some difficulty in understanding it because they used an American typewriter."

Index